DUNEDIN YOUTH GUILD, INC.

of Dunedin, Florida

presents

A Culinary Collection

Suncoast Seasons

Post Office Box 1453
Dunedin, Florida 34697-1453

First Printing November, 1984 10,000 books
Second Printing October 1988 10,000 books

The primary purpose of the Dunedin Youth Guild is to serve the youth of the greater Dunedin area and to further the civic and cultural progress of the community.

International Standard Book Number 0-9613858-0-4
The Library of Congress Catalog Number 84-72350

Printed in the United States of America
MORAN PRINTING COMPANY
9125 Bachman Road
Orlando, Florida 32824

Suncoast Seasons

Original Cookbook Committee

CHAIRMEN	Mrs. Anthony S. Brancato Mrs. Dean N. McFarland
RECIPE EDITORS	Mrs. Stanley H. Dawson Mrs. J. Wallace Lee Mrs. Bill Ritchey Mrs. J. J. Suddath, Jr. Mrs. Jack Wilson
COORDINATORS	Mrs. Arthur M. Borham Mrs. Janet Joyce Mrs. Gregory H. Keuroghlian Mrs. Lynn Lees
HISTORIAN	Mrs. Stanley H. Dawson

****

DUNEDIN YOUTH GUILD PRESIDENTS FROM INCEPTION THROUGH PUBLICATION	Mrs. Janet Joyce, 1981-1982 Mrs. Arthur M. Borham, 1982-1983 Mrs. Douglas Guilfoile, 1983-1984 Mrs. Robert Haverkos, 1984-1985

****

WINE ADVISOR	Mr. Peter W. Kreuziger Owner, Bon Appétit and Jamaica Inn Dunedin, Florida President, Florida Restaurant Association, Pinellas Chapter

****

REPRINT CHAIRMEN	**Joann E. Hensley** **Jeanne M. Gregg** **Paula Guilfoile**

Cover Design and Illustrations

Mrs. Lawrence J. Tierney, Jr.

The Jacaranda tree on our cover is one of the most beautiful tropical and semi-tropical trees of our Suncoast. In Spring its lavender blossoms and feathery foliage resemble a huge bouquet and create a lavender illusion. The Jacaranda is an integral facet of our *Suncoast Seasons*.

Foreword

Suncoast Seasons –they come and go, ebb and flow like the gentle tides in our beloved Gulf of Mexico.

The casual or intermittent visitor to our region of Florida, which is bounded by the city of St. Petersburg on the south and Tarpon Springs on the north, might say we really have no seasons at all. But, those of us who live on the Suncoast year-round, many of us transplants from colder climes where the dramatic contrasts between winter and spring and between summer and fall are often spectacular in their diversity, would say otherwise.

We have seen the havoc a sudden freeze can wreak upon our region's citrus and strawberry crops and upon tender ornamental plants like the showy hibiscus and colorful croton.

We gauge the more subtle changes of spring into summer and summer into fall by our magnificent sunrises and sunsets, by the life-giving heat of the summer sun, and by the ferocity of thunder and lightning storms that flare out of the Gulf of Mexico or blow from Old Tampa Bay with decided regularity in July through September.

Many lifestyles are most compatible with the seasons of the Suncoast as well. Once deemed a retiree's paradise, our area has seen a tremendous influx of young families seeking a better way of life and mid-life businessmen and women making career and job changes.

Despite our various reasons for being here, we can all share in the myriad outdoor activities that have made our area famous. Picnics, pool parties, suppers at the beach can be enjoyed throughout the year.

There is, as the seasons gently flow into years, a sense of dynamic change and growth among our population. But, amidst the change, young and old alike find the reminders of our past. In Safety Harbor we can see the burial grounds of the Timucuan Indians who resided in the region from the early 1500's. The historic Belleview Biltmore Hotel in Belleair, the largest occupied wooden structure in the world, remains as serenely lovely as when it was built by railroad magnate, Henry Plant, in 1897. Original buildings at Largo's Heritage Park reflect various Florida lifestyles·at the turn of the century from a single-room cabin to the elegant "House of Seven Gables".

We invite you to journey through our *Suncoast Seasons* with us, gathering ideas and insights as one collects shells on our beaches.

Here's to expanding your vistas—culinary and beyond. Sample our seasons and enjoy!

Carol L. Swyers

Acknowledgments

Suncoast Seasons is a collection of over 750 recipes selected by our committee from approximately 1,500 submitted by our members, families and friends. All the recipes have been edited, tested and re-edited and have been enthusiastically approved by our committee. An emphasis was placed on fresh ingredients, and detailed instructions have been written for even the novice cook. Anecdotes and kitchen hints are interspersed throughout the book to assist you in the preparation of recipes. Many of our recipes have travelled with the submitters during moves across the United States or the world; or have been "family secrets," cherished through generations; or are old true Florida recipes handed down from the early Florida pioneers—all were generously given to us to be included in our book. Our menu and entertaining section reflects the seasons of the Suncoast from spring luncheons at poolside, to summer alfresco dining, to a winter cocktail party *Suncoast Seasons* style. Our special section "From Suncoast Restaurants" will surely delight the most discriminating gourmet. And, the eminent personalities who have graciously submitted their recipes for our "From the Famous" section have shared their favorites. For the support of our members who edited recipes, tested and re-tested recipes, typed and proofed recipes, we will be eternally grateful. We thank each and every one, and a special thank you from our hearts to our husbands and families who have been so supportive during the last two years. So, enjoy our *Suncoast Seasons,* as much as we have enjoyed compiling it for you.

Suncoast Seasons Committee

Table of Contents

...Spring...

The Red Knot, "champion migrater" of our Suncoast, turns into a "scarlet seductress" with its red head, neck and breast and whitish rump. Bald Eagle nests are often seen during this season. Azaleas, jasmine and gardenia blossoms perfume the air. Our avid fishermen await the word that the Tarpon are running.

Spring

The Belleview Biltmore

The Belleview Biltmore Hotel, Belleair, Clearwater, Florida, is the largest wooden structure in the world and has served four generations of those who have sought the warm sunshine, the gracious leisure, the wide variety of recreation, and the relaxing serenity of this spacious private resort estate. One still finds here the high bluff along the Bay and the "easy living" which originally attracted the Timucuan Indians, Captain Charles Wharton Johnson and Henry Bradley Plant.

From 1897 until 1942 the Atlantic Coast Line passenger trains operating from St. Petersburg backed across parts of the golf course discharging passengers, luggage and mail at the hotel.

From 1942 to 1944 the Biltmore was leased to the United States Air Force. As many as 3,000 personnel were housed at one time on the premises. Some fairways were even used as drill grounds. The Biltmore was reopened in 1947.

After eighty-seven years gracious hospitality continues to be the reputation of the Belleview Biltmore.

Spring Luncheon At The Belleview Biltmore

Sutter Home White Zinfandel
**Bourbon Slush Garnished with Mint Leaves*

**Asheville Shrimp Mousse on*
Bibb Lettuce with Cherry Tomato Rosettes

Croissants
Chateau St. Michelle Johannisberg Riesling (Washington State)

**Chicken Salad à la Rogers*

**Shredded Carrots*
Fresh Asparagus with Lemon Butter Sauce

**Café au Lait Dessert*
Coffee   Iced Tea

American Egret

This magnificent bird was once hunted for its fine feathers. Today, egrets are plentiful along the Florida Suncoast and other southern states. They are identified by large yellow beaks and black legs and feet. Their nests are usually platforms of sticks in marshlands. These birds are very graceful in flight as depicted in our picture.

Brunch At A Beach House

Bloody Marys with Celery Sticks

**Champagne Punch*
Domain Chandon Kir Royale
**Cheese Wafers*
Simi Rose of Cabernet Sauvignon
**Popovers with Raspberry-Strawberry Conserve*
**Bran Muffins with Molded Butter Flowers*

**Sausage Bread   *Fluffy Eggs with Shrimp*
**Cheese Grits*

Beringer Chenin Blanc
**Florida Seafood Casserole*
*Fresh Green Beans with Dill Sauce   *Asparagus Casserole*

Melon Balls Garnished with Mint and Orange Blossoms
Fruit or Honey Dressing
Fresh Strawberries and Kirsch with Custard Sauce
**Florida Pound Cake   *Danish Puff*
Coffee   Tea   Iced Tea

Roebling Mansion

The Roebling Mansion on the National Register of Historic Places was built by Donald Roebling, the youngest son of John August Roebling II, of the wealthy Roebling engineering family. Donald Roebling came to Harbor Oaks in Clearwater in 1929 at the age of 20.

Roebling personally supervised the building of his 2½-story mansion on the highest elevation of Florida's Suncoast, overlooking Clearwater Bay on seven acres. The estate was a gift to his prospective bride, Florence Spottswood Parker, and he affectionately named it "Spottis Woode." The mansion cost $600,000 to build; it took 1½ years to complete.

Despite all he had put into the mansion and grounds, Roebling walked away from his magnificent home in 1956. Since then it has been owned by four different owners, and all have enjoyed the magnificent English Tudor "castle" built by Donald Roebling many years ago.

"ACS 100"

Cocktail Party At The Roebling Mansion To Benefit The American Cancer Society

Moët and Chandon Champagne Cocktails of Choice
Robert Mondavi Fumé Blanc

Oysters on the Half Shell with Lemon Wedges
**Fevillete de Homard et Crevette en Crevette en Couronne*

Simi Chardonnay
*Pâté — *Tarama*
with Melba Toast Points
**Sausage Stuffed Mushroom Caps *Meatballs with Creamy Dill Sauce*

Chateau La Rose Trimtadon
*Turkey Breast with *Curried Fruit Filet of Beef with Port Butter*

Assorted Fruit and Cheeses
**Miniature Cream Cheese Tarts with Cherry Sauce*
Petite Meringues with Filberts Chocolate Cups with Assorted Liqueurs

"ACS 100" is comprised of 100 couples dedicated to win the fight against cancer by holding a benefit cocktail party annually under the auspices of 'A Thousand Plus' Committee of the American Cancer Society—Pinellas County Unit, Florida Division.

Annual Oyster Roast Of The Clearwater Bar Association

In 1949 the Honorable Judge V. Byrd of Clearwater organized a social event for the members of the Clearwater Bar Association and their wives. An oyster roast was the fare for the day, and the gathering was held at the Judge's home amidst the orange groves where "Top of the World" is located today. A Dunedin gentleman, Ted Kaminsky, took pride in roasting the oysters, as he was a seafaring fellow with a great deal of experience with edible treasures from the sea. Judge Byrd directed a young lawyer, B.J. Driver, to assist Mr. Kaminsky with the Oyster Roast, and Mr. Kaminsky was B.J.'s mentor until his death. B.J. Driver has been roasting the oysters for the Annual Bar Association outing held every spring on the luxurious tree-covered grounds of the Florida Gulf Coast Art Center, Belleair, Clearwater, Florida.

With over 30 years' experience at roasting oysters, B.J. Driver continues to use this method: "Hardwood is recommended for roasting although charcoal may also be used. *Do not use pine, as the oysters will have the taste of turpentine.* When the coals are hot, place the oysters on a grill or grate depending on the amount used. The grill should be 6 to 12 inches above the coals depending on how hot they are. In 10 or 15 minutes the oysters will crack open and steam. At that point roast another few minutes and remove. Serve with salt and pepper, cocktail sauce, drawn butter and crackers as preferred. Guests should use a cotton garden glove to hold the hot roasted oysters and pry them open with an oyster knife. The longer the oysters roast, the less juice they will exude. Some oyster lovers prefer their oysters browned and well done. In any event, the oysters may be enjoyed at various roasting stages from raw to well done.

An oyster roast is a wonderful time for a winning combination — fellowship and good eating!"

B.J. Driver

Oyster Roast At Sunset
Annual Oyster Roast Of
Clearwater Bar Association

Spirits

Oysters on the Half Shell
Coleslaw

Roasted Oysters
**Potato Salad*

Cocktail Sauce   Lemon Wedges   Crackers

Domaine de Muscadet de L'Hyverniere
Charles Le Franc Fumé Blanc

Philosophy has always been an important influence in the daily life of the Chinese. Many of the table customs of the Chinese date back thousands of years to Confucius who taught that good taste in food was to be cultivated. The harmonious mixture in their dishes has always been the unifying principle of Chinese cooking. The gastronomical experience of sweet and sour, smooth and crunchy, and salty and bland shows this philosophy, as does the importance of aroma and visual appeal. The larger the group of diners, the more dishes that are prepared; for example — two main dishes can be prepared for five.

All who dine will understand the Chinese philosophy that "eating is truly one of the joys of life".

Chinese Floral Garden

Poolside

Hibiscus and Magnolia Floating on the Pool with Oriental Lanterns Discreetly Around the Patio to Transport Your Guests to the Orient

**Shanghai Spring Rolls with Duck Sauce*

**Butterfly Shrimp with Sweet Tomato Sauce*
Simi Chenin Blanc
**Hot and Sour Soup*

*Watercress Salad with *Chinese Dressing*

Dynasty White Wine from Mainland China
**Szechwan Chicken with Peanuts*
Fetzer Zinfandel
**Flank Steak*
Mirassou Gewürztraminer
**Lee Lum's Lemon Chicken*
**Sweet and Sour Pork*
**Shrimp in Black Bean Sauce*
*Ham and Egg Fried Rice *Broccoli with Straw Mushrooms*
**Snow Peas with Tomatoes*

**Almond Float* *Vanilla Ice Cream with Mandarin Oranges and Fresh Grated Coconut*

Almond Cookies *Fortune Cookies*

Plain Basic Omelet

3 eggs, room temperature
1 tablespoon cold water
4 drops hot pepper sauce
1/4 teaspoon salt, scant
1 tablespoon lightly salted butter

Beat eggs until they begin to foam. Properly beaten, they look "stringy" and make threads when you lift up the beater or whisk. Heat pan over medium heat until hot. Flick a few drops of water on to the pan, if it hops around your pan is ready, if steam rises the pan is too hot. Add butter, buttering the sides all the way up to the top. Pour eggs into the hot pan. Using the flat sides of a fork, make circular motions around the bottom of the pan fast, as you would making scrambled eggs. Speed is of the essence for lightness and fluffiness. While the right hand makes a circular motion, shake the pan with the left hand, rocking it back and forth to keep the eggs loose. When the eggs are cooked and all the liquid is firm, spread the eggs evenly, but lightly, with a fork to cover any breaks in the surface. Pause briefly to allow the eggs to set. To turn the omelet out, grasp the handle of the pan with your left hand, palm side up; this makes it easier to tilt the pan, and finally roll the omelet out. Tilt the pan at a 45-degree angle and with a fork in your right hand begin to roll the omelet away from the handle to the opposite edge of the pan and onto a heated plate.

"Being able to make a perfect omelet is as necessary to the good life as making a good cup of coffee or tea."

Rudy Stanish
America's Omelet King

An Evening With Chef D'Oeuf
For The Benefit Of UPARC Foundation
(Upper Pinellas Association for Retarded Children)

"Omelet"

Smithfield Ham

Brandied Peach Halves with Chutney

Beef Stroganoff

Wild Rice

Marinated Vegetables

Mary Johnson's Rosettes with Sour Cream and Plant City Strawberries

Champagne

An Evening with Chef D'Oeuf originated in 1967 and has become an annual charity gala to benefit the Upper Pinellas Association for Retarded Children. Hosts have included Ruth and Jack Eckerd, Lorrie and Ken Flowers, Jeanette and Bill Hale, Ruth and Jim Leonard, and Doris and Tommy Scanlan. One couple hosts the benefit each year, and the guest list increases annually.

Rudy Stanish of New York City, America's "Omelet King," takes pride in his delicious omelets, which have become his therapy. His culinary expertise has kept him jetting from New York to London, Rio de Janeiro, Berlin and many other places, wherever the beautiful people want the perfect omelet.

...Summer...

Snook and flounder are plentiful for the fisherman's enjoyment. All the shorebirds have donned their summer finery. The Black-Bellied Plover wears its summer "tuxedo", and the Ruddy Turnstone's dramatic black belly emphasizes its curious face with its black mask. Our vibrant green lawns provide a striking background for the colorful leaves of the croton.

Summer

Ybor Square

Ybor City, Tampa's Latin Quarter, was once known as "the fine cigar capital of the world" and is now one of the nation's most historic districts.

During the ten years' war (1868-1878) which Cubans fought to gain their independence from Spain, thousands of Cubans fled to Key West rather than take up arms against their countrymen. Among the refugees were many cigar makers and traders including Don Vincenté Martinez Ybor, a cigar manufacturer.

Ybor established cigar making in America by starting a factory in Key West. Attracted to Tampa's excellent port and the Plant railroad, Ybor came to Tampa in 1885 with hope of building a planned community based on cigar making. Cubans who followed Ybor to Tampa brought with them not only their fine skills but their culture, Spanish-style brick buildings with arched windows and wrought iron.

Also attracted to Ybor's model and friendly community were the Germans who brought their good business sense and a brewery to the Latin Quarter. Italians brought their willingness to work as cigar makers, bakers, butchers, and grocers. The Spanish came too, although they were distrusted by the Cuban majority before the Spanish-American War in 1898. During this cigar heyday 20,000 Spanish, Cuban, and Italian artisans produced hand-rolled cigars in the area's forty or so factories.

Today most of the once active factories and social centers are closed with only a few brief memories etched on the historical markers. The aroma of tobacco still lingers in the air, and the people are as friendly as ever. The Latin culture, which founded this historic city, lives on with many displays of arts, crafts, festivals, music and other cultural events in the popular Ybor Square.

Ybor Square — Spanish Fare

Torres Gran Vina Sol
White Sangria **Red Snapper "Alicante"*
Cordornui Brut Classico
**Black Bean Soup*

Marques de Riscal (Red)
**Chicken and Yellow Rice "Valencia Style"*
Green Peas with Onions **Fire and Ice Tomatoes*

Spanish Flan **Churros*
Spanish Coffee

Tarpon Springs

To the millions of tourists who pour through Tarpon Springs each year, this area is an easy-going ethnic enclave that has found the recipe for uncomplicated old-style living. Old homes color Tarpon Springs like dabs of oil on a painter's canvas, each lending to the unique, historic flavor of the community.

The Sponge Exchange built in 1909 was the economic center of the famous sponging community of Greek immigrants who came to the area because there were sponges in the Gulf of Mexico. For over forty years the sponges were good, and life was good. But, in 1950 a sponge blight came, and the sponge industry on the West Coast of Florida turned as lifeless as sand. The Sponge Exchange, "the heart and soul," of the Greek community was like a ghost house. Then, in 1981 the Exchange was sold to the Pappas Brothers who built specialty shops and restaurants. They vowed to preserve the historic nature in the design of the new and keep "the heart and soul" of Tarpon Springs pulsating!

Life continues in Tarpon Springs as in years past. Epiphany is celebrated every January 6 with the young men of town traditionally diving for a Cross. The young Greek man who retrieves the Cross from the Spring Bayou is said to have good luck throughout his life.

The Greek people are a fun-loving people who enjoy good food and good times. This is truly evident in the Glendi, a Greek Food Festival, where all the traditional Greek specialties are served. One can find a touch of Greece in Tarpon Springs.

Glendi At Tarpon Springs Sponge Docks

**Greek Salad* **Spanakopeta*

Greek Bread
Achaia Clauss Domestica White
**Chicken with Feta Cheese*

Archaia Clauss Castel Daniel
**Butterflied Lamb*

Dolmathes **Pastitso* **Stefado*

**Baklava* *Kourabiedes* **Galatoboureko*
Oozo *Greek Coffee*
Retsina

Glendi is a Greek Festival with great abundances of food, music and gaiety.

Don CeSar Hotel

Don CeSar, the pink palace on St. Petersburg Beach, has had its ups-and-downs since T. J. Rowe erected it in the 1920's. F. Scott Fitzgerald and his wife, Zelda, were among its illustrious guests. The army bought the Don for use as a hospital during World War II. It was reincarnated into a hotel again in 1973 after being restored and modernized.

The hotel today is on the National Register of Historic Places and is a six-time winner of the prestigious Mobil Four-Star Award.

Today, all who visit the Don CeSar are finding that history does indeed repeat itself. There are many who venture to guess, it is better the second time around.

Alfresco Dining At The Don CeSar
St. Petersburg Beach, Florida

Mirassou Chardonnay
**Cucumber Soup*

Robert Mondavi Johannisberg Riesling
**Chicken with Wine and Vegetables*
**Rice Pilaf* — *Tomatoes Stuffed with Broccoli Soufflé*

Grand Marnier Mousse in Pastry Swans
**Viennese Coffee* — **Brandied Coffee*

Clearwater

There are places one goes on vacation that a visitor never wants to leave. Florida's Suncoast is such a place — sunshine, a fabulous subtropical climate, the sparkling Gulf of Mexico and twenty-eight miles of white sand beaches are the backdrop for some of the most scenic sunsets to be found anywhere.

The Clearwater area boasts sunshine ninety-nine percent of the year. Temperatures average 72 degrees during the day and only a little bit lower at night. Outdoor activities — sports, boating, festivals and tournaments — take place year around.

Palm trees, almost constant blooms on subtropical foliage and the sparkling water of the Gulf of Mexico have given Clearwater its nickname, "*Sparkling Clearwater*".

Debutante Tea

Moët & Chandon Champagne

Minted Ice Tea | *Lemon Iced Tea*

Tea Sandwiches

Watercress | *Salmon-Chive* | *Dilled Cucumber*

**Scones with Orange Marmalade with Almonds and Amaretto*

**Queen Anne Cake* | *Seedcake*

**Teatime Tassies* | **Lemon Bars*

**Linzer Tarts* | **Wedding Wafers*

Hot Tea

Milk | *Sugar* | *Lemon Wedges*

Caladesi Island
Dunedin, Florida

Caladesi Island is one of the few remaining barrier islands in Florida. Barrier islands lie parallel to the coast and are separated from the mainland by a shallow bay or sound. Caladesi is separated by St. Joseph Sound and protects the mainland from the high winds and waters of occasional storms which continue to shape the islands.

An Indian burial site on Caladesi excavated in the early 1900's bore evidence of Indians living on the island prior to the arrival of the Spanish in the early 1500's. The island has stood essentially unchanged except by nature. The hurricane of 1921 cut the island in two, forming Hurricane Pass which today separates Caladesi Island from Honeymoon Island to the north. The bay side of Caladesi is a mangrove swamp. Much of the interior is dominated by virgin pine flatwoods. Sea turtles nest on the beaches during summer nights, and Caladesi is a refuge for many wading birds and shorebirds. Ospreys are also a common sight. Visitors may view coastal strand plants, virgin south Florida slash pine flatwoods, live oak hammocks, fresh and brackish water ponds and a mangrove swamp.

In 1960 Caladesi became a state park. No roads or bridges lead to Caladesi; the only access is by boat. This inaccessibility will assure that Caladesi will remain as the Indians knew it over four hundred years ago.

Gourmet Picnic At Caladesi Island

Sutter Home White Zinfandel (Serve Chilled)
Brie and Assorted Crackers

**Artichokes Vinaigrette* | **Blue Lagoon Lobster Salad*
**Vichyssoise*
**Avocado Mousse Mold* | **Molded Gazpacho Salad*

Georges Duboeff Beaujolais Villages (Serve Chilled)
**Roast Beef Salad* | **Tomato and Broccoli Salad*
**Chicken Salad Elegantè*

Charles Le Franc Johannisberg Riesling
**Blond Brownies* | **Blueberry Cheesecake Macadamia*
**Pineapple Bars*

...Autumn...

The Spotted Sandpiper, still in its Summer suit of brown "polka dots", teeters along by himself with his head held low and tilted forward, his tail bobbing up and down almost constantly. In the heat of early Fall our residents cool off by diving for scallops or setting out their Stone Crab pots. The gold to pinkish-yellow blossoms of our Golden Rain Trees color the Suncoast skyline.

Autumn

Slash Pine

The Slash Pine is called Cuban Pine or Caribbean Pine. It is a common pine growing in slashes or swamps in Western Cuba and Central America, but especially in Florida. It is a fast growing tree in moist soil, reaching a height of 80 feet or more with a two foot thick trunk. The needles are 6 to 12 inches long in twos and threes and remain green for two or more years. It has small purplish flower cones about 1½ inches long.

The Slash Pine is valued for its wood and is one of the chief sources of turpentine. It is widely used in reforestation programs, and is as common to the Suncoast as the sea and the sand.

Gourmet Dinner In The Autumn

Georges Duboeuf Beaujolais Villages (Serve Chilled)
**Marinated Mushrooms on Toast Points *Artichoke Soup*

Robert Mondavi Cabernet Sauvignon
**Beef Wellington with Bearnaise Sauce*
Antinori Reserva Chianti Classico Marchese
**Veal Scallopine Florentine*

Linguini with Marinara Sauce **Fried Eggplant Parmigiana*
**Zucchini*
**Salt Sticks* *Assorted Rolls with Herb Butter*

Villa Bonfi Frascati
**Crustoli* **Frozen Nut Zuccotta*
Flaming Coffees

Dunedin

Dunedin is the oldest town on the West Coast of Florida between Cedar Key and Key West, overlooking St. Joseph Sound which is part of Clearwater on the Gulf of Mexico. Along the waterfront is a beautiful paved boulevard with white lights, many fine homes, palms, hibiscus and other tropical foliage. Edgewater Drive offers a fantastic view from early dawn to a majestic, flamboyant sunset.

A thousand years ago and more, this area was a village for Indians of the Muskhogean Timucuans. These people were mound builders, hunters and agriculturists, raising tobacco and corn. They were as tall as 6′5″. They used dugout canoes, and their stone tools are still being found in the area.

Credit for the European "discovery" of Florida in 1513 usually goes to Don Juan Ponce de Leon, a Spanish knight. But an Italian, John Cabot, may have been the first. Ponce de Leon probably visited Florida while searching for gold rather than the "Fountain of Youth". He found only death, as he died before he ever reported on his searches. In 1539 De Soto marched through the area with his 600 soldiers and 213 cavalrymen. In 1567 Timucuans again had Spanish visitors when Menandez set up a fort and mission. His men were massacred by the Timucuans, so the area was left to the Indians for over 100 years. All the Timucuans died out eventually from European diseases.

In 1870 Dunedin had a general store; supplies were brought down the coast by small sailing craft. The main section of the Dunedin we know today was a cotton field. At this time the name of the little settlement was Jonesboro. All the land in this part of Florida was government and state owned. Settlers could, under the Government Homestead Law, file on 160 acres, live on it for 5 years, and then upon payment of $1.25 per acre get a clear title. This incentive attracted many northern farmers. The first church service was in June, 1869, in a school house.

In 1880 the district changed from a vegetable and cotton growing section to one of citrus growing. In 1880 the first steamboat to enter Clearwater Bay landed at the dock, establishing the first real communications with the outside world. Another milestone in the growth of Dunedin was the coming of the first railroad train in 1888.

The population of Dunedin has grown enormously since 1900 when there were 113 residents to the present day total of 36,000.

New England Clam Bake
Florida Style

Robert Mondavi Fumé Blanc
Beringer Johannisberg Riesling

**Seafood Soup*

**Clam Bake*

**Hush Puppies*

Assorted Breads and Rolls

**Dublin Potato Salad*

**Pride of Iowa Cookies*

**Pineapple Bars*

Stone Crabs

The stone crab has claws about 2¾ inches long.* It is relatively easy to catch. It is most satisfying!! The satisfaction comes from knowing you can take from the sea one of the most tasty offerings and not have to kill the crab. You simply catch a stone crab, break off the claws and throw the crab back into the sea. The stone crab will swim away, looking a little awkward and helpless, but will grow new claws in about eighteen months. The season for these delectable morsels from the sea is October 15 to May 15. Everyone who has sampled stone crabs waits with great anticipation for stone crab season!

*Ruling from Florida Department of Natural Resources: Both claws of the stone crab may be removed provided the forearm joint measures at least 2¾ inches. The crab must then be returned to the water.

Seafood Buffet

Robert Mondavi Chenin Blanc

Conch Chowder | **Cold Avocado Crab Soup*

Joseph Drouhin Puligny-Montrachet

**Boiled Shrimp with Creole Remoulade Sauce*

*Stone Crabs with *Mustard Sauce*

**Soft Shell Crabs with Lemon Wedges* | **Scallops Amandine*

Parducci Johannisberg Riesling

Watercress with Cherry Tomatoes

**Riverhouse Cornbread* | **Hush Puppies*

**Brazilian Snow* | **Fresh Strawberry Cream Pie*

Coachman-McMullen Log House At Heritage Park

In 1842 Captain James Parramore McMullen came from Georgia to what is now Pinellas County. He married Elizabeth Campbell in 1844 in Brooksville, Florida, and during 1848 he returned to Clearwater in possession of a 240-acre government land grant. Elizabeth and their three oldest children lived in Tampa while "Captain Jim" and five slaves from Georgia camped in palm-thatched huts on the wooded property and built the log house. By 1852 the home was completed and occupied by the McMullen family. This was the birthplace of eight additional McMullen children. At least 1000 descendants of the McMullen brothers now live in Pinellas County.

The McMullen Log House was a two-story Georgian style log house which had four rooms, two downstairs (one with a fireplace) and two upstairs. The center section, called the "dog-trot", was completely open from the front porch to the back porch and contained the stairway. A kitchen and dining area was later added to the back porch. Much of the 240 acres was planted with citrus trees.

The home and groves were purchased in 1902 by S.S. Coachman. The building was "modernized", including filling the wall cracks between the logs. It remained the Coachman residence until 1920. Later the log home was restored, refurnished and opened to the public until World War II. The Clearwater Chapter of the Daughters of the American Revolution placed a plaque on the front porch with the inscription: "The oldest existing log house in Pinellas County." Damaged by fire in December, 1976, the remains were donated to Heritage Park by the Coachman family and moved to Heritage Park in Largo in 1977. Restoration began in 1978, and Captain James Parramore McMullen would find his ancestral home as he knew it.

Thanksgiving At McMullen Cabin

Charles Le Franc Chardonnay

**Hearts of Palm with Anchovy Dressing*
Southern Beaten Biscuits

**Coquina Chowder*
**Pumpkin Muffins*

**Fresh Oregon Apple Bread*

**Cranberry-Orange Bread*

**Pineapple-Zucchini Bread*

Sutter Home Zinfandel (Serve Chilled)
Chateau St. Michelle Johannisberg Riesling
*Roast Turkey with *Apple Stuffing and*
**Other Than Bread Stuffing*

Giblet Gravy

**Cranberry Relish*
Gourmet Spinach

**Sweet Potato Puff*
**Mushroom Medley*

Fluffy Potatoes

**Southern Pecan Pie*
**Pumpkin Chiffon*

**Baked Egg Custard Pie*
Old Fashioned Apple Pie

The Florida Orchestra

The Florida Orchestra, "the best in Florida," was formed in 1968 with musicians from The St. Petersburg Symphony and The Tampa Philharmonic Orchestra. Their leaders met on a tugboat in the middle of Tampa Bay; at this wet and windy meeting the Florida Orchestra was created.

The orchestra plays in three cities — Clearwater/Dunedin, St. Petersburg and Tampa. It is not dependent on governmental funding, but rather relies on the support of its three guilds and the public.

The orchestra plays ten concerts of its Masterworks Series and four Pop Concert Series in each city. Many free concerts are also offered as well as Youth Concerts, playing to 60,000 students.

The Suncoast area is indeed fortunate to have such a fine orchestra.

Late Dessert After Symphony

Champagne

**Fresh Peach Soufflé* | **Black Forest Trifle*

**Almond Brittle Torte* | **Chocolate Mousse Pie*

**Almond Pumpkin Charlotte*
**Luscious Coconut Cake*

Coffee Tea
After Dinner Liqueurs in Chocolate Cups

...Winter...

The Audubon Society holds its annual bird count in mid-December. In 1983 one-hundred and fifty-five different birds were spotted. In late Winter "tipsy" robins arrive, devouring the berries from our shrubs and trees. Many of our shorebirds begin to build their nests on the trees and lands of our spoil banks and cays. These include Cormorants, Black Skimmers, Sanderlings, Pelicans, Ospreys, Herons and Wood Storks. School after school of trout provide an abundance of taste delights for the lucky fisherman. Our landmark Kapok Tree becomes a giant floral arrangement of thousands of flame-colored blossoms springing from the top of each branch and visible for miles around. In later Winter the scent of orange blossoms pervades the Suncoast.

Winter

Dunedin Youth Guild's Annual Holiday Tour Of Homes

Since 1970 the Dunedin Youth Guild's Annual Holiday Tour of Homes has become a traditional part of the winter holiday festivities for year-round residents and winter visitors alike.

On the first Saturday in December selected homes are opened to the Guild's guests. Many homes on the Tour have historic interest: "The John O. Douglas House" on Edgewater Drive in Dunedin, which is listed in the National Register of Historic Places, is known as Dunedin's first structure of sawn lumber. It remains the oldest existing house in Dunedin. A step into the old Douglas House is like a step into the last century.

Another home on our Tour was the historic home on Victoria Drive built by a commodore in 1895. This bay front home enhances present-day living with memories of the past. These homes, decorated for the holidays, are examples of the many and varied life styles possible in the area, from rambling waterfront accommodations to contemporary high-rise condominiums. The architecture and decor of these homes reflect the owners' diverse personalities and tastes, while a joyous holiday spirit is common to all.

An elegant tea with home baked treats served during the Home Tour is the Guild's way of saying "Thank you" to the hundreds of people who support our projects throughout the year.

Holiday Home Tour Christmas Tea

**Spiced Tea* **Honey Egg Nog*
**Lebkuchen* **Date Nut Balls* **Sandies*

**Rugelach* **Coconut Macaroons* **Springerle*
**Cathedral Cookies* **Chocolate Madeleins* **Shortbread*
**Norwegian Spritz*

**Peanut Bark* **Pecan Candy Rolls* **Cinnamon Pecans*

Clearwater Beach Hotel

The lovely Clearwater Beach Hotel started life as a vacation cottage, a substantial brown shingle two-story structure, built by E.T. Roux, at the turn of the century. At that time the island was used as a picnic playground by those who dared to venture by boat from Dunedin to Clearwater Beach. Through the years rooms and porches were added.

In the 1930's the Clearwater Beach Hotel was known as a health spa — orange juice, the warm winter sun, and a daily plunge into the Gulf of Mexico gave certain "curative effects." With the negotiation of prohibition the owner gained notoriety for the hotel as a place where "bottled heat" was dispensed to the guests on chilly winter days.

In the 1940's the mode of operation was catering to a select group of clientele from various parts of the country. Throughout the years the guests developed a camaraderie among themselves looking forward to each winter season to come.

In the 1950's the hotel was popular for the string quartet at the evening meal and black tie Saturday nights. The quaint atmosphere combined with the reputation of the clientele are benefits that make the Clearwater Beach Hotel a popular year-round resort. Many traditions of the past are still a topic of conversation among the guests today.

The various renovations and additions have enhanced its beauty and upheld its traditional charm. Therefore, the nostalgic history of the Clearwater Beach Hotel will always remain a recognition of days gone by.

In 1988 the Clearwater Beach Hotel reopened after major renovation which added a new dining room. The various renovations and additions have enhanced its beauty and upheld its traditional charm. Therefore, the nostalgic history of the Clearwater Beach Hotel will always remain a recognition of days gone by.

Opening Of The Winter Season
Christmas Cocktail Party
Clearwater Beach Hotel

Cocktails
White Tillet on the Rocks with a Twist

**Turkey Party Ball*
**Spicy Shrimp*
**Stuffed Mushrooms*
Assorted Canapes

Deinhard Piesporter Riesling
*Baked Virginia Ham with Petite Biscuits and *Mustard Sauce*

*Prime Rib Roast with *Homemade Swedish Rye Bread and*
**Horseradish Sauce*
Chateau Chevalier Pinot Noir
Assorted Fruits and Cheeses

Suncoast Christmas Trees

The Christmas trees of our Suncoast residents are often decorated with ornaments from our beaches, such as sand dollars and shells. Of course, traditional ornaments adorn many of our northern-grown trees. The tree-trimming party is an annual tradition in many of our Suncoast homes.

Trim The Tree Open House

**Christmas Wassail* — *Old Fashioned Egg Nog*

Beringer Chardonnay

**Baked Clam Dip in a Bread Shell*

**Boursin Cheese Spread with Assorted Crackers*

L. Latour Beaujolais (Serve Chilled)

**Party Meatballs with Creamy Dill Sauce*

**Stuffed Mushrooms* — *Shrimp Christmas Tree with Sauces*

Chateau St. Michelle Fumé Blanc

**Chicken Breasts Amandine*

**Asparagus Casserole* — **Rice Pilaf*

**Chocolate Roll* — **Ambrosia*

Toffee

**Glazed Pecans* — **Peanut Butter Bon Bon*

Suncoast Christmas Traditions

All of the Holiday traditions of other parts of the country are also a part of the Suncoast Christmas season. We may miss the snow of the North, but some of our local traditions can only be found in our warm clime. Dunedin hosts a very colorful Christmas Parade of Boats to Edgewater Park at Dunedin Marina where the City Christmas tree is then lit, and carols pervade the air. Other yacht clubs and cities along the Suncoast have similar parades throughout the Intercoastal Waterway. Many residents spend Christmas Day on their boats, some picnicking on Caladesi or other islands and spoil banks along our Suncoast.

New traditions have become a part of many of the lives of Suncoast residents, but old Holiday traditions still are very much a part of the area. The remembered sights and sounds of the Christmas Holiday Season are everywhere on our Suncoast.

Christmas Dinner

Royal Esmeralda Sherry, Sandeman
Shrimp Bisque
Mirassou Johannisberg Riesling
Clas der Val, Zinfandel
**Rock Cornish Game Hens* | *Pheasant with *Smitane Sauce*

Robert Mondavi Reserve Chardonnay
**Baked Wild Rice with Fresh Mushrooms* | **Spinach Soufflé Garnished with Watercress*

**Swedish Rice Pudding* | **Amaretto Pie*
**White Fruit Cake*
Coffee and Tea | *After Dinner Liqueurs*

Ruth Eckerd Hall
At
Richard B. Baumgardner Center
For The Performing Arts

The Richard B. Baumgardner Center for the Performing Arts was made possible by a donation of a 38-acre parcel of land in 1977 to the city of Clearwater by June Baumgardner and Family. The Performing Arts Center is used to promote the arts for the enjoyment of area residents. The first building on the site is the Ruth Eckerd Hall, designed by the prestigious Frank Lloyd Wright Foundation and officially opened on January 7, 1984. It is already a landmark in our community. The Hall seating 2,181 is a multi-purpose theatre designed for a variety of programming in music, dance and theatre.

The Margaret Heye Great Room situated on the third floor is a beautiful innovative feature of the Ruth Eckerd Hall. This room can accommodate 300 guests. Glass walls with doors lead out to a wide terrace which provide a breathtaking view of the naturally beautiful land that leads to Alligator Lake and Old Tampa Bay directly behind the Center.

Many wonderful experiences will be etched in our memories at Ruth Eckerd Hall for generations to come.

Gala Opening Of Ruth Eckerd Hall
At
Richard B. Baumgardner Center
For The Performing Arts
January 7, 1984

Margaret Heye Great Room

Assorted Continental Cheeses *Fresh Tropical Fruits*
Garden Fresh Relishes
Smoked Seafood Dip *Pâté de Champagne*
Artichauts Printemp *Waldorf Salad with Cumberland Sauce*
Chicken Hash au Croute Florentine
Sweets from Around the World *Coffee*

West and East Galleries

Assorted Fresh Fruits *Cheeses, Relishes, Dips*
Pâté de Champagne

Waldorf Salad with Cumberland Sauce
Roast Strip Sirloin of Beef *Eggs with Tuna*
Assorted Sweets from Around the World *Coffee*

Beverages

Honey Eggnog

2 eggs, beaten
2 tablespoons honey
2 cups cold milk
½ teaspoon vanilla extract
Nutmeg
½ pint vanilla ice cream (optional)

In a medium bowl combine eggs and honey; mix well. Beat in milk and vanilla. Pour into glasses; sprinkle lightly with nutmeg. For a frosty eggnog, float a scoop of ice cream on top of each serving. Serves 2.

Note: Can also be made in a blender.

Mrs. Jerry Harris (Nancy)

Honey-Strawberry Nog

1 quart milk
1 cup crushed strawberries
½ cup honey
1 teaspoon vanilla extract
1 pint vanilla or strawberry ice cream

In a deep bowl or blender combine milk, strawberries, honey and vanilla. Beat thoroughly or whirl in blender until slushy. Serve in tall glasses. Top with 1 scoop of ice cream. Serves 4.

Mrs. Jerry Harris (Nancy)

Party Punch

2 (750 ml) bottles champagne
4 ounces brandy
1 quart orange sherbet
1 (28-ounce) bottle ginger ale
1 (28-ounce) bottle club soda

In a large punch bowl mix all ingredients; chill well. If desired, add a package of frozen strawberries to float on top. Serves 15.

Mrs. Michael Porter (Paula)

Champagne Punch

1 (6-ounce) can lemonade concentrate, thawed
½ (750 ml) bottle brandy, chilled
1 (28-ounce) bottle sparkling water, chilled
2 (750 ml) bottles champagne, chilled

In a punch bowl combine lemonade and brandy. Add sparkling water and champagne. Serve immediately. Serves 12.

Note: For a festive holiday punch float an ice ring molded with lemon slices and green and red maraschino cherries.

Mrs. Jack Wilson (Mary Jane Brown)

Dunedin Junior Service League "Bundles Coffee" Punch

1 gallon strong coffee
5 cinnamon sticks
1½ pints whipping cream, whipped (3 cups)
⅓ cup sugar
1½ tablespoons vanilla extract
1¼ cups brandy
½ gallon coffee ice cream, softened but not melted

Add cinnamon sticks to hot coffee. When coffee is cool, remove sticks. Pour into a large punch bowl. Stir in 2¼ cups of the whipped cream and remaining ingredients. Serve with dollops of whipped cream floating on top. Serves 30 to 40.

Note: This is traditionally served at the annual "Bundles Coffee" sponsored by the sustainers of the Dunedin Junior Service League.

Mrs. William Hale (Jeanette)
Dunedin, Florida

Sangria Punch

1 (1.5-liter) bottle of Sangria
2 (1-liter) bottles of lemon-lime carbonated drink
1 (6-ounce) can frozen lemonade concentrate, thawed
1 orange, sliced
1 lemon, sliced

Chill Sangria and soda. When ready to serve, pour together into punch bowl. Stir in lemonade. Garnish with orange and lemon slices. Makes 15 cups.

Joyce Gentry
New Port Richey, Florida

Banana Slush

4 cups sugar
6 cups water
1 (46-ounce) can pineapple juice
1 (46-ounce) can orange juice
5 bananas, mashed
½ cup lemon juice
5 (28-ounce) bottles ginger ale, chilled

In a large saucepan combine sugar and water. Bring to a boil, stirring constantly, until sugar dissolves; cool. Pour sugar mixture into a 5-quart freezer container. Stir in pineapple juice, orange juice, bananas and lemon juice; freeze overnight or until firm. Remove mixture from freezer several hours before serving (should be slushy). Pour into punch bowl; stir in ginger ale. Serve. *Perfect summer refresher!* Makes 2½ gallons.

Mrs. Douglas Guilfoile (Paula L. Tiezzi)

Bourbon Slush

Divine describes this Southern fare!

2 (6-ounce) cans frozen lemonade concentrate, thawed
1 (6-ounce) can frozen orange juice concentrate, thawed
2 cups strong tea (3 tea bags)
3 cups bourbon
1½ cups sugar
7 cups water

In a large bowl combine all ingredients. Pour into two ½-gallon containers; cover and freeze. (Plastic ice cream containers work great.) Serve directly from freezer. Keeps indefinitely. Makes 1 gallon.

Mrs. Jack Wilson (Mary Jane Brown)

Kahlua in the Dark

Delicious Over Ice Cream!

4 cups sugar
4 cups water
¾ cup instant coffee
1 teaspoon chocolate syrup
1 tablespoon vanilla extract
1 (750 ml) bottle vodka

In a large pot combine sugar and water; boil. Add coffee and chocolate syrup; cool. Add vanilla and vodka. Pour mixture into a large jug. Store in a dark place. Shake jug well each day for 3 weeks. Pour into small containers to give as gifts. Makes ½ gallon.

Mrs. Richard Benkusky (Judy)

Instant Russian Tea

2½ cups instant orange drink mix
1 cup instant tea mix with lemon and sugar
1 to 1½ cups sugar
2 teaspoons cinnamon
1 teaspoon allspice
1 teaspoon ground cloves

In a medium mixing bowl combine all ingredients; mix well. Store in an airtight jar or canister. Use 1 tablespoon of mix with water for hot or cold tea. Makes 5 cups of mix.

Mrs. Lynn Lees
Mrs. J. J. Suddath, Jr. (Eleanor Picken)

Christmas Wassail

6 tea bags
2½ cups boiling water
¼ teaspoon allspice
¼ teaspoon cinnamon
¼ teaspoon nutmeg
¾ cup sugar
2 cups cranberry juice
½ cup orange juice
⅓ cup lemon juice
1½ cups water
½ cup wine or brandy (optional)
10 peppermint canes

Steep tea and spices in 2½ cups boiling water for 5 minutes; strain. Stir in sugar until dissolved. Add juices, water and wine or brandy, if desired. Heat to boiling. Serve hot with peppermint canes. Serves 10.

Suncoast Seasons Committee

Roman Punch

2 cups sugar
2 cups water
2 cups strong tea
1¼ cups orange juice
1 cup lemon juice
2 teaspoons almond extract
2 teaspoons vanilla extract
1 quart grape juice

In a medium saucepan combine sugar and water; boil for 5 minutes. Mix with remaining ingredients in a 1-gallon container. Add sufficient water to fill container, if necessary. Makes 1 gallon.

Note: Excellent served hot at Christmas or cold with an ice ring in summer.

Mrs. J. J. Suddath, Sr. (Sarah)
Tampa, Florida

Fruit Slush

1 (12-ounce) can frozen orange juice concentrate, thawed
1½ cups water
1½ cups sugar
1 (30-ounce) can apricot halves, drained
3 medium bananas
3 (8-ounce) cans crushed pineapple, drained
½ cup rum (optional)

In a blender mix juice, water and sugar. In a medium bowl mash apricots and bananas together; add pineapple and rum. In a large mixing bowl combine all ingredients; mix well. Pour into individual containers; freeze until firm. Remove from freezer 15 minutes before serving. Serves 25.

Hint: Small plastic glasses work well.

Mrs. William Harris (Clara)
Dunedin, Florida

Hot Mulled Cider

1 gallon cider
1 cup brown sugar
Juice of 1 lemon
4 (3-inch) cinnamon sticks
1 teaspoon whole cloves
1 orange, thinly sliced, for garnish
1 (6-ounce) jar maraschino cherries, for garnish

Combine all ingredients except garnish in a large pot; bring to a boil. Reduce heat; simmer 20 minutes. Strain; discard spices. Serve in mugs topped with a thin orange slice and maraschino cherry. Serves 16.

Variation: Add dark rum to each mug for superb holiday cheer!

Mrs. Brian Cook (Lee)
Dunedin, Florida

Mocha Iced Coffee

6 ounces semi-sweet chocolate
1/2 teaspoon cinnamon
4 cups hot coffee
16 coffee ice cubes
Whipped cream
Sugar

In the top of a double boiler, over simmering water, melt semi-sweet chocolate. Stir in cinnamon and gradually add hot coffee; chill mixture. Pour into 4 tall glasses filled with coffee ice cubes; serve with cream and sugar. Serves 4.

Note: To make coffee ice cubes, fill an ice tray with cooled coffee and freeze until firm. Makes 16 cubes.

Suncoast Seasons Committee

Brandied Coffee

3 tablespoons brandy
1 teaspoon dark brown sugar
1/4 teaspoon cinnamon
1 cup hot, strong coffee
1/3 cup whipping cream, whipped

In a mug combine brandy, brown sugar and cinnamon. Stir in coffee and top with whipped cream. Especially good on a cold evening! Serves 1.

Suncoast Seasons Committee

Viennese Coffee

4 ounces semi-sweet chocolate
1/4 cup whipping cream
4 cups strong, freshly brewed coffee
Lightly whipped cream, to taste
Cinnamon

In the top of a double boiler, over simmering water, melt chocolate with cream, stirring until mixture is smooth. Add coffee; heat. Stir mixture until it just begins to froth. Pour coffee into 4 cups; top each serving with a dollop of whipped cream. Sprinkle with cinnamon. Serves 4.

Suncoast Seasons Committee

For an elegant touch of class! serve in demi-tasse cups. Prepare coffee in a drip pot using 2 tablespoons of coffee grounds for every 6 ounces of cold water rather than the normal 1 tablespoon of coffee per 6 ounces of water.

Appetizers and Hors d'oeuvre

Wine and Cheese Guide

Cheese is a living substance; and in order to enjoy it at its best, it is important to look after it properly. Keep the cheese in a cool, dark, well-ventilated place. Remember that all cheese should be served at room temperature. To prevent soft cheeses which have already been cut from running, place them upright in their boxes, or press a strip of wood against the cut surface.

Bel Paese—Beaujolais, Orvieto Seco, Moselle, Dutchess Rhine, Delaware

Brick, German—Rhones, St. Emilion, Chianti, Gattinera, Baco Noir Burgundy, Chelois and Beer

Brick, American—Bland enough to serve with any wine

Brie—Dry Sherry, Chianti, Red Burgundies, Chelois, Baco Noir Burgundy

Camembert—Hermitage, Red Burgundies, Sancerre, Vouvray, Pouilly Fume, Dutchess Rhine, Baco Noir Burgundy, Chelois, and Cabernet Sauvignon

Caraway—Bordeaux Reds, White Burgundies, Baco Noir Burgundy, Chelois, Chablis, Diamond

Cheddar—(including Black Diamond, Colby, Longhorn, Cheddar-Herkimer) Red Bordeaux or Burgundies, Baco Noir Burgundy, Chelois

Colby—Ruby Cabernet

Edam—Medium-Dry Sherry, Red Bordeaux or Burgundies, Port, Solers Dry Cocktail Sherry, Baco Noir Burgundy, Chelois

Gouda—Graves, Cote D'Beaune, Beaujolais, Grignolino, Chelois, Chablis

Gruyere—Red Burgundies, Rhone, Baco Noir Burgundy, Chelois

Monterey Jack—Gamay Beaujolais, Rhine Wine

Muenster—Red and White Bordeaux, Baco Noir Burgundy, Chelois

Port Du Salut—Red or White Burgundy, Rhine, Johannisberg Riesling, Dutchess Rhine, Chablis, Diamond, Delaware, Baco Noir Burgundy

Swiss—Red Burgundies, Rhone, Baco Noir Burgundy, Chelois

Place left-over pieces of cheese in a cheese crock; blend equal parts cheese and butter; moisten with wine or liquor.

Avocado Dip

1 ripe avocado, peeled and mashed
1 cup mayonnaise
½ cup French dressing
1 onion, minced
1 teaspoon wine vinegar

In a medium bowl combine all ingredients; mix well. Chill. Serve with raw vegetables. Easy! Makes 2 cups.

Mrs. Edward W. Roos (Mildred Seagren)

Hot Dried Beef Dip

1 (8-ounce) package cream cheese, softened
1 (2½-ounce) jar dried beef
2 tablespoons finely chopped onion
½ cup sour cream
2 tablespoons finely chopped green pepper
2 tablespoons milk
⅛ teaspoon pepper

In a medium bowl combine all ingredients; mix well. Pour into an 8-inch glass pie pan. Bake at 350 degrees for 15 minutes. Serve warm. Makes 2 cups.

Mrs. John Gardner (Jean)

Chicken Liver Dip

½ pound chicken livers
2 tablespoons butter
1 tablespoon finely chopped onion
½ teaspoon curry powder
¼ teaspoon paprika
1 teaspoon seasoned salt
¼ cup chicken broth
2 (8-ounce) packages cream cheese, softened
1 cup chopped, toasted walnuts

In a skillet sauté chicken livers in butter with onion, curry powder, paprika and salt until tender. Cool slightly. Put into blender; add broth and whirl smooth. Beat in cream cheese. Pour mixture into a bowl; cover. Chill several hours to mellow flavors. Stir in walnuts before serving. Makes 2½ cups.

Mrs. Robert D. Garretson (Charlene)
Denville, New Jersey

Baked Clam Dip in a Shell

1 large round loaf crusty bread, unsliced
2 (8-ounce) packages cream cheese, softened
3 (6½-ounce) cans chopped clams, drained (reserve liquid)
2 tablespoons grated onion
2 tablespoons beer
2 teaspoons Worcestershire sauce
2 teaspoons lemon juice
1 teaspoon hot pepper sauce, or to taste
½ teaspoon salt
Parsley sprigs for garnish (optional)
Raw vegetables for dipping

With a sharp knife cut top from bread; set aside. Hollow loaf leaving a 1½- to 2-inch shell. Cut removed bread into cubes; set both aside. In a large bowl beat cream cheese until smooth. Stir in drained clams, ¼ cup reserved clam liquid and remaining ingredients except parsley; mix until well blended. On baking sheet make a cross with two sheets of foil, each long enough to cover loaf. Center bread shell on foil. Pour clam mixture into shell; cover with bread top. Wrap loaf with the foil. Bake at 250 degrees for 3 hours for flavors to blend. Toast bread cubes in oven during last 5 minutes of baking time. Remove top; sprinkle dip with parsley. Serve loaf on large platter surrounded by the bread cubes and raw vegetables for dippers. When empty, the bread shell can be cut or torn apart and eaten. Serves 12.

Mrs. Jack Wilson (Mary Jane Brown)

Harvey's Delight

Sandwich Spread or Dip

1 (16-ounce) can whole tomatoes, undrained and mashed
1 (16-ounce) package pasteurized process cheese spread, cut into chunks
1 (4-ounce) package dried beef, finely cut
3 tablespoons cornstarch
1 teaspoon water

In a medium pan cook tomatoes on medium heat for 4 minutes; add cheese and beef. Heat until cheese is melted. In a small bowl combine cornstarch and water; add to cheese mixture. Cook until mixture thickens. Cool in refrigerator until ready to serve. Makes 1 quart.

Harvey Huston
Altoona, Pennsylvania

Creamy Spinach Dill Dip

1 cup sour cream
1 cup mayonnaise
1/2 cup chopped green onions
1/2 cup chopped parsley
2 teaspoons dill
1 teaspoon monosodium glutamate
1 teaspoon salt
1 (10-ounce) package frozen chopped spinach, thawed and squeezed

Mix all ingredients in a blender. Serve with a variety of fresh vegetables. Makes 3 cups.

Mrs. James Berfield (Sue Mautz)

Crab Dip with Sesame Toast

Superb!

3 (8-ounce) packages cream cheese, softened
1/2 cup mayonnaise
2/3 cup dry white wine
1/8 teaspoon garlic salt
2 teaspoons Dijon mustard
2 teaspoons powdered sugar
1 teaspoon onion juice
1/8 teaspoon seasoned salt
3 (6 1/2-ounce) cans crabmeat, drained
2 (4-ounce) cans water chestnuts, drained and finely chopped (optional)

In a blender mix all ingredients except crabmeat and water chestnuts until well blended. Fold in crabmeat and water chestnuts. Place in top of double boiler; heat. Serve in chafing dish.

Sesame Toast:

1 (16-ounce) loaf thin-sliced white bread
1 cup butter, room temperature
1/4 cup sesame seeds

Butter bread; cut each slice in half. Put on cookie sheet; sprinkle with sesame seeds. Bake at 250 degrees for 35 minutes or until just firm. Makes 48.

Note: Freezes well.

Mrs. C. Henry Foltz (Caryn), Cleveland, Ohio
Mrs. J. Douglas Fresh (Jane Nolan)

Florentine Dip in Pumpernickel

1 (4-ounce) can water chestnuts, drained and finely chopped
1 small onion, finely chopped
1 (10-ounce) package frozen chopped spinach, thawed and squeezed
1 (2.75-ounce) package Swiss-style vegetable soup mix
1 cup sour cream
1 cup mayonnaise
1 (16-ounce) loaf round pumpernickel bread

In a large bowl or blender mix all ingredients except bread. Refrigerate at least four hours. When ready to serve, cut off top of bread; hollow out loaf leaving a ½ inch shell. Pour dip into bread shell. Cube bread filling; use for dipping along with vegetable crudités. Serves 15.

Mrs. Arthur M. Borham (Nancy L. Thomson)
Mrs. Charles R. Grimm (Carol), Palm Harbor, Florida

Tex-Mex Dip

2 (10½-ounce) cans bean dip
3 large, ripe avocados, peeled and mashed
½ teaspoon salt
¼ teaspoon pepper
2 tablespoons lemon juice
1 (16-ounce) carton sour cream
¼ (1¼-ounce) package taco seasoning mix
¼ cup mayonnaise
1 cup chopped onion
1 (3¼-ounce) can pitted ripe olives, chopped
3 medium tomatoes, diced
8 ounces Cheddar cheese, shredded

Spread bean dip on a large platter. In a small bowl combine avocado, salt, pepper and lemon juice; mix well. Spread on top of bean dip. Combine sour cream, taco seasoning and mayonnaise in a small bowl; spread over avocado layer. Sprinkle remaining ingredients on top. Serve with large corn chips. Serves 16.

Mrs. Arthur M. Borham (Nancy L. Thomson)

Hot Clam Dip

1 (8-ounce) can minced clams, drained
½ (1.37-ounce) package dry onion soup mix
1 (8-ounce) package cream cheese, softened
1 (16-ounce) carton sour cream
1 tablespoon dill weed

In a large bowl combine all ingredients; mix well. Let stand in refrigerator for 1 hour. Pour into 1½-quart casserole. Bake at 350 degrees for 30 to 45 minutes until bubbly. Makes 4 cups.

Mrs. Charles R. Grimm (Carol)
Palm Harbor, Florida

Spinach Dip

1 cup sour cream
½ cup mayonnaise
1 package Swiss-style creamed vegetable soup
½ (10-ounce) package frozen chopped spinach, thawed and squeezed

In a medium bowl mix all ingredients. Serve with bugle-shaped corn snacks, crackers, or raw vegetables. Can be stored in the refrigerator for several days. Makes 2 cups.

Variation: For spread use whole package of spinach.

Mrs. Dean N. McFarland (Donna VanEwyk)

Hot Crabmeat Dip

1 (6½-ounce) can Alaskan king crab, drained
1 (8-ounce) package cream cheese, softened
2 tablespoons mayonnaise
2 tablespoons minced onion
1 to 2 tablespoons curry powder, or to taste
2 tablespoons Worcestershire sauce
2 tablespoons lemon juice
2 tablespoons grated Parmesan cheese

In a medium bowl combine first 7 ingredients; blend well. Pour into a 1-quart casserole; sprinkle with cheese. Bake at 400 degrees for 30 minutes. Makes 2 cups.

Alice Forrester, Madre, California
Mrs. David J. Kremske (Layle J. Feltman)

Nacho Hot Cheese Dip

1 (10-ounce) can jalapeño peppers
1 medium onion, chopped
1½ cloves garlic, crushed
1½ pounds pasteurized process cheese, softened
2 cups mayonnaise

Remove stems and seeds from peppers. Place peppers, onion and garlic in blender; mix well. Cut cheese into cubes and add with mayonnaise to blended mixture. Beat until smooth. Pour into jars; refrigerate. Serve hot or cold with nachos. Makes 5 cups.

Mrs. Mark J. Palmer (Martha)
Northvale, New Jersey

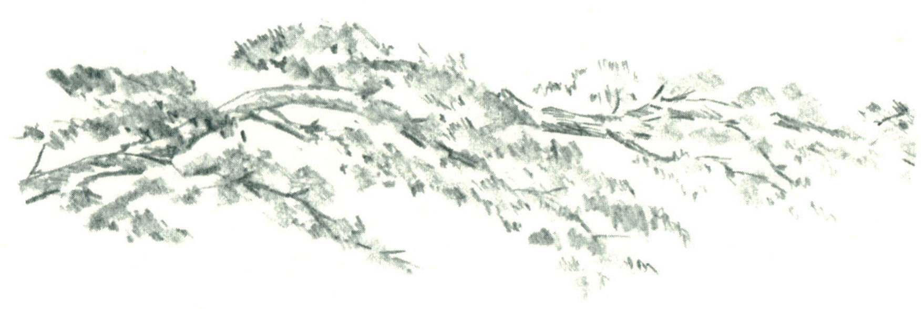

Salsa

3 large jalapeño peppers, roasted
1 bunch scallions, chopped (2 cups)
1 teaspoon basil
3 tablespoons chopped cilantro
2 to 3 large ripe tomatoes, chopped
¼ teaspoon freshly ground black pepper

Skin and finely chop roasted peppers. In a medium bowl mix peppers, scallions, basil, cilantro, tomatoes and pepper. Refrigerate 24 hours. Serve with nachos. Makes 3 cups.

Mrs. Michael Chandler (Dee)
Las Vegas, Nevada

Cilantro, coriander or Chinese parsley is an old world herb of the carrot family. The fresh dark green leaves are used in many cultures.

Vegetable Dip for Crudité

⅔ cup mayonnaise
⅔ cup sour cream
1 tablespoon parsley flakes
1 tablespoon minced onion
2 teaspoons Beau Monde seasoning
1 tablespoon dill weed

In a small bowl combine all ingredients; mix well. Chill at least 1 hour before serving. Makes 1½ cups.

Mrs. Robert Hartford (Linda)
Mrs. Mark J. Palmer (Martha), Northvale, New Jersey

Kitchen Hint: If celery or carrots go limp before you use them, soak in cold water one hour. Add lemon juice or vinegar. Drain vegetables. Place in plastic bag and put in refrigerator until crisp.

Mushroom Piroshkis

Filling:

½ cup finely chopped onions
¼ cup butter or margarine
½ pound fresh mushrooms, finely chopped
¾ teaspoon salt
¼ teaspoon freshly ground black pepper
1 hard-cooked egg, chopped

Pastry:

1 (11-ounce) package pie crust mix or 2 pie crust sticks, crumbled
½ cup sour cream

In a skillet sauté onions in butter until tender. Add mushrooms; sauté 3 minutes. Stir in salt, pepper and egg; mix gently. Cool. Prepare pastry by mixing pie crust and sour cream; form into ball. Roll onto floured surface; cut into 3-inch rounds. Spoon 1 teaspoon filling onto half of circle; moisten edges with water. Fold in half; press edges with fork. Bake on ungreased cookie sheet at 400 degrees for 12 to 15 minutes or until golden brown, serve hot.

Note: Mushroom Piroshkis can be frozen on cookie sheet before baking, then placed in plastic bags for longer storage. When frozen, increase baking time 15 to 18 minutes.

Mrs. Joseph L. Andreani (Sandra)
Oldsmar, Florida

Crabmeat Muffins

1/2 cup butter, room temperature
1 (5-ounce) jar sharp pasteurized process cheese spread
1 1/2 teaspoons mayonnaise
1/2 teaspoon garlic salt
1/2 teaspoon seasoned salt
1 (6 1/2-ounce) can crabmeat, drained
6 English muffins, cut in half

In a medium bowl combine all ingredients except muffins; mix well. Spread mixture on muffins; place in freezer at least 10 minutes. Remove from freezer 1 at a time; cut into 6 to 8 pieces; return to freezer. When frozen, store in plastic bags in freezer. To serve, broil on cookie sheet 10 minutes until brown. Makes 72 or more.

Dottie Mueller
Pleasant Plain, Ohio

Fried Cauliflower

1 head cauliflower, broken into flowerets
2 cups Italian breadcrumbs
1 (1 1/2-ounce) package grated Romano cheese
2 cloves garlic, finely diced, or 1 teaspoon garlic powder
2 eggs, beaten
Oil for frying

In a large saucepan cover cauliflower with water and cook until just tender; drain well. In a small bowl combine breadcrumbs, cheese and garlic. Heat oil in a skillet. Dip cauliflower in eggs; roll in breadcrumb mixture. Fry in oil until golden brown. Makes 40 small flowerets.

Mrs. Anthony Castrogiovanni (BeBe)

Chicken Livers in Wine

1/3 cup butter or margarine
1 large onion, chopped
1 (4-ounce) can sliced mushrooms, drained
1 clove garlic, minced
1 pound chicken livers
1/2 cup all-purpose flour or breadcrumbs
1/4 cup red wine

In a skillet sauté onions, mushrooms and garlic in butter. Coat chicken livers with flour or breadcrumbs. Add to skillet and brown; add red wine. Pour into a greased 1-quart casserole. Bake at 375 degrees for 15 minutes. Serves 4.

Mrs. Lawrence Feltman (Bertha)
Chicago, Illinois

Asparagus Rolls

4 ounces bleu cheese, softened
1 (8-ounce) package cream cheese, softened
1 egg
24 slices very thin bread
24 fresh asparagus spears, cooked and cooled
1/2 cup butter, melted

Mix bleu cheese, cream cheese and egg in blender until smooth. Trim crusts from bread and flatten with rolling pin. Spread each slice generously with cheese mixture. Roll one asparagus spear up in each slice of bread. Dip in melted butter to coat. Place on cookie sheet and freeze. Remove from freezer 40 minutes before baking. While firm, cut each roll in half and secure with a toothpick. Bake at 400 degrees for 10 to 12 minutes turning once. Makes 4 dozen.

Hint: You may use 1 (8-ounce) package frozen asparagus spears.

Alice Forrester
Madre, California

Herb-Stuffed Mushrooms

1 1/2 pounds large, fresh mushrooms
1/2 cup butter, divided
3 tablespoons finely chopped green onion
1/2 cup chopped parsley
1/2 cup breadcrumbs
1 teaspoon Italian seasoning or 1 teaspoon savory, oregano or basil
1/2 teaspoon salt
1/8 teaspoon pepper
1/8 teaspoon garlic salt
4 ounces Cheddar cheese, shredded
4 ounces Monterey Jack cheese, shredded
1/4 cup grated Parmesan cheese

Remove stems from mushrooms and chop very finely. In a skillet melt 1/4 cup butter; sauté stems. Remove stems from pan; set aside. Melt remaining butter in skillet; sauté onion, crumbs, parsley and spices. Add shredded cheeses; melt. Mix in stems. Stuff mixture into mushroom caps; sprinkle with Parmesan cheese. Bake on a cookie sheet at 350 degrees for 20 minutes. Can be fixed ahead and stored in refrigerator, then baked when ready to serve. Serves 50.

Mrs. Stanley Kincaid (Pat)
Ozona, Florida

Savory or summer savory is a European herb in the mint family, usually in leaves or ground. The aroma is pine-like.

Sausage-Stuffed Mushroom Caps

1 pound fresh mushrooms
1/4 pound bulk seasoned sausage
1/2 cup breadcrumbs
1 tablespoon butter, melted

Wash mushrooms gently. Remove stems; chop into fine pieces. In a skillet brown sausage; do not overcook. Add mushroom stems; sauté with sausage until tender. Add breadcrumbs and butter; mix well. Stuff mushroom caps with sausage mixture; place in 13x9x2-inch baking dish. Bake at 350 degrees for 15 to 20 minutes. Makes 25 to 30 caps.

Mrs. Douglas Guilfoile (Paula L. Tiezzi)

Stuffed Mushrooms

1 pound large fresh mushrooms
1 (8-ounce) package cream cheese, softened
2 teaspoons Worcestershire sauce
2 teaspoons lemon juice
1 small onion, finely chopped
10 strips bacon, fried crisp and crumbled
1/8 teaspoon garlic salt
1 tablespoon chopped parsley

Wash mushrooms; remove stems. In a medium bowl combine remaining ingredients. Stuff mushroom caps with cheese mixture; place on lightly greased cookie sheet. Bake at 350 degrees for 25 to 30 minutes; serve hot. Serves 6.

Mrs. Chris Demas (Jeannie)

Marinated Mushrooms

Great for parties!

40 small fresh mushrooms
2 tablespoons lemon juice
2 tablespoons wine vinegar
1 teaspoon salt
1/3 cup olive or salad oil
1 clove garlic, minced
1/8 teaspoon fresh ground pepper
1 bay leaf
1/8 teaspoon oregano

Clean mushrooms. Place in a saucepan with enough water to cover; simmer for 5 minutes. Drain and cool. Mix remaining ingredients in 1-quart jar with lid; shake well. Add mushrooms; marinate overnight in refrigerator. Makes 40.

Mrs. J. J. Suddath, Jr. (Eleanor Picken)

Escargots à la Française

Gourmet stuffed mushrooms!

16 large mushrooms
1/2 cup butter, room temperature
3 slices bacon, cooked and crumbled
1 teaspoon minced shallots
1 tablespoon chopped parsley
1 clove garlic, minced
16 bay scallops (4 ounces)
16 snails

Wash and dry mushrooms; remove stems. Put mushrooms into a baking dish, hollow side up. In a small bowl combine butter, bacon, shallots, parsley and garlic. Put one scallop and one snail in each mushroom cap. Cover with butter mixture using about 1 rounded teaspoon in each. Bake at 350 degrees for 20 to 25 minutes. Serve with rye toast points. Serves 16.

Mrs. Michael Porter (Paula)

Mussel Appetizer Salad

1 (10-ounce) can mussels, liquid reserved
1/2 cup olive oil
3 cups finely chopped onions
1/2 cup rice
1/4 to 1/2 teaspoon allspice
3/4 teaspoon salt
1/2 teaspoon pepper
1/2 cup currants
1 cup chopped walnuts or 1/4 cup pine nuts
1 tablespoon minced parsley (optional)

Drain mussels, reserving liquid. Add enough water to liquid to make 1 cup; set aside. Remove any black spots from mussels. In a skillet sauté onions in oil until light brown. Add rice, allspice, salt, pepper and reserved broth; cook for 10 minutes. Add mussels, currants and nuts; stir to blend. Cover; simmer 10 minutes more or until rice is cooked. Serve cold on a bed of lettuce or oyster shells. Sprinkle with parsley. Serves 8.

Variation: If more mussels are desired, 2 cans can be used. Two cans of whole baby clams may be substituted for mussels.

Mrs. Gregory H. Keuroghlian (Nora Ghazikian)

Shanghai Spring Rolls with Duck Sauce

Filling:

4 dried Chinese mushrooms
1 cup boiling water
1/2 pound lean ground pork
2 teaspoons cornstarch
1 tablespoon soy sauce
1/3 cup finely chopped raw shrimp
1 teaspoon sherry
2 tablespoons peanut oil
1/2 teaspoon salt
1/4 cup chicken broth
1 (13-ounce) can bean sprouts, drained, rinsed in cold water and dried with paper towels, or 3/4 pound fresh bean sprouts
8 whole scallions, finely chopped

In a small bowl cover mushrooms with boiling water; let stand 15 to 20 minutes. Squeeze the mushrooms to extract as much liquid as possible; cut off stems and discard. Shred mushrooms; set aside. In a small bowl combine pork with 1 teaspoon cornstarch and soy sauce; set aside. In a small bowl combine shrimp, sherry and 1 teaspoon cornstarch; set aside. In medium skillet heat oil; cook pork mixture, stirring well, until pork loses its color. Add mushrooms and salt; then add chicken broth, mixing well. Add shrimp and bean sprouts; briefly cook while stirring. Stir in scallions. Remove from heat and cool.

Preparation:

1 package Shanghai spring roll skins
1 beaten egg for sealing
Vegetable shortening for deep frying

Leave the spring rolls in one stack and keep them covered with a damp cloth as you work. Lay one spring roll shiny side down on a flat surface, one corner pointing toward you. Spoon about 2 tablespoons of the filling onto the mid-lower corner of the skin in a sausage shape. Fold the corner of the skin pointing toward you over the filling until just covered. Give it another turn to enclose the filling. Moisten the left and right corners of the triangle with beaten egg; fold over the corners. Press down firmly to seal, making a kind of envelope. Moisten the top flap with egg and turn until the cylinder is sealed firmly. Repeat, laying finished rolls on buttered baking pan. At this point spring rolls can be frozen or refrigerated after covering pan with aluminum foil. Heat shortening in wok or cast iron Dutch oven; when it is almost smoking, cook the spring rolls until crisp and golden brown. Drain on paper towel. Serve with duck sauce or hot mustard sauce.

Duck Sauce:

½ cup chopped chutney
½ cup apricot, plum or peach preserves
¼ cup plus 1 tablespoon brown sugar
1 teaspoon vinegar

In small bowl mix together all ingredients. Leftover sauce can be refrigerated in a covered jar.

Hint: Use a cleaver for finely chopping shrimp and onions.

Mrs. Jay Johnston, Princeton, New Jersey

Cheese Olives

1 (5-ounce) jar sharp pasteurized process cheese spread
3 tablespoons butter
¾ cup all-purpose flour
¼ teaspoon salt
½ teaspoon paprika
1 (5-ounce) jar medium-size stuffed green olives, drained

In a medium bowl combine all ingredients except olives. Mix until soft dough. If mixture is sticky, place in refrigerator for 1 hour or longer. Pinch off small amounts of dough; mold around olives forming balls. Place on ungreased cookie sheet. Bake at 400 degrees for 15 minutes. Makes 50.

Note: May be made ahead and frozen either before or after baking. Bake as above or reheat. *Excellent!*

Mrs. Dean N. McFarland (Donna VanEwyk)

Zucchini Appetizer

3 cups thinly sliced, unpeeled zucchini
1 cup biscuit baking mix
½ cup finely chopped onion
½ teaspoon seasoned salt
¼ teaspoon oregano or marjoram
⅛ teaspoon pepper
2 tablespoons chopped parsley
½ cup grated Parmesan cheese
¼ cup oil
4 eggs, slightly beaten
⅛ teaspoon garlic salt

In a large bowl mix together all ingredients; pour into greased 13x9x2-inch baking pan. Bake at 350 degrees for 30 to 35 minutes or until golden brown. Cut into finger-size portions. Makes 36.

Mrs. Walter D. Walker (Bettie Norris)
Mrs. John H. Mancini (Elizabeth), Clearwater, Florida

Barbecued Sausage Balls

1 pound bulk pork sausage
1 egg, slightly beaten
1/3 cup dry breadcrumbs
1/2 teaspoon sage

In a bowl mix sausage, egg, breadcrumbs and sage. Shape into 1-inch balls. In a skillet brown balls slowly on all sides, about 15 minutes. Drain off excess fat. Pour sauce over meat; cover. Simmer 30 minutes, stirring occasionally to coat balls. Makes 25 to 30 balls.

Sauce:

1/2 cup ketchup
2 tablespoons brown sugar
1 tablespoon vinegar
1 tablespoon soy sauce

In a bowl combine all ingredients; mix well. A small amount of water may be added if sauce is too thick.

Mrs. Phillip Chabot (Eva)
Royal Palm Beach, Florida

Cocktail Meatballs

Sauce:

1 (16-ounce) can whole cranberry sauce
1 (16-ounce) can tomato sauce

Combine cranberry sauce and tomato sauce. Cook slowly in large pot while preparing meatballs.

Meatballs:

1 pound ground chuck
1/4 cup Italian flavored breadcrumbs
1 teaspoon grated Parmesan cheese
1/4 teaspoon oregano
1/4 teaspoon parsley flakes
1/8 teaspoon garlic powder
1/2 teaspoon salt
1/4 teaspoon pepper
1 egg
Milk, just enough to moisten, if needed

Combine all meatball ingredients in a large bowl; mix well. Shape into small balls; place in sauce mixture. Cover; cook slowly for 2 hours. Serve hot on a tray with toothpicks. Makes 6 to 7 dozen.

Mrs. Robert Hall (Barbara)

Party Meatballs with Creamy Dill Sauce

1 1/2 pounds ground beef
1 pound ground veal
1 (4 1/2-ounce) can deviled ham
2/3 cup evaporated milk
2 eggs
1 tablespoon grated onion
1 cup soft whole wheat breadcrumbs (2 slices)
1/2 teaspoon salt
1/2 teaspoon allspice
1/4 teaspoon pepper
1/4 cup shortening
1/4 cup water

In a large bowl combine all ingredients except shortening and water. Mix lightly with a fork. Form into small meatballs. In a large skillet brown a few at a time in shortening. Drain fat from pan; return meatballs. Add water; cover. Simmer 20 minutes or until heated through. Spoon into chafing dish or server. Pour creamy dill sauce over meatballs; garnish with a sprig of fresh dill. Makes 6 dozen.

Sauce:

2 tablespoons butter or margarine
2 tablespoons all-purpose flour
1/2 teaspoon salt
1 cup water
1 cup sour cream
1 tablespoon ketchup
1 tablespoon dill weed

In a small saucepan melt butter; blend in flour and salt. Cook, stirring constantly, just until mixture bubbles. Slowly stir in water; continue cooking and stirring until sauce thickens and boils. Boil 1 minute more. Stir in sour cream, ketchup and dill weed. Heat just to boiling.

Mrs. William S. Sharpe (Wanda)

Baked Brie

Easy, Simple, Elegant!

6 (4 1/2-ounce) rounds of imported brie cheese
6 teaspoons butter
6 tablespoons lightly toasted, sliced almonds

Place brie rounds in individual ramekins; top each brie with teaspoon of butter and tablespoon of almonds. Bake about 4 minutes at 400 degrees, or until crusty on outside and runny inside. Serve with hot French bread, slices of Delicious apples and Anjou pears, and clusters of green grapes. Serves 6.

Suncoast Seasons Committee

A delightful accompaniment to baked brie would be dry sherry, chianti, red burgundy, chelois, or baco noir burgundy.

Sauerkraut Balls

1 (8-ounce) package pork sausage
¼ to ½ cup chopped onion
1 tablespoon mustard
1 tablespoon chopped parsley
¼ teaspoon garlic salt
⅛ teaspoon pepper
1 (3-ounce) package cream cheese, softened
1 (14-ounce) can sauerkraut, drained, liquid reserved
2 eggs, beaten well
¼ cup milk
¼ cup all-purpose flour
½ cup dry breadcrumbs
Oil for frying

In a skillet brown sausage; add onion and cook slightly. Drain fat from pan. Add mustard, parsley, garlic salt, pepper, cream cheese and sauerkraut; mix well. Put in refrigerator overnight. Refrigerate sauerkraut liquid. When ready to serve, remove mixture from refrigerator and form into small balls. Use reserved sauerkraut liquid, if needed for moisture, to make balls. In a small bowl combine eggs and milk. Mix together flour and breadcrumbs. Dip balls in egg mixture and roll in crumb mixture. Place balls in hot oil in a skillet, using enough oil to almost cover balls. Fry until golden brown for about 1 to 1½ minutes. Serve warm. Makes about 30 balls.

Note: Balls may be made ahead and kept in refrigerator or freezer. If frozen uncooked, thaw before frying. If cooked, thaw and bake at 375 degrees for 10 minutes or until warmed through.

Mrs. Dorman Duncan (Billi)

Mystery Muffins

6 English muffins, cut in half
8 ounces sharp Cheddar cheese, shredded
1 (3¼-ounce) can pitted ripe olives, finely chopped
1 medium onion, finely chopped
½ cup mayonnaise
2 teaspoons curry powder, or to taste

Cut each muffin half into quarters; place on a cookie sheet. In a medium bowl combine remaining ingredients; mix well. Spread mixture on muffin pieces. Bake at 375 degrees for 10 to 15 minutes until cheese is golden brown. Serve warm. Makes 4 dozen.

Note: A taste treat even non-curry lovers will love!

Danielle Lynn and Robert Nathan Borham
Palm Harbor, Florida

Pickled Shrimp

Great party dish!

1¼ pounds fresh shrimp, shelled
½ cup chopped celery tops
¼ cup mixed pickling spices
2 cups sliced onion
5 bay leaves
½ cup pickled sweet red peppers
1¼ cups salad oil
¾ cup white vinegar
2 tablespoons capers and liquid
1½ teaspoons celery seed
1½ teaspoons salt
⅛ teaspoon hot pepper sauce

Cover shrimp with boiling water. Tie celery tops and pickling spices loosely in a cheese cloth bag; add to shrimp. Cook 2 to 3 minutes or until pink. Remove spices; drain shrimp; cool. Arrange shrimp and onions in alternate layers in a bowl; add bay leaves and red peppers. In a medium bowl mix oil, vinegar, capers, celery seed, salt and hot pepper sauce. Pour over shrimp and onion. Cover; chill for 24 hours. Drain before serving. Serves 12 to 20.

Mrs. William Parmer (Jean Glasscock)

Capers are the flower buds of a Mediterranean caper bush; they are pickled and used for flavoring or garnish.

Pizza Bread Appetizers

1 package frozen bread dough (three 1-pound loaves)
¼ pound Swiss cheese, shredded
¼ pound provolone cheese, shredded
½ pound mozzarella cheese, shredded
2 (1-pound) sticks pepperoni, sliced

Thaw bread dough; roll out into three rectangles. Put a layer of Swiss, provolone, mozzarella and pepperoni on each rectangle; roll up. Slit top of each bread roll in 4 to 5 slashes. Bake at 350 degrees until golden brown, about 20 to 25 minutes. Slice as you would bread. Makes 30 slices.

Hint: May be baked ahead of time, wrapped in aluminum foil and frozen. Heat before serving.

Jeffrey Palmer Brancato
Oldsmar, Florida

Little Party Pizzas

2 pounds bacon, fried crisp and crumbled
2 bunches green onions, diced
2 (16-ounce) packages Cheddar cheese, shredded
1 cup mayonnaise
3 loaves party rye bread

Combine first four ingredients in a large bowl. Spread on individual slices of party rye; place on cookie sheet. Heat under broiler for 1 to 2 minutes until cheese is bubbly and lightly browned. Serve immediately. Serves 24 to 30.

Note: When dicing green onions, use 1 inch of the green stem.

Mrs. Bill Ritchey (Carol Eddington)

Smoked Fish Spread

1½ pounds smoked mullet
2 teaspoons minced onion
2 teaspoons finely chopped celery
1 clove garlic, minced
2 tablespoons finely chopped sweet pickle
1¼ cups mayonnaise
1 tablespoon mustard
⅛ teaspoon Worcestershire sauce
2 tablespoons chopped parsley

Remove skin and *carefully bone fish*; flake well. In a medium bowl mix all ingredients together. Chill at least one hour before serving. Makes 3½ cups.

Mrs. S. E. "Pete" Covey (Carol Daugherty)

Tipsy Wieners

2 tablespoons chopped onions
1 tablespoon butter
½ cup ketchup
⅓ cup brown sugar
1 cup bourbon
1 pound cocktail sausages

In a saucepan sauté onions in butter. Blend in ketchup, sugar and bourbon. Add sausages; simmer for 30 minutes. Makes 24.

Variation:

1 cup ketchup
1 cup brown sugar
1 cup bourbon
1 pound hot dogs, cut into fifths

Mix all ingredients together in a 2-quart saucepan. Simmer for 2 hours.

Nan J. Moffatt

Beet Ikra

Russian

1 large green pepper
3 to 4 tablespoons olive oil
1 large onion, finely chopped
4 beets, peeled and shredded
½ teaspoon salt
¼ teaspoon pepper
¼ teaspoon garlic powder
2½ tablespoons tomato paste
2½ tablespoons tomato sauce

Roast pepper in oven at 350 degrees until skin is slightly scorched and easily removed. Skin and chop. Heat enough olive oil to cover bottom of 10-inch skillet. Sauté onion; add remaining ingredients. Adjust seasoning to taste; mix well. Cover; steam about 25 minutes to soften beets. Remove cover; continue to sauté until oil separates and shows on side of pan. Chill mixture. Serve with crackers or pumpernickel party slices. Makes 1½ to 2 cups.

Mrs. H. Jack Bekarian (Stella)
Belmont, Massachusetts

Kitchen Hint: Alternate method to roast peppers: broil 1 inch below heat, turning frequently, until blistered and charred. Place in plastic bag; seal. Let sweat 15 to 20 minutes. Peel; seed; rinse.

Crispy Cheese Wafers

1 cup margarine, room temperature
2 cups shredded sharp Cheddar cheese, softened
½ teaspoon salt
1 teaspoon hot pepper sauce (optional)
2 cups all-purpose flour
2 cups crispy rice cereal

In a large mixing bowl cream together margarine and cheese. Add salt, hot pepper sauce, if desired, and flour; mix well. Stir in cereal. Form into 1-inch balls. Place on ungreased cookie sheet; press flat. Bake at 375 degrees for 15 minutes. Makes 6 dozen.

Note: May be frozen after baking and reheated to serve.

Mrs. David J. Kremske (Layle J. Feltman)
Nan J. Moffatt
Mrs. William Smoot (Helen), Dunedin, Florida

Spicy Cheese Wafers

¼ cup butter or margarine, room temperature
½ cup all-purpose flour, sifted
1 (6-ounce) roll sharp pasteurized process cheese food
½ teaspoon cayenne pepper
3 drops hot pepper sauce

In a medium bowl cream butter with flour and cheese using a pastry blender; stir in cayenne pepper and hot pepper sauce. Form into ½-inch balls. Place 1 inch apart on ungreased cookie sheet; refrigerate for 30 minutes. Heat oven to 350 degrees. With floured bottom of a measuring cup, press each wafer until thin. Bake for 10 minutes until slightly puffy and brown at the edges. Cool; remove to a paper towel. Store in a covered container. Makes 4 dozen.

Mrs. Dean N. McFarland (Donna VanEwyk)

Artichoke Spread

1 (8½-ounce) can water-packed artichokes, drained well and cut up
4 green onions, chopped
1 cup mayonnaise
½ teaspoon garlic salt
½ cup grated Parmesan cheese
2 teaspoons chopped parsley
½ teaspoon paprika

In a medium bowl combine first 5 ingredients; mix well. Spread in a 1-quart baking dish; sprinkle with chopped parsley and paprika. Bake at 350 degrees for 20 to 25 minutes. Serve with melba rounds or potato chips. Serves 6 to 8.

Edna L. White
Clearwater, Florida

Cheese Ball

1 (8-ounce) package cream cheese, softened
1 (3-ounce) package dried beef or corned beef, finely chopped
1½ teaspoons prepared horseradish
2 green onions, chopped
½ cup pecans or walnuts, chopped

Mix all ingredients except nuts; form into a ball. Roll ball in chopped nuts. Chill several hours. Makes 1 large ball.

Hint: Can be made several days ahead. Keeps quite well.

Mrs. John G. Dodson (Frankie Armitage)

Pineapple Cheese Ball

2 (8-ounce) packages cream cheese, softened
1 (8¼-ounce) can crushed pineapple, drained *well*
2 cups chopped pecans or walnuts, divided
¼ cup finely chopped green pepper
2 tablespoons finely chopped onion
1 tablespoon seasoned salt

In a medium bowl beat cream cheese until smooth. Gradually stir in pineapple, 1 cup nuts, green pepper, onion and seasoned salt; mix together. Refrigerate 1 hour. Shape mixture into a ball; roll in remaining nuts. Wrap in aluminum foil. Refrigerate overnight or until well chilled. Serves 40. *Keeps well in the refrigerator for at least 10 days!*

Mrs. Edward Staehle (Helen)
Dunedin, Florida

Turkey Party Ball

For curry lovers!

1 (8-ounce) package cream cheese, softened
¾ cup chopped walnuts
1 cup finely chopped, cooked turkey breast
⅓ cup mayonnaise
1 tablespoon curry powder
2 tablespoons chopped chutney
¼ teaspoon salt
Fresh parsley, chopped

In a medium bowl combine first 7 ingredients; mix well. Chill overnight or at least 4 hours. Form into a ball and roll in chopped parsley. Serve with crackers and pieces of French bread. Makes 3 cups.

From John Pillsbury, former Chef at Clearwater Beach Hotel

Mrs. J. Wallace Lee (Ida)

Asheville Shrimp Mousse

1 (10¾-ounce) can tomato soup
1 (8-ounce) package cream cheese, softened
2½ tablespoons unflavored gelatin
1 cup cold water
1 cup mayonnaise
½ cup finely chopped green pepper
1 small onion, grated
½ cup finely chopped celery
2 cups shrimp (frozen or canned), mashed

In a saucepan heat soup; dissolve cream cheese in soup. In a bowl dissolve gelatin in cold water; add to soup mixture. Add mayonnaise, green pepper, onion, celery and shrimp. Pour into lightly oiled 1½-quart mold. Place in refrigerator to set for several hours. Unmold and serve as a spread with crackers. Makes 5½ cups.

Variation: Tuna Mousse—Substitute 2 (7-ounce) cans tuna, drained.

Mrs. Chris Demas (Jeannie)
Susan Feltman, Chicago, Illinois
Marion Larsen, Dunedin, Florida

Chicken Mold

1 cup chopped, cooked chicken
1 (4-ounce) bottle stuffed olives, chopped
6 hard-cooked eggs, chopped
1 cup mayonnaise
1 (6½-ounce) jar mustard-mayonnaise flavored spread
2 teaspoons Worcestershire sauce
⅛ teaspoon hot pepper sauce, or to taste
½ small onion, grated
2 (¼-ounce) envelopes unflavored gelatin
¼ cup cold water
1 cup chicken broth

In a medium bowl combine chicken, olives and eggs. Add mayonnaise, flavored spread, Worcestershire sauce, hot pepper sauce and onion; mix thoroughly. In a saucepan soften gelatin in cold water; add chicken broth. Stir over heat until dissolved; add to chicken mixture. Blend well. Mold in 9x5x3-inch loaf pan. Chill until firm. Remove from mold; serve with crackers. Serves 12.

Mrs. Robert Leonard (Jeannie)
Largo, Florida

Tarama

Egg Roe Canapé Spread

7 slices stale bread
2 cups water
1 (7-ounce) jar tarama
2 tablespoons grated onion
3/4 cup oil
4 tablespoons lemon juice

Toast bread; trim edges. Soak in water; squeeze dry. Place tarama in blender. Blend at low speed until creamy. Add onions and bread; blend. Slowly add oil and lemon juice, alternating while blending. Turn blender to high speed; whip until tarama is light and creamy. Serve on crackers. Serves 10 to 12.

Note: Tarama is orange-colored mullet or carp roe. If 8-ounce jar is used, increase bread by 1 slice.

Mrs. Chris Demas (Jeannie)

Curry Sherry Cheese Pâté

2 (3-ounce) packages cream cheese
1 cup shredded sharp Cheddar cheese
4 teaspoons dry cocktail sherry
1/4 teaspoon salt
1/2 teaspoon curry powder
1 (8-ounce) jar chutney, finely chopped
1/2 bunch green onions, finely chopped

In a blender cream together cheeses, sherry, curry powder and salt. Spread mixture on a serving platter, shaping a layer about 1/2-inch thick. Chill until firm. At serving time spread with chutney and sprinkle with onions. Serve with wheat wafers or sesame crackers. Makes 2 cups. *Great! Nice change from traditional cheese spreads.*

Mrs. J. J. Suddath, Jr. (Eleanor Picken)

Mock Boursin Cheese Spread

Tastes imported!

1 (8-ounce) package cream cheese, softened
1 clove garlic, crushed
1 teaspoon caraway seed
1 teaspoon basil
1 teaspoon dill weed
1 teaspoon chopped chives

In a small bowl blend together cheese and seasonings. Pack into a small crock; cover. Refrigerate 24 hours to blend flavors. Serve at room temperature with assorted crackers. Makes 1 cup. *A great favorite. Simple but delicious.*

Mrs. Lawrence J. Tierney (Sue)

Eggplant Ikra

Russian

1 large eggplant
1 large onion, chopped
3 to 4 tablespoons olive oil
2 green peppers, roasted, peeled and chopped
2 cloves garlic, crushed
½ teaspoon salt
¼ teaspoon pepper
2½ tablespoons tomato paste
2½ tablespoons tomato sauce

Pierce eggplant all around and bake at 350 degrees for 30 minutes or until cooked through. Peel; cut lengthwise and remove as many seeds as possible. Chop and slightly mash eggplant. In an 8-inch skillet sauté onions in oil. Add eggplant and remaining ingredients; stir to blend. Sauté ikra, stirring constantly, until oil and tomato start to separate from sides of skillet and most of the liquid is cooked down. Cool. Serve with crackers or party bread. Makes 2½ cups.

Note: Can be served hot or cold.

Mrs. Gregory H. Keuroghlian (Nora Ghazikian)

Jezebel Sauce

1 (18-ounce) jar apple jelly
1 (18-ounce) jar pineapple preserves
1 (1¼-ounce) can dry yellow mustard
1 tablespoon red hot pepper flakes
1 (5-ounce) jar horseradish
1 (8-ounce) package cream cheese
Assorted crackers

Combine first 5 ingredients in a large bowl; mix well. Pour a portion of sauce over cream cheese; serve with crackers. Sauce will keep indefinitely in refrigerator. Makes 5½ cups.

Variation: Spread crackers with cream cheese and top with sauce.

Mrs. Paul Connor (Madeline), Palm Harbor, Florida
Donna M. Moore

Soups

Artichoke Soup

1 medium onion, finely chopped
2 tablespoons butter
2 tablespoons all-purpose flour
2 cups chicken stock or broth
1 (10½-ounce) can cream of celery soup
½ soup can milk
2 tablespoons finely chopped fresh parsley
¼ teaspoon curry powder
¼ teaspoon allspice
1 (16-ounce) can artichoke hearts, drained and rinsed
½ pint half and half or light cream
⅛ teaspoon salt, or to taste
⅛ teaspoon pepper, or to taste
⅛ teaspoon hot pepper sauce, or to taste

In a large saucepan sauté onion in butter until soft. Add flour and cook for 2 minutes, stirring constantly; remove from heat. Add chicken stock, celery soup, milk, parsley, curry powder and allspice. In blender or food processor chop artichoke hearts; add half to soup and cook for 5 minutes on medium heat. Purée soup mixture in blender or processor ½ at a time. Return to saucepan and add half and half or cream; add salt, pepper and hot pepper sauce to taste and remaining chopped artichokes. Cook for 5 minutes, stirring constantly. Refrigerate and serve cold. Makes 8 cups.

Mrs. Polly Leach
Kerville, Texas

Cheese Soup

¼ cup butter
½ cup finely diced carrots
½ cup finely diced celery
½ cup diced onions
¼ cup all-purpose flour
1½ tablespoons cornstarch
1 quart chicken stock or water and 4 bouillon cubes
1 quart milk or half and half
⅛ teaspoon baking soda
2 cups sharp Cheddar cheese, shredded
2 teaspoons salt
¼ teaspoon pepper
2 tablespoons finely chopped parsley (optional)

Melt butter in large pot. Add the carrots, celery and onions; cook until tender but not brown. Stir in flour and cornstarch; cook until mixture begins to bubble. Add broth; boil and stir 1 minute. Stir in milk; reheat just to boiling; remove from heat; add baking soda and cheese. Stir just until cheese melts. Season with salt and pepper. Add parsley a few minutes before serving. To reheat, stir constantly or soup will stick to bottom of pan. Makes 2 quarts.

Mrs. Michael Porter (Paula)

Beef Barley Soup

1½ pounds beef shin with bone
½ cup chopped celery tops
½ teaspoon salt
½ teaspoon pepper
2 quarts water
½ cup uncooked barley
3 cups chopped cabbage
1 cup sliced carrots
1 cup sliced celery
2 cups sliced parsnips
2 cups chopped onions
1 (12-ounce) can tomato paste
4 beef bouillon cubes

In a large saucepan simmer bone, celery tops, salt and pepper in water for 1 hour; add barley and cook 30 minutes longer, stirring occasionally. Add rest of ingredients and cook 30 minutes longer. Serves 8 to 10.

Mrs. Douglas Guilfoile (Paula L. Tiezzi)

Cream of Carrot Soup

2 (1-pound) packages fresh carrots
½ cup butter
1 (13¾-ounce) can chicken broth
1 quart half and half
2 pints whipping cream
½ cup milk
1 teaspoon salt
½ teaspoon pepper
3 tablespoons seafood seasoning (optional)
2 teaspoons curry powder

Grate carrots, put in food processor or blender. In a large saucepan melt butter and sauté carrots until tender. Pour in can of chicken broth. Add half and half and whipping cream. Dilute with milk to consistency of thin white sauce. Heat; add seasonings. Serves 12.

Karen Gauthier
Columbia, Maryland

Cucumber Soup

1 medium onion, chopped
1 medium cucumber, peeled and cubed
¾ cup chicken broth
1 (10¾-ounce) can cream of chicken soup
1 cup sour cream
1 teaspoon Worcestershire sauce
¼ teaspoon celery salt
Chives or parsley

Blend all ingredients, except seasonings, in blender. Add seasonings and chill 2 or 3 hours. Garnish with chopped chives and/or parsley. Makes 3½ cups.

Mrs. Preston Packard (D'Lou)

French Onion Soup

5 medium onions, sliced
3 tablespoons butter
2 (10¾-ounce) cans beef bouillon
2 soup cans of water
1 bay leaf
1 teaspoon Worcestershire sauce
½ teaspoon salt
¼ cup white wine
4 to 6 slices French bread
4 to 6 slices Swiss cheese
½ to ¾ cup Parmesan cheese

In a large saucepan sauté onions in butter until tender. Stir in bouillon, water, bay leaf, Worcestershire sauce and salt. Cook 1 hour. Remove bay leaf; add wine. Ladle into ovenproof crocks; top with a slice of French bread and a slice of Swiss cheese; sprinkle with 2 tablespoons Parmesan cheese. Bake at 350 degrees until cheese melts. Serves 4 to 6.

Mrs. Harry Lambert (Sue)
Clearwater, Florida

Gazpacho Soup

1 small stalk celery
1 bunch green onions
1 cucumber, unpeeled
3 medium tomatoes
1 large green pepper
¼ cup vegetable oil
¼ cup wine vinegar
¼ cup Worcestershire sauce
1 tablespoon lemon juice
1 tablespoon white horseradish
⅛ teaspoon pepper
1 teaspoon salt
1 (46-ounce) can tomato juice

Grate or chop vegetables fine by hand or use a food processor. Mix remaining ingredients thoroughly and combine with vegetables. Refrigerate several hours or overnight. Serves 8.

Violet T. Bernard

Fresh French Onion Soup

1½ pounds onions, thinly sliced (5 cups)
¼ cup butter
6 cups beef broth or bouillon
¼ teaspoon salt, or to taste
⅛ teaspoon pepper, or to taste
Grated Parmesan cheese
Toasted bread cubes

In a large pot brown onions lightly in butter. Add bouillon and simmer 30 minutes. Season with salt and pepper. Serve sprinkled with cheese and toasted bread cubes. Serves 4 to 6. *Quick and easy!*

Mrs. William Parmer (Jean Glasscock)

Guild Gazpacho

½ cup finely diced celery
½ cup finely diced green pepper
½ cup finely diced onion
½ cup peeled, seeded, diced fresh cucumber
1 cup peeled, diced tomatoes
1 (10¾-ounce) can tomato soup, undiluted
1 soup can water
1½ cups cocktail vegetable juice
1 tablespoon wine vinegar
1 tablespoon Italian salad dressing
¼ teaspoon salt
⅛ teaspoon fresh ground pepper, if desired
4 dashes hot pepper sauce, or to taste
⅛ teaspoon Worcestershire sauce, or to taste
⅛ teaspoon garlic salt, or to taste

Combine all ingredients in a large bowl. Cover and refrigerate for at least 4 hours—overnight or longer is best. Serve ice cold. Serves 6 to 8.

Hint: Food processor works very well for preparation of vegetables.

Mrs. J. Wallace Lee (Ida)

Hot and Sour Soup

2 tablespoons dried tree ear mushrooms
3 or 4 dried Chinese mushrooms
8 dried tiger lily buds
1 large pork chop, shredded
1 tablespoon peanut oil
4 to 5 cups chicken broth
⅓ cup shredded bamboo shoots
1 teaspoon soy sauce
½ teaspoon sugar
1 teaspoon salt
¼ teaspoon pepper
2 tablespoons wine vinegar
2 tablespoons cornstarch
3 tablespoons water
1 pad fresh bean curd, sliced
1 egg, lightly beaten
1 teaspoon sesame oil

In a small bowl soak tree ear mushrooms, Chinese mushrooms and tiger lily buds for 15 to 20 minutes in boiling water. Drain and cut into shreds, discarding mushroom stems; place in a large saucepan. Heat ⅓ cup shredded pork in small skillet in oil. Add pork, broth and bamboo shoots to saucepan; bring to a boil and simmer 10 minutes. Add soy sauce, sugar, salt, pepper and vinegar. Combine cornstarch and water in a small bowl; add to soup. Heat soup to a boil, stirring often; add bean curd and heat 2 minutes. Turn off heat. Just before serving stir in egg; add sesame oil and serve. Serves 4 to 6.

Mrs. Jay Johnston
Princeton, New Jersey

"This recipe will introduce you to the many delights of a Chinese food market."

Marshall Field's Cream of Mushroom Soup

1/4 cup butter or margarine
2 teaspoons chopped onion
1 3/4 cups finely chopped mushrooms
1 quart chicken broth or use 2 (13 3/4-ounce) cans chicken broth and add water to make 1 quart
2 tablespoons all-purpose flour
1/2 to 3/4 teaspoon salt
1 cup half and half

In a large saucepan melt 2 tablespoons butter; add onion and mushrooms. Cook until soft; about 2 minutes. Add chicken broth. Cover tightly and simmer 15 minutes. In a small saucepan melt remaining butter; stir in flour and salt. Cook 30 seconds or until bubbly. Blend in hot mushroom mixture; pour into the large saucepan with half and half; beat well; heat to boil, stirring continually. Makes 1 quart.

Note: Each serving may be garnished with whipped cream.

Mrs. Stanley H. Dawson (Ruth)

Cream of Broccoli Soup

1 (10-ounce) package frozen broccoli pieces
1 or 2 large onions, diced
3 cloves garlic, finely chopped
1/2 cup butter
1/2 cup water
1/2 gallon milk
1 (13-ounce) can evaporated milk
3 tablespoons all-purpose flour
3 tablespoons water
4 tablespoons seafood seasoning salt
1 teaspoon salt
1/2 teaspoon pepper

Place broccoli, onion, garlic, butter and water in kettle. Cook for 20 to 30 minutes or until tender. Whip with a whisk or mash with potato masher. Add milks and seasonings. Make a thin paste with flour and water. Add to above mixture. Heat through; do not boil. Serve hot. Makes 3 quarts.

Note: Quick, pressure-cooker method. Cook 10 minutes in cooker and proceed as above. Cook slowly. Watch for burning.

Mrs. Samuel Fisher (Mardel)
Dunedin, Florida

Mushroom-Barley Soup

1 pound fresh mushrooms
6 tablespoons margarine, separated
1 cup finely chopped onions
1 clove garlic, finely chopped
2 (10½-ounce) cans condensed beef broth
6½ cups water
3 tablespoons tomato paste or ketchup
¾ teaspoon salt
¾ teaspoon pepper
1 bay leaf
½ cup barley
¼ cup chopped parsley
1½ cups chopped celery and leaves
1½ cups sliced carrots
4 tablespoons dry sherry
1 (16-ounce) carton sour cream

Chop half of mushrooms; slice remaining half; set aside. In large pot melt 4 tablespoons margarine; add chopped mushrooms, onions and garlic; sauté 5 minutes. Stir in broth, water, ketchup, salt, pepper and bay leaf. Heat to boiling; stir in barley. Reduce heat; simmer 1 hour. Add vegetables; cook another ½ hour. In skillet sauté remaining mushrooms in 2 tablespoons margarine; add to soup with sherry. Serve with a dollop of sour cream in each serving. Serves 8.

Mrs. Lynn Lees

Hearty Lentil and Barley Soup

2 quarts water
1 cup lentils
½ cup barley (fine)
½ teaspoon salt
¼ teaspoon pepper
1 marrow bone or ½ pound lean beef
1 parsnip, thinly sliced
Few sprigs parsley
2 carrots, thinly sliced
1 large onion, finely chopped
2 stalks celery, thinly sliced

In a large pot bring water to a boil. Strain lentils and barley through strainer and place into the rapidly boiling water together with salt and pepper to flavor; add bone or beef. Add onion, and remaining ingredients, cooking on high heat and stirring frequently for first 10 minutes. Cover and continue cooking on a low flame making sure water boils continuously. Cook for 1½ hours stirring occasionally. Serves 6 to 8.

Optional: Remove bone or beef and put soup through a blender, making a lovely puree.

Lila K. Nenner
Dunedin, Florida

Turkey Spinach Soup

A really colorful delicious soup!

1/4 cup margarine
2 medium onions, chopped
2 tablespoons all-purpose flour
1 teaspoon curry powder
3 cups chicken broth
1 cup diced potatoes
1/2 cup thinly sliced carrots
1/2 cup sliced celery
2 tablespoons chopped fresh parsley
1/2 teaspoon sage or poultry seasoning
2 cups cubed, cooked turkey
1 1/2 cups half and half
1 (10-ounce) package frozen chopped spinach, thawed
1 teaspoon seasoned salt
Freshly ground pepper to taste

Melt margarine in a large saucepan over medium-high heat; add onions and sauté until translucent, about 10 minutes. Stir in flour and curry powder; cook 2 to 3 minutes. Add broth, potatoes, carrots, celery, parsley and sage; bring to boil. Reduce heat to low; cover and simmer for 10 minutes. Add turkey, half and half and spinach. Cover and simmer for 7 minutes more until heated through. Season with salt and pepper. Serve hot with crusty bread. Serves 6 to 8.

Janet Joyce

Collard Green Soup

2 small ham hocks
2 (2-ounce) chorizos (Spanish hot sausage)
2 short ribs of beef
1/2 cup chopped onion
1/2 green pepper, chopped
1 medium tomato, chopped
1 garlic clove, minced
1 bay leaf
2 (1-pound) cans Great Northern beans
1/2 teaspoon sugar
6 cups water
2 (1-pound) packages frozen collards
2 cups cubed potatoes
1 1/2 teaspoons salt

In a large soup kettle combine ham hocks, chorizos, short ribs, onion, green pepper, tomato, garlic, bay leaf, beans, sugar and water; simmer about 1 hour. Remove meat and cool. Strip meat from bones and fat. Cut sausage and meat into small pieces; return to broth. Add collards, potatoes, and salt; cook about 2 hours on low. Makes 12 cups.

Mrs. Jerry Harris (Nancy)

Midwestern Fish Chowder

1 pound fish fillets, fresh or frozen
¼ cup chopped bacon
½ cup chopped onion
½ cup chopped green pepper
1 cup chopped celery
2 cups boiling water
1 cup diced potatoes
¼ teaspoon thyme, or to taste
1 teaspoon salt
⅛ teaspoon cayenne pepper
2 cups tomato juice

Thaw frozen fillets; cut into ½-inch pieces. Fry bacon until lightly brown; add onion, green pepper and celery; cook until tender. Add water, potatoes, seasonings and fish. Cook about 15 minutes or until potatoes are tender. Add tomato juice; heat. Serves 4 to 6.

Variation: For New England fish chowder, omit green pepper, celery and thyme. Substitute 2 cups whole milk for tomato juice and black pepper for cayenne. Add a little butter and chopped parsley to each bowl before serving.

Hint: Add more fish and vegetables to make this chowder heavier. Delicious!

Mrs. Vito Grasso (Aurora)
Dunedin, Florida

Corn and Sausage Chowder

1 pound bulk pork sausage
1 cup chopped onion
4 cups pared and diced potatoes
2 teaspoons salt
1 teaspoon basil
⅛ teaspoon pepper
2 cups water
1 (17-ounce) can cream-style corn
1 (12-ounce) bag frozen corn
1 (13-ounce) can evaporated milk

In a medium skillet brown sausage. Remove sausage and drain on paper towel. Pour off grease; reserve small amount and sauté onions in skillet. In large kettle stir in potatoes, onions, salt, basil, pepper and water to cover. Simmer 15 minutes. Add cooked sausage, corn and evaporated milk; cover and heat until mixture starts to boil. Serve hot. Makes 9 cups.

Note: Canned corn may be substituted for frozen. Serve with crisp crackers or crusty French bread.

Karen Gauthier
Columbia, Maryland

Italian Sausage Soup

3 pounds tomatoes
1 pound Italian sausage, cut into ¼-inch slices
1 cup chopped onion
1 green pepper, chopped
2 cups sliced mushrooms
6 cups beef broth
1 teaspoon Italian seasoning
1 teaspoon sugar
1 teaspoon salt
1 cup rice

Use tomatoes held at room temperature until fully ripe. Drop tomatoes into boiling water for 30 seconds; remove skins. Dice tomatoes (makes about 4½ cups); set aside. In large kettle brown sausage on both sides, about 5 minutes. Remove from pan and set aside. Add onions, peppers and mushrooms to meat grease; sauté until tender, 3 to 5 minutes. Add beef broth, Italian seasoning, sugar, salt and sausage. Bring to boil; add rice and tomatoes. Simmer covered about 20 minutes. Serves 8 to 12.

Donald Rice
Palm Harbor, Florida

Turkey Noodle Soup

Leftover cooked carcass from turkey
5 quarts water
1 cup chopped celery
½ cup chopped celery leaves
1 cup chopped onion
7 chicken bouillon cubes
1 tablespoon salt
¼ teaspoon ground black pepper
1 bay leaf
½ cup chopped parsley
1 cup fresh, frozen or canned peas
1 cup sliced carrots
1 cup cut green beans
1 (8-ounce) package egg noodles
¼ cup butter or margarine
¼ cup all-purpose flour

In 8-quart stock pot or Dutch oven, place turkey carcass, water, celery, celery leaves, onion, bouillon cubes, salt, pepper and bay leaf. Heat to boiling; lower heat; cover and simmer 1 hour. Remove carcass; let cool. Add parsley, peas, carrots and green beans to soup; heat to boiling; reduce heat and simmer 10 minutes, until vegetables are just tender. Remove meat from carcass; return pieces to soup. Discard bones. Heat soup to boiling; add noodles; cook, uncovered, 10 minutes. Melt butter in small skillet, stir in flour. Cook over low heat, stirring constantly until flour is browned. Stir into boiling soup. Reheat to boiling and stir. Reduce heat; simmer 5 minutes. Makes 5 quarts.

Mrs. Jerry Harris (Nancy)

Spanish Black Bean Soup

2 pounds black beans
2 teaspoons salt
2 medium onions, chopped
4 medium green peppers, cut into chunks
6 cloves garlic, mashed
2 tablespoons oregano
6 bay leaves
½ cup olive oil
2 tablespoons wine vinegar

Wash beans; place in a large pot and cover with water. Add salt and soak overnight. Early the next day add onions, green peppers, garlic, oregano and bay leaves. Bring to a boil and reduce heat to simmer. Simmer on low heat all day, stirring often. When beans are medium soft add olive oil. Cook until thick and beans are done. At this point you may add more salt, if desired. With a fork remove green pepper skins and bay leaves. Add vinegar. Serve over rice. Serves 4 to 6.

Note: Fresh chopped onions are usually sprinkled over black beans. This freezes well. Reheat on very low heat.

Mrs. Juan Cueva (Hilda), Clearwater, Florida
Ann Arquitt, Clearwater, Florida

Quick Spanish Hamburger Soup

¼ pound ground beef
¼ teaspoon salt
⅛ teaspoon pepper
1 (8-ounce) can tomato sauce
1 medium carrot, sliced
1 (2-ounce) can mushroom stems and pieces
2 tablespoons chopped onion
2 tablespoons sliced pimento-stuffed olives
½ teaspoon sugar
½ cup water
¼ cup dry red wine
Grated Parmesan cheese (optional)

In saucepan cook ground beef until browned. Drain off fat. Stir in salt and pepper. Add tomato sauce, carrot, mushrooms, onion, olives and sugar. Stir in water and wine. Cover and simmer for 30 to 35 minutes or until carrot is tender, stirring occasionally. Sprinkle individual servings with Parmesan Cheese, if desired. Serves 2.

Mrs. William R. Barnes (Vickie)

Creamy Potato Soup

4 cups peeled, cubed potatoes
1 cup 3/4-inch sliced celery
1 cup coarsely chopped onion
2 teaspoons salt
2 cups water
1/8 teaspoon thyme
1/8 teaspoon oregano
1 cup milk
1 cup whipping cream
1 tablespoon butter, melted
1 tablespoon chopped fresh parsley
1/2 teaspoon caraway seeds
1/8 teaspoon pepper

In a large Dutch oven combine potatoes, celery, onions, salt and water. Simmer, covered about 20 minutes or until potatoes are tender. Mash mixture once or twice with a potato masher, leaving some vegetable pieces whole. Stir in remaining ingredients; return to heat; cook stirring constantly until thoroughly heated; do not boil. *Best a few days after making it.* Serves 6 to 8.

Note: Dried parsley flakes may be substituted if fresh parsley is not available.

Mrs. Greg Santa (Cathy)

Vichyssoise

4 leeks, tops only, chopped fine
1 medium onion, chopped fine
2 tablespoons sweet butter
5 medium potatoes, peeled and finely sliced
1 tablespoon salt
4 cups water or chicken broth
2 cups milk
2 cups half and half
1 cup whipping cream
1/2 teaspoon salt
1/8 teaspoon pepper
3 tablespoons chopped chives (optional)

In a large saucepan lightly brown leeks and onions in butter; add potatoes, water and salt. Boil gently 30 to 45 minutes. Puree in blender; return to heat; add milk and half and half; season with salt and pepper. Bring to boil; cool; strain through a sieve. Add cream; blend well. Chill. Garnish with chopped chives. Serves 8.

Mrs. Chris Demas (Jeannie)

Summer Yogurt Soup

Armenian

1 quart yogurt
1/2 cup barley
1 1/2 cups water
1 small onion, grated
1 to 2 cucumbers, grated
1 teaspoon salt
1/4 teaspoon white pepper
1/2 teaspoon garlic powder
1 1/2 cups milk, for thinning yogurt
1 pint whipping cream
1 bunch scallions, finely chopped
1/4 cup chopped parsley (optional)
2 tablespoons crushed, dried mint (optional)

Strain yogurt overnight in cheesecloth. Cook barley in water to cover and let cool overnight. Beat drained yogurt; add onion, cucumber, salt, pepper and garlic powder. Stir until all ingredients are well blended. Add enough milk to desired consistency (medium light soup) and enough cream to enhance flavor. Mix in scallions, parsley and mint. Makes 12 cups. *Excellent summer soup!*

Mrs. Gregory H. Keuroghlian (Nora Ghazikian)

Coquina Chowder

1 kettle coquinas, (6 quarts), rinsed several times
Water to cover
3 stalks celery, thinly sliced
3 medium potatoes, diced
1 medium onion, chopped
1 tablespoon butter
2 cups milk or half and half
1/2 teaspoon salt, or to taste
1/4 teaspoon pepper or to taste

Cover coquinas with water; boil until shells open and broth is milky looking. Drain juice off through cheese cloth or fine sieve so only broth comes through. Place broth in saucepan with celery, potatoes, onion and butter. Cook until potatoes are tender. Stir in milk and seasonings; heat thoroughly. Serves 6 to 8. *Real Florida Fare!*

Evelyn Ruth Carver
Dunedin, Florida

Coquinas are little native periwinkle clams in rainbow colors that may be collected in a sieve at ebb tide on Florida beaches.

Seafood Soup

1 pound medium fresh shrimp, peeled and deveined
1 pound grouper (any other white fish may be used)
1 medium onion, finely chopped
5 cloves garlic, finely chopped
2 tablespoons olive oil
6 large tomatoes or 2 (1-pound) cans tomatoes
½ bunch parsley
½ teaspoon allspice
2 teaspoons salt
½ teaspoon pepper
½ (1-liter) bottle dry white wine
1 (3-ounce) can tomato paste
8 mussels (optional)
8 clams (optional)

Wash fish; cut into bite-sized pieces; set aside. In a large saucepan sauté onion and garlic in olive oil until onion is opaque but not browned. Add remaining ingredients, except fish and shrimp; bring to a boil. Simmer about 20 to 30 minutes until mixture reduces to consistency of cream soup. (Consistency may be adjusted by adding tomato puree or tomato paste). Place mixture in blender; blend on high speed for 1 minute; return to saucepan. Add fish and shrimp; cook over medium heat until fish and shrimp are tender. Serves 4.

Hint: As this is a hearty soup, it makes an excellent meal when served with a tossed salad and garlic bread. Add 1 or 2 steamed mussels or clams to the top of each serving to give it an elegant touch.

Jacqueline Crowne
Sarasota, Florida

Salads and Salad Dressings

Avocado Mousse Mold

Gourmet Fare!

2 very ripe avocados
1/4 cup mayonnaise
1 1/2 teaspoons gelatin, softened in lemon juice
1 1/2 teaspoons fresh lemon juice
1 1/2 to 2 1/2 teaspoons grated onion
1/2 teaspoon Worcestershire sauce
1/2 teaspoon salt
1/4 teaspoon freshly ground pepper
1/4 teaspoon paprika
4 drops hot pepper sauce
2 to 3 tablespoons sour cream
Cucumber slices (optional)

Place pitted and peeled avocados in food processor or blender. Add all remaining ingredients except sour cream and cucumbers; turn into glass serving bowl. Whip sour cream lightly with fork; spread over mousse to prevent discoloration. Refrigerate until set. Garnish with cucumber slices, if desired. Serves 8.

Marilyn McDonald

Hint: Place unripe fruit in brown paper bag to speed ripening.

Gazpacho Salad Ring

4 1/2 cups tomato juice
2 (1/4-ounce) envelopes unflavored gelatin
1/4 cup red wine vinegar
1 teaspoon minced garlic
2 teaspoons salt
1/4 teaspoon pepper
1/8 teaspoon hot pepper sauce
2 large tomatoes, peeled, seeded, chopped and drained
1/2 cup chopped onion
3/4 cup chopped green pepper
3/4 cup chopped cucumber
1/4 cup chopped pimento
1 (16-ounce) carton sour cream

Pour 1 cup tomato juice into small saucepan; sprinkle with gelatin. Mix and let stand 5 minutes. Heat mixture over moderate heat until gelatin is dissolved. Pour into a large bowl; add remaining tomato juice, vinegar, garlic, salt, pepper and hot pepper sauce. Chill for 1 hour until mixture begins to set. Stir in remaining vegetables. Spoon into an oiled 6-cup mold. Chill until set. Serve with sour cream. Serves 8 to 10.

Mrs. Lawrence J. Tierney (Sue)

Heavenly Apple Salad

2 (3-ounce) packages lemon gelatin dessert
2 cups boiling water
16 large marshmallows, diced
1 cup cold water
2 large apples, peeled, diced
1 (8-ounce) can crushed pineapple, drained
1/2 cup chopped nuts

Dissolve gelatin in boiling water. Add marshmallows; stir until smooth. Add cold water; chill until mixture is the consistency of unbeaten egg whites. Add diced apples, pineapple, and nuts; chill until firm in a large mold or bowl. Cover with dressing. Serves 20.

Dressing:

3/4 cup sugar
2 eggs, slightly beaten
Juice of 1 lemon
1 (8-ounce) carton whipping cream, whipped or 1 (1.25-ounce) envelope prepared whipped topping mix

Combine in top of double boiler sugar, eggs and lemon juice. Cook, stirring constantly, until thick. Cool; fold in whipped cream or prepared whipped topping. Spread on cool salad. Chill until serving time.

Mrs. Edward W. Roos (Mildred Seagren)

Peaches and Cream Salad

2 cups sliced canned peaches, drained
1 (3-ounce) package lemon gelatin dessert
1/2 cup hot orange juice
2/3 cup cream-style cottage cheese
2 cups whipping cream
1/2 cup pecans
1 cup cracked ice

Line the bottom of a 6-cup mold with peaches. Place lemon gelatin and hot orange juice in blender and blend on High for 20 seconds. With blades spinning, add cottage cheese. Slowly add cream and cracked ice. Blend until on the verge of setting; add pecans. Turn blender off the second the last pecan is drawn down into blades. Pour over peaches. Chill 20 minutes. Serves 8.

Mrs. Paul J. Donahue (Sigrid)
Dunedin, Florida

Corned Beef Salad

1 (10½-ounce) can beef consommé
1 (3-ounce) package lemon gelatin dessert
1 medium onion, finely chopped
1 cup finely chopped celery
1 green pepper, finely chopped
3 hard-cooked eggs, finely chopped
1 (12-ounce) can corned beef, shredded
1 tablespoon lemon juice
⅛ teaspoon salt (optional)
1 cup mayonnaise

In a small saucepan boil consommé; add gelatin. Chill until slightly thickened. In a large bowl combine remaining ingredients with consommé mixture and mix well. Spoon into a 13x9x2-inch glass pan; chill until set. Serves 8 to 10.

Bente Lupion
Dunedin, Florida

Dallas Lime Asparagus Salad

1 (10¾-ounce) can cream of asparagus soup
½ soup can water
1 (3-ounce) package lime gelatin dessert
1 (8-ounce) package cream cheese, softened
½ cup mayonnaise
¾ cup chopped celery
½ cup chopped green pepper
1 tablespoon grated onion
½ cup walnuts, finely chopped

In a medium saucepan heat soup and water. Add gelatin; stir until gelatin is dissolved. Add cream cheese by chunks; mix with a beater until well blended. Add all remaining ingredients. Pour into a 9-inch square pan or 2-quart casserole; chill. Serves 8.

Mrs. Stanley H. Dawson (Ruth)

Crab Shrimp Salad

1 (1-pound) loaf white bread, crusts removed and cubed very small
2 cups mayonnaise
1 cup chopped celery
1 small onion, chopped
3 hard cooked eggs, chopped
2 (6½-ounce) cans crabmeat
1 (6½-ounce) can shrimp

Mix first 5 ingredients together in a 2½-quart casserole. Refrigerate overnight. In the morning add crabmeat and shrimp; mix well; refrigerate until cold. Serves 6.

Mrs. Kenneth Thomson (Elsie)
Leawood, Kansas

Red, White and Blue Salad

First Layer:

1 (3-ounce) package raspberry gelatin dessert

Prepare gelatin as directed on package; pour into a 13x9x2-inch glass pan or a large salad mold and refrigerate until set.

Second Layer:

1 cup coffee cream
1 (1/4-ounce) package unflavored gelatin
1/4 cup water
1 cup sour cream
1/2 cup sugar
1 teaspoon vanilla extract

Heat coffee cream to boiling point; remove from heat. Dissolve gelatin in water. In a small bowl beat sour cream until runny; add sugar and vanilla; beat one minute. Add gelatin and sour cream mixtures to coffee cream; pour over first layer; refrigerate for 2 hours.

Third Layer:

1 (3-ounce) package lemon or blackberry gelatin dessert
1 cup boiling water
1 (16-ounce) can blueberries, undrained

Mix gelatin with boiling water; add blueberries and syrup from can. Pour mixture over second layer; refrigerate for 4 to 6 hours. If a mold is used, unmold before serving. Otherwise, cut into squares. Serves 16.

Mrs. Donald Behm (Marion)

Hot Chicken Salad

2 cups cubed, cooked chicken (preferably breast)
2 cups chopped celery
1/2 cup cashew nuts
1 tablespoon minced onion
1 cup mayonnaise
1/8 teaspoon salt
1 tablespoon lemon juice
1 cup shredded Cheddar cheese
1 cup crushed potato chips

In a large mixing bowl combine first four ingredients. Blend mayonnaise, salt and lemon juice; add to vegetables and mix well. Spread in a 1½-quart casserole. Sprinkle with cheese, then with potato chips. Bake at 350 degrees for 20 minutes. Serves 4 to 6.

Mrs. Robert Haverkos (Ginny)

Grape-Molded Salad

2 (3-ounce) packages lemon gelatin dessert
1 cup sugar
2 cups boiling water
2 cups sour cream
2 cups green grapes, cut in half

Crust:

1 cup margarine
2 cups all-purpose flour
½ cup sugar
¾ cup slivered almonds

Mix gelatin and sugar together. Add boiling water; stir until dissolved. Using low speed on electric mixer, add sour cream. Refrigerate until thick, but not set; fold in grapes. In a skillet melt margarine. Add flour and sugar; brown lightly on low heat, stirring continuously. Put half of mixture in a 13x9x2-inch pan; add gelatin mixture. Add almonds to the remaining crust mixture; sprinkle over gelatin mixture. Refrigerate overnight. Serves 12.

Variation: To use as a dessert serve with non-dairy whipped topping on the side.

Arlene Karnuth

Apple, Pepper and Carrot Salad

1 large bunch carrots, peeled
1 green pepper, seeded
2 to 3 apples, finely chopped
Juice of 2 lemons
½ cup sugar

In a blender or chopper grind carrots and green pepper. Pour into a serving bowl. Add apples, lemon juice and sugar; stir. Chill before serving. *Unusual and delicious!* Serves 8 to 10.

Mrs. Robert Raab (Leila)
Evanston, Illinois

Kitchen Hint: To get maximum amount of juice from lemon, warm in water. Press down firmly and roll on hard surface before juicing.

Crab Salad

2 cups cooked crabmeat
½ cup diced cucumber
¼ cup finely chopped celery
½ cup mayonnaise
1 teaspoon lemon juice

Combine ingredients. Serve on crisp lettuce leaves. Serves 6.

Note: May be served with thin bread and butter or cream cheese sandwiches.

Mrs. Thomas Shaw (Helen)

Cranberry Salad

4 cups water
4 (3-ounce) packages red gelatin dessert
2 cups sugar
4 oranges, peeled and seeded
1 orange rind
1 pound raw cranberries, washed
1 (20-ounce) can crushed pineapple
1 pound chopped pecans

In a saucepan bring water to a boil; add gelatin and sugar; heat just until dissolved. Place oranges and orange rind in blender; process. Add cranberries to blender; grind. Add pineapple; blend until smooth. Stir in nuts and pour into 2 large or 3 small molds. Refrigerate until set. Unmold on serving plate. Serves 20 to 24.

Note: Recipe may be cut in half. Freezes well.

Mrs. William Parmer (Jean Glasscock)

Apple-Cinnamon Salad

Different and Easy

1/4 pound cinnamon candy hearts (1/4 cup plus)
1 cup water
1 (3-ounce) package red gelatin dessert
1 cup boiling water
2 unpeeled red apples, diced
1/2 cup chopped nuts
1/4 cup minced celery

Boil cinnamon candy hearts in water until dissolved. Dissolve gelatin in 1 cup boiling water. Add enough water to dissolved cinnamon to make 1 cup; add to gelatin. When gelatin is partially set, add apples, nuts and celery. Refrigerate overnight. Serves 4.

Mrs. Joe Hensley (Joann)

Cabbage Slaw

1 medium cabbage, shredded
2 medium onions, cut into rings
1 green pepper, chopped

Dressing:

1 cup sugar
1 cup white vinegar
1/2 cup salad oil
1 teaspoon salt
1 teaspoon dry mustard

Combine dressing ingredients and pour over cabbage, onion and green pepper. Marinate in refrigerator for 3 hours before serving. Serves 12 to 16.

Mrs. Brown Coleman
Paris, Texas

Honeyed Fruit Bowl

4 oranges, cut into "wheels"

Marinade:

½ cup honey
1 teaspoon grated orange peel
2 tablespoons lemon juice

Fruit:

1½ cups blueberries
2 cups honeydew melon, cubed
1½ cups sliced strawberries
Few sprigs mint

Mix marinade; pour over sliced orange wheels; marinate overnight. Pour off liquid and save. Place oranges in glass bowl. Add rest of fruit in order, for a beautiful layered look. Garnish with mint. Serves 8 to 10.

Note: Reserved liquid may be used to sweeten iced tea or lemonade.

Mrs. Stanley H. Dawson (Ruth)

Jewel's Salad

¼ pound mushrooms, sliced
1 cup broccoli flowerets
1 cup cauliflower flowerets
½ cup ½-inch sliced celery
2 green onions, cut into ¼-inch pieces

Dressing:

1 cup oil
⅓ cup wine vinegar
1 teaspoon sugar
2 teaspoons oregano
1 teaspoon salt
½ teaspoon pepper
½ teaspoon dry mustard
½ teaspoon dry garlic or 2 cloves of garlic, minced

Mix all dressing ingredients in small bowl. Pour over vegetables. Let set an hour or two before serving. Serves 8.

Mrs. Stanley H. Dawson (Ruth)

Tropical Seas Salad

1 (3-ounce) package orange gelatin dessert
1 cup boiling water
1/3 cup sugar
1 teaspoon vanilla extract
1 (8-ounce) carton sour cream
1 (8-ounce) can crushed pineapple
1 (11-ounce) can mandarin oranges, drained
1/3 cup sliced almonds
1/2 cup flaked coconut

Dissolve gelatin in 1 cup boiling water. Add sugar; stir until dissolved. Add vanilla and sour cream; blend until smooth. Add crushed pineapple, oranges, almonds and coconut. Pour into an oiled 4-cup mold or dish. Chill until set. Unmold onto serving dish. Serves 8 to 12.

Mrs. Robert Leonard (Jeannie)
Largo, Florida

Chicken Salad Elegantè

4 cups cubed, cooked chicken breast
1 cup chopped celery
1/2 to 1 cup slivered almonds, toasted
1 cup seedless green grapes, halved
1 teaspoon salt
1/4 teaspoon pepper
3/4 cup mayonnaise
1 cup sour cream

In a large mixing bowl combine chicken, celery, almonds and grapes. Sprinkle with salt and pepper. Add mayonnaise and sour cream. Mix thoroughly. Chill. Serves 6 to 8.

Mrs. Carl Ness (Myrtle)
Dunedin, Florida

Green Bean Seven Layer Salad

1/2 large head of lettuce, shredded
1 cup chopped celery
1/2 cup chopped green pepper
1/2 large sweet onion or red onion, sliced into thin rings
1 (16-ounce) can French style green beans, drained
2 cups salad dressing
1/2 cup Parmesan cheese
1/2 pound bacon, cooked and crumbled

In a 13x9x2-inch glass dish or large glass bowl, layer salad ingredients in order given. Refrigerate 24 hours before serving. Serves 8 to 10.

Mrs. William Parmer (Jean Glasscock)

Artichoke Salad

6 canned or fresh artichoke hearts, halved and dried
4 ounces fresh pea pods, cut into ½-inch pieces
4 ounces fresh mushrooms, sliced
2 teaspoons Dijon mustard
1 teaspoon salt
1 teaspoon pepper
¼ cup red wine vinegar
¼ cup salad oil
1 teaspoon chopped dill
1 teaspoon fresh garlic, finely chopped
1 cup half and half cream
1 ounce sliced almonds, toasted

In a large bowl combine artichokes, pea pods and mushrooms. In a small bowl thoroughly mix together remaining ingredients except cream and almonds. Slowly stir in cream. Pour dressing into vegetables and coat well. Add almonds. Serves 6.

Mrs. Anthony S. Brancato (Georgine E. Palmer)

Chinese Vegetable Salad

1 cup sugar
¾ cup vinegar
¼ teaspoon salt
1 (16-ounce) can French style beans, drained
1 (8½-ounce) can English peas, drained
1 (14-ounce) can Chinese vegetables, drained
1 small onion, diced

In a small saucepan boil together sugar, vinegar and salt; cool thoroughly. Combine vegetables in a serving bowl. Pour vinegar sauce over vegetables. Serves 6 to 8.

Note: Diced green pepper and celery salt may be added, if desired.

Beatrice Davis
Dunedin, Florida

Fresh Broccoli Salad

2 bunches fresh broccoli
½ pound bacon, cooked and crumbled
4 hard-cooked eggs, chopped
1 small onion, chopped
Juice from 1 lemon
1½ cups real mayonnaise

Cook broccoli in boiling water for 5 minutes. (Broccoli should still be a little crunchy.) Chop broccoli while warm; add remaining ingredients. Refrigerate several hours before serving. Serves 8.

Mrs. Harvey Heimann (Jean)

Hearts of Palm

Swamp Cabbage

1 pound salt pork
1 tablespoon sugar
3 cups water
Hearts of Palm (Swamp Cabbage), chopped

Fry salt pork in a Dutch oven until browned on all sides. Add sugar, water and cabbage. Cook 30 minutes to 1 hour, or until tender; drain. Serves any number depending upon how much cabbage is cooked.

Note: Serve chilled with your favorite vinaigrette dressing.

Variation: Serve hot with fried fish and hush puppies.

The cabbage palm must be cut when very small—about 8 feet high and 4 feet in diameter at the trunk. After cutting down the tree, remove boots until you reach the center or buds of the palm, known as the Hearts of Palm.

Mrs. Denver Bass (Eunice)
Dunedin, Florida

Dublin Potato Salad

A Pleasant Change from Ordinary Potato Salad

2 tablespoons vinegar
1 teaspoon celery seed
1 teaspoon mustard seed
3 pounds potatoes
2 teaspoons sugar
½ teaspoon salt
2 cups cabbage, shredded
¼ cup chopped dill pickle
¼ cup sliced green onion
1 cup mayonnaise
¼ cup milk
½ teaspoon salt
1 (12-ounce) can corned beef, chilled and cubed

Combine vinegar, celery seed and mustard seed; set aside. Peel and cook potatoes until barely done; drain and cube. While potatoes are still warm, drizzle with vinegar mixture. Sprinkle with sugar and salt; chill thoroughly. Combine remaining ingredients just before serving. Add to potato mixture; toss lightly. Serves 6 to 8.

Mrs. J. J. Suddath, Jr. (Eleanor Picken)

Quick 'N Delicious Potato Salad

3 pounds potatoes, cooked peeled and cubed
1 large green pepper, diced
1 medium onion, diced
2 teaspoons onion salt, or to taste
1/4 teaspoon celery salt, or to taste
1/2 teaspoon pepper, or to taste
1/3 cup red cider vinegar
1 cup mayonnaise

Mix potatoes, green pepper and onion in a large bowl. Blend seasonings, vinegar and mayonnaise; add to vegetables; mix well. Refrigerate. Serves 6 to 8.

Note: This salad is better if made 2 or 3 hours ahead.

Mrs. Vincent Borham (Rose) and Ellen M. Borham
Elmont, New York

Tomatoes Vinaigrette

3 large tomatoes
2 cloves of garlic, pressed or minced
1 teaspoon salt
1/2 teaspoon pepper
2 teaspoons oregano
1/2 teaspoon dry mustard
1/3 cup wine vinegar
1 cup olive oil
2 tablespoons minced onion
2 tablespoons chopped parsley

Remove stems and bottoms from tomatoes. Cut each tomato into 3 thick slices. Arrange in an 8-inch square glass dish. In a small bowl combine garlic, salt, pepper, oregano, dry mustard, wine vinegar and olive oil. Spoon mixture over tomatoes. Cover; refrigerate 2 to 3 hours, basting occasionally. To serve, sprinkle with minced onion, parsley and some of the viniagrette dressing. Serves 8.

Mrs. Donald Behm (Marion)

Pennsylvania Dutch Pepper Cabbage

2 pounds cabbage, finely shredded
1 stalk celery, chopped
1 green pepper, chopped
1 carrot or red pepper, chopped
1 cup sugar
1 teaspoon salt
1/2 cup water
1/2 cup vinegar

In a mixing bowl combine cabbage, celery and peppers. In a small bowl combine sugar, salt, water and vinegar. Taste mixture to be sure you have enough vinegar. Pour over vegetables; toss. Serves 6 to 8. *Easy to do. Even better the next day!*

Violet T. Bernard

Whole Green Bean Salad

2 (16-ounce) cans whole Blue Lake green beans, drained
6 tablespoons vinegar
½ cup salad oil
1 medium onion, sliced
½ teaspoon salt
½ teaspoon pepper
8 slices bacon, fried and crumbled
8 hard-cooked eggs, diced
6 tablespoons salad dressing
4 teaspoons vinegar
4 teaspoons prepared mustard

Combine first 6 ingredients; let stand several hours or overnight. Add remaining ingredients; mix well, stirring several times. Serves 8.

Mrs. Dean N. McFarland (Donna VanEwyk)

Hot German Potato Salad

8 large potatoes, unpeeled and cooked
½ pound bacon, cut into small pieces
½ cup bacon drippings
2 tablespoons all-purpose flour
½ cup vinegar
1½ cups water
1½ teaspoons salt
2 tablespoons sugar
½ teaspoon dry mustard
⅛ teaspoon freshly ground pepper
1 medium onion, diced

In medium skillet fry bacon until crisp. Remove and drain on paper towels. Pour off all but ½ cup of drippings; add flour and blend. Add remaining ingredients; cook until mixture thickens. Taste; if too sour, add a little more sugar and water. Pour over peeled, sliced, warm potatoes. Sprinkle with bacon. Serves 8 to 10.

Mrs. Francis A. VanEwyk (Lorraine)
Ozona, Florida

Sweet and Sour Sauerkraut

1 (16-ounce) can sauerkraut, drained
½ green pepper, finely chopped
3 stalks celery, finely chopped
3 green onions, finely chopped
1 (2-ounce) jar pimento, finely chopped
½ cup sugar
½ cup vinegar

In a mixing bowl combine first 5 ingredients. Combine sugar and vinegar in a saucepan and bring to a boil. Pour over sauerkraut mixture. Place in refrigerator and let stand for 24 hours. Serves 6.

Note: Leftover liquid may be used in coleslaw or reheated for more sauerkraut.

Mrs. Douglas Guilfoile (Paula L. Tiezzi)

Tabouleh Salad

1 cup fine bulgur (cracked wheat)
1 cucumber, peeled
3 tomatoes
2 medium onions or 1 bunch scallions
1 bunch parsley
1 bunch radishes (optional)
2 cloves garlic, crushed
1 tablespoon dried mint leaves or 1/2 cup fresh mint leaves, minced
1/4 cup olive oil
1/2 teaspoon pepper
1 tablespoon salt
1/2 cup lemon juice

Soak bulgur in water to cover for 1 hour. Strain well; squeeze out any excess. Mince all vegetables; add bulgur, liquids and seasonings; chill for at least 2 hours. Line a large bowl with romaine lettuce; fill with mixture. Serves 8 to 10.

Note: Bulgur can be purchased at a health food store.

Variation: Can be served as finger food for a buffet by filling romaine lettuce leaves and rolling.

Mrs. Gregory H. Keuroghlian (Nora Ghazikian)

"Nifty Nine" Layered Lettuce Salad

1 small head lettuce
1/2 cup chopped green pepper
1 cup chopped celery
1/2 cup chopped onion
4 hard-cooked eggs, chopped
1 (10-ounce) package frozen peas, unthawed
1/2 pound bacon, cooked and crumbled
1 cup mayonnaise
1 cup creamy Italian salad dressing
1/2 cup shredded Cheddar cheese

Tear clean lettuce into bite-size pieces; place in a 13x9x2-inch glass dish. Layer next 6 ingredients in order given. Combine mayonnaise and salad dressing; mix well. Spread on top of salad ingredients; top with cheese. Wrap tightly with plastic wrap. Refrigerate 8 hours or overnight. Serves 8 to 10.

Note: Use a glass dish for enhanced appearance.

Mrs. Jack Wilson (Mary Jane Brown)

Greek Salad

4 cups Romaine lettuce, washed and torn into bite-sized pieces
1 clove garlic, minced
4 to 6 anchovy fillets
1/3 cup imported olive oil
1/3 cup red wine vinegar
1/2 teaspoon oregano
1/4 teaspoon fresh ground pepper, or to taste
1 medium onion, sliced
1 large tomato, cut into 8 wedges
4 ounces feta cheese, crumbled
8 black olives, imported

In a large serving bowl place lettuce and all ingredients except tomato wedges, cheese and olives. Toss lightly. Add remaining ingredients; toss again. Serve immediately. Serves 4 to 6.

Mrs. Anthony S. Brancato (Georgine E. Palmer)

Feta cheese is a Greek cheese and has a crumbly white consistency and is made of goat's milk.

Mexican Salad Bowl

Dressing:

1/2 cup real mayonnaise
1/4 cup minced green onion
2 tablespoons chili sauce
2 teaspoons cider vinegar
1 teaspoon onion salt
1/2 teaspoon chili powder
4 drops hot pepper sauce

Salad:

2 cups shredded lettuce
1 (12-ounce) can whole kernel corn, drained
1 (8-ounce) can red kidney beans, drained
1 (7-ounce) can pitted ripe olives, drained

In a small bowl mix dressing ingredients; cover; chill. Line a medium serving bowl with lettuce. Combine corn, beans and olives; spoon into lettuce-lined bowl. Serve with dressing. Serves 6.

Mrs. John W. Vassel, Jr. (Eleanor)

A Different Spinach Salad

1 cup spinach, cooked and drained
2 hard-cooked eggs, chopped
1 ounce wheat toast, cut into ½-inch cubes
1 (4-ounce) jar pimentos, drained
2 tablespoons wine vinegar
1 tablespoon Italian dressing
¼ teaspoon salt
⅛ teaspoon black pepper
⅛ teaspoon nutmeg
Croutons (optional)

In a bowl combine spinach, eggs, toast cubes and pimentos. Toss lightly; chill. Mix wine vinegar, Italian dressing, salt, pepper and nutmeg. Pour dressing over spinach mixture; toss. Add croutons just before serving. Serves 4.

Variation: Substitute diet Italian dressing, if desired.

Suncoast Seasons Committee

Kitchen Hint: For quick croutons, butter bread and sprinkle with spices such as sage, thyme, garlic salt or oregano. Cut into cubes and toast under broiler, stirring occasionally for even browning. Use in salads, soups or vegetables. Or use in dressings with meat.

Spinach Salad

Dressing:

1 cup salad oil
¼ cup vinegar
½ cup ketchup
¾ cup sugar
1 tablespoon Worcestershire sauce
¾ to 1 cup chopped onion

In a bottle or jar combine ingredients; refrigerate overnight. Shake or stir well; pour over salad.

Salad:

1 (10-ounce) bag spinach, washed
1 (8-ounce) can water chestnuts, sliced
1 (14-ounce) can bean sprouts, drained
8 ounces fresh mushrooms, sliced
4 hard-cooked eggs, sliced
¼ pound bacon, fried crisp and crumbled

In a large bowl toss salad ingredients; add dressing. Serves 8 to 10.

Variation: Fresh bean sprouts may be substituted for canned sprouts.

Mrs. William Campbell (Darlene)
Palm Harbor, Florida

Tomato and Broccoli Salad

1 bunch fresh broccoli flowerets, chopped
2 green onions with stems, chopped
2 medium tomatoes, chopped
1 teaspoon salt
½ teaspoon pepper
1 tablespoon lemon juice

Dressing:

½ cup sour cream
½ cup mayonnaise

Combine first 6 ingredients. Mix dressing; add to salad mixture; toss lightly. Serves 4 to 6.

Mrs. Robert Russ (Carol Hodapp)

Sweet and Sour Carrot Salad

1 pound carrots, sliced in ½-inch pieces
1 medium onion, thinly sliced
1 medium green pepper, thinly sliced
1 (10¾-ounce) can tomato soup
1 cup sugar
1 cup vinegar
1 teaspoon salt
⅛ teaspoon pepper
1 teaspoon dry mustard

Place carrots in a saucepan; cover with water. Cook until tender; drain. Add onions and green pepper. Combine remaining ingredients in a separate saucepan; bring to a boil. Pour hot mixture over carrots, onions and peppers. Place mixture in a bowl; marinate in refrigerator 24 hours before serving. Serves 8.

Mrs. William Parmer (Jean Glasscock)
Mrs. Robert Leonard (Jeannie), Largo, Florida

Carol's Mexican Salad

1 medium head lettuce, torn into bite-sized pieces
1 large tomato, diced
1 small red onion, thinly sliced
1 (16-ounce) can dark red kidney beans, drained
½ cup shredded Cheddar cheese
1 cup corn chips
¼ cup spicy tomato salad dressing

In a large salad bowl place lettuce; add tomato, onion and kidney beans. Toss and chill. Just before serving, toss salad with salad dressing; top with Cheddar cheese and whole corn chips. Serves 6 to 8.

Mrs. Ronald Bliss (Judy)

Fire and Ice Tomatoes

Salad:

6 tomatoes, quartered
1 onion, sliced and separated into rings
1 green pepper, seeded and cut into thin strips
1 cucumber, sliced

Toss salad ingredients together in a large bowl; set aside.

Marinade:

3/4 cup vinegar
1/4 cup water
4 1/2 teaspoons sugar
1/8 teaspoon red pepper
1/8 teaspoon black pepper
1 teaspoon mustard seed
1 1/2 teaspoons celery salt
1/2 teaspoon salt

In a medium saucepan combine marinade ingredients; heat to boiling. Continue to boil for 1 minute. Immediately pour marinade over salad ingredients; toss well. Cover and refrigerate for 2 to 3 hours, or until *ice cold.* Serves 12.

Mrs. J. Wallace Lee (Ida)

Spinach-Lettuce Toss

5 slices bacon
3 cups lettuce
3 cups spinach
1/4 cup chopped celery
2 tablespoons bleu cheese, crumbled
1 tablespoon chopped green onion
1/4 cup red wine vinegar
2 teaspoons sugar (optional)
3/4 teaspoon Worcestershire sauce

In a skillet cook bacon until crisp. Drain; reserve drippings. Crumble bacon and set aside. Combine lettuce, spinach, celery, bleu cheese and green onion. To bacon drippings add vinegar, sugar and Worcestershire sauce; bring to a boil. Toss salad with dressing; sprinkle with bacon. Serves 6.

Variation: Substitute an additional 3 cups of spinach for lettuce, if desired.

Mrs. John G. Dodson (Frankie Armitage)

Plaki

Armenian Bean Salad

1½ cups Great Northern beans, washed
6½ cups water
4 carrots, cubed
1 green pepper, chopped
¼ cup chopped parsley
¼ cup chopped celery with leaves
3 cloves garlic, minced
1½ tablespoons salt
½ tablespoon black pepper
2 tomatoes, finely chopped
1 tablespoon tomato paste
½ cup olive oil

In a large saucepan or Dutch oven simmer beans in water for 1½ hours. Add the next 7 ingredients; continue to cook 30 minutes more. Add tomatoes and tomato paste; cook 10 minutes or until beans are soft. Add olive oil; cook for 15 minutes. Serve hot or cold. Serves 6 to 8.

Mrs. Gregory H. Keuroghlian (Nora Ghazikian)

Italian Salad

1 head cauliflower, separated into flowerets
4 carrots, sliced
1 green pepper, sliced
3 stalks celery, sliced
½ cup green olives, sliced
½ cup black olives, sliced
¾ cup olive oil
½ cup vinegar
¼ cup water
2 tablespoons sugar
¼ to ½ teaspoon oregano
⅛ teaspoon garlic salt
⅛ teaspoon salt
⅛ teaspoon pepper

Place all vegetables in a large skillet; mix oil, vinegar, water and seasonings in separate container; pour over the vegetables and cook over medium heat for 5 minutes. Chill 24 hours, stirring occasionally. Serves 12 to 16.

Note: This salad will keep in the refrigerator for 1 month.

Mrs. Joe Hensley (Joann)

Anchovy Salad Dressing

1 (2-ounce) can flat anchovies, drained
1 clove garlic
1 stalk celery, cut up
1 small onion
3 eggs
1 tablespoon pepper
1 tablespoon monosodium glutamate
1 teaspoon sugar
2 tablespoons lemon juice
2 tablespoons horseradish mustard
1 teaspoon garlic salt
2 cups oil

In a blender combine all ingredients, except oil. Mix on slow speed until thoroughly blended. While blender is running, slowly add oil; mix well. Makes 5 cups.

Mrs. Harvey Heimann (Jean)

Chesley's Salad Dressing

1½ cups oil
½ cup sugar
¾ cup vinegar
1 clove garlic, sliced
1 small to medium onion, cut in half
1 teaspoon salt
1 (10¾-ounce) can tomato soup
2 tablespoons Worcestershire sauce

Combine all ingredients in a quart jar; secure with lid or top; shake well. Refrigerate overnight for best flavor. Serve over tossed green salad. Makes 1 quart.

Mrs. Dorman Duncan (Billi)

Plantation Dressing

1 pint real mayonnaise
½ pint French oil dressing
1 (3-ounce) can grated Parmesan cheese
2 or 3 garlic cloves, crushed

In a blender mix all ingredients; chill. Serve with sliced tomatoes. Makes 2½ cups.

Mrs. James J. VanEwyk (Janice)
Villa Park, Illinois

Dill Dressing

1 tablespoon vinegar
½ teaspoon salt
⅛ teaspoon pepper
2 teaspoons sugar
1 teaspoon dill weed
1 cup sour cream

Combine all ingredients. Mix well and chill to blend flavors. Makes 1 to 1½ cups.

Note: Good for sliced tomatoes and cucumbers, or cold cuts. To use as dip, serve in hollowed out purple cabbage.

Mrs. Deanna McFarland Campbell
Milwaukee, Wisconsin

Fifty Dollar Spinach Salad Dressing

½ cup sugar
¼ cup white or red wine vinegar
¼ cup Dijon mustard
1 small onion, minced
1 teaspoon salt
½ teaspoon celery seed
½ teaspoon paprika
¼ teaspoon pepper
1 cup salad oil

Blend together all ingredients. Pour over spinach greens. Garnish with mandarin orange slices and peanuts, cashews or slivered almonds. Makes 1½ cups.

Sally Paul
Joliet, Illinois

Honey Salad Dressing

⅓ cup honey
⅓ cup cider vinegar
½ cup peanut or safflower oil
1 teaspoon Italian seasoning

In a bottle or jar combine all ingredients; shake well. Serve on lettuce or spinach salad. Makes 1⅓ cups.

Mrs. Jerry Harris (Nancy)

Mustard Salad Dressing

1 (8-ounce) bottle Italian salad dressing
2 tablespoons mustard
1 teaspoon celery seed

In a medium bowl mix all ingredients until well blended; chill. Beat again before serving. Makes 1 cup.

Mrs. James Long (Eva Fandrich)

Poppy Seed Dressing

1½ cups sugar
2 teaspoons dry mustard
2 teaspoons salt
⅔ cup white vinegar
3 tablespoons onion juice or finely-grated fresh onion
2 cups salad oil
3 tablespoons poppy seeds

In a blender or food processor mix dry ingredients; add onion juice or finely-grated onion and vinegar. Add oil slowly; blend until thick; add poppy seeds. Makes 3½ cups.

Note: This salad dressing is good on fruit salad or cole slaw with pineapple and white grapes.

Mrs. Dean N. McFarland (Donna VanEwyk)

Kitchen Hint: To peel and section Florida grapefruit and oranges: chill grapefruit and oranges before preparing. To section the fruit — (1) Cut slice from top; cut off peel in strips from top to bottom, cutting deeply enough to remove white membrane. Cut slice from bottom; (2) Cut alongside each dividing membrane from outside to middle of core; and (3) Remove section by section over bowl to retain juice from fruit.

Chinese Salad Dressing

1 teaspoon sesame seed oil
¼ teaspoon monosodium glutamate
1 tablespoon sugar
1 tablespoon soy sauce
1 tablespoon wine vinegar

In a small bowl mix together all ingredients. Pour over salad just before serving. Makes 2 servings.

Serving Suggestions:

Serve over a tossed salad; over a watercress and fresh mushroom salad or watercress and sliced water chestnut salad; over a cucumber salad made as follows:

1 cucumber
½ teaspoon salt
2 cups shredded Chinese celery cabbage

Peel cucumber; cut into very thin slices. Place in a small bowl; sprinkle with salt; let stand 20 minutes. Drain; arrange cabbage on plates with cucumber; pour dressing over salad at the very last minute.

Mrs. Jay Johnston
Princeton, New Jersey

Fruit-Veggie Dressing

2/3 cup sugar
1 teaspoon dry mustard
1 teaspoon paprika
1 teaspoon celery seed
1/4 teaspoon salt
1/3 cup honey
1/3 cup vinegar
1 teaspoon lemon juice
1 teaspoon grated onion
1 cup salad oil

In a medium bowl combine dry ingredients. Pour in honey, vinegar and lemon juice; add onion. Pour in oil while slowly beating with rotary or electric beater. Use immediately or chill, if desired. Makes 2 cups.

Note: A tasty dressing for cottage cheese, fruit, prunes or vegetable salad.

Mrs. Frank Sanson (Claudia)
Clearwater, Florida

Thousand Island Dressing

1 cup mayonnaise
3 tablespoons chili sauce
1 tablespoon chopped green pepper
1 teaspoon chopped pimento
1 teaspoon chopped chives

In a bottle or jar combine ingredients; blend thoroughly; chill. Serve on wedge of lettuce or any salad you like. *Simple to prepare!* Makes 1¼ cups.

Mrs. Dorman Duncan (Billi)

Blue Cheese Dressing

4 ounces blue cheese
1 cup mayonnaise
1/4 cup salad oil
1/4 cup sour cream
1/4 cup buttermilk
1 tablespoon white vinegar
1/4 teaspoon salt
1 teaspoon garlic powder
1/8 teaspoon pepper

Crumble blue cheese into a large bowl. Add mayonnaise and salad oil; blend thoroughly. Add sour cream and blend again. Add buttermilk, vinegar, salt and garlic powder; blend well. Add more salt and pepper to taste, if desired. For the best flavor store covered in refrigerator for at least 24 hours before serving. Makes 2 to 2½ cups.

Mrs. James Long (Eva Fandrich)

Dieter's Delight Mayonnaise

1 cup salad oil
2 egg whites
2 tablespoons vinegar, lemon or lime juice
½ teaspoon salt
½ tablespoon sugar
⅛ teaspoon pepper
½ teaspoon curry powder (optional)
¼ cup hot water

Place ¼ cup oil and all other ingredients in blender. Add remaining oil in a slow stream, until mixture reaches the consistency of butter.

Note: 1 tablespoon equals only 75 calories. Makes 1 pint.

Suncoast Seasons Committee

Piquant Dressing

⅓ to ½ cup sugar
½ to 1 teaspoon salt
1 teaspoon prepared mustard
1 teaspoon paprika
¼ teaspoon celery salt
⅓ cup ketchup
¼ cup vinegar
Juice of 1 lemon
10 drops hot pepper sauce
¼ cup grated onion
¾ cup salad oil

In a medium bowl blend dry ingredients; add remaining ingredients; beat thoroughly. Chill in covered container. Shake or stir before serving on your favorite salad greens. Makes 1 pint.

Mrs. William S. Sharpe (Wanda)

Kitchen Hint: Put 2 tablespoons oil, 1 tablespoon vinegar and ⅛ teaspoon Italian seasoning in bottom of almost empty ketchup bottle. Shake well; use as salad dressing.

Roquefort Dressing

1 (8-ounce) package Roquefort cheese, crumbled
1¼ cups mayonnaise
2 tablespoons light cream or milk
1 teaspoon Worcestershire sauce
¼ teaspoon salt
⅛ teaspoon garlic powder
⅛ teaspoon white pepper

Combine all ingredients; blend well and chill. Makes 1½ cups.

Mrs. Gregory H. Keuroghlian (Nora Ghazikian)

Breads

Baking Powder Biscuits

2 cups all-purpose flour
¾ teaspoon salt
2½ tablespoons sugar
3 teaspoons baking powder
½ cup vegetable shortening
½ cup milk

Sift dry ingredients and cut in shortening. Add milk, mixing to a soft dough. Place on floured board and roll ¾-inch thick. Use biscuit cutter or 2½- to 3-inch diameter glass. Place on ungreased baking sheet. Bake at 450 degrees for about 12 minutes. Makes 1 dozen.

Note: Perfect cut in ½ and used for strawberry shortcake! Can also be used for plain biscuits by omitting sugar.

Mrs. Lewis N. McFarland (Blanche)
Villa Park, Illinois

Hush Puppies

Florida Style

2 cups white self-rising cornmeal
1 cup all-purpose flour
1 teaspoon sugar
½ teaspoon salt
¼ teaspoon pepper
1 (8-ounce) can tomato sauce
1 medium onion, chopped
1 green pepper, chopped
2 stalks celery, chopped

In a large bowl mix together cornmeal, flour, sugar, salt and pepper. Add tomato sauce; mix well. Add onions, peppers and celery. Batter should be stiff. If too dry, add a little water. Drop mix by tablespoonfuls into hot oil and cook until reddish brown. For added flavor, fry with fish. Serves 7 to 10.

Mrs. Denver Bass (Eunice)
Dunedin, Florida

Beer Biscuits

4 cups biscuit baking mix
1 (12-ounce) can of beer
2 tablespoons sugar

In a large mixing bowl combine biscuit baking mix, beer and sugar; beat 1 minute. Place in greased muffin tins and bake at 375 degrees for 20 minutes. Makes 1½ dozen.

Note: They are as good the next day as the day you made them!

Mrs. R. C. Rilott (Melba)
Dunedin, Florida

Apple-Carrot Bread

1½ cups peeled and shredded apples
½ cup shredded carrots
¼ cup margarine, softened
½ teaspoon lemon extract
2 eggs
1¾ cups all-purpose flour
⅔ cup sugar
1 teaspoon baking powder
1 teaspoon baking soda
½ teaspoon salt
½ cup chopped walnuts

In a large bowl blend first 5 ingredients together; add remaining ingredients, except walnuts, and beat by hand 3 minutes, blend in walnuts. Pour into well-greased 9x5x3 or 8x4x3-inch loaf pan and bake at 375 degrees for 50 to 60 minutes or until done. Makes 1 loaf.

Mrs. Robert M. Blair (Elizabeth)
Dunedin, Florida

Banana Bread

½ cup margarine
1 cup sugar
2 eggs, beaten
3 large bananas, mashed
2 cups all-purpose flour
1 teaspoon baking soda
¾ teaspoon baking powder
1 teaspoon vanilla extract
½ cup chopped nuts

In a large bowl cream margarine and sugar; add eggs, one at a time, beating well. Add bananas; mix well. Stir flour, baking soda, baking powder, vanilla and nuts into batter. Pour batter into a well-greased 9x5x3-inch loaf pan and bake at 350 degrees for 45 to 60 minutes. Remove from pan and cool on rack. Serves 12.

Mrs. Charles Shupe (Jewel), Park Forest, Illinois
Mrs. Douglas Guilfoile (Paula L. Tiezzi)

Beer Bread

3 cups self-rising flour
2 tablespoons sugar
1 (12-ounce) bottle of beer

Preheat oven to 375 degrees. Grease a 9x5x3-inch loaf pan. In a large bowl mix together flour and sugar; add beer; mix well. Form into loaf; place into pan. Bake 1 hour; let cool. Makes 1 loaf.

Note: Quick and easy!

Mrs. Lynn Lees

Fresh Oregon Apple Bread

2 cups all-purpose flour
3 teaspoons baking powder
1 teaspoon salt
½ teaspoon cinnamon
¼ teaspoon grated nutmeg
½ cup butter or shortening
1¼ cups sugar
2 eggs
1½ cups peeled, finely grated apples
½ cup chopped walnuts or pecans

Preheat oven to 350 degrees. Sift together first 5 ingredients; set aside. In large bowl of mixer cream butter and sugar together until light and fluffy. Beat in eggs, one at a time, beating well after each addition. Stir in dry ingredients and apples, one half at a time. Fold in nuts. Pour into a well-greased and floured 9x5x3-inch loaf pan. Bake for 1 hour or until done. Cool in pan for 10 minutes; turn on to a wire rack. Cool completely before serving. Makes 1 loaf.

Mrs. Lynn Lees

Cranberry Nut Bread

2 cups all-purpose flour, sifted
1 cup sugar
1½ teaspoons baking powder
½ teaspoon baking soda
1 teaspoon salt
¼ cup shortening
¾ cup orange juice
1 tablespoon grated orange rind
1 egg, well beaten
½ cup chopped nuts
2 cups fresh cranberries, chopped

In a large bowl sift together flour, sugar, baking powder, baking soda and salt. Cut in shortening until mixture resembles coarse cornmeal. Combine orange juice and grated rind with well beaten egg. Pour into dry ingredients; mix just enough to dampen. Carefully fold in chopped nuts and cranberries. Spoon into greased 9x5x3-inch loaf pan. Spread corners and sides slightly higher than center. Bake 350 degrees about 1 hour until crust is golden brown and toothpick inserted comes out clean. Remove from pan; cool. Store overnight for easy slicing. Keep in refrigerator. Makes 1 loaf.

Mrs. Robert Fletcher (B. J.), Pound Ridge, New York
Catherine C. Lees, Dunedin, Florida

Chocolate Bits Bread

1/4 cup butter
1/4 cup shortening
1 cup sugar
2 eggs
2 cups sifted all-purpose flour
1 teaspoon baking soda
3 bananas, mashed
1/4 cup chopped nuts
1/4 cup chocolate chips

Grease and flour a 9x5x3-inch loaf pan. In a bowl cream butter and shortening together; add sugar and eggs. Add other ingredients; mix together. Bake at 350 degrees for 45 minutes or until done. Makes 1 loaf.

Mrs. Brian Cook (Lee)
Dunedin, Florida

Toasted Coconut Bread

1 cup coconut, toasted
1 cup milk
1 egg, beaten
1/4 cup oil
1 teaspoon vanilla extract
2 cups all-purpose flour
1 tablespoon baking powder
1/2 teaspoon salt
3/4 cup sugar

In a large bowl mix milk, egg, oil and vanilla extract together. Add coconut, flour, baking powder, salt and sugar; stir until blended. Pour into a greased and floured 9x5x3-inch loaf pan. Bake at 350 degrees for 1 hour. Cool on rack.

Note: Toast coconut at 350 degrees for about 10 minutes or until lightly brown.

Mrs. George Ghazikian (Gladys)
Springfield, Pennsylvania

Hot Herbed Bread

1 loaf French bread
1/2 cup soft margarine
1/2 teaspoon paprika
1/2 teaspoon dried rosemary leaves
1/4 teaspoon dried thyme leaves
1/4 teaspoon dried marjoram leaves
1/8 teaspoon salt

Preheat oven to 400 degrees. Make diagonal cuts three-quarters through bread at 1-inch intervals. Combine other ingredients until well blended. Spread mixture between bread slices. Wrap bread in foil; bake 15 to 20 minutes until margarine is melted and bread is hot. Serves 10.

Mrs. Brown Coleman
Paris, Texas

Glazed Lemon Bread

Bread:

2½ cups sifted all-purpose flour
3 teaspoons baking powder
1 teaspoon salt
⅓ cup butter
1 cup sugar
1 tablespoon grated lemon peel
2 eggs
1 cup milk
½ cup chopped walnuts

Grease and flour 9x5x3-inch pan. Into a large bowl sift flour, baking powder and salt. In another large bowl cream butter, sugar and lemon peel. Add eggs, one at a time. Add dry ingredients and milk alternating each. Fold in nuts. Pour into prepared pan and smooth top with a knife. Bake 60 to 70 minutes at 325 degrees.

Glaze:

1 tablespoon lemon peel
¼ cup sugar
⅓ cup fresh lemon juice

Just before end of baking time combine peel, sugar and juice in saucepan. Heat slowly until sugar dissolves, stirring constantly. Glaze bread with syrup immediately upon removing from oven. Use *all* syrup. It will be absorbed when bread cools. Cool in pan on rack 30 minutes. Remove from pan and cool completely on rack before slicing, about 2 to 4 hours. Makes 1 loaf.

Catherine C. Lees
Dunedin, Florida

Kitchen Hint: To get maximum amount of juice from lemon, warm in water. Press down firmly and roll on hard surface before juicing.

"No Need to Knead" Whole Wheat Bread

1½ cups warm water
3 tablespoons honey
1½ tablespoons butter, melted
1½ tablespoons salt
1½ tablespoons yeast
3 cups whole wheat flour

In a large bowl mix first 5 ingredients; add whole wheat flour and mix thoroughly. Place batter in a 9x5x3-inch greased loaf pan; cover. Let rise about 45 minutes. Bake at 350 degrees for one hour. Makes 1 loaf.

Mrs. John W. Vassel, Jr. (Eleanor)

Pineapple Zucchini Bread

3 eggs
1 cup oil
2 cups sugar
2 teaspoons vanilla extract
2 cups shredded zucchini
1 (8-ounce) can crushed pineapple, drained
3 cups all-purpose flour
2 teaspoons baking soda
1 teaspoon salt
1/4 teaspoon baking powder
1 1/2 teaspoons cinnamon
3/4 teaspoon nutmeg
1 cup chopped nuts
1 cup white raisins

In a large bowl beat eggs, oil, sugar and vanilla until thick. Stir in zucchini and pineapple; blend well. Add dry ingredients slowly; mix well. Pour into 2 well-greased and floured 9x5x3-inch loaf pans. Bake at 350 degrees for 1 hour. Makes 2 loaves.

Note: You may also use 5 mini loaf pans; bake 20 to 25 minutes or until done.

Great for gift-giving!

Mrs. Robert M. Blair (Elizabeth), Dunedin, Florida

Variation: Eliminate cinnamon and nutmeg and add 1 extra teaspoon of vanilla extract.

Catherine C. Lees, Dunedin, Florida

Poppy Seed Bread

1/4 cup poppy seed
1 (14 1/2-ounce) can evaporated milk
2 cups sugar
1 1/2 cups cooking oil
4 eggs
1 teaspoon vanilla extract
3 cups all-purpose flour
1 1/2 teaspoons baking soda
1 teaspoon salt
1 cup chopped nuts (optional)

In a small bowl soak poppy seeds in evaporated milk for 2 hours or overnight. In large bowl beat sugar and oil together. Add eggs and vanilla extract. Sift together flour, baking soda and salt. Add to liquid mixture. Mix well; add poppy seed mixture; add nuts, if desired. Grease and flour two 9x5x3-inch loaf pans or 1 (10-inch) tube pan. Bake at 350 degrees for 1 hour 10 minutes or until done. Makes 2 loaves.

Mrs. Robert Zinn (Shirley), Largo, Florida
Mrs. Anthony Castrogiovanni (BeBe)

Graham Bread

2 cups sour milk
2 cups graham flour
1 cup yellow cornmeal
1 teaspoon salt
½ cup white or brown sugar
1 teaspoon baking powder
1 teaspoon baking soda

In a large mixing bowl stir milk, flour, cornmeal and salt. Add sugar, baking powder and soda to batter. Pour batter into a greased 9x5x3-inch loaf pan. Bake at 350 degrees for one hour. Cool on rack after removing from pan.

Note: Whole wheat flour can be substituted.

"From my Great Grandmother Bromeley about 1875 or maybe even from her mother."

Mrs. Charles Shupe (Jewel)
Park Forest, Illinois

Kitchen Hint: To sour milk add 1 teaspoon vinegar per cup of milk.

Strawberry Bread

3 cups all-purpose flour
1 teaspoon baking soda
1 teaspoon salt
2 teaspoons cinnamon
2 cups sugar
2 (10-ounce) packages frozen strawberries, thawed and partly drained
4 eggs, beaten
1½ cups oil
1½ cups chopped pecans

In a large bowl mix dry ingredients and strawberries. Make well in center of mixture. Mix eggs, oil and pecans; add to dry ingredients; stir until moistened. Pour mixture into two 9x5x3-inch greased loaf pans. Bake at 350 degrees for 1 hour.

Hint: Good with equal amounts (2 tablespoons each) of sugar and cinnamon sprinkled on top when warm. *Different! Great hostess gift!*

Mrs. Joe Hensley (Joann)

Swedish Bread

½ cup butter, melted
⅔ cup sugar, separated
1 teaspoon salt
2¼ cups hot milk
1 (¼-ounce) package dry yeast
¼ cup warm water
1 egg, well beaten
1 teaspoon almond extract
7 cups all-purpose flour, separated

Mix the butter, sugar, salt and hot milk in a large bowl; let cool to lukewarm. Stir the yeast into the water with ¼ teaspoon sugar; let stand 5 minutes to dissolve. Add the yeast, egg, almond extract and 3 cups flour to the first mixture and mix vigorously. Add 3 more cups flour; mix well. Turn out onto a lightly floured board; knead for a minute or two; let rest for 10 minutes. Add the remaining flour a little at a time only if the dough is too sticky. Resume kneading until dough is smooth and elastic. Put the dough in a large, buttered bowl; cover and let rise in a warm place until double in bulk, approximately 1½ hours. Punch down; knead for a minute or two and shape into two loaves. Place in buttered loaf pans; cover and let rise until double in bulk once again. Bake at 375 degrees for 40 to 50 minutes. Remove from pans and cool on racks. Makes 2 loaves.

Braided Breads (two braids): After the dough has risen for the first time, punch it down; knead for a minute or two and divide into six equal pieces. Stretch and roll each piece with hands until you have six long rolls of uniform size. Make two braids with them, pinching the three pieces of dough firmly together when starting the braiding and again when finishing. Leave as is or form each bread into a ring. Place on buttered cookie sheets; cover and let rise until double in bulk. Brush with a lightly beaten egg yolk with 1 teaspoon cold water and sprinkle with blanched, chopped almonds. Bake for only 25 to 30 minutes.

John Vignola
Dunedin, Florida

Herbed Bread

½ cup butter, softened
2 teaspoons basil
1 teaspoon chives
1 loaf French bread

Mix first 3 ingredients. Slice French bread three-quarters through loaf and spread mixture on slices and on top. Wrap in foil and heat in oven at 350 degrees about 15 minutes. Serves 6 to 8. *Delightful, light change from garlic bread.*

Mrs. William J. Armstrong (Tish)
New Market, Maryland

Suncoast Orange Bread

2 cups all-purpose flour
1 teaspoon baking powder
1 teaspoon baking soda
½ teaspoon salt
½ cup boiling water
2 tablespoons margarine
⅓ cup orange juice
1 cup sugar
3 tablespoons orange marmalade
2 teaspoons orange extract
1 egg, slightly beaten
½ cup chopped walnuts

In a medium bowl mix flour, baking powder, baking soda and salt. In a large bowl mix boiling water, margarine, orange juice, sugar, marmalade, orange extract and egg. Sift flour mixture over orange mixture and add nuts. Stir until dry ingredients are dampened. Batter will be lumpy. Pour into a greased 9x5x3-inch loaf pan; bake at 350 degrees for 40 minutes or until done. Cool on rack. Makes 1 loaf.

Mrs. Gregory H. Keuroghlian (Nora Ghazikian)

Swedish Rye Bread

1 cup scalded milk
2½ teaspoons salt
2 tablespoons molasses
2 tablespoons margarine
1 cup water
1 (¼-ounce) package active dry yeast
3½ cups all-purpose flour
1 tablespoon caraway seeds
2 cups rye flour

Measure salt, molasses and margarine into a large bowl; pour milk over ingredients in bowl. Add water; cool to lukewarm. Add yeast and all-purpose flour; beat until smooth. Stir in caraway seeds. Gradually add the rye flour; mix to make a medium stiff dough. (The dough will be sticky.) Knead dough on a floured surface until smooth, about 10 minutes. Place in a buttered bowl; rub top with softened butter and cover; let rise until doubled, about 2 hours. Punch down; let rise again. Shape into 2 oblong loaves; place on buttered cookie sheets that have been sprinkled with cornmeal. Let rise until doubled. Rub top with softened butter and bake at 375 degrees for 30 to 40 minutes. Makes two 1-pound loaves.

Mrs. Wilford R. Poe (Mollye Redmon)

French Bread

2 (1/4-ounce) packages dry yeast
1/2 cup warm water
8 cups all-purpose flour
1 tablespoon salt
3 tablespoons sugar
3 tablespoons oil
3 cups warm water
1/4 cup cornmeal

Dissolve yeast in warm water; set aside. In a large bowl mix together flour, salt and sugar. Make a well in the flour; add yeast, oil and 3 cups warm water; mix well. Knead on floured board until no longer sticky (approximately 15 minutes). Cover and let rise 15 minutes. Punch down and repeat 4 more times at 15 minute intervals. Divide dough into fourths. Roll dough out into a triangle (approximately 6x8-inches). Roll up; seal under edge like a jelly roll. Grease lightly 2 cookie sheets. Sprinkle with cornmeal. Cut 4 diagonal slits across each loaf. Grease with butter; sprinkle with cornmeal. Cover; let rise 1½ hours. Bake at 350 degrees approximately 25 minutes. Remove from oven; butter top side lightly. Makes 4 loaves. *Excellent! You will say out of this world!*

Mrs. Anthony Castrogiovanni (BeBe)

Caraway Cheese Twist

1 (1/4-ounce) package active dry yeast
3/4 cup warm water
1 tablespoon sugar
1 teaspoon salt
1 egg
1 cup shredded sharp Cheddar cheese
2 tablespoons caraway seeds
2½ cups all-purpose flour

In a large mixing bowl dissolve yeast in ¾ cup warm water plus 1 tablespoon sugar. Then add salt, egg, cheese, caraway seeds and flour. Knead this until well mixed; put in a greased bowl to rise in a warm place until double. Divide dough and place in 2 greased 9-inch loaf pans to rise again. Bake 10 minutes at 425 degrees or 20 minutes at 350 degrees. Makes 2 loaves.

Mrs. Robert Fletcher (B. J.)
Pound Ridge, New York

Fluffy Pancakes

Melt-In-Your-Mouth

1 egg, separated
1 cup all-purpose flour
½ teaspoon salt
½ teaspoon baking soda
1 to 2 teaspoons sugar (optional)
1 cup buttermilk
1 tablespoon oil

In a small bowl beat egg white until stiff. Measure flour, salt, baking soda and sugar into bowl and mix. Make a well in center and add slightly beaten egg yolk, buttermilk and oil; mix until flour is moistened. Fold in egg white. If batter is too thick, add a little more buttermilk. Pour 2 to 3 tablespoons batter on greased griddle or skillet. Cook until middle starts to bubble. Turn and cook until golden brown. Serves 2.

Helen S. Glass

Cherry Orange Butter: Cream ½ cup butter thoroughly. Add 1 (4-ounce) jar maraschino cherries which have been drained and minced. Add 1 tablespoon maraschino cherry syrup and 2 teaspoons grated orange peel; beat until blended. Makes 1 cup.

Casserole Onion Bread

1 cup milk, scalded
3 tablespoons sugar
1½ tablespoons butter or margarine
¾ cup warm water
2 packages active dry yeast
1 (1.375-ounce) envelope onion soup mix
4 cups unsifted all-purpose flour

In a medium bowl mix together milk, sugar and butter. Cool to lukewarm. Sprinkle dry yeast into warm water in measuring cup; stir until dissolved. Add yeast mixture to milk mixture; then add soup mix and flour; stir and blend, about 2 minutes. Cover bowl; let rise in a warm place, free from draft until double in bulk, about 45 minutes. Preheat oven to 375 degrees. Stir batter down; beat vigorously about ½ minute; turn into greased 1½-quart casserole. Bake uncovered 1 hour. Serves 8 to 10.

Mrs. Dean N. McFarland (Donna VanEwyk)

Banana Muffins

2 cups sifted all-purpose flour
1 teaspoon baking soda
½ teaspoon salt
¾ cup sugar
1 egg, well beaten
1 cup mashed banana
½ cup shortening, melted
1 tablespoon vinegar
6 tablespoons milk

In a large bowl sift together flour, baking soda, salt and sugar; add remaining ingredients. Stir lightly and quickly until just mixed. Grease muffin tins and fill ⅔ full. Bake at 400 degrees for 20 minutes. Makes 18 to 20 muffins.

Mrs. James Long (Eva Fandrich)

Wild Blueberry Muffins

Topping:

⅓ cup brown sugar
¼ cup all-purpose flour
½ teaspoon cinnamon
3 tablespoons firm margarine

Mix with fork until crumbly; set aside.

Muffins:

2 eggs
1 cup milk
½ cup oil
3 cups all-purpose flour
1 cup sugar
4 teaspoons baking powder
1 teaspoon salt
1 (15-ounce) can wild blueberries, drained

Grease 24 medium muffin tins (2¾ inches in diameter) or line with paper cups. In a large bowl beat eggs; stir in milk and oil. Mix in flour, sugar, baking powder, and salt until flour is moistened. Stir in blueberries. Do not over mix. Fill muffin tins ⅔ full. Sprinkle tops with 1 teaspoon topping. Bake at 400 degrees for 20 to 25 minutes or until brown. Remove from pan immediately. Makes 2 dozen.

Helen S. Glass

Variations:
Apple Muffins: Stir in 2 cups grated apple with the oil, and add 1 teaspoon cinnamon to the flour.

Cranberry-Orange Muffins: Fold into batter, 2 tablespoons grated orange peel and 2 cups cranberries cut in half.

Suncoast Seasons Committee

Orange Blossoms

4 eggs, unbeaten
1½ cups sour cream
½ teaspoon baking soda
2 cups sugar
2 cups all-purpose flour
1 cup butter or margarine, melted
2 teaspoons baking powder
2½ teaspoons vanilla extract

Add enough sour cream to eggs to make 2 cups. In a large bowl combine all ingredients, mixing well. Pour batter into well-greased miniature muffin tins. Bake at 350 degrees for 18 minutes. Remove from tins and cool slightly. Makes 7 dozen.

Glaze:

6 cups powdered sugar
Juice and rind of 2 oranges
Juice and rind of 2 lemons

Mix all ingredients together and glaze cooled muffins.

Mrs. Dean N. McFarland (Donna VanEwyk)

Manyway Muffins

3 cups whole bran cereal
1 cup boiling water
2 eggs, beaten
2 cups buttermilk or plain yogurt
½ cup salad oil
1 cup raisins, currants, chopped dates or chopped prunes
2½ teaspoons baking soda
½ teaspoon salt
½ cup honey, brown sugar, molasses or sugar
2½ cups unbleached flour

In large mixing bowl mix cereal with water; set aside until cooled, then add eggs, buttermilk, oil and fruit. Blend well. In another bowl mix together soda, salt, honey and flour. Stir this mixture into the bran mixture. Fill well-greased muffin tins about ⅔ full. Bake at 425 degrees for 20 to 25 minutes. Makes 2½ to 3 dozen.

Note: You may bake all of the muffins now or use what you need now and refrigerate the remainder to be used later. Batter keeps for 6 weeks.

Donna Buchanan
Ozona, Florida

Finnish Nisu

Raised Sweet Rolls

4 eggs
2 cups sugar
1½ tablespoons salt
2 teaspoons vanilla extract
2 teaspoons almond extract
4 cups lukewarm milk
10 cups all-purpose flour, halved
4 (¼-ounce) packages dry yeast
1 tablespoon cardamom seeds, crushed
½ pound butter, melted

In a very large bowl mix eggs, sugar, salt and extracts. Pour in lukewarm milk and mix thoroughly. Add flour, yeast and crushed cardamom seeds to milk mixture. Add half of the butter to milk mixture. Mix well and let rise in warm place for 1 hour; cover with tea towel. Punch dough and add rest of flour and melted butter. Knead for 10 or 12 minutes making sure all flour is mixed. If dough remains sticky and sticks to your hands, add ½ to 1 cup more flour and continue to knead until mixed well. Let rise for another hour. Grease 5 (8-inch) cake pans. Divide dough into 5 parts; any shape can be used for dough, such as braids and twists. Place desired dough shape into pan and let rise for 1 hour, covered. Bake at 350 degrees for 30 to 40 minutes. Glaze with a powdered sugar frosting and nuts. Makes 5 loaves.

Note: 1 cup cooked raisins and/or 1 cup finely chopped candied fruit may be added for a variation.

Mrs. Fay Jacobson
Dunedin, Florida

Six-Week Bran Muffins

1 (15-ounce) box raisin bran flakes
5 cups all-purpose flour
3 cups sugar
2 teaspoons salt
5 teaspoons baking soda
4 eggs, well beaten
1 quart buttermilk
1 cup vegetable oil (or melted butter)

In a large mixing bowl combine raisin bran flakes, flour, sugar, salt and baking soda; stir to blend. Add buttermilk, oil and beaten eggs to dry ingredients; mix well. Pour batter into greased muffin tins, or line tins with paper cups; fill half full. Bake at 400 degrees for 15 minutes. Makes 4½ dozen.

Note: Batter can be prepared ahead and stored in a covered-container in refrigerator for up to six weeks, using as needed. More raisins and/or nuts may be added if desired. One half-cup raw bran can be substituted for ½ cup flour.

Mrs. Bill Ritchey (Carol Eddington)
Mrs. James Berfield (Sue Mautz)

Pumpkin Muffins

1 cup sifted all-purpose flour
1/2 cup sugar
2 teaspoons baking powder
1/2 teaspoon cinnamon
1/2 teaspoon nutmeg
1/4 teaspoon salt
1/4 cup butter
1 egg, beaten
1/2 cup canned pumpkin
1/2 cup evaporated milk
1/2 cup small seedless raisins

In a large bowl sift the dry ingredients and cut in butter until mixture resembles cornmeal. In a medium bowl combine beaten egg, pumpkin and milk. Stir in raisins. Add to the dry ingredients, stirring just to moisten. Grease and flour muffin tin. Fill muffin cups 2/3 full. Bake at 400 degrees for 20 to 25 minutes. Makes 1 dozen.

Mrs. John W. Vassel, Jr. (Eleanor)

Sour Cream Coffee Cake

1/4 cup margarine
1 cup sugar
3 eggs
2 cups all-purpose flour
1 teaspoon baking powder
1 teaspoon baking soda
1/4 teaspoon salt
1 cup sour cream
1/2 cup golden raisins
Pecan topping

In a large bowl cream margarine and sugar. Add eggs, one at a time, beating after each addition. Sift flour, baking powder, baking soda and salt. Add to creamed mixture alternately with sour cream, blending well. Sprinkle raisins over top and stir in. Spread in a greased and floured 13x9x2-inch baking pan and sprinkle with topping. Bake at 350 degrees for 30 minutes. Cut into squares for serving. Serves 12.

Pecan Topping:

3/4 cup firmly packed brown sugar
1 tablespoon all-purpose flour
1 teaspoon cinnamon
2 tablespoons butter or margarine
1 cup chopped pecans

Mix together sugar, flour and cinnamon. Cut in butter or margarine until mixture resembles cornmeal. Add pecans.

Mrs. Robert Baker (Alice)
Hebron, Indiana

Cranberry Coffee Cake

½ cup butter or margarine, softened
1 cup sugar
2 eggs
2 cups all-purpose flour
1 teaspoon baking powder
1 teaspoon baking soda
½ teaspoon salt
1 (8-ounce) carton sour cream
1 teaspoon almond extract
1 (16-ounce) can whole berry cranberry sauce
½ cup chopped pecans
Glaze (optional)

Cream butter and sugar until fluffy. Add eggs, one at a time, beating after each. Combine flour, baking powder, soda and salt; add to creamed mixture. Alternate with sour cream, beating well after each addition. Add almond extract and mix well. Spoon ⅓ of mixture into greased and floured 10-inch tube pan. Spread ⅓ of cranberry sauce over batter. Repeat twice, ending with cranberry layer. Sprinkle with pecans. Bake at 350 degrees for 1 hour or until cake is done. Let cool 5 minutes before removing from pan. Drizzle glaze over top, if desired.

Glaze:

¾ cup powdered sugar
½ teaspoon almond extract
1 tablespoon warm water

Combine all ingredients. Stir well. Serves 12.

Mrs. Anthony S. Brancato (Georgine E. Palmer)

French Breakfast Puffs

½ cup oil
½ cup sugar
1 egg
1½ cups all-purpose flour
1½ teaspoons baking powder
½ teaspoon salt
¼ teaspoon nutmeg
½ cup milk
¼ cup butter or margarine, melted
¼ cup sugar
½ teaspoon cinnamon

In a medium bowl blend oil, sugar and egg. Sift together flour, baking powder, salt and nutmeg; add to mixture alternating with milk. Pour into greased muffin tins, filling ⅔ full. Bake at 350 degrees 20 to 25 minutes. Immediately after baking, dip top into melted butter, then into mixture of sugar and cinnamon. Serve hot. Makes 15 muffins.

Mrs. Ralph Madden (Ann)
Dunedin, Florida

Cinnamon Puffs

2 cups biscuit baking mix
1/4 cup sugar
1/4 teaspoon nutmeg
3/4 cup milk
1 egg
2 tablespoons margarine, softened

In a large mixing bowl mix biscuit baking mix, sugar and nutmeg. Add milk, egg and margarine; beat hard. Drop into greased tassie pans (small miniature pans), ½ to ⅔ full. Bake at 400 degrees for 15 minutes.

Topping:

3/4 cup margarine, melted
1/2 cup sugar
1 tablespoon cinnamon

Roll puffs in melted margarine. Mix together sugar and cinnamon; dip puffs into mixture. Puffs can be made ahead, reheated and dipped into margarine and cinnamon mixture. Makes about 3 dozen.

Mrs. Addison Bender (Josephine Andrews)

Tropical Coffee Cake

1 1/2 cups all-purpose or unbleached flour
1 cup sugar
2 teaspoons baking powder
1/2 teaspoon salt
1/2 cup oil
2 eggs
1 (8-ounce) carton pineapple, apricot or orange yogurt or 1 cup dairy sour cream

Heat oven to 350 degrees. Grease a 9-inch square pan or 11x7x2-inch pan. In large bowl mix all ingredients, stir just until dry ingredients are moistened. Pour batter into prepared pan; set aside. Make topping; sprinkle over batter. Bake at 350 degrees for 35 to 45 minutes, or until toothpick inserted in center comes out clean. *Topping tends to brown quickly: cover loosely with foil after topping browns.* Serves 9.

Topping:

1 cup coconut or chopped nuts
1/3 cup sugar
1 teaspoon cinnamon

In a small bowl combine all ingredients.

Mrs. William R. Barnes (Vickie)

Chocolate-Chip Coffee Ring

1 cup sugar
3/4 cup butter or margarine
2 1/2 cups all-purpose flour
1 cup sour cream
2 eggs
1 teaspoon baking powder
1 teaspoon baking soda
1 teaspoon vanilla extract
1 cup semi-sweet chocolate pieces
1/2 cup packed light brown sugar
1 1/2 teaspoons cocoa
1 1/2 cups chopped walnuts

Preheat oven to 350 degrees. Grease a 10-inch tube pan. In a large bowl with mixer at medium speed, beat sugar with 1/2 cup butter until light and fluffy. Add 2 cups flour, sour cream, eggs, baking powder, baking soda and vanilla extract; beat at low speed until blended, constantly scraping bowl with rubber spatula. Increase speed to medium, beat 3 minutes, occasionally scraping bowl. With a spoon stir in 1/2 cup chocolate pieces. Spread batter evenly in pan. In a medium bowl measure 1/2 cup flour, brown sugar and cocoa. With pastry blender or 2 knives used scissor-fashion, cut in 1/4 cup butter or margarine until mixture resembles coarse crumbs and ingredients are well blended; stir in walnuts and remaining chocolate pieces. Crumble mixture evenly over batter in pan. Bake 60 to 65 minutes until cake pulls away from sides of pan. Cool cake completely in pan on wire rack. Serves 8 to 10.

Mrs. Robert D. Garretson (Charlene)
Denville, New Jersey

Refrigerator Coffee Cake

2 cups all-purpose flour
2 teaspoons baking powder
3/4 teaspoon salt
1/2 cup sugar
6 tablespoons butter
1 egg, beaten
1/2 cup milk

Grease and lightly flour an 8-inch square pan. In a large bowl blend flour, baking powder, salt, sugar, butter, egg and milk. Pour batter into prepared pan.

Topping:

1 1/2 tablespoons butter, melted
4 tablespoons sugar
1 tablespoon all-purpose flour
1 teaspoon cinnamon

In a small bowl combine melted butter, sugar, flour and cinnamon. Spread over batter. Cover and refrigerate overnight. Bake at 350 degrees for 25 to 30 minutes. Serves 6 to 8.

Mrs. Charles Shupe (Jewel)
Park Forest, Illinois

Cheese Pastry

2 (8-ounce) cans refrigerated crescent rolls
2 (8-ounce) packages cream cheese
2 eggs, separated
¾ cup sugar
1 teaspoon vanilla extract

Spread one can of crescent rolls in the bottom of a 13x9x2-inch pan. Mix together cream cheese, egg yolks, sugar and vanilla. Spread mixture over crescent rolls in pan. Spread second can of crescent rolls on top of mixture. Brush rolls with egg whites. Bake at 350 degrees for 25 to 30 minutes or until golden brown. Top with powdered sugar and serve. Serves 12 to 15.

Mrs. John W. Vassel, Jr. (Eleanor)

Salt Sticks

1 (8-ounce) package refrigerated biscuits
2 tablespoons milk
2 teaspoons salt
1½ cups crisp rice-type cereal, coarsely crushed
2 tablespoons sesame, caraway or celery seeds

Cut biscuits in half; roll each part into pencil-thin sticks (about 4 inches long). Brush with milk. Mix salt, cereal crumbs and seeds. Roll sticks in mixture. Bake on greased cookie sheet at 450 degrees about 20 minutes, until lightly browned. Makes 20 sticks. *Quick and easy!*

Mrs. Joe Hensley (Joann)

Viennese Pancakes

3 eggs
1 cup small-curd cottage cheese
4 tablespoons butter, melted
3 tablespoons all-purpose flour
¼ teaspoon salt
1 teaspoon sugar

In a medium bowl beat eggs until foamy; stir in sieved or very small-curd cottage cheese and butter. Add flour, salt and sugar; mix well. Cook on hot buttered griddle. Serve with syrup or fresh fruit. Serves 4.

Note: Very good with a sauce made with 2 cups applesauce heated to boiling with ¼ teaspoon each of cinnamon and nutmeg and 2 tablespoons brown sugar.

This is a high-nutrition, low-fat pancake. Whole wheat flour may be used which will change taste. The batter will keep in a refrigerator for a few days.

Donna M. Moore

German Apple Pancakes

1 cup all-purpose flour
1 egg
1 cup milk
1 teaspoon baking powder
1/4 cup sugar
2 or 3 apples, peeled and sliced
Shortening for frying

In medium bowl mix together all ingredients. Fry in vegetable shortening until done. Drain on paper towel; dust with powdered sugar. Serves 4.

Mrs. Anthony S. Brancato (Georgine E. Palmer)

Jo's Waffles

3 cups sifted all-purpose flour
3 1/2 teaspoons baking powder
3/4 teaspoon salt
1 cup margarine
3 egg yolks, well beaten
2 cups milk
3 egg whites, stiffly beaten
2 teaspoons sugar (optional)

In a large bowl sift flour with baking powder and salt. Cut in margarine until mixture is as fine as cornmeal. Combine beaten egg yolks and milk; add to flour mixture and mix until smooth. Fold in beaten egg whites. Bake in hot waffle iron. Add more milk for crisper waffle. Same recipe can be used for pancakes or corn fritters. Serves 6.

Jo Brooks
Dunedin, Florida

Churros

Spanish Crullers

Vegetable oil
1 cup water
1/2 cup butter or margarine
1/4 teaspoon salt
1 cup all-purpose flour
3 eggs
1/4 cup sugar
1/2 teaspoon cinnamon

In a large skillet heat oil to 360 degrees (1- to 1 1/2-inches deep). In a 3-quart saucepan heat water, butter and salt to a rolling boil; add flour and stir vigorously over low heat until mixture forms a ball. Remove from heat. Beat in eggs all at one time; continue beating until smooth. Spoon mixture into decorator's tube with large star tip. Squeeze 4-inch strips into hot oil. Fry until golden brown, turning once (about 2 minutes on each side). Drain on paper towels; roll in sugar and cinnamon which has been mixed together. Makes 15.

Carol Dawson Clarke
Columbus, Mississippi

Giant Popovers with Rhubarb-Strawberry Conserve

3 eggs
1 cup milk
3 tablespoons butter or margarine, melted
1 cup all-purpose flour
½ teaspoon salt

Place eight well-greased 6-ounce custard cups on a jelly roll pan or large cookie sheet. In medium bowl with mixer at low speed, beat eggs until frothy; beat in milk and margarine or butter until blended. Gradually beat in flour and salt. Pour about ⅓ cup batter into each cup. Bake 50 minutes at 375 degrees; then quickly cut small slit in top of each popover to let out steam; bake 10 minutes longer. Immediately remove popovers from cups. Serve piping hot. Serves 8.

Rhubarb-Strawberry Conserve:

4 cups rhubarb, sliced
1 cup sugar
1 cup water
2 cups strawberries, hulled
1 (¼-ounce) envelope gelatin
Few drops red food coloring

In a saucepan simmer rhubarb, sugar and water until rhubarb is almost soft. Add strawberries and gelatin; cook until conserve thickens. Then add red food coloring. May be frozen.

Mrs. Anthony S. Brancato (Georgine E. Palmer)

Scotch Scones

Modern Method

4 cups all-purpose flour
6 teaspoons baking powder
1 teaspoon baking soda
¾ teaspoon salt
¼ cup margarine
1 egg
1½ cups buttermilk

In a large bowl mix dry ingredients together; cut in margarine. Beat egg and add enough buttermilk to make 1½ cups; stir into dry ingredients with a fork until blended. Divide dough into 4 parts. On a floured board roll each part into a circle; cut into 4 triangles. Bake on an ungreased griddle or non-stick skillet using medium heat until light brown; turn and brown other side. Makes 16.

Effie Lange
Dunedin, Florida

Danish Puff

1 cup sifted all-purpose flour
½ cup butter, softened
2 tablespoons water
1 cup water
½ cup butter
2 teaspoons almond extract
1 cup all-purpose flour
3 eggs
Powdered sugar frosting
Coconut and nuts

Measure first cup of flour into a small bowl; cut in ½ cup butter. Sprinkle with 2 tablespoons water and mix with fork or hands. Form mixture into a ball and divide in half. Pat each half into a 12x3-inch strip. Place 3 inches apart on an ungreased baking sheet. Mix 1 cup water and ½ cup butter in a saucepan; bring to a rolling boil. Add almond extract and remove from heat. Stir in 1 cup flour immediately to keep it from lumping. When smooth and thick add one egg at a time; beat until smooth. Divide in half; spread over each piece of pastry. Bake at 350 degrees for 1 hour until topping is crisp and nicely browned. Frost with powdered sugar frosting; top with coconut or nuts. Makes two 13x2-inch pastries.

Icing:

½ cup powdered sugar
2 teaspoons hot milk
¼ teaspoon vanilla extract

Mix all ingredients in a bowl. Pour on top of Danish Puff.

Variation: Instead of almond extract add ½ to ¾ cup shredded Cheddar cheese after adding eggs. Bake as above; delete frosting and garnish.

Amy Marie Guilfoile, Dunedin, Florida
Mrs. Lynn Lees

Scotch Scones

Original Method

4⅔ cups all-purpose flour
1 teaspoon salt
1 teaspoon baking soda
1 teaspoon cream of tartar
2 cups buttermilk

In a large bowl sift 4 cups flour with dry ingredients; add buttermilk and blend until moistened. Use the remaining flour as needed to make dough easy to handle. Cut dough into 4 parts and roll each into a circle; cut circles into 4 triangles each. Bake on dry griddle, using medium heat, until light brown; turn and brown on other side. Makes 16.

Effie Lange
Dunedin, Florida

Pumpkin Bread

3 cups sugar
1 cup corn oil
4 eggs
1 (16-ounce) can pumpkin
3½ cups all-purpose flour
1 teaspoon baking powder
2 teaspoons salt
1 teaspoon cinnamon
2 teaspoons baking soda
½ teaspoon ground cloves
1 teaspoon nutmeg
1 teaspoon allspice
⅔ cup water

In a bowl combine sugar, oil and eggs. Add pumpkin; sift together dry ingredients; add to pumpkin mixture. Add water and mix well. Pour into three greased 1-pound coffee cans or two 8x4x3-inch well-greased loaf pans. Bake at 350 degrees for 1 hour.

Mrs. Jimmie Bryan (Donna)
Mrs. Edwin Everett (Barbara)

Squash Bread

2 cups sugar
4 eggs, beaten
1 cup vegetable oil
1½ teaspoons salt
1 teaspoon baking powder
1 teaspoon baking soda
1 teaspoon cinnamon
1 teaspoon nutmeg
2 cups grated summer squash (about ¾ pounds)
3½ cups all-purpose flour
½ cup chopped pecans

In a large mixing bowl mix sugar, eggs, oil, salt, baking powder, baking soda, cinnamon and nutmeg. Add squash and mix well. Stir in the flour and pecans until well blended. Pour batter into well greased 8x4x3-inch or 9x5x3-inch loaf pans. Bake at 350 degrees for 45 to 55 minutes or until toothpick inserted in center comes out clean. Remove bread from pans. Cool on rack. Makes 2 loaves.

Mrs. S. E. "Pete" Covey (Carol Daugherty)

Pepperoni Bread

1 pound bread dough

Filling:

1 4- to 6-ounce pepperoni stick, thinly sliced
2 cups shredded mozzarella cheese
2 eggs (reserve 1 egg white)
¼ cup grated Romano cheese

Let dough rise until doubled. Punch down and roll out dough; cut into 4 squares. In a medium bowl mix all ingredients for filling. Divide the mixture and place on each square. Roll up into a log. Beat reserved egg white and brush on breads. Let rise again. Bake at 350 degrees for 30 minutes. Cut diagonally and serve hot. Serves 4 to 6.

Mrs. Charles Nikitas (Theresa)
Williamstown, Massachusetts

Sausage Bread

1 (16-ounce) loaf frozen bread
1 pound mild or hot pork sausage (bulk)
1 (12-ounce) jar fried peppers and onions
1 egg, beaten
¼ cup grated Parmesan cheese

Thaw dough. Let rise about 4 hours. In a skillet brown sausage; drain; add peppers and onions to sausage; sauté 5 minutes. Roll dough on lightly floured board to fit in a 15x10x1-inch jelly roll pan. Brush dough with beaten egg. Sprinkle with grated cheese, then with meat mixture. Roll lengthwise; seam sides down and place in pan. Brush with remaining egg. Bake at 350 degrees for 20 minutes. Makes 15 slices.

Mrs. Dorman Duncan (Billi)

Best-Ever Pizza

Dough:

1/2 teaspoon active dry yeast
3/4 cup plus 2 tablespoons warm water (110 to 115 degrees)
3 to 3 1/4 cups all-purpose flour, sifted

Dissolve yeast in warm water. Blend in flour to make a stiff dough. Knead on lightly floured surface. (A mixer with kneader bar works great!) Place in a greased bowl; turn to grease top. Cover; let rise in a warm place (about 85 degrees) until doubled about 1 1/2 to 2 hours. Divide into two parts; roll each part into a circle or rectangle about 1/8-inch thick. Place on pizza pan or oblong pan with shallow sides.

Sauce:

1 (15-ounce) can tomato sauce or 2 (8-ounce) cans
1 teaspoon oregano
1 teaspoon garlic salt
1 tablespoon parsley flakes
3/4 teaspoon crushed red pepper
2 tablespoons grated Parmesan cheese
1 teaspoon anise seed

Simmer tomato sauce with next 6 ingredients for about 30 minutes. Spread over dough.

Topping:

1/2 pound mozzarella cheese, shredded
1/2 pound provolone cheese, shredded
2 links Italian sausage, crumbled
1/2 stick pepperoni, sliced
1 small onion, chopped
Olives, peppers, sliced mushrooms or whatever you desire

Bake at 500 degrees for 10 minutes or until bubbly. Makes 2 medium.

Mrs. J. J. Suddath, Jr. (Eleanor Picken)

Cheese, Eggs and Pasta

Breakfast Casserole

4 or 5 slices sour dough bread, trimmed
2 cups shredded American or Cheddar cheese
1 pound link sausage
4 large eggs
3/4 teaspoon dry mustard
2 1/4 cups milk
1 (10 3/4-ounce) can cream of mushroom soup, diluted with 1/2 can milk
1/4 cup shredded American or Cheddar cheese

Place bread in buttered 13x9x2-inch pan. Sprinkle with cheese. Brown sausage; drain. Cut sausage into small pieces; place on top of cheese. Beat together eggs, dry mustard and milk. Pour over other ingredients; refrigerate overnight. Before baking, pour diluted mushroom soup overall. Sprinkle 1/4 cup cheese on top. Bake at 300 degrees for 1 hour. Serves 8.

Alice Forrester
Madre, California

Eggs Benedict

Brunch Style

3 tablespoons butter
3 tablespoons all-purpose flour
1 1/2 cups milk
1/2 pound pasteurized process cheese spread
1/8 teaspoon pepper
3/4 teaspoon salt
1 teaspoon dry mustard
1/2 teaspoon Worcestershire sauce (optional)
6 eggs
3 English muffins, halved
6 slices of Canadian bacon, or 12 slices bacon, cooked

In a medium saucepan mix the first 8 ingredients; cook until thickened. Pour 1/2 of the mixture into a 12x8x2-inch baking dish; break eggs one at a time over the mixture; carefully pour remainder of sauce over eggs. Bake at 325 degrees for 40 minutes or until eggs are set. Toast muffin halves. Place a slice of bacon over each muffin half; top with 1 egg and sauce. Serves 6.

Note: This is great for company brunch!

Mrs. Kenneth Thomson (Elsie)
Leawood, Kansas

Cheese Strata

14 slices day-old bread, crusts removed
1 pound hot sausage or ham, cooked, drained and crumbled
3/4 pound shredded sharp Cheddar cheese
6 eggs
4 cups milk
1 teaspoon salt
1 teaspoon dry mustard
1/2 teaspoon paprika

Heavily butter a 13x9x2-inch baking dish. Cut bread into 1/2-inch cubes and place a layer in bottom of dish. Add a layer of sausage, then cheese. Repeat. In a bowl beat eggs, milk, salt, mustard and paprika; pour over ingredients in baking dish. Refrigerate for 24 hours. Remove and let stand 4 hours. Bake at 350 degrees for 1 hour. Serves 15 to 20.

Mrs. Jack Clapp (Anne Kathleen)
Clearwater, Florida

Classic Cheese Pie

1 unbaked 9-inch pie shell
1 1/2 cups (6-ounces) shredded Swiss cheese
4 scallions, chopped
4 slices boiled ham, cut into small pieces
3 eggs, beaten
1 cup whipping cream
1/2 cup milk
1/2 teaspoon salt
1/4 teaspoon pepper
1/2 teaspoon dry mustard
1/8 teaspoon cayenne pepper

Mix Swiss cheese, scallions and ham; put in bottom of pie shell. Mix eggs, whipping cream, milk, salt, pepper, dry mustard and cayenne pepper; pour into pie shell. Bake at 375 degrees for 45 minutes, until firm and golden brown on top. Serve warm or cold. Serves 6.

Janet Joyce

Spinach Quiche

1 (10-ounce) package frozen chopped spinach
2 tablespoons butter or margarine
1 small onion, chopped
1 (4-ounce) can chopped mushrooms, drained
2 cups shredded Swiss cheese
2 tablespoons all-purpose flour
3 eggs, beaten
1 cup milk
½ teaspoon salt
⅛ teaspoon pepper
⅛ teaspoon nutmeg
1 (9-inch) deep-dish pie shell (1½ inches deep), unbaked

Cook spinach according to package directions; drain. Sauté onion and mushrooms in butter. Toss cheese with flour. Combine eggs, milk and seasonings. Add cheese mixture, spinach, onion and mushroom mixture; mix well; pour into pie shell. Bake at 350 degrees for 50 to 60 minutes. Serves 6.

Mrs. S. E. "Pete" Covey (Carol Daugherty)

Easy Quiche Lorraine

12 slices bacon, fried crisp and crumbled
1 cup shredded natural Swiss cheese
⅓ cup minced onion
1 (9-inch) pie shell
4 eggs
2 cups whipping cream
¼ teaspoon salt
¼ teaspoon sugar
⅛ teaspoon cayenne red pepper

Preheat oven to 425 degrees. Sprinkle bacon, cheese and onion in the pie shell. Beat eggs and then beat in remaining ingredients. Pour mixture into pie shell. Bake 15 minutes at 425 degrees. Reduce temperature to 300 degrees; bake 30 minutes longer or until knife inserted 1 inch from edge comes out clean. Let stand 10 minutes before cutting. Serves 6 to 8.

Mrs. James Berfield (Sue Mautz)

Crab Quiche

1 (9-inch) pie shell, unbaked
1 cup shredded Swiss cheese
1 (6½-ounce) can crabmeat, drained, flaked and cartilage removed
2 scallions, sliced
3 eggs, beaten
1 cup light cream
½ teaspoon salt
½ teaspoon grated lemon peel
¼ teaspoon dry mustard
⅛ teaspoon mace
¼ cup sliced almonds

Sprinkle cheese evenly over bottom of unbaked pie shell; top with crabmeat and scallions. Combine eggs, cream, salt, lemon peel, dry mustard and mace; pour over crabmeat; top with almonds. Bake at 375 degrees for 45 minutes. Remove from oven and let stand 10 minutes before serving. Serves 6.

Mrs. David Foster (Elaine)
Dunedin, Florida

Zucchini Quiche

2 (9-inch) pie shells, unbaked
2 small unpeeled zucchini, grated
1 teaspoon salt
2 teaspoons butter
½ cup whole scallions, sliced
3 eggs, beaten
1 cup whipping cream
½ cup shredded Gruyère cheese
¼ to ½ teaspoon dill weed
2 tablespoons chopped fresh parsley
⅛ teaspoon pepper

Bake pie shells for 5 minutes at 450 degrees. Sprinkle zucchini with salt; place in a fine strainer to drain. In a small skillet melt butter and sauté scallions until tender. Spread scallions over pie shells. Mix eggs and cream. Press water out of zucchini; add to egg mixture along with cheese, dill weed, parsley and pepper. Pour the mixture into pie shells. Place the quiches on a cookie sheet; bake at 375 degrees for about 30 minutes. Makes 2 pies.

Mrs. Dean N. McFarland (Donna VanEwyk)

Quiche Unique

3/4 cup shredded Swiss cheese
3/4 cup shredded mozzarella cheese
1/2 cup chopped pepperoni
1 tablespoon chopped green onion
1 (9-inch) pie shell, unbaked
3 eggs, beaten
1 cup half and half
1/2 teaspoon salt
1/4 teaspoon oregano
Few sprigs of parsley

Combine cheese, pepperoni and onion. Sprinkle in pie shell. Combine eggs, half and half, salt and oregano. Mix well; pour into pie shell. Bake at 325 degrees for 45 minutes. Allow to stand at least 10 minutes before cutting. Garnish with parsley. Serves 6 to 8.

Mrs. Robert Hall (Barbara)

Chili Egg Puff

10 eggs
1/2 cup all-purpose flour
1 teaspoon baking powder
1/2 teaspoon salt
1 (16-ounce) carton small curd cream-style cottage cheese
1 pound Monterey Jack cheese, shredded
1/2 cup butter, melted
2 (4-ounce) cans green chilies, chopped

In bowl of electric mixer beat eggs until light; add flour, baking powder, salt and cottage cheese; mix well. Add remaining ingredients. Pour mixture into a buttered 13x9x2-inch baking pan. Bake at 350 degrees for 35 minutes. Serves 10.

Regina Howard
Amherst, New Hampshire

Fluffy Eggs with Shrimp

1 pound medium shrimp, shelled, deveined and cut into 4 equal pieces
6 tablespoons peanut oil
10 eggs, lightly beaten
7 green onions, chopped (about 3/4 cup)
2 teaspoons salt

In a heavy skillet or wok heat 2 tablespoons of oil; add shrimp; stir fry 10 seconds or until shrimp begins to turn pink. Remove; drain off any liquid. In a large bowl mix eggs, green onions and salt until well blended. Heat remaining oil. When hot, add egg mixture; stir gently, letting the uncooked egg work its way to the bottom of the pan. Add shrimp; mix thoroughly. Continue to cook until eggs are set. Serves 6.

Mrs. Bill Ritchey (Carol Eddington)

Tiropita

Greek Cheese Pie

10 sheets fillo dough
1/2 cup butter, melted
2 (16-ounce) cartons small curd cottage cheese, or ricotta cheese, drained
1 (8-ounce) package cream cheese, softened
4 eggs, beaten
1/4 pound feta cheese, crumbled

Thaw fillo according to package directions. Layer a 15x11x1-inch pan, or equivalent, with 5 sheets fillo. Butter between each sheet. Mix remaining ingredients; pour mixture on fillo. Top with remaining 5 sheets of fillo, buttering between sheets and top layer. With a sharp knife, score top layer only into a 3-inch square. Bake at 350 degrees for 30 minutes. Cut into squares; serve at once. Serves 15.

Mrs. Chris Demas (Jeannie)

Spanakopeta

Greek Spinach Pie

10 sheets fillo
1/2 cup butter, melted
3 (10-ounce) packages frozen chopped spinach, thawed and drained
1 onion, chopped
4 eggs, beaten
1 (16-ounce) carton cottage cheese, drained
1/4 pound feta cheese, finely crumbled

In a 15x11x2-inch baking pan layer 5 sheets of fillo, brushing with butter between each sheet. In a mixing bowl combine remaining ingredients. Pour over fillo. Top with remaining 5 fillo sheets, buttering between each sheet. With a sharp knife score top layer only into 3-inch squares. Pour remaining butter over fillo. Bake at 350 degrees for 45 minutes. Cut squares through and serve hot. Serves 10 to 12.

Mrs. Chris Demas (Jeannie)

Crêpes

1 cup cold water
1 cup cold milk
4 eggs
½ teaspoon salt
2 cups all-purpose flour
4 tablespoons melted butter

Whirl ingredients in electric blender in order given for 2 minutes, or until well blended. Chill for 2 hours. Pour chilled crêpe batter into a wide-mouth plastic pitcher. Heat non-stick crêpe skillet on high until water sizzles and evaporates. Remove skillet from heat; pour batter to barely cover bottom of pan. Place skillet back on burner for 1 minute or until bubbles form in batter and edges of crêpe come away from the pan. Flip crêpe to other side in the skillet for 30 seconds; slide onto waxed paper. This process makes a perfect thin crêpe that is almost transparent. Makes 24.

Mrs. Lawrence J. Tierney (Sue)

Pasta Primavera

2 cups fresh broccoli flowerets
2 cups unpeeled, cubed zucchini
2 cups fresh cut green beans
⅓ cup imported olive oil
2 cloves garlic, crushed
¼ to ½ cup minced shallots
3 tablespoons chopped fresh parsley
2 tablespoons chopped fresh basil or ¾ teaspoon dried basil
1 pound mostaccioli or ziti cooked al denté according to package directions
¼ cup freshly grated Romano cheese
¼ cup freshly grated Parmesan cheese
¼ cup freshly grated Locatelli cheese
Freshly ground pepper to taste
Cherry tomatoes, for garnish (optional)

Steam vegetables 5 to 6 minutes, should remain crunchy. Sauté garlic and shallots in olive oil until transparent. Add parsley, basil and vegetables; mix with pasta; blend in cheeses. Serve immediately. Serves 6 to 8.

Suncoast Seasons Committee

Manicotti

Manicotti:

4 eggs
1 cup all-purpose flour
1 cup water
1/8 teaspoon salt
1/8 teaspoon pepper

In a medium bowl combine all ingredients; beat well with wire whisk. Fry in crêpe pan or small frying pan (non-stick preferred). Place on waxed paper when done.

Filling:

1 1/2 pounds ricotta cheese
1/2 pound mozzarella cheese, shredded
1/2 cup grated Parmesan cheese
2 eggs
1/8 teaspoon salt
1/8 teaspoon pepper
1 tablespoon chopped parsley

In a medium bowl combine all ingredients; mix well. Put 2 heaping tablespoons of filling in each manicotti and roll. Use a 13x9x2-inch baking dish and your favorite tomato sauce recipe. Bake at 350 degrees for ½ hour or until bubbly. Makes 12 to 15 manicotti.

Mrs. Vito Brancato (Nicolina)
Garfield, New Jersey

Spaghetti with Shredded Zucchini

Ginny's Special Spaghetti

1 (8-ounce) package spaghetti
2 tablespoons butter or margarine
2 medium zucchini (about 1 pound), shredded
1 (8-ounce) package mozzarella cheese, shredded
1/2 cup half and half or milk
1/2 teaspoon salt
1/8 teaspoon basil

About 30 minutes before serving, prepare spaghetti in saucepan according to package directions. In a 10-inch skillet over medium heat, melt butter; cook zucchini until tender, about 5 minutes. When spaghetti is done, drain. Return spaghetti to saucepan; add zucchini and remaining ingredients. Over low heat, toss spaghetti mixture until cheese is melted. Serve immediately. Serves 4.

Mrs. Robert Haverkos (Ginny)

Cappelletti

Excellent! Well worth time!

Dough:
Makes 1 pound

2 cups unsifted all-purpose flour
2 eggs
1 tablespoon oil
1 teaspoon salt
Few drops of water

Filling:

½ pound chopped ham or 2 chicken breasts, boned, skinned and cooked for 15 minutes
½ cup freshly grated imported Parmesan cheese
2 eggs, beaten
⅛ teaspoon nutmeg
1 teaspoon salt
⅛ teaspoon pepper

Mix ingredients for dough and keep in bowl covered with damp cloth. Mix ham or chicken, cheese, eggs and nutmeg in medium bowl, until thoroughly combined. Season with salt and pepper. Break off ¼ of the pasta dough; keep rest moist in bowl. Roll out the dough on a floured board until it is paper thin; cut into 2-inch rounds with a biscuit cutter. Place ¼ teaspoon of ham mixture in the center of each round; moisten the edges of each round. Fold the circles in half; press the edges firmly together. Shape into little rings by stretching the tips of each half circle slightly and wrapping the ring around your index finger. Gently press the tips together. Bring water and salt to a boil in a heavy saucepan. Drop in the cappelletti; stir gently with a wooden spoon for a moment to make sure they do not stick to one another. Boil, stirring occasionally, for about 8 minutes. Drain cappelletti into a large sieve or colander. Serve with tomato sauce, butter and grated Parmesan cheese, or in hot beef or chicken stock. Serves 6 to 8.

Note: The cappelletti are best if they are cooked at once, but they may be covered with plastic wrap and refrigerated for a day or so.

Mrs. Giordano Tiezzi (Ida)
Meriden, Connecticut

These tiny pasta are made in the shape of a Cardinal's cap, thus the name cappelletti.

Mostaccioli

Kids will love this!

1/2 cup chopped onion
1/2 cup chopped green pepper
2 tablespoons oil
1/2 pound ground chuck
1 (16-ounce) can tomatoes
1 (6-ounce) can tomato paste
1/2 cup water
1/2 teaspoon salt
1/4 teaspoon pepper
1 bay leaf
1/2 pound package mostaccioli type pasta
1/2 pound pasteurized process cheese, thinly sliced
1/4 cup grated Parmesan cheese, or to taste

In a large skillet sauté onion and green pepper in oil until tender. Add ground chuck; cook until brown; drain. Stir in tomatoes, tomato paste, water, salt, pepper and bay leaf. Simmer 5 minutes. Cook pasta according to directions on package. In a 2-quart casserole arrange alternate layers of pasta, meat and pasteurized process cheese. Sprinkle with Parmesan cheese. Bake at 350 degrees for 30 minutes. Serves 6 to 8.

Mrs. Robert Hall (Barbara)

Gnocchi

Italian Dumplings

9 baking potatoes, boiled, peeled, mashed and cooled
1/2 teaspoon nutmeg
1 egg, beaten
3 cups all-purpose flour

In a large bowl beat potatoes, nutmeg and egg until smooth; mix in flour to dry dough consistency. Roll into sticks 1/2-inch thick; cut sticks into 1-inch lengths. Boil 6 cups of salted water; drop in pieces of dough. Cook 3 to 5 minutes or until gnocchi float on top. Serves 10 to 12.

Note: Serve with Italian tomato sauce or melted butter and Parmesan cheese.

Mrs. Douglas Guilfoile (Paula L. Tiezzi)

Sailors' Linguini

- 6 slices bacon, cut into ½-inch strips
- ¼ cup sliced green onions
- 2 cloves garlic, minced
- 6 tablespoons butter or margarine
- 2 (7½-ounce) cans minced clams, drained
- ½ cup sliced ripe olives
- ¼ cup snipped fresh parsley
- ⅛ teaspoon pepper
- 12 ounces linguini
- ½ cup grated Parmesan cheese
- Lemon wedges

In a skillet cook bacon until crisp, reserving ¼ cup of the drippings. Remove bacon; set aside. Cook onions and garlic in drippings until tender but not brown. Stir in butter or margarine until melted. Add bacon and remaining ingredients, except cheese and lemon wedges. Heat sauce thoroughly. Cook linguini according to directions on package. Toss sauce with pasta; garnish with Parmesan cheese and lemon wedges. Serves 4.

Mrs. Robert Hall (Barbara)

Busy Day Lasagne

- 1 pound ground beef
- 4 to 5 cups spaghetti sauce
- ½ package (8-ounces) lasagne noodles
- 1 pound cottage cheese, drained, or ricotta cheese
- 8 ounces mozzarella cheese, shredded
- 1 cup grated Parmesan cheese

In a large skillet brown ground beef and drain; add spaghetti sauce. In a 13x9x2-inch baking dish spread about 1 cup of above mixture in bottom of pan. Arrange a layer of uncooked lasagne; top with sauce, cottage or ricotta cheese, mozzarella and Parmesan cheeses and sauce. Repeat, gently pressing lasagne into cheese mixture ending with a final layer of lasagne. Pour remaining sauce over, making sure the lasagne are covered with sauce; top with remaining mozzarella and Parmesan cheese. Bake at 350 degrees for 45 to 55 minutes. Allow to stand 15 minutes. Cut in squares to serve. Serves 6 to 8.

Mrs. William R. Barnes (Vickie)

Jo Jo's Quick Lasagne

1 pound lean ground beef
10 green onions, chopped or 1 large onion, chopped
2 (8-ounce) cans tomato sauce
1/4 teaspoon oregano
1/4 teaspoon basil
1/8 teaspoon pepper
1 clove garlic, minced
1 1/2 teaspoons salt
1 (8-ounce) package wide noodles, cooked and drained
1 cup cottage cheese
1 cup sour cream
1/3 cup shredded Cheddar cheese

In a large skillet brown beef; drain fat. Add onions; cook lightly. Add tomato sauce, oregano, basil, pepper, garlic and salt; simmer 10 minutes. Combine noodles, cottage cheese, sour cream and Cheddar cheese in large bowl. In a 3-quart baking dish alternate layers of noodle mixture and meat sauce, starting with noodles and ending with meat sauce. Bake at 350 degrees for 25 to 30 minutes. Serves 6 to 8.

Nan J. Moffatt

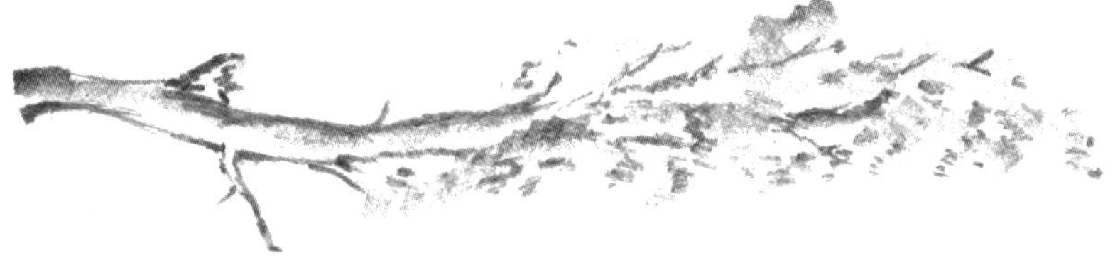

Celia's Spaghetti Alla Carbonara

4 slices prosciutto, cut into small pieces
3 tablespoons olive oil
1/2 teaspoon freshly ground pepper
1 (16-ounce) package spaghetti
6 teaspoons salt
3 large eggs
1/2 cup grated Parmesan cheese

In small skillet sauté prosciutto in oil; add pepper. Cook spaghetti in salted water until firm but tender; drain, reserving some liquid. Beat eggs in a large serving bowl until foamy. Pour drained spaghetti on beaten eggs; toss until the heat of the spaghetti has cooked eggs and spaghetti is coated. Be sure spaghetti is very hot or eggs will not be cooked. If dish is too dry, add some of the reserved pasta water. Add prosciutto and oil; mix and season with additional pepper to taste. Add Parmesan cheese and toss. Serves 5.

Mrs. Paul Palazzola (Celia), Dunedin, Florida
Donna M. Moore

Fettucine Plus

½ pound fresh mushrooms, thinly sliced
¾ cup butter, divided
1¼ pounds zucchini, cut into julienne strips
¾ cup whipping cream
1 (12-ounce) package fettucine
¾ cup freshly grated Parmesan cheese
½ cup chopped fresh parsley
1 teaspoon salt
1 teaspoon freshly ground pepper

In a large skillet sauté mushrooms in ¼ cup butter for 2 minutes. Add zucchini, cream and remaining butter. Bring to a boil; simmer for 3 minutes. Cook fettucine; drain; add to the skillet. Add Parmesan cheese and parsley. Toss with wooden spoon. Add salt and freshly ground pepper. Serves 6.

Mrs. Anthony S. Brancato (Georgine E. Palmer)

Cheese Kugel Noodles

2 cups broad noodles
1 (8-ounce) carton sour cream
1 (8-ounce) carton cottage cheese
1 cup milk
½ teaspoon salt
⅛ teaspoon cinnamon
½ cup raisins
3 eggs, beaten
2 tablespoons butter, melted
1 teaspoon sugar

Prepare noodles according to package directions; drain. Combine noodles with remaining ingredients. Pour into a buttered 9-inch square baking dish. Bake at 400 degrees for 45 minutes or until a brown crust forms on top. Serves 8.

Mrs. Douglas Guilfoile (Paula L. Tiezzi)

Oriental Noodle Casserole

1 (8-ounce) package fine noodles
1 cup margarine
2 cups instant rice
2 (10¾-ounce) cans onion soup
2 (10¾-ounce) cans chicken broth
1 teaspoon soy sauce
1 cup water
1 (8-ounce) can water chestnuts, drained and sliced

In a medium or large skillet brown noodles in margarine. Mix in all other ingredients. Remove from skillet; place in a 2-quart casserole. Cover; cook for 45 minutes at 350 degrees. Serves 8.

Sarah Noparstak
Chicago, Illinois

Meats,
Poultry and
Game

Beef Mandarin

3 tablespoons vegetable oil
1 (10-ounce) package frozen pea pods
1 pound sirloin steak, cut into 3-inch strips
1½ teaspoons onion powder
1 teaspoon monosodium glutamate
½ teaspoon salt
¼ teaspoon garlic powder
1 (1-ounce) package brown gravy mix
1 cup water
2 tablespoons brown sugar
2 tablespoons soy sauce
1 (4½-ounce) jar sliced mushrooms, drained

Heat oil in heavy skillet; sauté pea pods for two minutes and remove. Put steak and seasonings in skillet and cook, stirring constantly, just until redness disappears. Sprinkle gravy mix over meat; stir in water, brown sugar and soy sauce; continue cooking until thickened. Add mushrooms and pea pods. Cook until heated. Serve over hot rice. Serves 4 to 5.

Mrs. Stan Dawson, Jr. (Kathy)
Oak Lawn, Illinois

Beef Wellington

2 to 2½ pounds center cut of beef tenderloin or equivalent cut of tender beef
½ teaspoon salt
¼ teaspoon pepper
1 (8-ounce) sheet of ready-to-use frozen puff pastry or 1 (10-ounce) package frozen patty shells, thawed
1 (4½-ounce) can of pâté (optional)
2 ounces sliced fresh mushrooms or duxelles (optional)
1 egg, beaten

Season beef with salt and pepper and sear on all sides in a very hot skillet; remove and allow to cool. Thaw pastry according to package directions and roll out on a floured surface until roughly 3 times the size of the beef. Spread pâté over top and sides of beef; then cover with sliced mushrooms or duxelles. Place beef, pâté-side down in center of pastry. Fold dough around meat, encasing meat without overlapping; trim off excess pastry. Pinch seams together firmly to seal and brush with beaten egg. Place seam-side down in a 13x9x2-inch baking dish. Decorate with dough trimmings shaped into leaves, braids and so forth to enhance appearance. Bake 40 minutes at 400 degrees for medium beef. Allow to cool 10 minutes before carving. Serves 6.

Mrs. Gregory H. Keuroghlian (Nora Ghazikian)

Crock Beef Burgundy

3 pounds top round steak, cut into cubes
2 (1.37-ounce) envelopes onion soup mix
1 (4-ounce) can sliced mushrooms, drained
2 (10¾-ounce) cans golden mushroom soup
1⅓ cups Burgundy wine

Combine ingredients in a crockpot. Cook on low for 8 to 9 hours or until done. Thicken if necessary. Serves 8.

Mrs. Robert Hartford (Linda)

Flemish Carbonnades

1½ pounds round steak, cut ¾-inch thick
½ cup all-purpose flour
½ teaspoon salt
⅛ teaspoon pepper
2 tablespoons shortening
¾ cup beer
1 (10¾-ounce) can onion soup
2 teaspoons sugar

Mix flour, salt and pepper and pound into round steak. Cut steak into serving-size pieces. In a skillet brown floured steak pieces in shortening. Drain off fat. Add beer; stirring to loosen bits in bottom of pan. Add soup and sugar. Cover and simmer for one hour. Serves 4.

Note: If desired, gravy may be thickened with 2 teaspoons cornstarch.

Mrs. Mike Dawson (Mary)
Chicago, Illinois

Flank Steak Teriyaki

Marinade:

¾ cup vegetable oil
⅓ cup soy sauce
2 tablespoons dried onion
1 clove garlic, mashed
¼ cup honey
2 tablespoons vinegar
1 teaspoon ginger
1 to 1½ pounds flank steak

In a small bowl mix marinade ingredients well. Place meat in a 12x8x2-inch glass baking pan. Pour marinade over meat. Marinate for 6 hours turning occasionally. Broil for 5 minutes on the first side and 4 minutes on the second side. Allow to stand 2 minutes before carving. Slice very thin diagonally. Serves 4.

Marilyn McDonald

Marinated Chuck Roast

Best marinade you'll ever taste!

3 pounds chuck roast
1 teaspoon monosodium glutamate
1/3 cup wine vinegar
1/4 cup ketchup
2 tablespoons cooking oil
2 tablespoons soy sauce
1 tablespoon Worcestershire sauce
1 teaspoon mustard
1 teaspoon salt
1/4 teaspoon pepper
1/4 teaspoon garlic powder

Sprinkle both sides of roast with monosodium glutamate. Place in shallow baking dish. Combine remaining ingredients; pour over meat. Marinate for 3 hours turning once or twice. Remove from marinade; place on broiler pan. Broil about 6 inches from heat turning roast and basting it with the marinade every 10 to 15 minutes. Broil until desired doneness, approximately 35 to 45 minutes for medium rare. Serves 6 to 8.

Note: The marinade may be used with other meats grilled outside.

Mrs. Jack Wilson (Mary Jane Brown)

Round Steak Dinner

2 pounds beef round steak cut 1/2- to 3/4-inch thick
3 tablespoons all-purpose flour
1 teaspoon salt
1/8 teaspoon pepper
1/4 cup shortening
1 beef bouillon cube
1 cup boiling water
1 (10 3/4-ounce) can tomato soup
1 bay leaf
3 large potatoes, pared and quartered
2 medium onions, sliced
2 (16-ounce) cans French-style green beans, drained

Cut round steak into serving pieces. Combine flour, salt and pepper; pound into meat. In a large skillet, brown meat in hot shortening. Transfer to a 3-quart casserole. Dissolve beef bouillon cube in boiling water and combine with tomato soup. Pour over meat; add bay leaf; cover. Bake at 350 degrees for 45 minutes. Remove bay leaf. Arrange potatoes and onions around edge of casserole. Season with salt and pepper. Pour tomato sauce over vegetables; cover. Bake 45 minutes longer at 350 degrees. Add green beans in center; cover. Bake 15 minutes longer. Serves 6 to 8.

Mrs. Edwin Everett (Barbara)

Kitchen Hint: For very thin slices of beef, slightly freeze beef before cutting. Cut slices across grain.

Tomato Beef Stroganoff

1/2 teaspoon unseasoned meat tenderizer
1 1/2 pounds round steak
1/4 cup all-purpose flour
1/2 teaspoon salt
1/4 teaspoon pepper
4 tablespoons shortening or oil
1/2 cup chopped onions
1 (6-ounce) can mushrooms, undrained
1 cup sour cream
1 (10 3/4-ounce) can tomato soup
1 tablespoon Worcestershire sauce
1/4 teaspoon hot pepper sauce
1 (8-ounce) package egg noodles

Sprinkle meat tenderizer on one side of meat. Prick all over with fork. Turn meat over and repeat on other side. Let stand about 10 minutes. Cut meat into strips and dust lightly with flour, salt and pepper. In a large skillet brown meat in oil; add onion and mushrooms. Combine sour cream, soup and sauces. Pour over meat. Cover and cook over high heat until bubbling. Reduce heat to simmer; cook for 1 to 1½ hours. Cook noodles according to package directions. Serve over noodles. Serves 6.

Mrs. Edward McEvilly (Mary)
Algonquin, Illinois

Flank Steak Oriental

2 to 2 1/2 pounds flank steak
1 clove garlic, minced
1 tablespoon brown sugar
1 tablespoon sugar
1/2 teaspoon pepper
1/2 teaspoon ginger
1 tablespoon cooking oil
2 tablespoons water
1/4 cup soy sauce

In a small mixing bowl combine all ingredients except flank steak. Pour over flank steak and marinate in the refrigerator for 3 to 4 hours or overnight, turning occasionally. Remove steak from refrigerator; bring to room temperature. Broil 5 to 10 minutes on each side, according to thickness. Can be cooked on a barbecue grill over low coals for up to 5 minutes a side. Use leftover marinade to baste meat while cooking. Serves 4 to 5.

Mrs. Joseph L. Andreani (Sandra)
Oldsmar, Florida

Savory Swiss Steak

1½ to 2 pounds round steak, cut approximately 1½-inches thick
2 tablespoons all-purpose flour
2 tablespoons bacon drippings
3 large onions, chopped
½ green pepper, chopped
1 medium stalk of celery, chopped
¾ cup chili sauce
2 tablespoons Worcestershire sauce
½ teaspoon salt
¼ teaspoon pepper
¾ cup water

Dredge steak with flour. In a large skillet brown meat on both sides using drippings. Remove and place in a 2-quart casserole. Add onions, pepper and celery. Combine chili sauce, Worcestershire sauce, salt and pepper. Pour into casserole; cover tightly and bake at 350 degrees for 1½ hours. To serve, remove meat to a platter. Make a gravy by adding ¾ cup water to juice in casserole and heat to thicken. Good served with mashed potatoes. Serves 4.

Variation: Try a California roast as a change—also less expensive cut of beef.

Irva Schweighauser
Holiday, Florida

Sweet and Sour Beef

4 tablespoons rum
2 pounds boneless chuck, cut into chunks
4 tablespoons butter (divided in half)
8 medium carrots, cut into bite-size pieces
8 small white onions, peeled
2 tablespoons all-purpose flour
1½ teaspoons salt
1 (6-ounce) can mushrooms with liquid
1 tablespoon ketchup
1 crumbled bay leaf
1 tablespoon currant jelly
1 tablespoon wine vinegar
2 cups water

Sprinkle 2 tablespoons rum over meat. Let stand 1 hour. Brown meat in butter; then sprinkle with remainder of rum and cook two minutes. Place meat in a Dutch oven. Add carrots and onions. In a small skillet melt 2 tablespoons butter and add flour, blending well. Add salt, mushrooms with liquid, ketchup, bay leaf, jelly, wine vinegar and water. Pour sauce over meat and vegetables. Cover tightly. Bring to boil, then simmer gently for 45 minutes or until meat is tender. Serves 4 to 6.

Mrs. Michael Porter (Paula)

Round Steak Ranchero

1/2 cup oil
1/2 cup red wine vinegar
2 tablespoons bottled steak sauce
1/2 large onion, sliced
1 clove garlic, crushed
1/2 teaspoon thyme
1/4 teaspoon pepper
1/2 teaspoon salt
1 1/2 pounds round steak

For marinade combine all ingredients except steak. Marinate steak several hours or overnight in refrigerator. Broil steak until cooked, using marinade as a basting sauce. Serves 4.

Helen S. Glass

Beef Barbecue

1/3 cup brown sugar
1 medium onion, chopped
1/2 teaspoon hot pepper sauce
1/2 teaspoon garlic powder or 1 clove garlic, minced
1 (14-ounce) bottle ketchup
1 tablespoon celery salt (optional)
1 teaspoon Worcestershire sauce
1 teaspoon chili powder (optional)
1 cup water
3 to 4 pound chuck roast
Hamburger buns

In a medium bowl mix sauce ingredients and pour over meat. Bake at 250 degrees for 6 hours or until meat tests done with fork. Serve on hamburger buns. Serves 8 to 10.

Mrs. William Harris (Clara)
Dunedin, Florida

Poor Boy Sandwiches

5 pound chuck roast
5 medium onions, thinly sliced
1 tablespoon garlic salt
1 tablespoon celery salt
1 tablespoon Worcestershire sauce
1 teaspoon hot pepper sauce
1 teaspoon pepper
5 cups water
8 poor boy (submarine) rolls

Combine all ingredients in a Dutch oven. Cover and let simmer on stove for 4 to 5 hours; uncover and simmer 1 hour longer, or until meat is tender. Slice meat and serve on rolls. Serves 8.

Hint: Will serve 18 to 20 people, using hamburger rolls.

Mrs. Bill Ritchey (Carol Eddington)

Country Pot Roast

Microwave Oven/Clay Pot

2½- to 3-pound beef chuck roast
1 tablespoon chopped parsley
1 tablespoon Worcestershire sauce
½ teaspoon garlic salt
¼ teaspoon pepper
2 medium onions, quartered
2 stalks celery, cut into pieces
3 carrots, peeled and cut into pieces
6 to 8 small red potatoes

Thoroughly soak clay pot in water. Remove and place roast inside. Sprinkle with all the seasonings. Cover with water soaked lid. Microwave for 15 minutes on High. Turn roast over; add vegetables and re-cover. Microwave for 50 to 55 minutes on simmer or until meat and vegetables are tender. Let stand, covered, 30 minutes before serving. Serves 4.

Mrs. John W. Vassel, Jr. (Eleanor)

Country French Onion Beef Stew

2 pounds beef stew meat, cut into 1½-inch cubes
2 medium onions, peeled and cut into eighths
3 stalks celery, cut into large pieces
4 medium carrots, cut into large pieces
1 cup tomato juice
1 tablespoon sugar
1 tablespoon salt
¼ teaspoon pepper
½ teaspoon basil or 1 teaspoon pickling spice
⅓ cup quick-cooking tapioca
2 large potatoes, peeled and quartered

Place beef in a 2½-quart casserole; add onions, celery and carrots. In a small bowl combine tomato juice, sugar, salt, pepper, basil and tapioca; pour over meat and vegetables. Cover casserole; cook at 325 degrees for 2½ hours. Remove casserole from oven; add potatoes. Bake one hour longer, uncovered, stirring occasionally. Serves 4 to 6. *Works like magic—tapioca thickens stew and disappears!*

Mrs. Robert Hall (Barbara)
Michael Boucher, Riverside, California

Oven Stew

1 (10½-ounce) can cream of mushroom soup
1 (10½-ounce) can tomato soup
2 soup cans of water
½ cup burgundy cooking wine
1 (1.375-ounce) package dry onion soup mix
1 pound lean beef stew meat, frozen or thawed
6 potatoes, cut into large pieces
6 carrots, cut into large pieces
1 large onion, cut into eighths
1 pound fresh mushrooms

In a large bowl mix soups, water, wine and dry soup mix. In a 3-quart casserole place meat, soup mixture, potatoes, carrots, onions and mushrooms. Bake covered at 300 degrees for six hours. Serves 6.

Mrs. Robert Russ (Carol Hodapp)

Stefado

Greek Beef Stew

3 pounds beef chuck
3 pounds small white onions, or large onions, cut into wedges
1 tablespoon salt
½ teaspoon pepper
½ teaspoon paprika
2 tablespoons chopped parsley (optional)

Cut meat into 1-inch cubes. Place meat, onions, salt, pepper and paprika in large Dutch oven; (no water needed). Cook over medium heat for 20 minutes, stirring often. Simmer covered for 2 hours. Uncover and simmer until liquid cooks down to gravy, approximately 15 minutes. Serve over noodles or rice. Sprinkle with parsley before serving. Serves 6.

Mrs. Chris Demas (Jeannie)

Short Ribs à la Esther

8 lean short ribs of beef
½ cup chili sauce
3 tablespoons soy sauce
2 cloves garlic, chopped
2 tablespoons brown sugar
1 teaspoon salt
½ teaspoon freshly ground pepper

Place ribs in Dutch oven. Cover and bake at 350 degrees for 1½ hours. Drain fat from pan. Mix remaining ingredients; add to meat. Cover and continue baking for about 30 minutes, or until tender. Serves 4.

Mrs. Lawrence Feltman (Bertha)
Chicago, Illinois

Chili

- 2 medium onions, chopped
- 1 green pepper, coarsely diced
- 1 tablespoon salad oil
- 2 pounds ground chuck
- 1 (16-ounce) can stewed tomatoes
- 1 (15-ounce) can tomato sauce
- ½ cup ketchup
- 1 tablespoon chili powder
- 2 teaspoons salt
- ¼ teaspoon pepper
- 2 (16-ounce) cans red kidney beans, partly drained

In a large kettle or Dutch oven, sauté onions and green pepper in oil until tender. Add beef, stirring lightly to break up. Cover; simmer about 30 minutes or until meat loses color. Add tomatoes, tomato sauce, ketchup, chili powder, salt and pepper. Simmer uncovered for 30 minutes, stirring occasionally. Add kidney beans; simmer an additional 15 minutes. Makes 2½ quarts.

Note: Recipe makes a mild-flavored chili. Additional chili powder may be added for a spicier dish.

Mrs. Robert Haverkos (Ginny)
Mrs. Charles Shupe (Jewel), Park Forest, Illinois

Skyline Chili

- 2 pounds ground beef
- 5 cups tomato juice
- 1 teaspoon cinnamon
- 1 teaspoon ground cumin
- 1 large whole onion
- ⅛ teaspoon Worcestershire sauce
- 1 clove garlic or ⅛ teaspoon minced garlic
- 1 teaspoon allspice
- 1 to 2 tablespoons chili powder
- ½ teaspoon salt
- ½ teaspoon pepper
- ¼ to ½ teaspoon crushed red pepper
- 1½ teaspoons vinegar
- 5 whole bay leaves
- 2 cups shredded Cheddar cheese

In a 5-quart Dutch oven brown ground beef and drain off excess grease. Add all remaining ingredients except cheese and cook uncovered for 2 hours. Remove onion and bay leaves before serving. Serve over spaghetti. Sprinkle cheddar cheese over each serving. Serves 10.

Note: Can be served with kidney beans added. Freezes well!

Mrs. Lynn Lees

Cincinnati Chili

4 cups water
2 pounds ground beef
2 medium onions, finely chopped
2 (8-ounce) cans tomato sauce
5 whole allspice
½ teaspoon crushed red pepper
1 teaspoon ground cumin
4 tablespoons chili powder
½ ounce unsweetened baking chocolate
4 cloves garlic, minced
2 tablespoons cider vinegar
1 whole bay leaf
5 whole cloves
2 teaspoons Worcestershire sauce
1½ teaspoons salt
1 teaspoon cinnamon

Place water in a 5-quart Dutch oven. Add beef; stir until beef separates to a fine texture. Boil slowly for 30 minutes. Add the remaining ingredients; stir to blend. Bring to a boil; reduce heat and simmer uncovered 3 hours. Refrigerate overnight; remove the fat before reheating. Heat and serve alone or over macaroni. Serves 6 to 8.

Mrs. Louis Doty (Faylene)
Palm Harbor, Florida

Chili Elegantė

1 pound ground beef
2 tablespoons oil
2 onions, chopped
1 clove garlic, minced
2 cups diagonally-cut celery (1-inch pieces)
1 green pepper, cut into thin strips
1 (28-ounce) can tomatoes
2 teaspoons salt
⅛ teaspoon cayenne pepper
½ to 1 tablespoon chili powder, or to taste
½ cup red wine
2 (16-ounce) cans kidney beans, drained, reserving liquid
1 (4-ounce) can of mushrooms drained, reserving liquid

In Dutch oven brown meat in oil; add onions, garlic, celery and green peppers. Sautė lightly; add tomatoes and liquid from beans and mushrooms. Combine salt, pepper, chili powder and wine; add and mix well. Heat to boiling; reduce to simmer and cover. Simmer for 1½ hours. Add beans and mushrooms. Reheat to boiling; reduce to simmer; keep at low for at least 10 minutes. Serves 6 to 8.

Mrs. Joe Hensley (Joann)

Prize Winning Barbecue Meat Loaf

1½ pounds ground beef
1 cup dry fresh breadcrumbs
1 onion, finely chopped
1 egg
1½ teaspoons salt
¼ teaspoon pepper
2 (8-ounce) cans tomato sauce
½ cup water
3 tablespoons vinegar
3 tablespoons brown sugar
2 tablespoons mustard
2 teaspoons Worcestershire sauce

Mix meat, breadcrumbs, onion, egg, salt, pepper and half can of tomato sauce together in large bowl. Form into loaf and place in 9½-inch baking pan or 2-quart casserole. Combine in bowl remaining 1½ cans of tomato sauce with water, vinegar, brown sugar, mustard and Worcestershire sauce and pour mixture over meat loaf. Bake for 1 hour and 15 minutes at 350 degrees. Serves 4 to 6.

Mrs. William Parmer (Jean Glasscock)

Texas Style Meat Loaf

10 Saltine crackers, crushed
1 pound ground beef
½ cup chili sauce
1 medium onion, finely chopped
1 teaspoon salt
¼ teaspoon pepper
1 egg
12 Saltine crackers
3 strips bacon

Thoroughly mix the first 7 ingredients together in a large bowl. Shape into a loaf and place in a 9x5x3-inch loaf pan. Place a layer of crackers over the meat loaf. Place 3 strips of bacon over crackers. Bake at 350 degrees for 1 hour. Serves 4 to 6.

Mrs. Armen Bezjian (Barbara)
Novato, California

Best-Ever Meat Loaf

2 pounds ground beef
1 (1.37-ounce) envelope onion soup mix
1½ cups soft breadcrumbs
2 eggs
¾ cup water
1 (8-ounce) can tomato sauce

Combine all ingredients in a large bowl and mix well. Transfer to a 9x5x3-inch loaf pan. Bake at 350 degrees for 1 hour and 15 minutes. Serves 6 to 8.

Mrs. Norval Dawson (Donna)
Lockport, Illinois

Meat Loaf for a Crowd

10 pounds ground beef
3 quarts breadcrumbs
1/4 cup salt
1 tablespoon pepper
2 tablespoons Worcestershire sauce
1 teaspoon hot pepper sauce
2 1/2 quarts milk
2 cups chopped onions
12 eggs

Mix all ingredients thoroughly in extra large bowl. Form into five loaves in 9x5x3-inch loaf pans. Bake at 350 degrees for 1 hour. Serves 50.

Mrs. Ronald D. Kimball (Hope)

Midget Meat Loaves

1 1/2 pounds ground beef
3/4 cup crushed corn flake cereal
1 teaspoon salt
3/4 teaspoon pepper
1 (10-ounce) can onion soup
3 stuffed olives, halved
6 cubes Cheddar cheese, 3/4-inch thick

In a large bowl combine meat, cereal, seasonings and soup; mix well. Divide equally between twelve 3-inch muffin tins; press lightly to shape. Press olive halves into 6 meat loaves; press cheese cubes into remainder. Bake at 400 degrees for 20 minutes. Serves 6.

Note: May be frozen and used at a later date.

Helen Wood
Dunedin, Florida

Texas Hash

2 tablespoons oil
1 large onion, chopped
1 pound ground beef
1 (16-ounce) can tomatoes
1/2 cup rice
2 teaspoons salt
1 teaspoon chili powder
1 cup whole kernel corn, drained
1 cup shredded Cheddar cheese

In a large skillet heat oil; sauté onion; add ground beef and brown. Add tomatoes, rice, salt, chili powder and corn. Pour into a 2-quart casserole; bake at 375 degrees for 45 minutes, covered. Uncover; add Cheddar cheese; bake until melted. Try medium sharp Cheddar cheese. *Fast and Easy!* Serves 4 to 6.

Mrs. Dorman Duncan (Billi)

Faggots

English Meatballs

1 (6-ounce) package chicken flavored stuffing mix
2½ pounds ground beef
2 cups chopped onion
¼ cup dried parsley
1 teaspoon pepper
1 teaspoon salt
1 egg, beaten

Make stuffing according to package directions; set aside to cool. In a large skillet brown ground beef; remove to large bowl using slotted spoon. Discard all but ¼ cup drippings; add onions and sauté until lightly browned. Add to beef, then add all remaining ingredients. Mix together thoroughly. Using a ½ cup measure, scoop out mixture and form into balls, shaping with hands. Makes 12 large balls. (At this point, faggots may be frozen.) To serve bake in a 13x9x2-inch baking pan at 350 degrees for 30 minutes. Pour heated gravy overall and bake 15 minutes more. Serves 6 to 8.

Gravy:

2 tablespoons all-purpose flour
1 tablespoon dried beef extract
1½ cups water or stock

In a small pot mix flour and beef extract to a smooth paste with a little of the water. Add remaining stock or water and bring to a boil or use 1 (16-ounce) jar prepared beef gravy.

Note: Recipe can be doubled, stored in plastic bags and frozen.

Janet Joyce

Chinese Jambalaya

1 pound ground beef
1 cup beef bouillon
3 stalks celery, cut diagonally
1 onion, chopped
1 green pepper, chopped
4 ounces fresh or canned mushrooms
½ teaspoon garlic salt
2 tablespoons soy sauce
1 tomato, chopped
½ head of lettuce, chopped

In a large skillet brown beef; drain, remove and set aside. In skillet combine beef bouillon, celery, onion, pepper and mushrooms; cook for 5 minutes. Add browned beef, garlic salt, soy sauce. Cook another 5 minutes. Just before serving, add tomato and lettuce. Serve with rice. Serves 4.

Edna L. White
Clearwater, Florida

Ground Steak Casserole

1½ pounds ground steak (preferably sirloin)
½ cup chopped onions
2 tablespoons butter
1 (10¾-ounce) can cream of mushroom soup
½ cup milk
2 cups cooked noodles
½ cup shredded Cheddar cheese
1 tablespoon Worcestershire sauce
5 stuffed olives, cut in half
½ cup ground peanuts

In a large skillet sauté ground steak and onions in butter; drain off fat. Add mushroom soup, milk, noodles, cheese and Worcestershire sauce. Pour into greased 3-quart casserole. Place olive halves on top, red slice down. Push in so only top shows. Sprinkle ground peanuts over the top. Bake at 350 degrees for 35 to 40 minutes. Serves 6.

Mrs. James Long (Eva Fandrich)

Russian Cutlet

2 eggs, beaten
¼ cup milk
1¼ cups plain breadcrumbs
1 small onion, finely diced
2 tablespoons finely diced green pepper (optional)
1 teaspoon salt
½ teaspoon pepper
½ teaspoon garlic powder (optional)
1 pound lean ground beef
½ cup butter or margarine and oil mixed

In a large bowl combine eggs, milk, ¼ cup breadcrumbs, onion, green pepper, salt, pepper and garlic powder. Stir to blend. Add meat and knead to make a soft texture. Add more breadcrumbs if too soft. Shape meat into ½-inch patties and dip in remaining breadcrumbs. Refrigerate at least ½ hour for flavor to set. Melt butter in a 10-inch skillet on medium-high heat. Add cutlets and sauté turning frequently to cook and brown meat, approximately 5 minutes. (Cutlets will swell and double their size and inside juices will seep out of center.) Can be served hot or cold. Serves 6.

Try Menu: Serve with mashed potatoes, lemon-butter string beans, tomato-cucumber-onion salad and pumpernickel bread.

Mrs. Gregory H. Keuroghlian (Nora Ghazikian)

Kitchen Hint: Oatmeal or applesauce can stretch hamburger patties. Use one part applesauce or oatmeal to four parts hamburger.

Pastitso

Baked Macaroni with Beef and Cheese

1 (8-ounce) package elbow macaroni
1½ pounds ground beef
1 small onion, chopped
1 (8-ounce) can tomato paste
⅓ cup water
3 teaspoons salt
¼ cup grated Parmesan or Romano cheese
⅛ teaspoon nutmeg
⅛ teaspoon cinnamon
2⅓ cups milk
⅓ cup butter or margarine
4 eggs, beaten

Cook macaroni according to package directions; drain and set aside. In a large skillet cook and stir meat and onion until meat is brown and onion is tender; drain off fat. Stir in tomato paste, water and 2 teaspoons salt; set aside. In a small bowl mix cheese, nutmeg, cinnamon and 1 teaspoon salt. In a 13x9x2-inch greased pan spread half the macaroni; cover with the meat mixture. Sprinkle meat with cheese mixture; cover with remaining macaroni. Measure milk and butter into a 2-quart saucepan; cook and stir until butter is melted. Remove from heat. Gradually stir at least half the hot milk into beaten eggs; mix into hot milk mixture in saucepan. Pour over macaroni. Bake at 325 degrees until bubbly, about 55 minutes. Serves 6.

Note: Garnish with parsley if desired.

Mrs. Robert Haverkos (Ginny)

Spinach Fandango

2 (10-ounce) packages frozen spinach, cooked and drained
1 medium onion, chopped
1 pound ground beef
2 cloves garlic, minced
¼ teaspoon hot pepper sauce
½ to 1 teaspoon oregano
½ teaspoon salt
⅛ teaspoon pepper
1 (10-ounce) can mushrooms, drained
1 cup sour cream
1 (10¾-ounce) can cream of celery soup
8 ounces mozzarella cheese, sliced

In a large skillet sauté onion, beef and garlic until meat browns and onion is tender. Add hot sauce, oregano, salt, pepper and mushroom; simmer 5 minutes. Add spinach, sour cream and soup, mixing well. Pour into a buttered 8-inch baking dish. Top with cheese. Bake at 350 degrees for 15 to 20 minutes. Serves 6.

Edna L. White
Clearwater, Florida

Corned Beef Casserole

3 tablespoons butter
½ cup chopped onion
½ cup chopped green pepper
1 (8-ounce) package medium noodles, cooked and drained
2 cups shredded Cheddar cheese
1 (12-ounce) can corned beef, broken into pieces
1 (10¾-ounce) can condensed cream of chicken soup
1 cup milk
1 tablespoon butter, melted
¼ cup breadcrumbs
1 green pepper, cut into rings

In a skillet melt butter; add onion and green pepper. Sauté 5 minutes or until tender. In a greased 3-quart casserole layer onion, noodles, Cheddar cheese and corned beef. In a medium bowl combine soup and milk; pour over the layered mixture. Mix butter and breadcrumbs; sprinkle on top. Garnish top with green pepper rings. Bake at 350 degrees for 40 minutes. Serves 6 to 8.

Mrs. William Parmer (Jean Glasscock)

Stuffed French Bread

1 loaf French bread
1½ pounds ground beef
¾ cup chopped onion
¾ teaspoon oregano
½ teaspoon salt
¼ teaspoon pepper
1½ cups breadcrumbs
¼ teaspoon mustard
⅓ cup chopped parsley
1 egg, beaten
1½ cups shredded Cheddar cheese

Cut off ends of the bread and hollow out the center with a fork, leaving thick crust as a shell. In a medium skillet combine beef, onion, oregano, salt and pepper; brown. Remove from heat; add crumbs, mustard, parsley, egg and Cheddar cheese. Mix thoroughly. Fill loaf with mixture; replace cut ends and secure with tooth picks. Brush with butter, and wrap in aluminum foil. Bake at 400 degrees for 10 to 15 minutes. Serves 6.

Sauce:

1 cup cheese soup
½ cup milk

In a small saucepan mix cheese soup and milk. Heat to boiling. Serve bread by slicing and pouring cheese mixture over each serving.

Mrs. Anthony Castrogiovanni (BeBe)

Barbecued Hamburgers

1 pound ground beef
1 onion, minced
1 (8-ounce) can tomato sauce
1 tablespoon Worcestershire sauce
1 tablespoon prepared mustard
1/4 teaspoon vinegar
2 tablespoons brown sugar
1/4 cup ketchup
1/2 teaspoon salt
1/4 teaspoon pepper
6 hamburger buns

In a medium skillet brown ground beef. Drain off fat. Add remaining ingredients; mix well; simmer over low heat for 20 minutes. Serve on toasted hamburger buns. Serves 6.

Mrs. John Dodson (Frankie Armitage)

Pizzaburgers

1 pound ground beef
1 teaspoon salt
1/4 teaspoon pepper
3 hamburger buns
1 large tomato, sliced
1 teaspoon oregano
1/4 cup chopped onion
6 slices mozzarella cheese

Add salt and pepper to ground beef and make into 6 patties. Place each patty on bun and top with tomato; sprinkle with oregano and chopped onion. Top with a slice of cheese. Bake in 13x9x2-inch baking dish at 400 degrees for 20 minutes.

Note: Canned tomato slices or 1 (4-ounce) can of tomato sauce may be substituted for tomatoes. Serves 4 to 6.

Mrs. Lynn Lees

Carol's Mexican Burgers

1 medium onion, chopped
1/3 cup chopped green pepper
2 tablespoons butter
1 pound ground beef
1 (6-ounce) can tomato paste
1/3 cup water
1 1/2 teaspoons salt
1/8 teaspoon pepper
1 to 2 teaspoons chili powder
1 (16-ounce) can pork and beans
6 toasted hamburger buns

In a large skillet sauté onion and green pepper in butter for about 5 minutes or until tender. Add ground beef and cook until browned. Drain off fat. Add tomato paste, water, salt, pepper, chili powder and pork and beans. Simmer 5 minutes. Serve on toasted hamburger buns. Serves 6.

Mrs. Ronald Bliss (Judy)

Bleu Cheese Stuffed Hamburgers

½ cup crumbled bleu cheese
2 tablespoons light or heavy cream
1 teaspoon grated onion
1 pound ground round or chuck
½ teaspoon salt
⅛ teaspoon pepper
1 tablespoon vegetable oil
4 hamburger buns, split, toasted and buttered
Cherry tomatoes (optional)

Combine bleu cheese, cream and onion in a small bowl; cream well. Tear off a 6-inch piece of waxed paper. (You will have a 12x6-inch rectangle.) Flatten meat evenly on the waxed paper. Dip a knife in cold water and cut the meat lengthwise into two 6-inch strips; then crosswise into eight 3-inch squares. Divide bleu cheese mixture evenly onto 4 of the meat squares to within ¼ inch of edges. Top with remaining squares. Lightly moisten hands with water and crimp the edges together so that the filling will not seep out during cooking. Shape into hamburger rounds. Sprinkle both sides with salt and pepper. Heat oil in large skillet; fry burgers over medium heat about 5 minutes on each side or until as done as you like them; or broil or grill 5 to 6 inches from heat; turning once. Place between halves of hamburger buns. Garnish with cherry tomatoes. Serves 4.

Mrs. Bill Ritchey (Carol Eddington)

Poor Man's Meat Pie

Pastry for 2-crust pie

Filling:

1 pound ground beef
¼ cup chopped onion
½ cup chopped green pepper
3 hot dogs, cut into slices
1 (16-ounce) can stewed tomatoes
½ (10-ounce) box frozen mixed vegetables, cooked, drained
½ teaspoon sugar
1 tablespoon butter, melted

In a medium skillet brown meat, onion and pepper; drain off fat. Add remaining ingredients; heat and simmer for 5 minutes. Line an 8x8x2-inch or a 9- or 10-inch pie pan with pastry. Pour in meat mixture. Cover with top crust; brush with melted butter. Bake at 400 degrees for 30 minutes or until crust is brown. Makes 10 to 12 pieces.

Lois Glass
Dunedin, Florida

Hamburger Stroganoff

½ cup onions, chopped
1 clove of garlic, sliced
¼ cup butter
1 pound ground beef
2 tablespoons all-purpose flour
1 teaspoon salt
⅛ teaspoon pepper
1 (4-ounce) can of sliced mushrooms or ½ pound fresh mushrooms, sliced
1 (10¾-ounce) can cream of chicken soup
1 cup sour cream

In a skillet cook onions and garlic in butter. Add ground beef, flour, salt, pepper and mushrooms. Cook 10 minutes. Add chicken soup; cook 10 minutes. Add sour cream and heat. Serve over noodles or shell macaroni. Serves 4.

Mrs. J. J. Suddath, Jr. (Eleanor Picken)

Corn Pone Pie

1 pound ground beef
⅓ cup chopped onion
1 tablespoon shortening
2 teaspoons chili powder
¾ teaspoon salt
1 teaspoon Worcestershire sauce
1 cup canned tomatoes
1 cup drained kidney beans
1 cup whole kernel corn
1 (8½-ounce) box cornbread mix

In a medium skillet brown meat and onion in shortening. Add seasonings and tomatoes; cover and simmer for 15 minutes. Add kidney beans and corn. Pour meat mixture into a 1½-quart casserole. Top with cornbread batter, mixed according to package directions. Bake at 425 degrees for 20 minutes. Serves 4.

Mrs. Thomas Parsons, Jr. (Gerrie)
Tampa, Florida

Calico Beef 'N Beans

½ pound bacon, cut into small cubes
1 pound ground beef
1 cup chopped onion
2 tablespoons mustard, or to taste
¾ cup ketchup
½ cup brown sugar
1 (16-ounce) can pork and beans
1 (16-ounce) can lima beans
1 (15½-ounce) can kidney beans
1 (15½-ounce) can butter beans
½ teaspoon salt
¼ teaspoon pepper

In large skillet brown bacon, ground beef and onion. In 4-quart greased baking dish combine browned mixture and remaining ingredients. Bake at 350 degrees for 1 to 1½ hours. Serves 12.

Jo Brooks
Dunedin, Florida

Cabbage Rolls

3 pounds ground beef
2 teaspoons salt
¾ teaspoon pepper
2 teaspoons celery salt
½ cup ketchup
2 eggs
½ cup cracker crumbs
1 head cabbage
3 cups chopped onion

Sauce:

2 cups chili sauce
1 cup grape jelly
¼ cup water

In a large bowl combine first 7 ingredients; set aside. Pour boiling water over 1 large head of cabbage; let set for 5 minutes. Core and separate the cabbage leaves. Take 2 to 3 tablespoons of the mixture and roll in each cabbage leaf. Fold sides of leaves over mixture as you roll so filling will not spill out. Put onions in the bottom of a greased 13x9x2-inch pan and lay the cabbage rolls on top. Combine chili sauce, jelly and water over heat. Pour over rolls. Cover pan and bake at 375 degrees for 2 hours. Uncover and brush rolls with sauce; bake 40 minutes longer. Makes 24 rolls.

Mrs. Jack Wilson (Mary Jane Brown)

Stuffed Peppers

1½ pounds ground beef
½ cup rice
6 green peppers, halved and seeded
2 eggs
8 ounces sharp Cheddar cheese, shredded
1 (15-ounce) can tomato sauce
¼ teaspoon oregano
½ teaspoon dried parsley flakes
2 drops hot pepper sauce
1 teaspoon seasoning salt

In a medium skillet brown beef; drain and cool. Cook rice according to package directions; cool. In a large pot parboil peppers 2 to 3 minutes; drain and cool. In a large bowl combine meat, rice and all other ingredients, reserving ½ cup tomato sauce and 3 ounces of the cheese for topping. Mix well. Stuff pepper halves with mixture; arrange in a large buttered 13x9x2-inch baking dish. Pour remaining tomato sauce over peppers. Bake uncovered at 350 degrees for 30 minutes. Sprinkle remaining cheese over peppers; bake 10 minutes more. Serves 6.

Mrs. Robert Haverkos (Ginny)

Quince Stew

2 pounds lamb, cut for stew (shank, neck)
8 quinces
1 teaspoon lemon juice
1 large onion, finely chopped
1 teaspoon salt
½ teaspoon pepper
1 tablespoon tomato sauce (optional)
1 tablespoon sour salt, or to taste
⅓ cup sugar, or to taste
1 cup hot water or enough to cover meat

Core, peel and slice each quince into 12 pieces; cover with cold water to which 1 teaspoon lemon juice has been added until ready to use. In a large (4- to 5-quart) saucepan braise meat with onion; season with salt and pepper; add hot water to cover meat. Cover and simmer 45 minutes, or until meat is tender. Remove ¼ cup meat broth and mix with tomato sauce, salt and sugar; set aside. Drain quince and add to meat, quickly bring to a fast boil, then lower heat and simmer 15 minutes. Add tomato sauce mixture to stew and cook 15 minutes longer. Serve with pilaf or bulgur. Serves 4 to 5.

Mrs. Gregory H. Keuroghlian (Nora Ghazikian)

Butterfly Leg of Lamb

1 (5- to 6-pound) leg of lamb, boned and butterflied
2 to 3 tablespoons fresh lemon juice
2 cloves garlic, minced
1 tablespoon rosemary, crushed
¼ teaspoon dry mustard
2 tablespoons Worcestershire sauce
2 tablespoons oil
Dash soy sauce
¼ teaspoon fresh ground pepper

Have butcher bone and butterfly leg of lamb. Put leg in a large stainless steel roasting pan. Sprinkle all ingredients in order given over both sides of leg of lamb. Cover and refrigerate overnight, turning once. Prepare barbecue grill; cook lamb over medium-hot charcoal coals, basting often with left over marinade. Cook 40 to 45 minutes; do not overcook. Serves 6.

Hint: Crush rosemary in palm of hands to release oil in the herb.

Mrs. Mark J. Palmer (Martha)
Northvale, New Jersey

Savory Stuffed Cabbage

1 pound cooked lamb, ground
2 cups cooked rice
1 egg
1 clove garlic, crushed
1 teaspoon salt
1/4 teaspoon thyme, crumbled
1/4 teaspoon rosemary, crumbled
1/8 teaspoon pepper
1 (15-ounce) can tomato sauce
1 head (3 1/2 pounds) cabbage
2 tablespoons butter
1 cup chopped onion
2 teaspoons sugar
1/2 teaspoon salt
1/2 cup water
1 tablespoon sour cream per serving

In a large bowl combine lamb, rice, egg, garlic, salt, thyme, rosemary, pepper and 2/3 of the tomato sauce; mix well. Trim outside leaves from cabbage. Cut a small slice about 3 inches in diameter from top end; set aside. With a sharp knife and hands, hollow out cabbage leaving a shell about 1/2-inch thick. Chop cut-out pieces coarsely and cook separately to serve along with stuffed cabbage. Spoon lamb mixture into shell, pressing down firmly. Fit top of cabbage back into place; tie with string. Sauté onion in hot butter in medium-size skillet until soft, about 5 minutes; add remaining tomato sauce, sugar, salt and water. Bring to a boil, stirring constantly. Remove from heat. Place cabbage, core end down, in a deep flame-proof casserole or Dutch oven. Pour sauce over cabbage; cover. Bake at 350 degrees for 1 hour and 30 minutes, basting 2 or 3 times with sauce. To serve, place cabbage on serving platter; remove string. Spoon some of the sauce over cabbage; pass remaining sauce in gravy boat. Cut cabbage into wedges. Garnish with a tablespoon of sour cream. Serves 6.

Note: A favorite of the Tierney family!

Mrs. Lawrence J. Tierney (Sue)

Deviled Pork Chops

6 pork chops, cut 1-inch thick
2 to 3 tablespoons bacon drippings
3 tablespoons chili sauce
1 1/2 tablespoons lemon juice
1 tablespoon grated onion
1/4 teaspoon dry mustard
2 teaspoons Worcestershire sauce
1/8 teaspoon curry powder
1/2 teaspoon salt
1/4 teaspoon paprika
1/2 cup water

In a large skillet brown pork chops well on both sides in about 2 tablespoons bacon drippings. Combine remaining ingredients; mix well; pour over chops. Cover skillet tightly; cook slowly until chops are tender and cooked through, about 1 hour. Serves 6.

Mrs. Lynn Lees

Delicious Baked Pork Chops

6 pork chops, cut 1-inch thick
½ cup all-purpose flour
1 teaspoon salt
¼ teaspoon pepper
1 large onion, thinly sliced
⅛ teaspoon thyme
⅛ teaspoon rosemary
¾ cup white wine
½ cup water

Dredge pork chops with flour, salt and pepper. Fry in a skillet until well browned on both sides. Remove to a 13x9x2-inch roasting pan. Cover with onion. Combine remaining four ingredients; pour over chops; cover and bake at 350 degrees, 1½ hours or until fork tender. Baste occasionally.

Note: This recipe can be prepared in advance and frozen. Serves 6.

Mrs. Del Coller (Helen)
Clearwater, Florida

Pork Curry

5 pounds of pork, cut into small pieces
2 tablespoons cornstarch
2 egg whites
2 medium red peppers, cut into pieces
2 medium green peppers, cut into pieces
2 large onions, cut into wedges
8 cloves garlic, crushed
⅔ cup vegetable oil
2 to 4 tablespoons curry powder
½ teaspoon crushed red pepper
4 teaspoons tomato paste
4 tablespoons sherry
4 teaspoons sugar
2 teaspoons salt
2 tablespoons soy sauce

Place meat in a large bowl; add cornstarch and egg whites; stir until well coated. Heat 1 tablespoon of oil in a small saucepan. Stir in curry powder and crushed red pepper. Cook and stir 1 minute; add tomato paste; stir and remove from heat. In a large skillet add oil; heat and brown the pork well. Remove meat from skillet; add curry mixture, sherry, sugar, salt and soy sauce; blend; return onions and garlic. Stir fry until peppers and onions are done. Serve on rice. Serves 12. *This recipe is for curry lovers!*

June Burns
Dunedin, Florida

Sweet and Sour Pork

Batter:

1 egg, lightly beaten
1 tablespoon dry sherry
1 tablespoon cornstarch
2 tablespoons all-purpose flour
1/2 teaspoon salt
1 pound pork tenderloin, cut in 1-inch cubes

In large bowl combine all ingredients except pork, and mix well until smooth. Add pork to batter; mix well. Refrigerate for 30 minutes before deep frying.

Pork Preparation:

8 dried Chinese mushrooms
2 medium carrots, sliced
8 small broccoli flowerets
1 cup chicken broth
1/2 teaspoon chili paste with garlic
3 tablespoons sugar
1 tablespoon soy sauce
3 tablespoons white rice vinegar or white vinegar
3 tablespoons ketchup
2 tablespoons peanut oil
1 teaspoon minced fresh ginger root
1/2 teaspoon minced clove garlic
4 cups peanut oil
1 tablespoon cornstarch dissolved in 2 tablespoons cold water

In small bowl cover mushrooms with boiling water; soak for 30 minutes. Rinse mushrooms; discard stems and cut into quarters; set aside. Bring 2 quarts water to boil; add carrots and broccoli; boil 2 minutes. Drain and rinse in cold water; set aside. In small bowl combine broth, chili paste, sugar, soy sauce, vinegar and ketchup; set aside. Put 2 tablespoons oil into wok or large skillet; add ginger and garlic and stir. Add carrots, broccoli and mushrooms; stir. Add broth mixture; stir until boiling. Set aside. Heat 4 cups oil in Dutch oven, wok or deep fryer to 350 degrees; add pork, half at a time, and fry for about 6 minutes until golden brown. Drain on paper towels. Reheat sauce mixture; stir in dissolved cornstarch, stirring for 1 minute. Add cooked pork; remove from heat. Serve immediately. Serves 3 to 4.

Note: Pork cubes can be fried well ahead of time and then refried briefly to recrisp them just before serving.

Mrs. Lynn Lees

Maria's Pork Chop Casserole

4 pork chops, cut 1-inch thick
1 cup rice
1 medium onion, chopped
½ green pepper, chopped
2 pimento, chopped
1 (10½-ounce) can condensed beef consommé
½ cup Sauterne wine (or other white table wine)
⅛ teaspoon thyme
⅛ teaspoon marjoram
⅛ teaspoon pepper
¼ teaspoon salt

Trim excess fat from chops and use to grease large heavy skillet; brown chops slowly on both sides. Mix rice, onion, green pepper and pimento; spread on bottom of 2-quart casserole. Place chops on top. Mix consommé and wine; add enough water to make 2 cups liquid; add seasonings. Heat to boiling; pour over chops and rice. Cover and bake at 375 degrees for 30 minutes. Remove chops and stir rice gently with fork; replace chops, cover and continue baking for about 30 minutes, or until chops are tender and rice has absorbed all liquid, turning chops occasionally. Serves 4.

Mrs. Lynn Lees

Ham Squares

1 pound cooked ham, ground
½ pound ground beef
1 cup soft breadcrumbs, about 1½ slices
¾ cup milk
1 egg
2 tablespoons chopped onions
2 teaspoons snipped parsley
1 teaspoon dry mustard
½ teaspoon salt
⅛ teaspoon pepper

In a large bowl combine all ingredients and mix thoroughly; lightly pack into an 8-inch square pan; bake at 325 degrees for 1 hour. Drain off fat; allow meat to stand a few minutes; then cut into 6 pieces. Remove to warm serving platter; top with Curried Creamed Peas. Serves 6.

Curried Creamed Peas:

1 (10-ounce) package frozen peas
2 tablespoons butter or margarine
1 tablespoon all-purpose flour
¼ teaspoon curry powder
¼ teaspoon salt
⅛ teaspoon white pepper
1 cup milk

Cook peas according to package directions; drain; set aside. Melt butter in saucepan over low heat; blend in flour, curry powder, salt and pepper. Add milk, cook stirring constantly until mixture thickens; cook 1 minute more; stir in the peas. Serve over ham squares.

Helen Wood
Dunedin, Florida

Pork Chops Special

2 pork chops
1 tablespoon all-purpose flour
1 tablespoon oil
$2^1/_2$ tablespoons Parmesan cheese
$^1/_4$ teaspoon salt
$^1/_8$ teaspoon pepper
2 cups thinly sliced potatoes
1 medium onion, thinly sliced
2 beef bouillon cubes
$^1/_4$ cup plus 2 tablespoons hot water
$1^1/_2$ teaspoons lemon juice

Dredge chops in flour; brown in oil in medium skillet. Combine cheese, salt and pepper. Sprinkle 1 tablespoon cheese mixture over chops. Arrange potatoes over meat. Sprinkle 1 tablespoon cheese mixture over the potatoes. Arrange onion on top. Dissolve bouillon cubes in water. Stir in lemon juice and pour over vegetables. Sprinkle remaining cheese mixture over top. Cover and simmer on stove for 40 minutes or until chops are tender. Serves 2.

Mrs. S. E. "Pete" Covey (Carol Daugherty)

Smoked Ham Steak

2 tablespoons sweet butter
2 tablespoons brown sugar
4 tablespoons Dijon mustard
$^3/_4$ cup dry sherry
1 (2-pound) ham steak, bone in

Preheat oven to 325 degrees. On top of stove melt butter in an ovenproof skillet or casserole. Add sugar, mustard and sherry; stir until sauce is smooth. Place ham in pan and spoon sauce over it. Cover and bake in oven 30 to 40 minutes. Uncover, baste and continue to bake until ham is glazed, about 5 to 10 minutes. Serves 4 to 6.

Mrs. Brown Coleman
Paris, Texas

Hot Ham and Cheese Rolls

$^1/_2$ pound ham, diced
$^1/_2$ pound cheese, diced
$^1/_3$ cup sliced scallions
2 hard-cooked eggs, diced
$^1/_2$ cup Spanish olives, sliced
3 tablespoons mayonnaise
$^1/_2$ cup chili sauce
12 frankfurter rolls

In a large bowl combine ham and cheese with scallions, eggs and olives. Blend mayonnaise with chili sauce; add to the ham and cheese mixture. Spread in 12 split rolls; wrap in foil. Bake 10 to 20 minutes at 400 degrees or until hot. May be prepared ahead and refrigerated for 4 to 6 hours. Serves 12.

Mrs. Donald Behm (Marion)

Savoy Ham Bake

2 cups diced, cooked ham
2 cups cooked, medium egg noodles
1 (10¾-ounce) can cream of vegetable soup
½ cup milk
1 (11-ounce) can peas with onions
1 teaspoon minced parsley
½ teaspoon mustard
½ teaspoon celery flakes, crushed
¾ cup crushed cheese crackers
2 tablespoons butter, melted

Combine first eight ingredients and place in a 1½-quart casserole. Mix crushed crackers with butter and sprinkle over casserole. Bake at 350 degrees for 30 to 35 minutes. Serves 6.

Bea Vass
Holiday, Florida

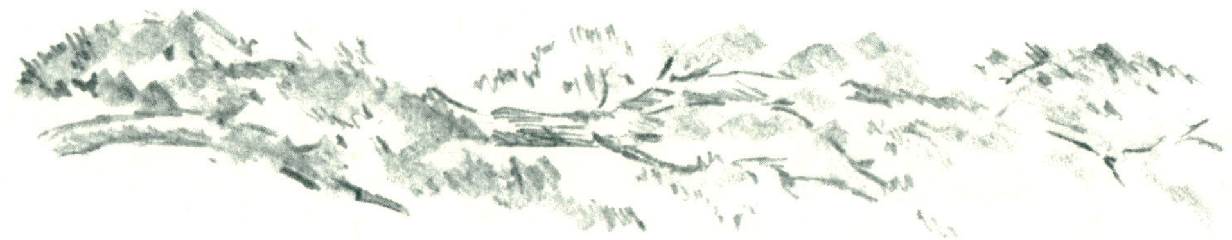

Polynesian Ribs

Polynesian Sauce:

½ cup soy sauce
½ cup ketchup
3 tablespoons brown sugar
2 to 3 teaspoons grated ginger root

Combine all ingredients in a small bowl. Refrigerate overnight before using.

Meat:

3 pounds pork loin chops or meaty spare ribs
½ cup sugar

Rub meat on both sides with sugar; let stand for 2 hours. Brush meat with Polynesian sauce; let stand for at least one hour, preferably longer. Bake in a 13x9x2-inch baking pan at 350 degrees for about 45 minutes or until meat is tender. Brush meat with sauce every 15 minutes while baking. Serves 4.

Douglas G. Guilfoile
Dunedin, Florida

Spareribs and Caraway Kraut

3 pounds pork spareribs, cut in serving-size pieces
2 teaspoons salt
1/4 teaspoon pepper
3 1/2 cups (1 pound 11-ounce can) sauerkraut
1 medium tart apple, unpared and chopped
1 1/2 cups tomato juice
2 tablespoons brown sugar
2 to 3 teaspoons caraway seed

Stuffing Balls:

1 1/3 cups water
1/2 cup margarine
1 (8-ounce) package herb-seasoned stuffing mix (3 1/2 cups)
2 eggs, slightly beaten

Season ribs with salt and pepper; place in Dutch oven and thoroughly brown. In a medium bowl combine remaining ingredients; spoon over the ribs. Simmer, covered for 1½ hours, basting with juices several times. Skim off fat. While ribs and kraut mixture is cooking, make stuffing balls. In a 2-quart saucepan, heat water and margarine. Add stuffing mix and toss lightly until stuffing is moistened. Stir in eggs. Shape into 6 balls. If desired, smaller ones can be made to increase the number served. When rib-kraut mixture has cooked for 1½ hours, place the stuffing balls on top of the mixture and continue cooking for 15 minutes. Serves 6.

Mrs. Robert Hall (Barbara)

Spareribs with Dry Red Wine

4 to 5 pounds of spareribs
1/2 teaspoon salt
1/8 teaspoon pepper
3 apples, peeled, cored and sliced
1/2 cup chopped onion
1 cup burgundy or dry red wine
1/2 cup chili or barbecue sauce
3 tablespoons brown sugar
1/2 cup dry red wine

Place spareribs in roasting pan; sprinkle with salt and pepper. Cover with apples and onions. In a medium bowl mix wine, chili or barbecue sauce and sugar. Pour over spareribs. Cover roasting pan; bake at 450 degrees for 1 hour. Skim off excess fat; add additional ½ cup wine; return to oven; cook additional 15 minutes, uncovered. Serves 4.

Donna M. Moore

Veal Antonino

- 2 pounds veal, cut into thin slices
- 1½ cups all-purpose flour for dredging
- 2 teaspoons salt or to taste
- 2 teaspoons fresh ground pepper, or to taste
- ½ cup butter
- 1 pound fresh mushrooms, sliced
- 1 (16-ounce) can artichoke hearts, drained
- ¼ pound prosciutto
- ½ cup marsala wine
- ¼ cup beef stock or broth

Pound veal lightly until thin. Mix flour, salt and pepper together and dredge veal slices. Heat half the butter in a skillet; add the veal; brown on both sides. Remove veal from skillet; heat remaining butter; sauté mushrooms, artichoke hearts and proscuitto for about 3 minutes. Add marsala wine and beef stock; stir; return veal to skillet; simmer another 10 minutes, scraping particles from bottom of skillet. Sprinkle with fresh parsley. Serve on heated platter. Serves 6 to 8.

Mrs. Anthony S. Brancato (Georgine E. Palmer)

Prosciutto is Italian-style ham, pressed and aged in spices; may be purchased in Italian specialty stores.

Veal Rolls à la Porter

- 2 pounds veal round, cut ¼-inch thick
- 1 cup finely chopped, cooked ham
- 2 tablespoons finely chopped shallots
- 1 clove garlic, minced
- ½ teaspoon dried rosemary
- 2 tablespoons clarified butter
- 1 cup white wine
- 2 cups chicken broth
- 1 tablespoon cornstarch
- 2 tablespoons cold water
- Minced parsley

Cut veal into 16 even-sized pieces. Pound each piece to ⅛-inch thickness. Sprinkle with salt and pepper. Combine ham, shallots, garlic and rosemary; top each veal slice with about 1 tablespoon of mixture. Roll veal around filling and secure with toothpicks. Melt butter in a large skillet over medium heat; add veal rolls and brown quickly. Add wine and simmer for 3 minutes; then add chicken broth; cover and simmer 20 minutes more. Remove veal rolls to a warm serving platter. Boil broth rapidly until reduced to about 1½ cups. Combine cornstarch and water; stir into hot broth; continue to cook and stir until slightly thickened. Spoon sauce over veal and sprinkle with parsley. Serves 8.

Mrs. Michael Porter (Paula)

Fettine di Vitello Piccata

Slices of Veal

2 pounds veal, cut in 3-inch pieces
1/3 cup all-purpose flour
6 to 8 tablespoons butter
1/4 teaspoon salt
1/8 teaspoon pepper
3/4 cup dry white wine
2 tablespoons minced shallots
1 tablespoon fresh lemon juice
2 teaspoons minced parsley
1/2 cup butter

Pound veal pieces until very thin. Dip both sides in flour. Heat 3 tablespoons of butter in a skillet over medium heat. Quickly sauté a few pieces of veal at a time, turning to lightly brown on both sides; add butter as needed. Remove meat; keep warm on heated plate until all veal is cooked. Season with salt and pepper. Pour excess butter out of pan; add wine, shallots and lemon juice; reduce liquid to ⅓. Take off heat; add parsley and ½ cup butter, quickly blending with whisk to a creamy texture. Pour sauce over veal. Serve immediately. Serves 6 to 8.

Mrs. Michael Porter (Paula)

Veal Scaloppine Florentine

4 tablespoons butter, divided
2 tablespoons chopped shallots
1 (10-ounce) package of chopped spinach, drained
2 tablespoons grated Parmesan cheese
1/4 cup all-purpose flour
1/2 teaspoon salt
1/4 teaspoon pepper
1 pound veal scallopine
1/2 pound fresh mushrooms, sliced
1/2 cup white wine
1 cup water
1 chicken bouillon cube
1/4 pound proscuitto
1/4 pound mozzarella cheese, shredded
2 tablespoons chopped fresh parsley

In a small skillet sauté shallots in 1 tablespoon of butter; add spinach; sauté until tender; add cheese. Set aside. Dust veal lightly with flour seasoned with salt and pepper. In a large skillet sauté veal in 2 tablespoons butter until lightly brown. Remove veal; keep warm. Add mushrooms and 1 tablespoon of butter; sauté lightly; add wine, water and bouillon cube; simmer until tender. Remove mushroom-wine mixture; set aside. In the skillet over medium heat add a little mushroom-wine mixture; layer in order veal, proscuitto, spinach; and top with cheese. Cover skillet to melt cheese. Sprinkle with parsley just before serving. Serves 4.

Mrs. Anthony S. Brancato (Georgine E. Palmer)

Oven Barbecued Spareribs

3 pounds spareribs, cut into serving-size pieces
1 tablespoon margarine
2 cups sliced onions
2 cloves garlic, minced
½ cup vinegar
½ cup water
¼ cup chili sauce
2 tablespoons lemon juice
2 tablespoons Worcestershire sauce
3 tablespoons brown sugar
1½ teaspoons salt
1 teaspoon dry mustard

Bake ribs in 13x9x2-inch baking pan at 450 degrees for 30 minutes. Melt margarine in medium saucepan; sauté onions and minced garlic until tender but not brown. Add remaining 8 ingredients and simmer for 10 minutes. Brush ribs with sauce. Reduce oven temperature to 350 degrees. Continue baking uncovered for 1 hour. Brush occasionally with sauce. Serves 6 to 8.

Variation: Try beef ribs. Bake at 450 degrees for 30 minutes or until desired doneness.

Mrs. Robert Hall (Barbara)

Barbecue Sauce I

For Steaks, Roasts, Spareribs and Chicken

2 tablespoons butter
1 medium onion, chopped
1 clove garlic, minced
½ cup ketchup
2 tablespoons vinegar
½ teaspoon hot pepper sauce
1 tablespoon black strap molasses
1 teaspoon salt
1 teaspoon dry mustard
¼ cup water

Combine all ingredients in heavy saucepan. Bring to boil. Spread over meat.

Mrs. James Long (Eva Fandrich)

Barbecue Sauce II

1 cup butter
1 cup vinegar
2 cups ketchup
4 tablespoons Worcestershire sauce
1 tablespoon hot pepper sauce
1 tablespoon salt
3 tablespoons mustard
⅛ teaspoon pepper
Juice of 1 lemon

In a medium saucepan melt butter; add the rest of the ingredients; simmer for a few minutes. Serve over your favorite meat or poultry. Makes 2½ cups.

Mrs. William Parmer (Jean Glasscock)

Barbecued Spareribs

1 cup water
2 tablespoons salt
5 to 6 pounds spareribs
2½ tablespoons chili sauce
2 tablespoons chopped onions
1½ cups pure maple syrup
1 tablespoon Worcestershire sauce
2 teaspoons salt
½ teaspoon dry mustard
¼ teaspoon chili powder
⅛ teaspoon pepper

In a small bowl mix water and salt. Place spareribs on a grill over low heat. Baste ribs frequently with salt mixture for about 45 minutes. Mix last 8 ingredients together in a medium bowl. Cook ribs 15 minutes longer basting with barbecue sauce. Serves 4 to 6.

Mrs. Anthony S. Brancato (Georgine E. Palmer)

Sausage and Wild Rice Casserole

5 stalks celery, chopped
1 cup chopped onion
3 tablespoons margarine
1 pound hot sausage
1 teaspoon sage
1 (5-ounce) package wild rice mix, cooked
½ teaspoon salt

In a large skillet sauté celery and onions in margarine. Add sausage; brown. Drain well in a colander. Return to skillet and add sage. Mix with cooked rice and add salt. Place in 1½-quart casserole. Bake at 350 degrees for 20 minutes or until hot. Serves 6.

Note: Serve with hot peaches and currant jelly. Arrange canned peach halves in a dish. Fill centers with a 1 teaspoon jelly each. Heat along with casserole until hot.

Variation: Could substitute mild sausage, if preferred.

Mrs. Richard Benkusky (Judy)

Ratatouille with Sausage

2 large eggplants, peeled and cut into strips
8 medium zucchini, cut into ½-inch slices
Flour and olive oil
5 large onions, sliced
6 garlic cloves, minced
6 green peppers, seeded and diced
8 large tomatoes, peeled and cut into strips
1 cup finely chopped parsley
½ to 1 cup black olives, sliced
2 teaspoons oregano
2 teaspoons thyme
2 teaspoons basil
½ teaspoon salt
¼ teaspoon pepper
2 pounds sweet Italian sausage
Chopped parsley for garnish

Dredge eggplant and zucchini in flour. Heat oil in large, heavy skillet; sauté eggplant and zucchini over medium high heat about 5 minutes. Remove and drain on paper towels. Sauté onion, garlic and green pepper in same oil until soft; add more oil if needed. Use skillet to sauté sausages. Preheat oven to 350 degrees. Layer sautéed vegetables, tomatoes, parsley, olives and seasonings in 6-quart casserole. Stir gently to mix. Bake uncovered for 35 minutes. Meanwhile sauté sausages in reserved skillet until browned; remove and drain on paper towels and cool. Slice ¼-inch thick; return to skillet. Sauté slices 2 to 3 minutes on each side. After vegetables have baked 35 minutes, add sausage, pushing most of the slices down into the mixture, but reserving some for casserole top. Return to oven and bake; uncovered, for 20 minutes. Garnish with parsley. Serves 12.

Hint: Tastes better when chilled overnight. Bring to room temperature before reheating.

Excellent company dinner served with green salad, crusty French bread, fruit and cheese!

Mrs. Richard Goldstein (Maureen)
Dunedin, Florida

Italian Sausage and Peppers with Spinach Noodles

6 links mild or hot Italian sausage (about 1 pound)
2 or 3 medium green peppers, cut into 1-inch pieces
½ (8-ounce) can tomato sauce
1 (16-ounce) package spinach noodles
3 tablespoons butter
¼ cup grated Parmesan cheese

Cut sausage links into 1-inch slices. In a large skillet saute until brown; add tomato sauce and cook 10 minutes, stirring occasionally. Add green peppers and simmer 5 minutes. Cook spinach noodles 7 minutes, drain and return to pan. Add butter and Parmesan cheese. Place on serving platter; top with sausage or serve noodles separately. Serve with additional cheese on the side. Serves 6.

Donna M. Moore

Zucchini and Smoked Sausage

4 cups sliced zucchini
1/4 cup diced celery
1/4 cup diced onion
1/4 cup diced green pepper
2 large tomatoes, chopped
1 cup smoked sausage, cut into rings
1 tablespoon parsley flakes
1 teaspoon salt
1/2 teaspoon pepper
1/2 cup pasteurized process cheese or mozzarella cheese, cut into strips

Overlap half of squash slices in greased 1½-quart casserole dish. Sprinkle with half of celery, onion, pepper, tomatoes, sausage and seasonings. Repeat in layers. Place strips of cheese on top. Bake at 350 degrees for 35 to 40 minutes or until vegetables are tender. Serves 6.

Mrs. Annie B. McClellan
Wetumpka, Alabama

Coq au Vin

10 pieces of chicken—legs, thighs, breasts
1 teaspoon garlic salt, or to taste
2 to 3 tablespoons margarine
3 carrots, diced
1 large Spanish onion, finely chopped
4 stalks celery, diced
2 tablespoons dried parsley flakes
2 tablespoons all-purpose flour
2 teaspoons marjoram
1 teaspoon thyme
1/2 teaspoon salt
1/2 teaspoon pepper
3 slices bacon, cooked and crumbled
1 cup beef broth
1 1/2 cups dry red wine

Place chicken on broiling pan; sprinkle with garlic salt. Broil on both sides until brown; set aside. In a large, covered skillet or Dutch oven sauté carrots, onions and celery in margarine. Stir in parsley, flour, marjoram, thyme, salt, pepper, bacon, broth and wine. Bring mixture to a boil; add browned chicken. Cover and simmer for at least one hour. Serves 5 to 6.

Variations: Small peeled potatoes may be added with the chicken. Add ½ pound sliced mushrooms 10 minutes before serving. Chicken broth and white wine may be substituted for beef broth and red wine.

Janet Joyce

The Best Baked Chicken

3/4 cup dry breadcrumbs
1/4 cup minced parsley
1/3 cup grated Parmesan cheese
1/4 cup butter
1 clove garlic, minced
4 chicken breasts
1/2 teaspoon salt
1/4 teaspoon pepper

In a small bowl mix crumbs and parsley with cheese. Melt butter in a skillet; add minced garlic. Dip chicken in butter; roll in breadcrumb mixture. Salt and pepper each piece; arrange in a single layer in greased 8-inch square baking dish. Bake at 350 degrees for 1 hour or until chicken is crispy brown. Serve with JB's rice. Serves 4.

JB's Rice:

1 1/2 cups instant rice
2 tablespoons butter
1/8 teaspoon celery seed
1 teaspoon dried onion flakes
1/4 scant teaspoon curry powder
1/8 teaspoon tumeric
1/2 teaspoon salt
1/8 teaspoon paprika
1 1/2 cups water
3 chicken bouillon cubes
1/2 (10-ounce) package frozen peas, cooked

In a skillet brown rice in butter. In a 2-quart saucepan bring water to a boil; add remaining ingredients except peas. Stir in rice; let stand covered until water is absorbed, about 5 minutes. Stir in the peas. Serve immediately with chicken breasts.

June Burns
Dunedin, Florida

Chicken Breasts with Macadamia Nuts

6 chicken breasts, skinned and boned
1/4 teaspoon salt
1/8 teaspoon pepper
1/2 cup finely ground macadamia nuts
1/2 cup all-purpose flour
2 tablespoons butter
1 cup whipping cream

Salt and pepper chicken breasts; place in a 13x9x2-inch buttered baking pan. Combine nuts and flour; sprinkle over chicken. Place 1 teaspoon butter on each breast; pour cream overall. Cover; refrigerate overnight. Bake, uncovered, at 400 degrees for 15 minutes. Reduce temperature to 350 degrees; bake, covered, for 30 minutes. Serves 6.

Mrs. Harvey Heimann (Jean)

Chicken Breasts with Grapes

6 chicken breasts
2 teaspoons salt
1/2 teaspoon pepper
3 tablespoons butter or margarine
2 teaspoons tarragon leaves
2 cups seedless green grapes
1/2 cup dry white wine
1 tablespoon all-purpose flour
2/3 cup light cream
2 large egg yolks

Rub chicken breasts with salt and pepper. In a skillet brown on all sides in butter. Place chicken in a 13x9x2-inch baking pan, adding all pan drippings. Sprinkle with tarragon; add grapes and wine. Bake at 325 degrees for 40 minutes or until chicken is tender. Remove chicken from pan; keep warm. In a small bowl blend flour with a little of cream; add remaining cream and egg yolks. Beat well; add to pan drippings. Cook over medium heat for 5 minutes; do not boil. Serve sauce separately or pour over chicken and garnish with grapes. Serve on toast or with rice. Serves 6.

Mrs. John Dronzek (Pat)

Chicken Breasts with Almond Rice

6 boneless chicken breasts
1/4 cup butter
1/2 pound fresh mushrooms, sliced
1/4 cup chopped onions
2 tablespoons all-purpose flour
1/8 teaspoon pepper
1 3/4 cups chicken broth
1/2 cup light cream
2 tablespoons butter
1/4 cup sliced blanched almonds
1 1/3 cups rice, cooked

In a medium skillet brown chicken in 1/4 cup butter. Add mushrooms and onions; sauté until lightly browned. Remove chicken; blend in flour and pepper. Gradually, add broth and cream, stirring until thickened. Add chicken; simmer, covered, until tender about 25 to 30 minutes. In a small skillet sauté almonds in butter; add to hot rice. Serve chicken breasts on rice topped with sauce. Serves 6.

Note: Sherry may be added to sauce, if desired.

Mrs. John G. Dodson (Frankie Armitage)

Party Chicken

Great company dish!

1 (16-ounce) carton sour cream
2 (10¾-ounce) cans cream of mushroom soup
1 (5-ounce) jar dried beef
8 chicken breasts, skinned and boned
8 strips of bacon
1 (4-ounce) package sliced toasted almonds

In a large bowl combine sour cream and mushroom soup to make a sauce; set aside. Line a greased 13x9x2-inch casserole dish with dried beef. Wrap each chicken breast in a strip of bacon; put into casserole. Pour sauce over chicken. Bake at 300 degrees for 1½ hours. Sprinkle with toasted almonds before serving. Serves 8.

Note: May be prepared early in the day and refrigerated. Looks like you spent all day in the kitchen, but very simple to prepare.

Variation: Use cream of celery soup in place of mushroom soup.

Variation: Spread chicken breasts flat; cover with dried beef and top with a spoonful of sauce. Roll up jelly-roll fashion; wrap each breast with a slice of bacon and secure with a toothpick. Put into casserole; top with remaining sauce.

Mrs. Edwin Everett (Barbara)
Mrs. Robert Hall (Barbara)
Mrs. William S. Sharpe (Wanda)

Lemon Chicken

1 (6-ounce) can frozen lemonade, thawed
3 tablespoons ketchup
3 tablespoons brown sugar
3 tablespoons white vinegar
¼ teaspoon ground ginger
1 teaspoon soy sauce
1 (2 to 2½-pound) chicken, cut up
½ cup all-purpose flour
¼ cup oil

In a medium bowl combine lemonade, ketchup, brown sugar, vinegar, ginger, and soy sauce; set aside. Dredge chicken with flour. In a large skillet brown chicken in oil. Drain excess oil from skillet. Pour sauce over chicken; cover. Simmer 30 to 45 minutes or until chicken is tender. Serve over brown rice. Serves 4.

Mrs. Joe Hensley (Joann)

Chicken Parmesan

1 chicken, cut up
1 (8-ounce) bottle garlic salad dressing
1/2 to 3/4 cup biscuit baking mix
2 to 3 tablespoons shortening
1/2 teaspoon oregano
2 tablespoons grated Parmesan cheese

In a medium bowl marinate chicken in garlic dressing at least 2 hours. Roll chicken in biscuit baking mix. In a skillet brown in shortening. Place chicken in a 12x8x2-inch baking dish; sprinkle with oregano and Parmesan cheese. Bake at 350 degrees for 1 hour. Serves 4.

Mrs. Lawrence Feltman (Bertha)
Chicago, Illinois

Chicken with Feta Cheese

1 medium eggplant, peeled and sliced 3/4-inch thick
4 boneless chicken breasts
1 teaspoon garlic powder
1 (8-ounce) can tomato sauce
1 teaspoon oregano
1 teaspoon basil
1/8 teaspoon pepper
3/4 pound feta cheese, crumbled

In an 8x8-inch baking dish arrange eggplant slices in a single layer. Broil for 10 minutes on both sides; set aside. Sprinkle chicken with garlic; in a skillet sauté in oil until lightly browned on both sides. Put chicken on top of eggplant. In a saucepan combine tomato sauce, oregano, basil and pepper; cook for 5 minutes. Sprinkle feta cheese over chicken; pour sauce overall. Bake at 350 degrees for 20 minutes. Serves 4.

Mrs. Charles Nikitas (Theresa)
Williamstown, Massachusetts

Chicken Livers with Mushrooms

1 1/2 pounds chicken livers
1/4 cup butter or margarine
3 cups sliced fresh mushrooms
4 tablespoons all-purpose flour
1 1/2 cups chicken broth or bouillon
3/4 cup white wine
1 tablespoon lemon juice

In a skillet sauté livers in butter, reserving 1 tablespoon butter. Remove from pan; keep warm. Add mushrooms and reserved butter to skillet; sauté for 5 minutes. Stir in flour; slowly add broth and wine. Cook, stirring constantly, until sauce thickens. Add lemon juice and livers; heat through. Serve with wild rice. Serves 6.

Donna M. Moore

Chinese Chicken and Nuts

1 teaspoon sherry
1/4 teaspoon onion powder
1/8 teaspoon pepper
1 tablespoon cornstarch
2 slices ginger root or 1/4 teaspoon ginger powder
2 1/2 tablespoons soy sauce
1 pound chicken breasts, skinned, boned and diced
4 tablespoons oil
1/4 to 1/2 cup walnuts or cashews, peanuts, almonds
1/2 small onion, diced or 2 cloves garlic, crushed
1 tablespoon soy sauce
1 cup diced celery
1/2 cup sliced water chestnuts, or 1/2 cup bamboo shoots, diced
1 cup diced red peppers (green may be used)
1 tablespoon cornstarch mixed with 1 tablespoon water
1/2 cup water
1/8 teaspoon pepper
1/8 teaspoon sugar

In a medium bowl blend together first 6 ingredients. Add chicken pieces; marinate. Heat oil in wok or skillet. Stir in nuts; fry until light brown. Remove nuts to small bowl. Add chicken to wok in remaining oil, stirring until color turns. Remove chicken to side dish. Sauté onion or garlic in remaining oil; add soy sauce and vegetables, stirring constantly. Add cornstarch paste, water, pepper and sugar; stir and mix 1 minute. Add cooked chicken; mix well. Remove to serving dish. Garnish with fried nuts. Serve immediately with rice. Serves 6.

Note: Chicken may be cut up and marinated early in the day. Cut up vegetables should all be the same size.

Donna M. Moore

Honey Nutty Chicken

1/4 cup honey
2 tablespoons Worcestershire sauce
2 tablespoons oil
1 tablespoon lemon juice
1 3/4 teaspoons salt, divided
2 1/2 pounds chicken pieces
3/4 cup corn flake crumbs
1/3 cup finely chopped nuts

In a small bowl combine honey, Worcestershire sauce, oil, lemon juice and 1 1/4 teaspoons of salt. Pour over chicken; coat completely. Cover; refrigerate 24 hours, turning once. Combine corn flake crumbs, nuts and remaining 1/2 teaspoon salt. Remove chicken from marinade; coat with crumb mixture. Arrange on rack in 13x9x2-inch baking pan. Bake at 325 degrees until chicken is fork tender, about 1 hour. Serves 4 to 5.

Mrs. Jerry Harris (Nancy)

Chicken Cacciatore

1/4 cup olive oil
1 (2 1/2- to 3-pound) chicken, cut up
2 medium onions, cut into 1/4-inch slices
2 cloves garlic, minced
1 (16-ounce) can tomatoes
1 (8-ounce) can seasoned tomato sauce
1 teaspoon salt
1/4 teaspoon pepper
1/2 teaspoon celery seed
1 teaspoon crushed oregano or basil
1 or 2 bay leaves

In a large skillet or Dutch oven, heat oil until hot. Add chicken pieces; brown slowly, turning once. Remove chicken from pan. Cook onions and garlic in oil until tender but not brown. Return the browned chicken to the pan. In a medium bowl combine remaining ingredients. Pour tomato mixture over chicken; cover pan and simmer gently for 45 minutes. Cook chicken, uncovered, turning occasionally for 20 minutes more or until fork-tender and sauce has thickened. Discard bay leaf; skim off excess fat. Arrange chicken on platter and top with sauce. Serves 4.

Mrs. Edwin Everett (Barbara)

Chicken Breasts Amandine

10 boneless chicken breasts
2 1/2 cups water
1/2 teaspoon salt
1/8 teaspoon pepper
2 tablespoons all-purpose flour
1/4 cup water
1 cup sour cream
1/2 cup white wine
1 cup sliced or slivered almonds

In a pot simmer chicken breasts in water seasoned with salt and pepper until tender. Remove breasts and place in a 13x9x2-inch baking dish. Make a paste of flour and 1/4 cup water. Add to chicken broth, stirring constantly, to make a light cream sauce. Stir in sour cream and wine. Pour sauce over chicken. Cover baking dish; refrigerate overnight. Sprinkle almonds over chicken. Bake at 325 degrees for 1 hour. Serves 10.

Note: Additional seasonings such as onion, celery or rosemary may be added to sauce to taste, if desired.

Joan Bentley
New Port Richey, Florida

Chicken Primavera

1 (3-pound) broiler-fryer chicken, cut up
1/2 cup all-purpose flour
1 teaspoon ground ginger
1 teaspoon salt
1/4 teaspoon pepper
1/4 cup oil
3 cloves garlic, minced
1/2 cup chicken broth
1 pound fresh asparagus spears or 1 (10-ounce) package frozen spears
2 medium zucchini, cut into 1-inch pieces
2 medium yellow squash, cut into 1-inch pieces
2 medium sweet red peppers, cut into 1-inch pieces
1/2 pound fresh mushrooms, sliced
1/4 cup soy sauce
3 tablespoons dry sherry
1/2 teaspoon ground ginger

Shake chicken in a plastic bag with flour, ginger, salt and pepper until coated. Fry chicken in oil in a large skillet, turning frequently, about 5 minutes or until golden brown. Add garlic and chicken broth. Cover; simmer 15 minutes. Trim and cut asparagus into 1-inch pieces. Add all vegetables to skillet. Add soy sauce, sherry and ginger; stir gently to mix. Cover; simmer 10 minutes or until vegetables are crisp tender. Excellent served with rice. Serves 4 to 6.

Mrs. Mark J. Palmer (Martha)
Northvale, New Jersey

Kitchen Hint: Chill chicken before coating with flour. Coating sticks better.

Chicken with Riesling

1 (2 1/2- to 3-pound) frying chicken, cut up
1/2 teaspoon salt
1/4 teaspoon white pepper
3 tablespoons butter
1 small onion, studded with 4 whole cloves
1/2 bay leaf
1/2 cup chicken broth or stock
1 cup Riesling wine
1/2 cup half-and-half
1 1/2 tablespoons lemon juice

Season chicken with salt and pepper. In a skillet melt butter; brown chicken well. Add onion, bay leaf, chicken broth and wine. Cover; simmer until chicken is tender, about 30 minutes. Remove chicken to platter; keep warm. Discard bay leaf and onion from skillet; reduce liquid to about 1/2 cup. Gradually add half-and-half and lemon juice; heat through. Pour sauce over chicken. Serves 4 to 6.

Note: Excellent served with fine noodles drizzled with browned butter.

Mrs. Lynn Lees

Chicken with Shrimp

1 pound boned chicken breasts, cut into thin strips
2 tablespoons oil
2 cloves garlic
1 green pepper, cut into thin strips
1 (8-ounce) can bamboo shoots, drained
¾ cup chicken broth
1 teaspoon salt
2 tablespoons cornstarch
¼ cup molasses
2 tablespoons soy sauce
¼ cup vinegar
1 (8½-ounce) can pineapple slices, drained
1 pound medium raw shrimp, peeled

In a large skillet cook chicken in oil and garlic until partially done. Remove garlic; add green pepper, bamboo shoots, broth and salt. Cover; simmer 10 minutes. In a small bowl combine the cornstarch, molasses, soy sauce and vinegar. Pour over chicken; cook until mixture thickens. Add pineapple and shrimp; cook approximately 5 minutes or until shrimp is done. Serve over noodles or with rice and snow peas. Serves 6.

Mrs. Michael Porter (Paula)

Cheesy Chicken Olé

8 chicken breasts
½ pint sour cream
1 (10¾-ounce) can cream of chicken soup
1 (10¾-ounce) can cream of mushroom soup
1 cup drippings from chicken
½ cup milk
1 large onion, chopped
3 (3-ounce) cans chilies, whole
6 corn tortillas
1 pound sharp Cheddar cheese, shredded

Bake chicken breasts, covered with foil, at 350 degrees for 1 hour. Reserve drippings. When breasts have cooled, skin and bone chicken, leaving meat in fairly large pieces. In a medium bowl combine sour cream, soups, milk, onion and chicken drippings. Remove seeds from chilies. Cut tortillas into 1-inch strips. In a greased 3-quart casserole begin layering ⅓ of soup mixture, ½ of tortillas, ½ of the chicken, ½ of the chilies, ½ shredded cheese; repeat. Pour remaining soup mixture over casserole. Cover with foil; refrigerate for 24 hours. Bake at 300 degrees for 1½ to 2 hours. Serve with rice. Serves 8 to 10.

Jackie Ballert
San Diego, California

Baked Chicken and Rice

1¼ cups rice
½ cup chopped celery
½ cup chopped onion
2 tablespoons butter
2 large or 3 medium chicken breasts, cooked and cubed
1 (10-ounce) package frozen chopped broccoli, par-boiled and drained
1 (8-ounce) package pasteurized process cheese, cubed, or 1 (8-ounce) jar pasteurized process cheese spread
1 (10¾-ounce) can cream of mushroom soup
1 (10¾-ounce) can cream of chicken soup
1 (2.8-ounce) can French fried onions or 1 cup crunchy-type cereal

Cook rice according to package directions; set aside. In a small skillet sauté celery and onion in butter; set aside. In a large mixing bowl combine chicken, rice, broccoli, cheese and soups; add celery and onion mixture. Pour into a 13x9x2-inch baking dish. Bake at 350 degrees for 1 hour. Sprinkle with fried onions or cereal for last 10 minutes of baking. Serves 8.

Note: Dark chicken pieces can be used instead of white meat or use a mixture of both.

Mrs. Stanley H. Dawson (Ruth)

Chicken and Wild Rice

4 pounds chicken breasts
1 (6-ounce) box wild rice
3 medium onions, chopped
1 cup butter
3 tablespoons all-purpose flour
1½ (10¾-ounce) cans cream of mushroom soup
1 cup milk
1 (6-ounce) jar sliced mushrooms
¼ teaspoon salt
⅛ teaspoon pepper
1 pound sharp cheese, shredded

In a large pot cook chicken breasts in water until tender; cool. Remove skin and bone; tear into bite-size pieces. Cook rice as directed on package. In a skillet sauté onions in butter; stir in flour; add soup and milk, stirring constantly. Add mushrooms; season with salt and pepper. In a 13x9x2-inch casserole alternate layers of chicken, rice, sauce and cheese, ending with cheese. Bake at 350 degrees for 35 minutes or until bubbly. Serves 12 to 14.

Mrs. William Parmer (Jean Glasscock)

Chicken à la King on Noodle Squares

Chicken:

1/4 cup butter
1/4 cup all-purpose flour
1 teaspoon salt
1/4 teaspoon pepper
1 1/2 cups milk or chicken broth
1/2 cup whipping cream
2 cups diced, cooked chicken or turkey
1 (4-ounce) can mushrooms
2 tablespoons chopped pimento
1 cup peas, cooked and drained

In a large saucepan melt butter; add flour, salt and pepper to make a paste; stir constantly. Add milk or chicken broth and cream. Add chicken or turkey, mushrooms, pimento and peas. Cook until heated through. Serve on noodle squares.

Noodle Squares:

1 (6-ounce) package medium noodles
3 eggs, slightly beaten
1/3 cup cream
1 tablespoon butter, melted
1/2 teaspoon salt
Paprika

In a large pot cook noodles according to package directions; drain; rinse with cold water. In a medium bowl combine eggs, cream, butter and salt; add noodles. Pour mixture into greased 8x8-inch baking pan. Sprinkle with paprika. Bake at 350 degrees for 45 minutes. Cut into squares. Makes 4 servings.

Note: Good and easy company dish.

Mrs. Robert Hall (Barbara)

Chicken in Beer

2 pounds chicken breasts, skinned and boned
1/2 cup all-purpose flour
1/2 cup butter
1 pound fresh mushrooms, sliced
6 ounces beer
1/2 teaspoon salt
1/4 teaspoon pepper
1/8 teaspoon garlic powder

Freeze chicken slightly; slice in half crosswise, then into thirds lengthwise. Dredge chicken pieces in flour. In a medium skillet brown in 1/4 cup butter. Remove and set aside. Melt remaining butter; sauté mushrooms for 10 minutes, stirring occasionally. Add chicken pieces; mix. Add beer and seasonings, cover; cook over low heat for 5 minutes. Serves 4.

Mrs. John Vignola (Franca)
Dunedin, Florida

Baked Chicken Soufflé

- 8 or 9 slices white bread, crusts removed
- 4 cups diced, cooked chicken
- 8 ounces fresh mushrooms, sliced
- 1/4 cup butter
- 1 (8-ounce) can sliced water chestnuts, drained
- 1/2 cup mayonnaise
- 8 or 9 slices American cheese
- 4 eggs
- 2 cups milk
- 1 (10 3/4-ounce) can cream of mushroom soup
- 1 (10 3/4-ounce) can cream of chicken soup
- 2 cups coarse breadcrumbs, buttered

Line a buttered 13x9x2-inch baking pan with bread slices. Top with chicken. In a skillet cook mushrooms in butter for 5 minutes; spoon over chicken. Add water chestnuts. Dot with mayonnaise; add layer of cheese slices. In a medium bowl combine eggs and milk, beating slightly. Pour over chicken. In a small bowl combine soups; pour overall. Refrigerate overnight. Bake at 350 degrees for 1 1/2 hours. Add breadcrumbs the last 15 minutes. Serves 12 to 15.

Mrs. William B. Harris (Clara)
Dunedin, Florida

Szechwan Chicken with Peanuts

- 2 cups boneless chicken breast, cut into 1-inch cubes
- 3 tablespoons soy sauce
- 1 tablespoon cornstarch
- 3 whole dry red peppers (or more, if desired)
- 1 tablespoon sherry
- 1 teaspoon vinegar
- 2 teaspoons sugar
- 1 teaspoon sesame seed oil
- 1/4 cup peanut oil
- 1 teaspoon finely chopped ginger
- 2 whole scallions, chopped
- 1/2 cup skinless peanuts, roasted at 250 degrees for 30 minutes

In a medium bowl mix together chicken, 1 tablespoon soy sauce and cornstarch; marinate for 30 minutes. Wipe red peppers clean with a wet towel; remove tips and seeds; set aside. In a small bowl mix together remaining soy sauce, sherry, vinegar, sugar and sesame oil; set aside. In a wok or large skillet heat peanut oil; add red peppers and fry until black; discard peppers. Add chicken and stir-fry over high heat for 2 to 3 minutes; remove chicken. In same wok add ginger and scallions; stir-fry a few minutes. Add chicken and stir for one minute; pour in seasoning sauce. Stir and fry for another minute; add peanuts and mix well. Serve hot over rice. Serves 3 to 4.

Mrs. Jay Johnston
Princeton, New Jersey

Chicken Mexicana

1 (2½- to 3-pound) chicken, cut up
1 cup butter, melted
1 teaspoon salt
½ teaspoon paprika
1 teaspoon pepper
1 (6-ounce) package tortilla chips, crumbled
1 (4-ounce) can enchilada sauce
1 cup shredded Cheddar cheese
½ cup chopped green onion
1 (2¼-ounce) can pitted black olives, sliced

Arrange chicken in a single layer, skin side up in a 13x9x2-inch baking pan. Pour butter over chicken. Sprinkle with salt, paprika and pepper. Bake at 375 degrees for 1 hour. Sprinkle tortilla chips over chicken. Add enchilada sauce; sprinkle evenly with cheese, then onion and olives. Return to oven for 15 minutes, or until cheese is melted. Serves 6.

Mrs. Douglas Guilfoile (Paula L. Tiezzi)

Pineapple Chicken with Rice

1 medium chicken, cut up
½ teaspoon salt
4 tablespoons strained, fresh lime juice
4 tablespoons oil
¼ cup raisins
2 tablespoons rum
⅛ teaspoon hot pepper sauce
1 (16-ounce) can tomatoes, undrained and mashed
1 (15½-ounce) can pineapple chunks, undrained
¼ to ½ teaspoon salt
⅛ teaspoon pepper
1½ cups rice
1 orange, sliced

Rub chicken pieces with salt; marinate in lime juice 1 to 4 hours before cooking. In a large skillet heat oil; fry chicken quickly until browned. Reduce heat; cook additional 10 minutes. Add raisins, rum, hot sauce, tomatoes and pineapple. Season with salt and pepper. Cover; simmer 20 to 30 minutes. Cook rice according to package directions. Arrange rice on a large serving platter to form a bed. Place chicken on rice; pour sauce overall. Garnish with orange slices. Makes 5 servings.

Mrs. S. E. "Pete" Covey (Carol Daugherty)

Walnut Chicken

Chinese Style

3 chicken breasts
2½ tablespoons soy sauce
¾ cup condensed chicken broth
2 teaspoons cornstarch
3 tablespoons oil
1½ cups snow peas
1½ cups sliced fresh mushrooms
1 cup sliced celery
1 medium onion, cut into wedges
¼ cup green pepper strips
½ cup large walnut pieces

Remove skin and bone from chicken; cut into strips. Toss with 1½ teaspoons soy sauce; set aside. Combine broth with cornstarch and remaining soy sauce; mix well. Heat 1 tablespoon oil in a skillet or wok; add chicken. Cook until brown and tender. Remove chicken; add remaining oil to skillet; add vegetables; heat 5 minutes. Add broth mixture; bring to a boil. Return chicken; add walnuts. Heat 1 minute. Serves 4.

Mrs. Norval Dawson (Donna)
Lockport, Illinois

Baked Chicken Sandwiches

½ pound fresh mushrooms, sliced
¼ cup thinly sliced green onions and tops
¼ cup butter or margarine
3 tablespoons all-purpose flour
¾ cup milk
1 (10¾-ounce) can cream of mushroom soup
3 cups diced, cooked chicken
1 (2-ounce) jar chopped pimento (optional)
12 slices sandwich bread
3 eggs, slightly beaten
⅓ cup milk
2 cups or more lightly crushed potato chips
½ cup slivered almonds

In a small skillet sauté mushrooms and onions in butter. Stir in flour; blend in milk. Cook, stirring constantly, until thick and smooth. Add soup, chicken and pimento. Place 6 slices of bread in a 13x9x2-inch pan. Spread chicken mixture on top; cover with remaining bread. Cover with plastic wrap or foil; chill for at least 8 hours or overnight. Mix eggs and ⅓ cup milk. Cut sandwiches into halves; dip both sides in egg mixture and then in potato chips. Arrange on buttered cookie sheet. Bake at 350 degrees for 25 minutes. Top with almonds last 10 minutes of cooking time. Serves 6.

Mrs. William Harris (Clara)
Dunedin, Florida

Spiced Chicken

1 cup orange juice
1½ cups canned peaches
2 tablespoons brown sugar
2 tablespoons vinegar
1 teaspoon sweet basil
1 teaspoon nutmeg
1 clove garlic, minced
1 (2- to 3-pound) frying chicken, cut up
½ cup all-purpose flour
1 teaspoon salt
⅛ teaspoon pepper
Oil

In a medium saucepan combine orange juice and peaches with next five ingredients; cook slowly for 10 minutes. Dredge chicken pieces in flour seasoned with salt and pepper. In a skillet brown chicken in oil. Remove chicken; pour off oil, retaining the browned particles in skillet. Replace chicken; pour fruit sauce over chicken. Cover; simmer about 20 minutes. Serves 4.

Mrs. Lynn Lees

Chicken Crunch

4 cups cubed, cooked chicken
½ cup chicken broth
2 (10¾-ounce) cans cream of mushroom soup
1 medium onion, diced
1 cup diced celery
1 (4-ounce) can water chestnuts, drained and sliced
1 (5-ounce) can chow mein noodles

In a large mixing bowl combine chicken, broth, soup, onion, celery, water chestnuts and ½ can of chow mein noodles. Pour into buttered 13x9x2-inch baking dish; top with remaining noodles. Bake at 325 degrees for 40 minutes. Serves 6 to 8.

Variation: Leftover turkey may be substituted for the chicken.

Mrs. Jack Wilson (Mary Jane Brown)

Rye Stuffing Balls

Great with pork!

¼ cup finely chopped onions
3 tablespoons butter
1 egg, beaten
2 teaspoons Dijon mustard
½ teaspoon caraway seeds
6 cups cubed rye bread (about 9 slices)
¾ to 1 cup boiling water

In a medium skillet sauté onions in butter until tender. Combine with egg, mustard and caraway seeds. Add bread cubes and water to moisten. Lightly shape into balls. Bake at 325 degrees for 20 minutes. Serves 6.

Suncoast Seasons Committee

Lee Lum's Lemon Chicken

"A Unique Taste Treat!"

4 whole chicken breasts, skinned and boned
2 tablespoons soy sauce
¼ teaspoon sesame oil
1 teaspoon salt
1 tablespoon gin or vodka
3 egg whites, beaten until frothy
1 cup water chestnut flour or powder
1 pint peanut oil
¼ head iceburg lettuce, finely shredded

Place chicken in a large bowl. Combine soy sauce, sesame oil, salt and gin or vodka in small bowl; pour over chicken. Toss and let stand 30 minutes. Prepare sauce. Drain chicken and discard marinade; cut chicken into 2-inch pieces. Dip into egg whites, then flour. Add peanut oil to wok or large heavy skillet to depth of ½ inch; heat to moderate. Add chicken pieces, a few at a time. Brown on all sides; drain on paper towels. Place lettuce on an ovenproof platter; cover with chicken pieces and keep warm in oven at 200 degrees.

Sauce:

¾ cup sugar
½ cup white vinegar
1 cup chicken broth
½ teaspoon monosodium glutamate
Juice of 1 lemon
Finely grated rind of 1 lemon
1 tablespoon cornstarch
2 tablespoons water
6 small carrots, peeled and cut into julienne strips
1 green pepper, cut into julienne strips
6 scallions, cut into julienne strips
½ cup shredded canned pineapple
¾ ounce lemon extract

In a medium saucepan combine sugar, vinegar, broth, monosodium glutamate, lemon juice and lemon rind. In small bowl mix together cornstarch and water; add to saucepan. Bring to a boil, stirring often, until mixture thickens. Add carrots, green pepper, scallions and pineapple; remove from heat and stir in lemon extract. Set aside and reheat when ready to serve chicken; pour over chicken. Serves 4 to 6.

Mrs. Jay Johnston
Princeton, New Jersey

Filipino Chicken Gizzards

2 pounds chicken gizzards
2½ cups water
½ cup vinegar
½ cup soy sauce
⅓ cup oil
1 clove garlic, minced

Place all ingredients in a deep saucepan (do not use an iron skillet). Cover; simmer until all liquid is gone and gizzards are tender, about 2 hours. Serve with gravy over white or brown rice. Serves 4 to 6.

Gravy:

2 tablespoons butter
2 tablespoons all-purpose flour
2 cups chicken bouillon

Melt butter in a medium saucepan; add flour. Slowly add bouillon; stir and cook until thick and smooth. Add gizzards; heat and serve.

Mrs. Ronald Bliss (Judy)

Apricot Chicken

1 (8-ounce) jar apricot preserves
1 (1.37-ounce) envelope dry onion soup mix
1 (8-ounce) bottle Russian or garlic French dressing
2 chickens, cut into pieces

In a medium bowl mix preserves, soup mix and dressing until well blended. Spoon half of sauce into foil-lined 13x9x2-inch pan. Add chicken pieces, skin side down; spoon remaining sauce overall. Cover with aluminum foil. Bake at 350 degrees for 45 minutes. Remove foil; continue baking an additional 45 minutes. For a company dish add apricot halves last 15 minutes of baking. Serve with rice pilaf. Serves 6 to 8. *Excellent as an hors d'oeuvre using chicken wings.*

Hint: If using plain French dressing, add garlic powder to taste.

Microwave: Cut larger pieces of chicken in half; place in glass dish. Add sauce mixture. Cover; cook 28 minutes on high or until done. Rotate dish half way through cooking.

Mrs. Gregory H. Keuroghlian (Nora Ghazikian)
Mrs. David J. Kremske (Layle J. Feltman)
Mrs. Bill Ritchey (Carol Eddington)

Roast Duckling with Green Peppercorn Sauce

2 (5- to 6-pound) ducklings
3 tablespoons shallots
2 tablespoons green peppercorns in vinegar
1/4 cup brandy
1 cup white wine
3 tablespoons pan drippings
1 1/2 cups chicken or beef stock
1 teaspoon salt
2 teaspoons cornstarch
1 tablespoon cold water
1 tablespoon whipping cream

Roast ducklings at 350 degrees about 20 minutes per pound or until tender; keep warm. In a medium saucepan combine shallots, 1/2 peppercorns, brandy, wine and pan drippings. Bring to a boil; reduce to about 3/4 cup. Add stock, remaining peppercorns and salt; bring to a boil. Combine cornstarch and water; stir into sauce. Boil; reduce sauce to 1 cup. Stir in cream. Cut ducklings in half. Under broiler crisp skin and heat. Serve with peppercorn sauce. Serves 4.

Mrs. Michael Porter (Paula)

Rock Cornish Hens

4 Cornish hens, about 1 pound each
1/4 teaspoon salt
1/8 teaspoon pepper
1/3 cup margarine, melted
1/4 cup condensed consommé soup
1/4 cup light corn syrup

Season hens inside and out with salt and pepper. Place breast side up on rack in a roasting pan; brush well with margarine. Bake at 400 degrees for 1 hour or until tender. During last 15 minutes of baking, baste several times with mixture of consommé and syrup. Serves 4.

Note: Serve with rice cooked in remaining consommé.

Mrs. William Parmer (Jean Glasscock)

Horseradish Sauce

1/2 cup whipping cream
1 tablespoon prepared horseradish
1 teaspoon sugar
1/2 teaspoon lemon juice

In a small bowl whip cream; fold in horseradish, sugar and lemon juice. Chill for several hours. *Excellent with prime rib of beef!*

Mrs. Robert Hall (Barbara)

Apple Stuffing

1/4 cup chopped onions
1/4 cup chopped celery
2 tablespoons margarine
4 cups dried bread cubes
1 cup diced unpeeled apples
1/2 teaspoon poultry seasoning
1/2 teaspoon sage
1/4 teaspoon salt
1/8 teaspoon pepper
1 chicken bouillon cube
1/2 cup hot water

In a large saucepan cook onions and celery in margarine for 5 minutes, or until tender. Remove from heat. Add remaining ingredients except water and bouillon; mix well. Dissolve bouillon cube in water. Add to dry mixture and toss lightly. This yields enough for a 10-pound turkey. Delicious stuffing for pork chops and chicken as well. Serves 8 to 10.

Mrs. Robert Haverkos (Ginny)

Other Than Bread Stuffing

8 cups toasted corn flakes
3 cups coarse, stale bread cubes
2 medium onions, finely chopped
2 teaspoons sage
1 teaspoon salt
1/8 teaspoon pepper
3 tablespoons butter or margarine
2 1/4 cups boiling water

Combine first six ingredients in a large saucepan. Dot with butter. Add boiling water; mix well. Cover; let steam for 10 minutes. This yields enough for a 10-pound turkey. *Excellent change from bread stuffing.*

Mrs. Jack Wilson (Mary Jane Brown)

Smitane Sauce

1 tablespoon butter
1/4 cup finely chopped onions
1/4 to 1/2 cup dry white wine
1 tablespoon chopped parsley
1/4 teaspoon chervil
1/4 teaspoon tarragon
1 (3/4-ounce) envelope brown gravy mix
1 cup sour cream

In small saucepan melt butter; sauté onions until transparent. Add wine and herbs; cook until mixture is slightly reduced. Prepare gravy according to package instructions; add to saucepan and blend well. Cook until thick. Add sour cream; do not boil. Serve over pheasant, Cornish game hens or poultry and wild rice. Makes 2 1/2 cups.

Suncoast Seasons Committee

Turkey Casserole

2 cups cooked spaghetti (approximately 4 ounces, dry)
2 tablespoons chopped onion
1 tablespoon butter or margarine
1 (10¾-ounce) can cream of mushroom soup
½ cup water
2 tablespoons pimento
1 tablespoon chopped fresh parsley
1½ cups cubed, cooked turkey
½ cup (2-ounces) shredded sharp Cheddar cheese

In a large saucepan cook spaghetti according to package directions. Do not overcook. Set aside. In a medium pan cook onions in butter until tender; add mushroom soup, water, pimento and parsley. Arrange spaghetti in bottom of 1½-quart casserole; spread turkey on top. Pour the soup mixture over turkey; sprinkle with shredded cheese. Bake at 350 degrees for 45 minutes. Serves 4. *Great for leftover turkey!*

Mrs. Robert Haverkos (Ginny)

Mustard Sauce

4 ounces dry mustard
1 cup white or red wine vinegar
1 teaspoon turmeric
4 eggs
1 cup sugar

In small bowl mix mustard, vinegar and turmeric; set aside for about 6 hours. In a separate bowl mix together eggs and sugar with a whisk. Place all ingredients in top of double boiler; cook over rapidly boiling water, stirring often until thickened. Cover and cool mixture completely. Refrigerate. Makes 9 ounces. *Wonderful with ham!*

Mrs. Lynn Lees

Raisin Sauce

½ cup brown sugar
1 teaspoon dry mustard
2 tablespoons cornstarch
2 tablespoons vinegar
¼ teaspoon grated lemon peel
2 tablespoons lemon juice
1½ cups water
½ cup golden raisins

In a medium saucepan mix sugar, mustard and cornstarch. Slowly add the other ingredients, stirring well. Cook over low heat until thick, stirring constantly. Serve with baked ham. Makes 2 cups.

Note: May be refrigerated and reheated.

Mrs. Gregory H. Keuroghlian (Nora Ghazikian)

Seafood

Clams di Zuppa

Italian Clam Soup

3 dozen cherrystone clams
2 tablespoons olive oil
2 cloves garlic, minced
1 cup chopped onions
2 (1 pound, 12-ounce) cans crushed, peeled tomatoes
1/2 cup dry white wine
1 teaspoon oregano
1/2 teaspoon crushed red pepper
1/4 teaspoon salt
1/2 teaspoon basil leaves
2 tablespoons chopped parsley
Clam broth, reserved (approximately 3 cups)

Scrub clams well; rinse about six times in water to remove sand. Place in large kettle in about 2 inches of water; cover kettle and steam clams until open. Discard any clams which do not open. Remove clams; set aside. Strain clam liquid; reserve. In a large saucepan sauté garlic and onions in oil until transparent; add remaining ingredients. Cook about 20 minutes; add broth; heat through. Add steamed clams; stir gently so sauce covers and gets into shells, heat thoroughly. Serve in bowls with crusty Italian or French bread. *Mangia! Enjoy! Enjoy!* Serves 4 to 6 entrée, 6 to 8 appetizer.

Hint: If you have leftover sauce, serve with linguini.

Mrs. Anthony S. Brancato (Georgine E. Palmer)

Jambalaya

New Orleans favorite

1 pound medium shrimp, cleaned
1/2 cup white wine
1/2 cup water
1/4 cup fat
1 large onion, sliced
1/2 cup sausage, cooked and broken into pieces
1 (26-ounce) can tomatoes
1 bay leaf
1 1/2 teaspoons salt
1/4 teaspoon pepper
1/8 teaspoon thyme
1 1/2 cups rice

Marinate shrimp in wine and water for 1 hour, turning occasionally. Sauté onions in fat until lightly browned; add cooked sausage meat and shrimp including marinade. Simmer 2 or 3 minutes; transfer to a 3-quart heavy pot. Add tomatoes, seasonings and rice. Cover pot tightly; bring just to a boil; simmer gently 20 minutes. Serves 6 to 8.

Mrs. Michael Porter (Paula)

Shrimp and Scallop Vol-au-Vent

Excellent dish for entertaining

Stock:

½ pound fresh mushrooms or 1 (3¼-ounce) can of mushrooms, drained
½ cup vinegar
2 tablespoons chopped parsley
1 clove garlic, minced
2 tablespoons olive oil
2 cups dry white wine
1 medium onion, sliced
1 bouquet garni (Wrap 2 tablespoons parsley, 1 teaspoon thyme and 1 bay leaf in cheese cloth; secure.)
1 teaspoon salt
½ teaspoon pepper
1 chicken bouillon cube
1 pound medium shrimp, peeled and deveined
1 pound scallops

Clean mushrooms; soak in vinegar for 15 to 30 minutes; pat dry; slice thin. In a skillet sauté mushrooms, parsley and garlic in olive oil over high heat for approximately 3 minutes, stirring frequently to blend ingredients. (Do not sauté canned mushrooms.) Place mushrooms and the next 6 ingredients in a large saucepan. Bring to a boil; reduce heat to medium and continue to cook for 15 minutes allowing mixture to thicken slightly. (Add a little more wine if mixture thickens too much.) Add cleaned shrimp and scallops; bring mixture to a boil; cook until shrimp and scallops are tender, 2 to 3 minutes. Do *not* overcook. Remove from stove; strain the stock; set aside.

Parisienne Sauce:

3 tablespoons all-purpose flour
3 tablespoons butter
1 cup whipping cream

In a medium saucepan blend flour with butter over medium heat. Add stock slowly to white sauce stirring constantly. Add cream; blend well. Add shrimp, scallops, onion and mushrooms; heat until warm, but do *not* boil. Serve over pastry shells or rice. Serves 6 to 8.

Variation: 4 cups cooked, cubed chicken and 1 cup diced ham may be substituted for shrimp and scallops for an interesting taste.

Jacqueline Crowne
Sarasota, Florida

H. H. Shrimp

For "His" and "Hers"

3 tablespoons oil
2 tablespoons butter
2 pounds shrimp in shell
1 ounce lemon juice
2 ounces dry vermouth

In an electric skillet place oil and butter; set temperature at 350 degrees. Add shrimp; cook until pink. Add lemon juice and vermouth; cover and cook at highest temperature for 1 minute. Serve at once with horseradish sauce or cocktail sauce, if desired. Serves 4.

Note: Takes 5 minutes to prepare.

Nan J. Moffatt

Fish and Shrimp

1 to 1½ pounds fresh or frozen flounder
1 (10¾-ounce) can cream of shrimp soup
¼ cup unsalted cracker crumbs
½ cup butter, softened

Place fish in a 13x9x2-inch glass baking dish; pour soup over fish. Bake at 350 degrees for 45 minutes. Mix butter and cracker crumbs; sprinkle over top. Bake in oven additional 15 minutes. Serves 6.

Mrs. Selwyn Chalker (Jane)

Kitchen Hint: Thaw frozen fish in milk for a good flavor.

Shrimp and Wild Rice

1 (6-ounce) package of wild rice mix (omit herb packet)
½ green pepper, chopped
½ onion, chopped
3 tablespoons butter, melted
1 tablespoon lemon juice
½ teaspoon Worcestershire sauce
1 teaspoon salt
¼ teaspoon pepper
1 (3¼-ounce) can mushrooms with liquid
1 (8-ounce) can sliced water chestnuts, drained
1½ pounds fresh or frozen shrimp

Prepare rice according to package directions. In a skillet sauté pepper and onion in melted butter. Combine all ingredients in a greased 2½-quart casserole. Bake at 375 degrees for 1 hour. Serves 4 to 6.

Mrs. Joseph Holder (Martha)

Shrimp Mozambique

An exotic shrimp for the grill

1 cup peanut oil
1 teaspoon salt
½ to 1 teaspoon peppercorns
3 cloves garlic, minced
2 pounds medium shrimp, cleaned, butterflied and dried

In a 1½- or 2-quart glass dish place peanut oil, salt, peppercorns, garlic and shrimp. Cover and marinate for 2 hours. Drain well. Place heavy foil over grill; poke holes in foil; add shrimp. Cook on grill for about 10 minutes, stirring shrimp often. Serves 4 to 6.

Note: May also be prepared in an electric skillet at medium heat. Leave a little of the marinade on the shrimp.

Mrs. Ronald Bliss (Judy)

Shrimp in Sauce

1 cup mayonnaise
3 teaspoons horseradish mustard
1 tablespoon chopped capers
1 tablespoon sweet relish
1 tablespoon chopped parsley
1 tablespoon chopped chives
1 tablespoon tarragon vinegar
½ teaspoon salt
¼ teaspoon pepper
3 pounds shrimp, cleaned, cooked and chilled

In large bowl mix all ingredients except shrimp until well blended; add shrimp. Blend thoroughly. Refrigerate at least 12 hours. Serves 6 to 8.

Mrs. J. Douglas Fresh (Jane Nolan)

Capers—the flower-buds of a Mediterranean caper bush; they are pickled and used for flavoring or garnish.

"Boiled" Shrimp

2 pounds raw, headless, unpeeled shrimp, fresh or frozen
5 cups water
¼ cup salt

Thaw shrimp, if frozen. Add salt to water and bring to boil; add shrimp and reduce heat. Cover and simmer 3 to 5 minutes, depending on size of shrimp; drain. Rinse shrimp under cold running water. Makes 2 pounds.

Note: If shrimp has been peeled, reduce salt to 2 tablespoons and cooking time to 2 to 3 minutes. Serve with favorite sauce and lemon wedges.

Suncoast Seasons Committee

Shrimp Curry and Green Rice

½ cup diced celery
½ cup diced green pepper
1 tablespoon butter
1 (10¾-ounce) can cream of shrimp soup
½ cup boiling water
1 pound shrimp, cleaned and cooked
1½ teaspoons curry powder
1½ teaspoons salt
⅛ teaspoon pepper
2 tablespoons sugar
½ cup ripe olives, sliced

In medium skillet sauté celery and green pepper in butter until tender. Add soup and water; bring to a boil. Add shrimp and seasonings. Heat through stirring continuously. Do not over cook. Just before serving add ripe olives. Serve with hot green rice, topped with toasted almonds. Serves 4.

Green Rice:

2 cups rice
⅔ cup chopped green pepper
1 cup chopped green onions and tops
⅓ cup minced fresh parsley
¼ cup oil
1½ tablespoons Worcestershire sauce
1 teaspoon salt
¼ teaspoon cayenne pepper
4 cups chicken or beef stock

Combine all ingredients in a 2-quart casserole with a tight fitting lid. Bake at 350 degrees without stirring for 45 minutes. Before serving, remove cover and toss with a fork. Makes 4 cups.

Note: Bouillon made from 6 cubes dissolved in 4 cups water may be used in place of stock.

Mrs. Dean N. McFarland (Donna VanEwyk)

Artichokes with Baked Shrimp

2 cups cooked rice
1 cup sliced black olives
2 cups boiled, shelled and deveined shrimp
1 (16-ounce) jar tomato sauce with mushrooms
1 (10-ounce) package frozen artichoke hearts, cooked and drained
1 teaspoon onion salt
¼ cup minced parsley
1 cup grated Cheddar cheese

In a large bowl combine all ingredients except cheese. Pour into a 2-quart casserole. Sprinkle cheese on top; bake at 350 degrees for 30 minutes. Serves 4.

Mrs. Douglas Guilfoile (Paula L. Tiezzi)

Shrimp Stroganoff

3 pounds medium-size raw shrimp, shelled and deveined
½ cup butter or margarine
½ pound fresh mushrooms, sliced
⅔ cup chopped onion
1 clove garlic, minced
2 tablespoons all-purpose flour
1 cup chicken broth or consommé
1 tablespoon tomato paste
¾ teaspoon Worcestershire sauce
1 tablespoon chopped fresh dill or 1 teaspoon dried dill weed
1½ teaspoons salt
1 cup sour cream
Cooked rice or noodles

Sauté shrimp in 6 tablespoons of butter or margarine in skillet 4 to 5 minutes. Remove shrimp and reserve. Add remaining 2 tablespoons butter or margarine, mushrooms, onion, and garlic; cook 5 minutes. Add flour; mix well. Stir in chicken broth or consommé, tomato paste, Worcestershire sauce, dill and salt. Simmer 2 minutes. Add sour cream; mix well. Add shrimp. Heat but do not boil. Serve on hot cooked rice or noodles. Serves 6.

Mrs. Lynn Lees

Shrimp in Black Bean Sauce

1 pound fresh raw shrimp, shelled and cleaned
2 tablespoons fermented salted black beans
2 tablespoons sherry
4 whole scallions, minced
2 cloves garlic, minced (or less, as desired)
12 thin slices fresh ginger, minced
2 cups peanut oil
½ teaspoon sugar

In a medium bowl cover shrimp with cold water. In small bowl combine black beans with 1 tablespoon sherry; crush lightly with spoon. Set scallions, garlic and ginger aside in separate bowls. In wok or large skillet heat oil until hot and almost smoking; add shrimp and fry over high heat, stirring often, for 3 minutes. Drain in a sieve-lined bowl, reserving 3 tablespoons of the oil. Add beans to the pan; cook over high heat about 10 seconds. Add garlic and ginger; cook about 5 seconds, stirring. Add sugar and remaining sherry and cook, stirring, 10 seconds. Return shrimp and drippings to pan; add scallions and toss quickly. Serve hot with rice. Serves 4.

Mrs. Jay Johnston
Princeton, New Jersey

Fermented salted black beans are available at any oriental grocery.

Spicy Shrimp in Shells

2 pounds large fresh shrimp in shells
1 teaspoon salt
2 teaspoons pickling spice
3 bay leaves
½ teaspoon cracked pepper
½ cup salad oil
¼ cup water
¼ cup vinegar

Wash shrimp in cold water; drain on paper towels. Place shrimp and remaining ingredients in a saucepan with tight fitting lid. Bring to boil; then simmer for 2 to 3 minutes. Place in a serving bowl that will keep them warm; and let your guests do the rest. Serves 4.

Note: Delicious and messy and great fun to eat! Great for casual gathering such as a football party or any informal event. Perfect for a large crowd if you want to multiply the recipe.

Mrs. J. Wallace Lee (Ida)

Kitchen Hint: To freshen guests fingers after eating seafood, offer individual finger bowls containing warm water and lemon wedge.

New England Clam Boil
Florida Style

6 small whole onions, tied in cheese cloth
4 medium whole potatoes, washed
4 small whole sweet potatoes, washed
1 pound chorizo (Spanish sausage) tied in cheese cloth or 1 pound pork and 1 pound hot dogs
4 ears corn
2 (8-ounce) bottles clam juice
1 (8-ounce) bottle water
2 quarts clams (Atlantic Steamers) in can, drained and tied in cheese cloth

In large steamer place ingredients in order given. Cook on high for 1 minute; then lower heat and steam until potatoes are cooked approximately 1 hour (all else will be done). Cook sweet corn in separate pot. When all is cooked, serve each item in separate bowls or place corn on top of other ingredients to steam. Serves 4.

Note: Lobster can be added last ½ hour of cooking time.

Mrs. Philip Chabot (Eva)
Royal Palm Beach, Florida

Gulf Shrimp Divine

Simply Divine!!

2/3 cup olive oil (no substitute)
1/2 cup lemon juice
1/2 teaspoon salt
1/8 teaspoon pepper
2 pounds fresh shrimp, shelled and deveined
3 tablespoons butter (no substitute)
1 clove garlic, crushed
1 cup blanched slivered almonds
Dash of hot pepper sauce
1/2 cup dry vermouth

Make marinade of olive oil, lemon juice and seasonings. Marinate shrimp for at least 2 hours. Melt butter in large skillet; add garlic and shrimp. Reserve marinade. Stir-fry shrimp over medium heat until pink. Discard garlic; remove shrimp to a hot platter. Sauté slivered almonds in butter until brown; add marinade, hot pepper sauce and vermouth. When well blended, pour sauce over shrimp. Serve over saffron rice mixed with chopped chives or finely chopped green onions. Serves 6 to 8.

Mrs. Paul J. Donahue (Sigrid)
Dunedin, Florida

Beered Shrimp and Sauce

24 ounces beer
1 teaspoon thyme
1 tablespoon dry mustard
2 bay leaves
1 tablespoon chopped chives
1 tablespoon salt
2 cloves garlic, minced
2 tablespoons chopped parsley
1/2 teaspoon ground pepper
3 pounds fresh headless shrimp

Place all ingredients except shrimp into a large saucepan; bring to boil. Add shrimp, return to boiling; simmer for 5 minutes; drain. Serve with shrimp sauce. Serves 4.

Sauce:

4 tablespoons lemon juice
2 tablespoons chopped scallions
2 tablespoons chopped parsley
2 teaspoons salt
1/2 cup butter

Mix all ingredients in a small saucepan; cook over low heat until butter melts.

Mrs. David Foster (Elaine)
Dunedin, Florida

Chinese Butterfly Shrimp

1 pound medium shrimp
1/8 teaspoon salt
1 teaspoon baking soda

Shell shrimp, leaving on the tails. Butterfly the shrimp by cutting down the back to flatten; wash and devein. Pat dry with paper towels. Place in a medium bowl; add salt and baking soda. Let stand 30 minutes. Rinse shrimp in cold water; drain well and dry again with paper towels.

Batter:

1 cup all-purpose flour
1 cup water
1/2 teaspoon salt
2 teaspoons baking powder
1 quart peanut oil or vegetable oil

Place flour in a medium bowl. Stir in water; blend until smooth. Add salt and baking powder and stir. Heat oil in wok, Dutch oven or deep fryer. Oil should be very hot (almost smoking). Dip shrimp in batter, one at a time; drop them in oil. Fry until golden brown and crisp; drain on paper towels. Serve hot with sauce.

Dipping Sauce:

1 tablespoon oil
2 tablespoons ketchup
1 teaspoon tomato paste
1 cup, plus 3 tablespoons, water
1 tablespoon soy sauce
3 tablespoons white vinegar
1/8 teaspoon salt, or to taste
1/4 cup sugar
1 1/2 tablespoons cornstarch

Place the oil, ketchup and tomato paste in a small saucepan and cook 1 minute, stirring. Stir in 1 cup water; add soy sauce, vinegar, salt and sugar. In small bowl blend cornstarch with 3 tablespoons water; stir in sauce. Cook until thickened. Serve warm. Serves 3 to 4.

Mrs. Jay Johnston
Princeton, New Jersey

Kitchen Hint: Baking soda sprinkled over uncooked shrimp and then washed off before cooking makes shrimp crisp.

Shrimp Creole

1/2 cup chopped onions
1 clove garlic, minced
1 tablespoon butter or margarine
1 tablespoon all-purpose flour
6 large tomatoes, peeled and chopped
1/2 cup chopped celery
1 1/2 teaspoons salt
1/4 teaspoon thyme
2 bay leaves
1/8 teaspoon cayenne pepper, or to taste
1/4 teaspoon hot pepper sauce, or to taste
2 pounds shrimp, cleaned and deveined

In a large skillet sauté onions and garlic in butter. Blend in flour. Add all other ingredients except shrimp; simmer 10 minutes. Add shrimp; simmer another 5 minutes or until shrimp are done. Serve over rice. Serves 6.

Mrs. Donald Behm (Marion)
Mrs. J. Douglas Fresh (Jane Nolan)

Scallops in a Shell

1 pound fresh sea scallops
1/2 teaspoon salt
1/2 teaspoon pepper
2 tablespoons chopped parsley
1/4 to 1/2 cup fine cracker crumbs
6 tablespoons butter
6 teaspoons cream

Wash; dry and cut scallops into 1/2-inch pieces; place in six baking shells. Sprinkle with salt, pepper and parsley. Cover with cracker crumbs; add 1 tablespoon butter and 1 teaspoon cream to each shell. Bake at 400 degrees until browned. Serves 4 for entrée and 6 for appetizer.

Mrs. R. C. Rilott (Melba)
Dunedin, Florida

Scallops Amandine

2 pounds fresh or frozen bay scallops
1/4 teaspoon salt
1/8 teaspoon pepper
1/2 cup all-purpose flour
1/2 cup slivered almonds
1/2 cup butter or margarine
2 tablespoons chopped parsley

Thaw scallops if frozen; rinse in cold water. Sprinkle scallops with salt and pepper; roll in flour. In large skillet fry almonds in butter until lightly browned; remove almonds. Add scallops and continue frying. When brown on one side, carefully turn over. (Cooking time: approximately 4 minutes.) Add parsley and almonds; serve immediately. Serves 6.

Mrs. Lynn Lees

Shrimp Gumbo

10 cups water
4 to 5 pounds shrimp
1 (3-ounce) package crab boil
1/4 teaspoon cayenne pepper
1/4 cup butter
2 cups finely chopped celery
2 medium onions, finely chopped
1 large bell pepper, finely chopped
4 cloves garlic, minced
1 tablespoon salt
1/2 teaspoon ground thyme
4 bay leaves
1 to 1 1/2 pounds okra, sliced 1/2-inch thick
1 (28-ounce) can whole, peeled tomatoes, quartered
2 teaspoons filé powder
5 tablespoons oil
5 tablespoons flour
2 pints oysters (use liquid from 1 pint; drain other)

Put water into a very large kettle; add shrimp, crab boil and cayenne pepper. Cook until shrimp turns a pink color, about 5 to 6 minutes. *Do not overcook!* Remove shrimp and rinse with cold water, saving liquid for later use. Peel shrimp; set aside. Sauté celery in butter in a medium skillet over medium heat; add onion, pepper and garlic; cook until tender. While the vegetables are cooking, return 8 cups of the reserved liquid to the kettle; add salt, thyme, bay leaves, okra, tomatoes and gumbo filé. Add the sautéed vegetables; bring to a boil. In skillet brown flour in oil and add to the kettle; cook for 15 minutes. Add reserved oyster liquid, drained oysters, undrained oysters and shrimp; bring to a boil and cook slowly for 30 minutes, stirring occasionally. Serve over cooked rice. Serves 8 to 10.

Mrs. Ray Windham (Ann)
Spring Hill, Florida

Maryland Crab Cakes

2 pounds fresh blue crab, boiled and cleaned or 2 cups crabmeat
2 to 3 slices of white bread with crust
Water to soak bread
1 tablespoon dry mustard
3/4 tablespoon salt
1/2 teaspoon pepper
1 tablespoon mayonnaise
1 egg, well beaten
Shortening for frying

To each pound of crabmeat use one slice bread with crust. Soak bread in water; squeeze dry and break into small pieces. Break up crabmeat into large lumps and add all ingredients; mix well. Form mixture into round cakes. In a 10-inch skillet carefully sauté cakes until lightly browned. Can also be deep-fried. Serves 6.

Mrs. J. Douglas Fresh (Jane Nolan)

Different Crab Imperial

1 cup mayonnaise
1/4 cup chopped green pepper
1/4 cup finely chopped onion
1/2 teaspoon dry mustard
2 tablespoons lemon juice
1/2 teaspoon salt
1/8 teaspoon pepper
2 cups cooked fresh, thawed frozen, or drained canned crabmeat
2 hard-cooked eggs, chopped
4 medium-sized avocados
1 tablespoon lemon juice
1 cup soft breadcrumbs
2 tablespoons melted butter

In a large bowl combine mayonnaise, green pepper, onion, dry mustard, lemon juice, salt and pepper; mix in crabmeat and eggs. Cut avocados in half; remove seed. Cut a thin slice off round side so it will rest on plate. Brush inside with lemon juice. Spoon crabmeat mixture into avocados. In a small bowl combine breadcrumbs and melted butter; sprinkle over crabmeat. Bake at 350 degrees for 10 to 15 minutes. Serves 8.

Mrs. Harvey Heimann (Jean)

Cheese and Crab Bake

8 slices bread
1/2 cup butter, softened
2 (4 1/2-ounce) cans crabmeat
1 tablespoon grated onion
1/4 cup chopped celery
2 tablespoons lemon juice
1/2 teaspoon Worcestershire sauce
1 (10 3/4-ounce) can cream of mushroom soup
2 eggs
1 cup milk
4 slices American cheese

Trim crust from bread and butter on both sides. Place four slices in greased 8-inch square baking dish. Combine crabmeat, onion, celery, lemon juice, Worcestershire sauce and mushroom soup in medium-sized bowl. Spoon mixture over bread. Beat eggs and milk together; pour over bread and crab mixture. Top with cheese slices and remaining bread. Cover dish and refrigerate for 12 hours. Bake at 350 degrees for 1 hour or until golden brown. Serves 4 to 6.

Note: Shrimp or tuna may be substituted for crabmeat.

Mrs. Michael Porter (Paula)

Soft Shell Blue Crab

A Suncoast favorite!

8 live soft shell crabs
1 cup all-purpose flour
1 teaspoon salt
¼ teaspoon pepper
⅛ teaspoon paprika (optional)
Oil for frying

Clean soft shell crabs by first cutting off the eyes with kitchen shears across face of the crab. Remove the mouth. Lift the points of crab and remove the sandbags and gills. Turn crab over and remove apron at lower part of shell. Wash thoroughly; pat dry. Mix flour, salt and pepper together. Dip crab in seasoned flour; dust off excess. Fry in oil 3 to 5 minutes or until golden brown, turning once. Drain on paper towels. Serve with lemon wedges and favorite seafood sauce. Serves 4.

Suncoast Seasons Committee

Soft shell crabs are crabs that have just molted and are not yet hard. The crabs harden within several days after shedding—hence, the name "shedders" in some parts of the country.

Deviled Crab

3 to 4 tablespoons butter, melted
¼ teaspoon salt
¼ teaspoon cayenne pepper
¼ teaspoon celery seed
1 pound flaked crabmeat
1 tablespoon mustard
1 teaspoon dry mustard
3½ tablespoons mayonnaise
2 tablespoons chopped parsley
3¼ tablespoons chopped green pepper
½ teaspoon lemon juice
2 tablespoons butter
Paprika

Preheat oven to 350 degrees. In a large bowl blend butter, salt, cayenne pepper and celery seed. Add crabmeat, mustard, dry mustard, mayonnaise, parsley, green pepper and lemon juice; mix. Place in sterilized crab shells or shallow casserole. Top with butter; sprinkle with paprika. Bake at 350 degrees for 20 to 30 minutes or until top is brown. Serves 4.

Clara MacWherter
Dunedin, Florida

Crabmeat Open Sandwiches

- 2 (6½-ounce) cans white crabmeat
- 3 tablespoons butter
- 8 imported Holland golden toasts
- 2 large tomatoes, cut into ¼-inch slices
- 2 (3-ounce) packages cream cheese
- 2 tablespoons mayonnaise
- 2 tablespoons ketchup or chili sauce
- 1 teaspoon Worcestershire sauce
- ⅛ teaspoon salt
- ½ pound sharp Cheddar cheese, shredded

Butter toasts; cover with tomato slice and put on a cookie sheet. In a small bowl combine cream cheese, mayonnaise, ketchup, Worcestershire sauce and salt; add crabmeat. Spread equal amounts on tomato-covered toasts. Cover with cheese. Bake at 350 degrees for 30 to 35 minutes. Serves 8.

Mrs. Robert E. Hoerter (Lynne)
Winter Park, Florida

Deviled Shell Fish

- ¼ cup green pepper, finely chopped
- ¼ cup onion, finely chopped
- ¼ cup celery, finely chopped
- 1 teaspoon Worcestershire sauce
- ½ teaspoon salt
- 1 cup chopped, cooked shrimp
- 1 cup crabmeat or 1 (7-ounce) can
- 2 cups herb-seasoned stuffing, crushed
- 1 cup mayonnaise

In medium bowl stir together all ingredients until blended. Spoon into a 1-quart casserole or 8 ovenproof shells. Bake at 350 degrees for 30 minutes or until browned. Serves 4.

Note: These can be made up ahead of time, wrapped in clear plastic-wrap and frozen. Thaw before baking.

Mrs. R. C. Rilott (Melba)
Dunedin, Florida

Coquilles St. Jacques

This is a Classic

1 pound bay scallops
2 tablespoons minced onion
1 tablespoon butter or margarine
1½ cups chopped fresh mushrooms
1 tablespoon lemon juice
¾ teaspoon salt
⅛ teaspoon marjoram
⅛ teaspoon paprika
¾ cup dry sherry
⅓ cup butter or margarine
¼ cup all-purpose flour
1 cup half and half cream
2 teaspoons snipped parsley
1 tablespoon butter or margarine
⅓ cup fine dry breadcrumbs

Wash scallops and drain. In medium saucepan cook and stir onions in butter until onion is tender. Add scallops, mushrooms, lemon juice, salt, marjoram, paprika and sherry; simmer uncovered exactly 2 minutes. Drain liquid from scallop mixture; set aside. In medium saucepan over low heat melt ⅓ cup butter; blend in flour; cook over low heat stirring until mixture is smooth and bubbly. Remove from heat; stir in reserved liquid and cream. Heat to boiling, stirring constantly for 1 minute; add parsley. Pour sauce over scallops. Spoon into 6 individual ½-cup baking shells or dishes. Melt 1 tablespoon butter in small skillet; add breadcrumbs, stirring until brown. Place shells on baking sheet. Sprinkle with crumbs. Bake 5 to 7 minutes or until bubbly and golden brown. Serve with herbed rice. Serves 6.

Helen S. Glass

Crab Casserole

2 tablespoons butter
2 tablespoons all-purpose flour
¼ teaspoon salt
¼ teaspoon white pepper
1 cup milk
2 egg yolks, beaten
1 teaspoon chopped chives or onions
1 teaspoon dry mustard
1 teaspoon Worcestershire sauce
1 cup crabmeat
¼ cup buttered breadcrumbs

Melt butter in top part of double boiler; add flour, salt, and pepper; cook until bubbly. Slowly add milk; stir briskly. Cook over hot water until thick and smooth, stirring occasionally. Continue cooking for about 5 minutes. Add egg yolks, then onions, mustard and Worcestershire sauce; stir in crabmeat. Pour mixture into 1-quart casserole dish; cover with buttered bread crumbs. Bake at 400 degrees for 45 minutes. Serves 2.

Mrs. Dean N. McFarland (Donna VanEwyk)

Suncoast Scallops

1/4 cup butter or margarine, melted
1 pound fresh bay scallops
1/3 cup fine soft breadcrumbs
1/8 teaspoon garlic salt
1/8 teaspoon dry mustard
1/8 teaspoon paprika
2 tablespoons dry sherry
Lemon wedges for garnish

Pour 2 tablespoons of butter into a shallow baking pan; arrange scallops in single layer. Combine breadcrumbs, garlic salt, mustard, paprika and remaining butter; sprinkle over scallops. Broil 4 inches from heat until lightly browned, 6 to 8 minutes. Drizzle sherry over scallops; serve hot with lemon wedges. Serves 6 to 8.

Note: Use as an appetizer or double the recipe for an entrée.

Suncoast Seasons Committee

Seafood en Coquilles

1 cup water
2 teaspoons lemon juice
1/2 cup butter or margarine, divided
1/2 pound mushrooms, sliced
1 cup dry white wine
1 small onion, sliced
1/2 bay leaf
6 sprigs parsley
1 teaspoon salt
1 (8-ounce) package frozen scallops
1 cup flaked crabmeat
1 cup cooked lobster, diced
1 cup peeled, deveined shrimp, cooked
1/4 cup all-purpose flour
1/8 teaspoon freshly ground pepper
6 tablespoons Gruyére cheese
1 cup breadcrumbs

In a medium saucepan combine water, lemon juice and 2 tablespoons butter; add mushrooms, simmer 10 minutes. Drain liquid from mushrooms; set mushrooms and liquid aside. Stir next 5 ingredients together in pan; bring to boil, add scallops; simmer 10 minutes. Remove onion, bay leaf and parsley; discard. Add liquid from scallops to mushroom liquid. Combine scallops, crab, lobster and shrimp. Measure 2 cups liquid, adding water if necessary. Melt 1/4 cup butter in top of double boiler. Blend in flour and pepper. Slowly stir in 2 cups liquid. Cook over low heat, stirring constantly, until thick and smooth. Add cheese; place over hot water and cook until melted, about 15 minutes. Stir in shell fish and mushrooms in sauce. Serves 10 to 12.

Hint: Fill ramekins; sprinkle with crumbs; dot with butter. Brown under broiler.

Mrs. William S. Sharpe (Wanda)

Lobster Thermidor

Magnificent for entertaining!

4 (1½-pound) live lobsters
¾ cup butter
1 cup chopped mushrooms
⅛ teaspoon salt, or to taste
⅛ teaspoon freshly ground black pepper
½ cup soft breadcrumbs
1 tablespoon Worcestershire sauce
1½ teaspoons liquid seasoning
⅛ teaspoon hot pepper sauce, or to taste
4 teaspoons chopped parsley
4 teaspoons chopped pimento
¾ cup sherry
¼ cup cognac
2 cups whipping cream
4 egg yolks
½ cup grated Parmesan cheese
Paprika, for garnish

Plunge the lobster, head first, into a large pot of boiling salted water. Cover the pot; return to boil; boil 12 to 15 minutes for a 1½ to 2-pound lobster. When done, remove from water with tongs and place lobster on its back. Slit the undershell lengthwise with a sharp knife or scissors. Remove and discard the dark vein, the sac near the head and spongy tissue, but save the green liver and coral (roe) if any. Twist off claws, reserving the small claws for garnish. Remove the meat from the bodies and cut into small pieces. Crack the large claws; remove the meat and cube. Reserve shells. Preheat oven to 350 degrees. Heat ½ cup of the butter; add mushrooms and cook 3 minutes. Season with salt and pepper. Add the lobster meat, crumbs, seasonings, sherry, cognac, cream and egg yolks. Mix well. Fill the lobster shells with the mixture; sprinkle with cheese; dot with the remaining butter; sprinkle with paprika. Place in shallow pan; bake 15 minutes. Garnish and serve immediately. Serves 4.

Suncoast Seasons Committee

Lobster Tails in Marinara Sauce

¼ cup olive oil
4 to 8 lobster tails
1 small onion, minced
2 cloves garlic, crushed
½ green pepper, sliced
1 (6-ounce) can tomato paste
1 (10- to 12-ounce) can whole tomatoes
½ teaspoon salt
⅛ teaspoon pepper

Sauté lobster tails, onion, garlic, and pepper in olive oil until lobster changes to orange color. Add paste and tomatoes; add seasonings. Cook over low heat for one hour. Serve over linguini prepared al dente. Serves 6 to 8.

Mrs. Giordano Tiezzi (Ida)
Meriden, Connecticut

Lobster in Sherry Sauce

4 tablespoons butter
4 tablespoons all-purpose flour
2 cups milk
½ teaspoon salt
¼ teaspoon white pepper
1 (4½- to 5-ounce) can lobster or crab
¼ cup dry sherry or to taste

In a skillet melt butter over low heat; add flour and stir until well blended. Add milk stirring continually until sauce thickens; add salt and pepper. Cook until done, about 5 minutes. Stir lobster into sauce; add sherry. Serves 4 to 6.

Note: Serve over thin noodles or toast points.

Mrs. Giordano Tiezzi (Ida)
Meriden, Connecticut

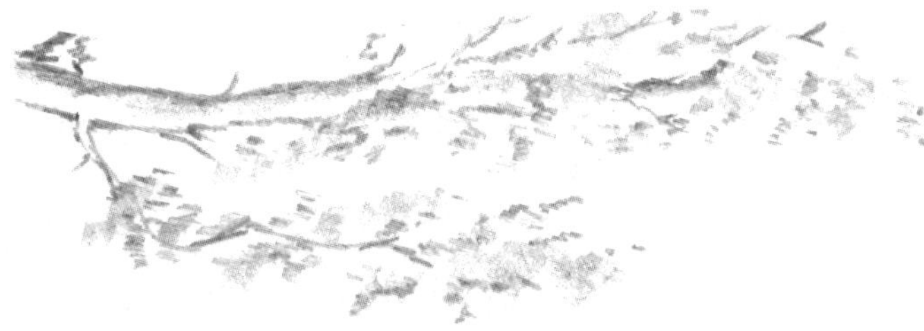

Lobster Fra Diavolo

Hot and Spicy!

1 (1½- to 2-pound) live lobster
3 tablespoons olive oil
2 cloves garlic, minced
⅛ cup finely chopped shallots
¼ cup dry white wine
¼ cup finely chopped green pepper
⅛ teaspoon salt, or to taste
⅛ teaspoon pepper, or to taste
⅛ teaspoon crushed red pepper
2 cups Italian plum canned tomatoes
¼ cup chopped fresh Italian parsley
½ teaspoon chopped dried basil or 1 teaspoon of chopped fresh basil
½ teaspoon thyme
½ bay leaf
½ teaspoon oregano

Kill lobster by plunging a knife into back of lobster, where tail meets body. Slit lobster in half; remove sac near the eyes. Set aside. In large saucepan sauté in oil, garlic and shallots; add all other ingredients; simmer for about 10 minutes. When boiling gently, add lobster; lower heat and simmer, stirring occasionally about 30 minutes. Turn lobster occasionally. Serve with linguini prepared *al dente*. Serves 2.

Mrs. Anthony S. Brancato (Georgine E. Palmer)

Suncoast Seasons Grouper Dijon

1 large tomato
2 (6- to 8-ounce) fillets of grouper, or any firm fleshed fish, skinned
1/4 cup all-purpose flour
1/4 cup clarified butter
1/2 teaspoon minced shallots
2 1/2 teaspoons Dijon-style mustard
1/4 cup dry white wine
1/2 cup whipping cream
1/4 teaspoon salt
1/8 teaspoon pepper, or to taste
2 teaspoons fresh lemon juice
1 teaspoon chopped fresh parsley

In saucepan of boiling water blanch the tomato for 10 seconds. Drain; peel; and cut crosswise into 6 thin slices. Sprinkle the grouper fillets with salt and pepper; dredge in flour, shaking off excess. In an ovenproof stainless steel or enameled skillet, sauté fish in clarified butter over moderately high heat for 3 minutes on each side or until golden. Remove skillet from heat and carefully pour off any remaining butter. Add shallots to the skillet. Spread each fillet with 1 teaspoon of mustard and top with 3 tomato slices. Add wine; cook over moderate heat for 5 minutes or until wine is almost evaporated. Add cream, salt and pepper to taste; swirl in remaining ½ teaspoon mustard. Bake at 425 degrees for 7 to 10 minutes or until sauce is smooth; sprinkle fish with lemon juice and transfer with a slotted spoon to a heated platter. Spoon sauce over fish. Sprinkle with parsley. Serves 2.

Mrs. J. Wallace Lee (Ida)

Fillet of Sole with Artichokes

2 (6-ounce) fillets of sole
1/2 cup all-purpose flour
1/8 teaspoon salt, or to taste
1/8 teaspoon pepper, or to taste
3 eggs, beaten
1/2 cup butter
6 mushroom caps, quartered
4 artichoke hearts, quartered
Juice of 2 lemons

Season flour with salt and pepper. Dip both sides of fish in the seasoned flour. Melt butter in skillet and sauté fillets on both sides until brown. Remove; place on serving platter. Keep hot. To skillet add mushroom caps and artichoke hearts; sauté until a little soft. Then add lemon juice. Let sear and pour over fish; serve. Serves 2.

Suncoast Seasons Committee

Kitchen Hint: To get maximum amount of juice from lemon, warm in water. Press down firmly and roll on hard surface before juicing.

Flounder Meunière

2 pounds fresh flounder fillets
1 teaspoon salt
1/8 teaspoon pepper, or to taste
1 cup all-purpose flour
1/2 cup butter
1 tablespoon lemon juice
1 tablespoon chopped fresh parsley

Cut fillets into serving-size portions. Sprinkle with salt and pepper. Roll in flour and sauté in butter. When fish is brown on one side, turn carefully and brown the other side. Cooking time will be approximately 10 to 15 minutes depending on thickness of fish. Remove fish and place on hot platter. Add lemon juice to browned butter; pour over fish. Sprinkle with parsley. *Delicious preparation for this delicate fish!* Serves 6.

Suncoast Seasons Committee

Fish Stew with Lemon Sauce

Fish Stew:

2 pounds flounder, perch or turbot fillets
1/4 teaspoon salt
1/8 teaspoon pepper
1/8 teaspoon oregano
Juice of 1 lemon
2 to 3 pounds small new potatoes
2 pounds small white onions
6 large stalks celery, cut into 2-inch pieces
1 cup sauterne or dry white wine
2 tablespoons chopped parsley

Sprinkle each fillet with salt, pepper, oregano and lemon juice. Roll up and secure with toothpicks. Refrigerate for several hours. Cook the vegetables, covered in boiling salted water for 20 to 25 minutes. Drain and add rolled fillets and sauterne to vegetables. Cook 5 to 10 minutes. Serve sprinkled with parsley and lemon sauce. Serves 6.

Lemon Sauce:

3/4 cup butter or margarine
2 tablespoons all-purpose flour
1/4 cup lemon juice

Melt butter; add flour to make a roux. Gradually stir in lemon juice. Serve hot.

Mrs. Chris Demas (Jeannie)

Buttery Baked Perch Fillets

2 pounds fresh or frozen perch fillets, thawed
1/4 cup butter or margarine
1/2 teaspoon paprika
1 tablespoon minced fresh basil
1/4 teaspoon salt, or to taste
1/4 teaspoon pepper, or to taste
Fresh basil leaves (optional)
Lemon wedges (optional)
Tartar sauce

Place fillets, skin side down, in a greased 13x9x2-inch baking dish; dot with butter. Sprinkle paprika, minced basil, salt and pepper over fillets. Bake at 350 degrees for 20 to 30 minutes or until fish flakes easily when tested with a fork. Arrange fish on a platter and garnish with basil leaves and lemon wedges, if desired. Serve with tartar sauce. Serves 6.

Hint: May substitute 1 teaspoon dried basil leaves for fresh.

Tartar sauce:

1/2 cup mayonnaise
2 tablespoons chopped sweet pickle
1 teaspoon instant minced onion
Juice of 1 lemon (3 to 4 tablespoons)

Combine all ingredients; mix well. Chill before serving. Makes about 2/3 cup.

Mrs. Bill Ritchey (Carol Eddington)

Salmon Soufflé

Pink and perfect for lunch

3 tablespoons butter
3 tablespoons all-purpose flour
1 cup milk
1/2 teaspoon salt
1/2 teaspoon paprika
1 teaspoon onion juice
2 tablespoons parsley
1/2 teaspoon celery salt
4 eggs, separated
1 (16-ounce) can salmon, drained and boned

In a medium saucepan melt butter; stir in flour until absorbed. Add milk to white sauce stirring constantly until thickened. Add salt, paprika, onion juice, parsley, and celery salt; heat through. Beat egg yolks and add to sauce along with salmon. While this mixture cools slightly, beat egg whites until they form peaks; fold into cooled salmon mixture. Pour into 1½-quart casserole. Bake at 350 degrees for 40 to 45 minutes. Serves 4 to 6.

Mrs. Dean N. McFarland (Donna VanEwyk)

Scalloped Oysters

2 cups crushed water biscuits
1 pint oysters and juice
½ cup butter, cut into pieces
⅛ teaspoon salt
⅛ teaspoon pepper
1 quart milk
¼ cup water

Butter 2-quart casserole well. Cut oysters in half if large; reserve juice. Place ⅓ of the crumbs in casserole; then layer ½ of the oysters topping with ⅓ of the butter. Sprinkle with salt and pepper. Repeat for next layers finishing with biscuit crumbs and butter on top. Pour milk overall and any remaining oyster juice. Let stand 3 or 4 hours in refrigerator. Add ¼ cup water just before baking. Bake at 350 degrees for 1 hour. Casserole should be brown and puffy. Serves 4 to 6.

Mrs. Preston Packard (D'Lou)

Salmon Loaf

1 (16-ounce) can salmon
4 eggs
1 small onion, grated
½ teaspoon salt
¼ teaspoon pepper
3 heaping tablespoons sour cream
1 cup corn flake crumbs

Drain, skin and flake the salmon. In a medium size bowl mash salmon; add remaining ingredients and mix well. Shape into a loaf; place in a greased 9x3x2-inch loaf pan. Bake at 325 degrees for 45 minutes. Makes 1 loaf.

Mrs. Lawrence Feltman (Bertha)
Chicago, Illinois

Stuffed Flounder Supreme

1 pound flounder fillets
½ cup French dressing
⅓ cup seasoned croutons, crushed
¼ cup finely chopped celery

Divide fillets into four servings. Using 2 tablespoons of dressing brush top side of fillets. In a small bowl combine ¼ cup of the dressing, croutons, and celery; equally divide mixture on fillets and roll up; brush with remaining dressing. Bake at 350 degrees for 35 minutes or until fish flakes. Makes 4 rolls.

Mrs. Joseph L. Andreani (Sandra)
Oldsmar, Florida

Grecian Broiled Fish

2 pounds Spanish mackerel fillets, fresh or frozen
1 teaspoon salt
½ teaspoon pepper
2 tablespoons margarine, melted or olive oil
3 tablespoons lemon juice
2 cloves garlic, finely minced
3 tablespoons margarine or olive oil
½ cup thinly sliced onion rings, cut into fourths
1½ cups chopped parsley
1 cup chopped fresh tomato
1 teaspoon lemon juice

Thaw fish if frozen; skin fillets and dry them. Sprinkle fillets with salt and pepper. Place on well-greased 15x10x1-inch baking pan. Combine 2 tablespoons melted margarine, lemon juice and garlic; pour over fillets. Broil fillets about 4 inches from heat source for 4 to 6 minutes. Turn carefully and baste fillets with pan drippings. Broil 4 to 6 minutes longer. In a 1-quart saucepan, melt 3 tablespoons margarine. Add onion; cook until tender, but not brown. Stir in parsley and tomatoes; cook just long enough to heat about 1 minute. Stir in lemon juice. Spread evenly over fillets. Serves 6.

Note: Try red snapper or trout fillets.

Mrs. Robert Haverkos (Ginny)

Trout Amandine

¼ cup all-purpose flour
1 teaspoon salt
¼ to ½ teaspoon freshly ground pepper
6 fresh trout, cleaned
1 cup butter
1 cup sliced blanched almonds
1 tablespoon fresh lemon juice
Lemon wedges

Combine flour, salt and pepper and roll trout in seasoned flour until thoroughly coated. Sauté three trout at a time in 12-inch skillet for about 5 minutes on each side. Use ¼ cup butter for each batch you cook. Carefully remove cooked trout to a heated platter; cover to keep warm. When all fish are cooked, discard the browned butter and wipe out the skillet. Add remaining ½ cup butter and almonds to the skillet; cook over the lowest heat possible, stirring frequently until almonds become a pale golden color. Remove from heat and stir in lemon juice. Pour almond mixture over trout. Serve immediately with lemon wedges. Serves 4 to 6.

Suncoast Seasons Committee

Greek Style Baked Fish

1 medium onion, chopped
6 stalks celery, chopped
1 green pepper, chopped
1 or 2 tablespoons oil
1 (16-ounce) can tomatoes
1 (8-ounce) can tomato sauce
1 teaspoon all-purpose Greek seasoning
1 teaspoon dill
1 teaspoon basil
1 cup chopped fresh parsley
1 pound haddock, grouper, snapper or similar fish

Sauté onions, celery and green pepper in oil. Add tomatoes, tomato sauce and seasonings. Cook for ½ hour. Place fish in baking pan. Pour sauce evenly over fish and bake at 350 degrees for 30 minutes. Serves 4.

Mrs. Charles Nikitas (Theresa)
Williamstown, Massachusetts

Baked Fish Fillets

1½ pounds fresh fish or fish fillets (about ⅓ pound per serving)
¼ cup milk
1 cup seasoned breadcrumbs
¼ cup butter, melted

Dip fish in milk, then in breadcrumbs. Let fish dry on a rack for 20 minutes. Preheat oven to 350 degrees. Bake in an ovenproof dish until firm and golden. Baste twice during baking with melted butter. Serves 4.

Mrs. Donald Behm (Marion)

Tomatoed Fish Fillets

1 pound fish fillets
¼ teaspoon thyme
½ (10¾-ounce) can cream of mushroom soup
1 medium tomato, sliced
1 teaspoon margarine, melted
¼ to ½ teaspoon dill weed, more if desired

Preheat oven to 350 degrees. Divide fish into 4 servings in ungreased baking pan. Stir thyme into soup; spoon over fish. Bake uncovered 20 to 30 minutes. Add tomato slices; brush with margarine and sprinkle with dill. Bake 5 minutes longer until fish flakes. Serves 4.

Helen S. Glass

Dressing for Fish

½ cup butter or margarine
¼ cup chopped onion
½ cup chopped celery
1 (8-ounce) package bread stuffing
½ cup pickle relish
1 cup boiling water

Sauté butter, onion and celery until tender. Add stuffing, relish, water and mix. Bake in pan with fish or separately 20 to 30 minutes at 350 to 400 degrees. Serves 6.

Helen S. Glass

Clarified Butter

1 cup unsalted butter

In small saucepan heat butter over low heat until melted and solids have separated from fat (10 to 15 minutes); remove from heat and let stand a few minutes. Skim off foam; slowly pour off clear yellow liquid, leaving behind the residue of milk solids that has settled to bottom of pan. Makes ¾ cup.

Note: Keeps well for several weeks in refrigerator or freezer.

Suncoast Seasons Committee

French Beer Batter for Shrimp or Fish

1⅓ cups all-purpose flour, sifted
1 teaspoon salt
1 tablespoon butter, melted
2 eggs, separated
¾ cups stale beer

Combine flour, salt, butter, egg yolks and beer. Beat only until smooth. Cover and let stand in cool place or refrigerate 1 to 12 hours. Just before using, beat egg whites until stiff and fold gently into batter. Dip shrimp and/or fish into batter. Sauté or deep fry. Makes 4 cups.

Mrs. Gregory H. Keuroghlian (Nora Ghazikian)

Kitchen Hint: To remove tastes from deep-frying fat, fry potato slices until brown. Removes taste so you can use fat again.

Batter for Deep-Fried Fish

1 egg, beaten
1/2 teaspoon salt
1/2 cup milk
1/2 cup all-purpose flour
1 teaspoon baking powder

Combine all ingredients in a large bowl; beat with mixer until smooth. Dip fish pieces in batter coating both sides. Fry about 12 minutes at 350 to 375 degrees. Makes enough to cover 1 pound of fish.

Mrs. Donald Rice (Linda)
Palm Harbor, Florida

Mustard Sauce for Seafood

2 teaspoons butter or margarine
1/2 cup sour cream
1 1/2 tablespoons creole mustard
1/2 teaspoon parsley flakes
1/8 teaspoon salt

In top of small double boiler melt butter; add remaining ingredients. Heat on low heat until warm, stirring occasionally; do not boil. Serve with cold or hot stone crab claws or boiled shrimp. Makes 2/3 cup.

Note: For a different taste use other kinds of mustard.

Mrs. Lynn Lees

Caper Sauce for Seafood

1 cup chopped fresh parsley
1/4 cup chopped green onion
2 tablespoons capers
1 clove garlic, finely chopped
2/3 cup mayonnaise
2 tablespoons olive oil
1 tablespoon lemon juice
1/2 teaspoon mustard

Combine parsley, onion, capers and garlic in blender or food processor; cover and process until finely chopped. Add remaining ingredients and blend well. Chill. Serve with hot or cold stone crab claws or boiled shrimp. Makes 1 1/4 cups.

Mrs. Lynn Lees

Creole Sauce

1/4 cup finely chopped green pepper
1/2 cup finely chopped green onions
2 stalks celery, finely chopped
1 clove garlic, minced
3 tablespoons bacon grease, strained, or 3 tablespoons butter
1/2 teaspoon salt
1/4 teaspoon cayenne pepper, or to taste
1 (16-ounce) can tomatoes
1 (8-ounce) can tomato sauce
1 tablespoon brown sugar
1 bay leaf
1/8 teaspoon basil
1/8 teaspoon rosemary
1/8 teaspoon thyme
1/8 teaspoon marjoram
1 tablespoon Worcestershire sauce

In a skillet sauté pepper, onion, celery and garlic in bacon grease until browned. Add tomatoes, tomato sauce and seasonings; simmer slowly for 40 minutes, stirring frequently. Makes 2½ cups.

Note: Excellent with seafood or rice!

Mrs. Kenneth Thomson (Elsie)
Leawood, Kansas

Vegetables

Asparagus Casserole

3 (10½-ounce) cans asparagus
1½ cups shredded sharp Cheddar cheese
1½ cups round butter crackers, broken by hand
1 (10¾-ounce) can cream of mushroom soup
¼ cup butter or margarine, melted
1 (8-ounce) can sliced water chestnuts
¼ cup sliced pecans or almonds

Drain asparagus reserving ⅔ cup of liquid. In a small bowl combine cheese and crackers. Combine soup, butter and asparagus liquid in a bowl. Spread a layer of cheese and cracker mixture in bottom of a 2-quart casserole. Add a layer of asparagus and nuts; cover with soup mixture. Continue layering ingredients ending with cheese mixture topped with soup. Bake at 350 degrees for 30 minutes. Serves 8 to 10.

Note: Can be made ahead and baked just before serving.

Phyllis Taylor
New Concord, Ohio

Creamed Brussels Sprouts and Celery

1 pound fresh brussels sprouts
2 cups sliced celery
1 medium onion, chopped
3 tablespoons butter or margarine
3 tablespoons all-purpose flour
½ teaspoon celery salt
1 (10¾-ounce) can condensed chicken broth

Place brussels sprouts in a small amount of boiling water; cover. Reduce heat; simmer 5 to 10 minutes or until tender. Drain; set aside. Melt butter in a saucepan. Add celery and onion; sauté until tender. Add flour and celery salt, stirring until smooth. Cook 1 minute, stirring constantly. Gradually add chicken broth; cook over medium heat, stirring constantly, until mixture is thickened and bubbly. Add brussels sprouts; stir gently. Cook 1 minute or until thoroughly heated. Serves 6.

Mrs. Jack Wilson (Mary Jane Brown)

Kitchen Hint: To ensure even cooking of brussels sprouts or small white boiling onions, cut a shallow "X" in each stem end before cooking. Boil or steam as desired.

Bubbly Three Bean Bake

5 slices bacon
1 medium onion, chopped
1 (16-ounce) can lima beans, drained
1 (16-ounce) can baked beans
1 (15½-ounce) can kidney beans, drained
¾ cup ketchup
¾ cup brown sugar
1 tablespoon Worcestershire sauce
1 cup shredded sharp Cheddar cheese

In a skillet fry bacon until crisp; remove and crumble. Drain skillet, reserving 2 tablespoons bacon drippings. Sauté onions in drippings until tender. In a mixing bowl combine all ingredients. Pour into a 2-quart casserole. Bake at 350 degrees for 1 hour or until bubbly. Serves 8.

Note: Great make ahead cookout dish—tastes even better the second day.

Mrs. Stanley H. Dawson (Ruth)

Beets with Orange Sauce

½ cup sugar
2 teaspoons cornstarch
½ cup boiling water
1 teaspoon grated orange rind
1 teaspoon lemon juice
¼ cup orange juice
1 tablespoon butter or margarine
1 (16-ounce) can whole beets, undrained

In a small saucepan combine sugar and cornstarch; add water, stirring until smooth. Cook over low heat 15 minutes. Stir in orange rind, lemon juice, orange juice and butter; set aside. Put beets with liquid into a saucepan; heat thoroughly. Drain off juice. Pour sauce over beets and serve. Serves 4 to 6.

Mrs. James Long (Eva Fandrich)

Double Corn Bread Casserole

1 (17-ounce) can cream-style corn
1 (17-ounce) can whole kernel corn, drained
1 cup sour cream
¼ cup butter, melted
2 eggs
1 (8½-ounce) package corn muffin mix
1 cup shredded Cheddar cheese (optional)

In a mixing bowl combine all ingredients except cheese; mix well. Pour into 1½-quart buttered casserole dish. Bake at 350 degrees for 45 to 60 minutes. Top with cheese, if desired, and bake 10 minutes more. Serves 6 to 8.

Suncoast Seasons Committee

Delicious Party Broccoli

3 (10-ounce) packages frozen chopped broccoli, cooked and drained well
½ cup butter
1 bunch green onions and tops, sliced
3 celery stalks, sliced
1 (8-ounce) can sliced mushrooms, drained
1 (10¾-ounce) can cream of mushroom soup
1 (6-ounce) roll garlic cheese spread
12 round butter crackers, crushed

In a skillet sauté onions, celery and mushrooms in butter; set aside. In a large saucepan melt garlic cheese in soup; add onion mixture and broccoli. Pour into a 2½-quart baking dish. Top with crushed crackers. Bake at 350 degrees for 15 minutes or until thoroughly heated. Serves 6 to 8.

Mrs. Paul J. Donahue (Sigrid)
Dunedin, Florida

Italian Baked Beans

A Little Different!

½ pound bacon, diced
1½ cups thinly sliced onions
1 teaspoon garlic powder or 1 clove garlic, crushed
1 (20-ounce) can red kidney beans, drained
1 (20-ounce) can chick peas or ceci, drained
1 (20-ounce) can cannellini white kidney beans, undrained
1 (15-ounce) can tomato sauce
1¼ teaspoons Italian seasoning
1 teaspoon salt
4 ounces mozzarella cheese

In a skillet cook bacon and onion until tender. In a large mixing bowl combine all ingredients except cheese. Pour into a 2-quart baking dish. Bake at 350 degrees for 1 hour. Top with cheese; bake 10 minutes more. Serves 6.

Suncoast Seasons Committee

Green Bean Casserole

3 tablespoons melted butter, divided
2 tablespoons all-purpose flour
1 teaspoon salt
1/4 teaspoon pepper
1 teaspoon sugar
1/2 teaspoon grated onion
1 cup sour cream
2 (10-ounce) packages frozen French-style green beans, cooked
2 cups shredded Cheddar cheese
1/2 cup corn flake crumbs

In a medium saucepan combine 2 tablespoons of butter and flour; cook gently. Remove from heat; stir in salt, pepper, sugar, onion and sour cream. Fold in green beans. Pour into 2-quart casserole. Cover with cheese and crumbs mixed with remaining butter. Bake at 350 degrees for 30 minutes. Serves 8.

Mrs. Joseph L. Andreani (Sandra)
Oldsmar, Florida

Green Peas with Onions

1 (10-ounce) package frozen peas
2 tablespoons water
3/4 teaspoon salt
1/4 cup butter, divided
8 to 12 green onions
2 teaspoons all-purpose flour
1/2 teaspoon sugar
1/8 teaspoon white pepper
1/2 cup milk or cream

In a saucepan cook peas in salted water with 1/2 of the butter until just tender, about 5 to 7 minutes. Drain; set aside. Cut onions, including tops, into 1/2-inch lengths; saute in a saucepan in remaining butter for 3 to 4 minutes, stirring constantly. Add flour, sugar, pepper and milk, stirring constantly. Cook until sauce is smooth and thick. Serve at once over drained peas. Serves 4.

Judy Nevrkla

Broccoli-Rice Casserole

1 cup rice, cooked
1 (10-ounce) package frozen chopped broccoli, cooked and drained well
1 (8-ounce) can sliced water chestnuts
1 (8-ounce) jar pasteurized process cheese
2 tablespoons instant onions
1 (10 3/4-ounce) can cream of mushroom soup

In a medium bowl combine all ingredients. Pour into a 2-quart baking dish. Bake at 350 degrees for 30 minutes or until bubbly. Serves 6 to 8.

Mrs. Jack Garber (Lois)
Mrs. Ronald Gordon (Linda)

Cauliflower with Double Cheese Sauce

1 medium head cauliflower
2 tablespoons butter
2 tablespoons all-purpose flour
½ teaspoon dry mustard
¼ teaspoon salt
⅛ teaspoon white pepper
1¼ cups milk
¾ cup shredded Monterey Jack cheese
½ cup shredded Cheddar cheese

Wash, trim and remove outer leaves of cauliflower. Cook whole, covered, in small amount of boiling salted water about 20 to 25 minutes or until just tender. While cauliflower is cooking, melt butter in a small saucepan. Blend in flour, mustard, salt, and pepper; add milk. Cook over medium heat, stirring constantly, until thick and bubbling. Remove from heat; stir in cheeses. Pour over cauliflower just before serving. Serves 6.

Note: Cheese sauce is also good over crêpes.

Mrs. James Martinelli (Robin)
Palm Harbor, Florida

Snappy Green Beans

4 slices bacon
¼ cup chopped onion
1 to 2 tablespoons tarragon vinegar
½ teaspoon salt
⅛ teaspoon pepper
2 cups cooked whole green beans, drained and hot

In a skillet fry bacon until crisp; remove. Drain drippings from pan reserving 2 tablespoons. Add onion; sauté until tender. Add vinegar, salt and pepper. Pour mixture over hot green beans. Crumble bacon on top and serve. Serves 3 to 4.

Variation: Use 1 (10-ounce) package frozen French-style green beans, cooked, in place of whole beans; add ¼ teaspoon dill weed to vinegar mixture.

Mrs. John G. Dodson (Frankie Armitage)
Mrs. Edward W. Roos (Mildred Seagren)

Garden Vegetable Medley

1 cup slivered almonds
1/4 pound bacon, cut into 1-inch pieces
1 pound zucchini, sliced
1 pound eggplant, diced
1 large onion, cut into wedges
1 tablespoon all-purpose flour
2 cups diced fresh tomatoes
1 teaspoon minced garlic
1 1/2 teaspoons salt
1/4 teaspoon pepper
1 teaspoon basil
1 (6-ounce) package sliced Swiss cheese

In a large skillet sauté almonds with bacon until almonds are lightly roasted and bacon is crisp. Remove from skillet; add zucchini, eggplant and onion. Cover; cook over medium-low heat 15 minutes, stirring often to prevent sticking. Mix in flour; add tomatoes, garlic, salt, pepper and basil. In a 2-quart casserole layer vegetable mixture, almonds and bacon and cheese, ending with bacon and almonds in a ring on top. Bake at 400 degrees for 20 to 25 minutes. Serves 6.

Note: To serve later cover and refrigerate. Uncover; bake for 30 to 35 minutes.

Mrs. Greg Santa (Cathy)

Kitchen Hint: Place tomatoes in brown paper bag, pour boiling water over sack until bag breaks. Tomatoes will be ready to peel.

Glorified Sauerkraut and Sausage Casserole

1 stick smoked sausage or 5 smokey links, chopped
2 medium onions, chopped
1 green pepper, chopped
1 stalk celery, chopped
1 (4-ounce) can sliced mushrooms (optional)
1 (16-ounce) can tomatoes, chopped
1/4 teaspoon nutmeg
1/4 teaspoon basil
1/4 teaspoon thyme
1/4 teaspoon marjoram
1/4 teaspoon salt, or to taste
1 tablespoon brown sugar (optional)
Dash of garlic powder (optional)
1/4 teaspoon pepper
1 (16-ounce) can sauerkraut, drained and rinsed

In a skillet sauté sausage; remove and set aside. Sauté onion, green pepper, celery and mushrooms in sausage fat. If not enough grease from sausage, add a little oil. Add tomatoes, seasonings, sausage and sauerkraut. Pour into a 12x8x2-inch baking dish. Bake, covered, at 350 degrees for 1 hour. Uncover; bake 30 minutes more. Serves 4.

Mrs. Elwood Reichart (June)
Chicago, Illinois

Austrian Red Cabbage

2 medium heads red cabbage
5 strips bacon, cut up
1 large onion, chopped
2 tablespoons sugar
¼ teaspoon salt
¼ cup water
1 tablespoon wine vinegar
2 tablespoons all-purpose flour
½ cup water

Shred cabbage fine. In a large skillet cook bacon, onion and sugar together over low heat until onion is golden. Add cabbage, salt and ¼ cup water. Cover; cook over low heat for 15 to 20 minutes or until cabbage is fork tender. Add additional water, if necessary, to keep mixture from sticking. In a small bowl make a paste of vinegar, flour and ½ cup water. Add to cabbage and cook, stirring until mixture is thickened. Serves 4 to 6.

Mrs. James Long (Eva Fandrich)

Sweet Skillet Cabbage

¼ cup bacon drippings
4 cups chopped or shredded cabbage
1 green pepper, chopped
2 cups diced celery
¾ cup chopped onions
2 tomatoes, chopped
2 tablespoons sugar
¼ teaspoon salt
⅛ teaspoon pepper

Heat bacon drippings in a large skillet. Add chopped vegetables, sugar, salt and pepper; mix well. Cover; cook over medium heat about 5 to 10 minutes or until vegetables are semi-tender. Good, especially with meat loaf or fish! Serves 6.

Mrs. Richard Benkusky (Judy)

Mushroom Medley

1 pound mushrooms, cleaned
1 large green pepper, chopped
1 large onion, chopped
5 tablespoons vegetable oil
¼ teaspoon salt, or to taste
⅛ teaspoon pepper, or to taste
¼ cup hot water
1 tablespoon tomato paste

Cut mushrooms into ¼-inch slices. Mix green pepper, onion, oil, salt, pepper, tomato paste and hot water in a pot; cook for 3 minutes on medium heat. Add mushrooms; mix well. Reduce heat to low; cook covered for ½ hour, stirring occasionally. Serve warm or cold as a side dish. Serves 4 to 6.

Rose Ghazikian
Dunedin, Florida

Broccoli with Straw Mushrooms

1 bunch broccoli
2 tablespoons peanut oil
1 teaspoon salt
½ teaspoon sugar
¼ teaspoon monosodium glutamate
½ cup water
1 (12-ounce) can straw mushrooms, drained and dried with paper towels

Wash and cut broccoli flowerets off stems; cut stems into 1-inch pieces. In medium pan or skillet parboil stems and flowerets. Rinse in cold water; drain; set aside. In same pan heat oil over high heat; add broccoli and stir well until covered with oil. Add salt, sugar and monosodium glutamate; mix well. Add water; cover pan. Cook over medium flame for 5 minutes; stir. Add straw mushrooms; cook over high heat until liquid is almost absorbed. Serves 2 to 3.

Mrs. Jay Johnston
Princeton, New Jersey

Creamed Celery Casserole

1 large bunch celery, sliced
1 (8-ounce) can sliced water chestnuts, drained
1 (10¾-ounce) can cream of mushroom or cream of chicken soup
¼ cup butter or margarine, melted
½ cup dry breadcrumbs
½ cup almonds, chopped (optional)

Cover celery with water in a saucepan and simmer for 8 to 10 minutes; drain. Add water chestnuts and soup. Pour into a buttered 2-quart casserole. Combine butter and breadcrumbs; spoon over celery. Top with almonds. Bake at 350 degrees for 45 minutes. Nice change of pace vegetable. Serves 8 to 10.

Violet T. Bernard
Mrs. Edward W. Roos (Mildred Seagren)

Kitchen Hint: If celery or carrots go limp before you use them, soak in cold water one hour. Add lemon juice or vinegar. Drain vegetables. Place in plastic bag and put in refrigerator until crisp.

Ratatouille I

Vegetables Stewed In Olive Oil

½ cup olive oil
5 garlic cloves, crushed
1½ cups chopped onion
1½ cups coarsely chopped green pepper
1½ cups coarsely chopped eggplant, unskinned
1½ cups sliced and quartered zucchini
1 teaspoon salt
1 teaspoon pepper
2 teaspoons basil
1½ cups peeled, seeded and coarsely chopped tomatoes

In a large skillet sauté garlic, onion and green pepper in oil. Add remaining ingredients. Cook until mixture is reduced to a thick consistency and vegetables are tender; stir occasionally. Serve hot or cold. Serves 8 to 10.

Mrs. Lawrence J. Tierney (Sue)

Kitchen Hint: Wrap fresh vegetables in damp paper towels and put in plastic bags before refrigerating. They'll last longer.

Spinach Soufflé

1 cup fresh breadcrumbs
½ cup milk
2 (10-ounce) packages frozen chopped spinach, cooked and squeezed
4 large egg yolks
5 tablespoons sweet butter, melted and cooled
¼ teaspoon nutmeg
4 large egg whites, room temperature
⅛ teaspoon cream of tartar
⅛ teaspoon salt

In a small bowl combine breadcrumbs and milk; let stand for 15 minutes. In a mixing bowl or blender combine spinach, egg yolks and 3 tablespoons butter. Add bread mixture; blend thoroughly. Transfer mixture to a large bowl; stir in nutmeg. In a separate bowl beat egg whites with cream of tartar and salt until they form stiff peaks. Stir ⅓ of the egg whites into spinach mixture. Fold in remaining egg whites gently, but thoroughly. Turn mixture into a well-buttered 1-quart ring mold; brush top with remaining butter. Put mold in baking pan; pour enough hot water in pan to reach half way up sides of mold. Bake at 325 degrees for 45 minutes, or until puffed and firm to the touch. Let cool 10 minutes before serving. Serves 6 to 8.

Mrs. Dean N. McFarland (Donna VanEwyk)

Ratatouille II

1 medium eggplant, peeled and sliced
1/2 cup olive oil
2 small summer squash, sliced
3 cloves garlic, crushed
3 medium onions, sliced
2 medium green peppers, cut into strips
1 teaspoon salt, or to taste
1/4 teaspoon pepper, or to taste
3 large tomatoes, peeled, seeded and diced
1/2 cup chopped parsley

Sprinkle eggplant with salt; let stand for 30 minutes. Wipe dry with paper towel. Heat half of olive oil in a large skillet. Sauté eggplant and squash until golden on both sides; remove and set aside. Heat remaining oil in skillet. Sauté garlic, onions and green peppers over medium heat for 10 minutes, stirring frequently. Sprinkle with salt and pepper. Top with tomatoes and simmer 5 minutes. Cover; simmer 10 minutes longer. Arrange alternate layers of eggplant and squash, tomato mixture and parsley in a 2-quart saucepan. Cover; simmer for 15 minutes; or layer in a casserole and bake, covered, at 350 degrees for 30 minutes. Serve hot or cold. Serves 6.

Note: Takes time to prepare, but is delicious!

Variation: Zucchini, peeled, may be used in place of summer squash.

Mrs. Richard Jaked (Jean), Wappingers Falls, New York
Mrs. Nicholas Scalise, Meriden, Connecticut

Herb-Baked Spinach

1 (10-ounce) package frozen chopped spinach, cooked and drained
1 cup cooked rice
1 cup shredded sharp process American cheese
2 eggs, slightly beaten
2 tablespoons butter or margarine, room temperature
1/3 cup milk
2 tablespoons chopped onion
1/2 teaspoon Worcestershire sauce
1 teaspoon salt
1/4 teaspoon crushed rosemary or thyme

In a medium bowl combine all ingredients; mix well. Pour into a 9-inch square baking dish. Bake at 350 degrees for 25 to 30 minutes or until knife inserted in center comes out clean. Cut into squares. Serves 6 to 8.

Hint: Ideal for buffet dinner. Can be made ahead and baked at the last minute.

Mrs. William S. Sharpe (Wanda)

Zucchini Casserole

1½ pounds small zucchini
1 large onion, finely chopped
4 tablespoons butter
1 cup shredded sharp Cheddar cheese
¾ teaspoon salt
⅛ teaspoon pepper
2 eggs, beaten
2 tablespoons butter, melted
½ cup soft breadcrumbs

Cook whole zucchini in a small amount of boiling water until crisp-tender, approximately 10 minutes; cool. In a skillet sauté onion in butter until golden. Cut unpeeled zucchini into fairly large cubes; add to onion. Stir in Cheddar cheese, salt and pepper. Remove from heat; mix vegetables lightly with beaten eggs. Spoon into buttered 1½-quart casserole. Combine melted butter and breadcrumbs; sprinkle over top of mixture. Bake at 350 degrees for 30 to 45 minutes. Serves 5 to 6.

Mrs. Preston Packard (D'Lou)

Southern Corn Pudding

2 cups fresh corn (5 to 6 ears) or canned cream-style corn
3 eggs, slightly beaten
2 cups milk
1 cup cracker crumbs
2 teaspoons sugar
2 teaspoons salt, or to taste
⅛ teaspoon pepper
¼ cup butter or margarine, melted
½ cup shredded Cheddar cheese (optional)
3 tablespoons pimento (optional)

Cut kernels from cob with sharp knife; scrape remaining corn from cob. In a medium bowl combine eggs and milk. Add cracker crumbs, sugar, salt and pepper; blend well. Add corn and melted butter. Pour mixture into a 2-quart casserole. Place casserole in a pan of water 1½ inches deep. Bake at 350 degrees for 1 to 1½ hours or until knife inserted in center comes out clean. Top with cheese and pimento last 20 minutes of baking time, if desired. Serves 6 to 8.

Note: 2 tablespoons of chopped green pepper may be added for color.

Violet T. Bernard
Alice Forrester, Madre, California
Mrs. Robert Haverkos (Ginny)

Cheese Topped Zucchini Halves

3 medium or 5 small zucchini
1 medium onion, thinly sliced
1 tablespoon oil
1/4 teaspoon salt, or to taste
1/8 teaspoon pepper, or to taste
1/2 to 1 teaspoon crushed oregano
1 (8-ounce) can seasoned tomato sauce
1 (8-ounce) package sliced mozzarella cheese
1 to 2 tablespoons grated Parmesan cheese (optional)

Wash zucchini and cut in half lengthwise. In a large skillet cook onion in hot oil until tender but not brown. Add zucchini, cut side up. Sprinkle with salt, pepper and oregano. Add tomato sauce; cover. Cook until just tender, about 10 minutes. Top with cheese slices. Sprinkle with Parmesan cheese and additional oregano, if desired. *Very easy!* Serves 4 to 6.

Mrs. Annie B. McClellan
Wetumpka, Alabama

Corn Fritters

1 (8-ounce) can cream-style corn
1 egg
1/2 teaspoon baking powder
1 1/2 cups pancake mix
1/2 cup oil

In a medium bowl combine corn and egg; mix well. Add baking powder and pancake mix. In a skillet heat oil to medium hot. Drop batter into oil by full tablespoons. Turn carefully when bubbles appear on top and fritters are light brown. Remove to paper towels to absorb oil; hold in warm oven until serving time. Makes 12.

Sonya Tatko
Dunedin, Florida

Fried Eggplant Parmigiana

2 eggplants
2 eggs
1/2 teaspoon salt
1/8 teaspoon pepper
2 cups Italian-style breadcrumbs
2 1/2 cups olive oil
1 (32-ounce) jar spaghetti sauce
1 pound mozzarella cheese, shredded

Peel and slice eggplants into 1/4-inch round slices. In a bowl beat eggs with salt and pepper. Dip eggplant into eggs then into breadcrumbs. In a skillet fry in oil until golden brown. Drain on paper towels. In a 10-inch square casserole layer eggplant, sauce and mozzarella cheese. Bake at 350 degrees for 20 minutes, or until heated through. Serves 8 to 10.

Mrs. Douglas Guilfoile (Paula L. Tiezzi)

Carrot Soufflé

3 large carrots, peeled, cooked and mashed (1 cup)
1/4 cup finely chopped onions
1 cup shredded Cheddar cheese
3 large eggs, separated
4 tablespoons breadcrumbs
2 tablespoons milk
1/2 teaspoon salt, or to taste
1/8 teaspoon pepper, or to taste
1/2 teaspoon sugar
1 tablespoon breadcrumbs
1/2 tablespoon butter

Butter a 1½-quart soufflé dish; set aside. In a medium bowl mix carrots, onions and cheese; blend in slightly beaten egg yolks. Add breadcrumbs, milk, salt and pepper; stir to blend. In a small bowl beat egg whites with sugar until stiff peaks form. Fold gently into carrot mixture and pour into soufflé dish. Sprinkle top with 1 tablespoon breadcrumbs and dot with butter. Bake at 350 degrees for 45 to 55 minutes or until golden on top. Serves 8.

Mrs. Lewis Allen (Catherine)
Memphis, Tennessee

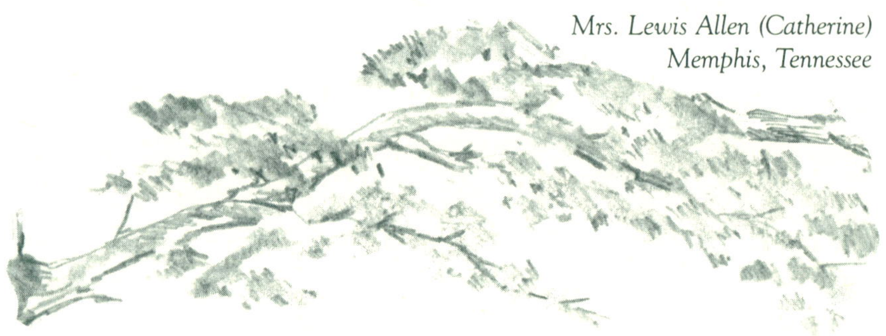

Country Style Tomatoes

1 clove garlic, minced
1/4 cup minced parsley
1/8 teaspoon salt
1 (8-ounce) package cream cheese, softened
1 teaspoon chopped fresh basil (optional)
4 large tomatoes
1/2 cup all-purpose flour
1 egg, beaten
2/3 cup dry breadcrumbs
3 tablespoons butter
3 tablespoons oil
Fresh basil or parsley (optional)

Beat together in mixer or food processor the garlic, parsley, salt and cream cheese; add basil, if desired. Cut tomatoes into 12 even slices, about ½-inch thick. Spread 6 slices with about 2 tablespoons of mixture; top with remaining slices to make 6 sandwiches. Dip each in flour, then egg and breadcrumbs. In a skillet fry over medium heat in mixture of butter and oil until brown, turning once. Garnish with fresh basil or parsley. Serves 6.

Mrs. Michael Porter (Paula)

Tomatoes Rockefeller

1 small onion, grated
1 clove garlic, crushed
½ teaspoon salt
4 tablespoons butter
1 (10-ounce) package frozen chopped spinach, cooked and drained
⅓ cup seasoned breadcrumbs
6 tomatoes, halved
Grated Parmesan cheese

In a small skillet sauté onion, garlic and salt in butter until lightly browned. Remove from heat; add spinach and seasoned breadcrumbs. Spread over tomatoes; sprinkle with cheese. Place tomatoes on cookie sheet. Bake at 350 degrees for 20 minutes. Serves 6 to 8.

Mrs. Lawrence Feltman (Bertha)
Chicago, Illinois

Snow Peas and Tomatoes

2 tablespoons peanut oil
¼ cup chopped onions
1 pound fresh snow peas or 2 (7-ounce) packages frozen snow peas
1 tablespoon soy sauce
1 teaspoon salt
1 teaspoon dried oregano leaves, crumbled
3 medium-size fresh tomatoes, cut into wedges

Heat peanut oil in a large skillet over medium heat. Sauté onion 1 minute. Add peas, soy sauce, salt and oregano. Cook, stirring constantly, until peas are just tender. Add tomatoes; cook 1 minute. Spoon into serving dish. Serves 8.

Variation: Sugar Snap peas may be substituted for snow peas. Add 1 tablespoon finely chopped fresh ginger, if desired.

Mrs. John Dronzek (Pat)
Dunedin, Florida

Curried Baked Tomato Slices

4 medium firm, ripe tomatoes
½ cup all-purpose flour
2 cups soft breadcrumbs
1 teaspoon salt
1½ teaspoons curry powder, or to taste
2 large eggs, slightly beaten
⅓ cup butter, melted

Line a 15x10x1-inch jelly roll pan with foil; butter well. Remove stems and bottoms from tomatoes. Cut each tomato into 2 or 3 thick slices. Mound flour on a sheet of waxed paper. In a shallow dish stir together breadcrumbs, salt and curry powder. Dip each tomato slice in flour, then in egg, then in crumb mixture; coat well. Place in a single layer in prepared pan. Drizzle with butter. Bake at 375 degrees for 10 minutes or until crisp and lightly browned. Serves 4 to 6.

Mrs. Stanley H. Dawson (Ruth)

Sausage-Flavored Mexican Rice

1 cup minced onion
½ cup sliced hot Italian sausage
½ cup sliced mushrooms
¼ cup oil, preferably olive
1 cup rice
1 teaspoon salt
1 tablespoon chili powder
3 to 4 cups tomato juice (or use part bouillon)

In a skillet sauté onions, sausage and mushrooms in oil for 2 or 3 minutes. Add remaining ingredients; bring to a boil. Reduce heat; cover. Simmer for 18 to 25 minutes or until rice is tender. Serves 4 to 6.

Note: For milder tastes reduce chili powder to 1 teaspoon.

Mrs. Ray Windham (Ann)
Spring Hill, Florida

Mexican Rice

⅔ cup chopped onion
3 tablespoons bacon drippings
1 cup converted white rice
1 cup chopped green pepper
1 teaspoon chili powder
1 (16-ounce) can whole tomatoes
1 teaspoon salt
2 cups water
4 tablespoons chopped raw tomato
2 tablespoons chopped green pepper

In a heavy skillet sauté onion in drippings. Stir in rice, green pepper, chili powder, tomatoes and salt. Add water; bring to a boil. Reduce heat; cover. Simmer 20 minutes or until liquid is absorbed and rice is tender. Garnish with raw tomato and green pepper. Serves 4 to 6.

Mrs. Jack Garber (Lois)

Arroz Frito Sabroso

Spanish Fried Rice

1/4 cup butter
1 1/4 cups long-grain rice
1 (8-ounce) can sliced water chestnuts, drained (reserve liquid)
1 (3-ounce) can sliced mushrooms, drained (reserve liquid)
2 (10 3/4-ounce) cans condensed onion soup
1/8 teaspoon salt
1/8 teaspoon pepper
1/4 cup cooking wine, preferably sauterne
1/8 teaspoon hot pepper sauce

Melt butter in a skillet. Brown rice in butter over low heat, stirring constantly. Add water chestnuts and mushrooms to browned rice; sauté for 10 to 15 minutes. Pour mixture into a 3-quart casserole. Add onion soup, reserved liquids, salt, pepper, hot pepper sauce and wine. Mix well. Bake, covered, at 325 degrees for 1 hour and 15 minutes. Serves 6. *Goes well with roast fowl, beef or pork.*

Mrs. William Parmer (Jean Glasscock)

Rice Pilaf

2 tablespoons butter or margarine
1/4 cup vermicelli, curled or fine egg noodles
1 cup long grain rice
2 cups chicken or beef broth, boiling hot
1/4 teaspoon salt, or to taste

Melt butter in a 2-quart saucepan. Break up vermicelli; sauté in pan until slightly brown, stirring constantly. Add rice; sauté together a few minutes more. Add broth and salt; mix well. Cover; cook over low heat for 20 minutes. When liquid is absorbed and rice is soft, remove from heat; stir once with a fork. Cover rice mixture with a double layer of absorbent paper toweling; replace cover. Let rest 15 minutes before serving. Stir once more with a fork. Serves 4.

Variations:

Red Pilaf: Follow above directions substituting 1 cup tomato juice for 1 cup broth. Omit vermicelli. Serve sprinkled with 1 medium chopped onion.

Bulgur Pilaf: Follow above directions substituting bulgur for rice. Omit vermicelli. Add 1 small chopped onion and 1 teaspoon dried, crushed mint leaves to mixture.

Mrs. Gregory H. Keuroghlian (Nora Ghazikian)
Rose Ghazikian, Dunedin, Florida

Chinese Fried Rice

½ pound bacon, fried crisp and crumbled
3 tablespoons reserved bacon drippings
½ cup chopped green onions and tops
1 cup diced celery
1 cup sliced mushrooms
3 cups cooked rice
2 tablespoons soy sauce
1 egg, slightly beaten

In a large skillet cook onions and celery in reserved bacon drippings until tender. Add mushrooms, rice and soy sauce. Sauté 10 minutes on low heat, stirring occasionally. Stir in beaten egg; cook only until egg is done. Add bacon; mix well. If a darker color is preferred, extra soy sauce may be added with the rice. Serves 6.

Variation: ½ cup finely diced, cooked ham, chicken, or pork may be used in place of bacon. Brown meat first using oil.

Helen S. Glass
Mrs. Elwood Reichart (June), Chicago, Illinois

Sweet Potato Puff

3 cups mashed, cooked sweet potatoes
½ cup butter, room temperature
½ cup sugar
½ cup milk
2 eggs
1 teaspoon vanilla extract

In a medium bowl mix all ingredients together until creamy. Pour into a buttered 2-quart casserole.

Topping:

⅓ cup butter
⅓ cup all-purpose flour
½ cup brown sugar
1 cup chopped nuts

Cut butter into flour until crumbly. Add brown sugar and nuts. Sprinkle over potatoes. Bake at 350 degrees for 35 to 40 minutes. Serves 8 to 10.

Mrs. Allen Wieska (Joy)
Bellwood, Illinois

Herbed Rice

2 tablespoons butter
2 tablespoons chopped onion
1/4 cup finely chopped celery
2 cups chicken broth or bouillon
1/2 teaspoon salt
1/2 teaspoon soy sauce
1/4 teaspoon rubbed sage
1/4 teaspoon basil
2 tablespoons chopped fresh parsley or 1 tablespoon dry parsley flakes
1 cup rice

In a large skillet melt butter; sauté onion and celery until tender. Add remaining ingredients; bring to a boil. Cover pan; reduce heat to low. Cook 15 minutes without stirring until liquid is absorbed. Serves 6.

Note: Good for dishes that do not have gravy and when plain rice is just not elegant enough. Seasonings are light and do not cover up flavor of main dish.

Helen S. Glass

Dotty's Italian Spinach

2 (10-ounce) packages frozen chopped spinach
7 eggs, lightly beaten
1 pound Ricotta cheese
4 ounces mozzarella cheese, shredded
1 cup yogurt
1/2 cup butter, melted
1/4 teaspoon salt
1/8 teaspoon pepper
1/2 teaspoon nutmeg
1/2 teaspoon thyme
Grated Parmesan cheese
Butter

Defrost spinach in a colander, pressing out all excess liquid; set aside. In a medium bowl beat together remaining ingredients except Parmesan cheese and butter. Add spinach; blend well. Pour into a buttered 13x9x2-inch baking dish. Top with Parmesan cheese; dot generously with butter. Bake at 350 degrees for 1 hour until firm and golden. Serve at room temperature. Serves 8.

Mrs. Harvey Heimann (Jean)

Sweet Potato Casserole

2 (17-ounce) cans sweet potatoes, drained and mashed, or 2 large sweet potatoes, baked and mashed
½ cup orange juice
1 teaspoon cinnamon
½ teaspoon nutmeg
¼ teaspoon ground cloves
¼ cup brown sugar
½ cup chopped nuts
2 tablespoons butter
Marshmallows (optional)

In a large bowl mix all ingredients except butter and marshmallows. Pour into a 1-quart casserole. Dot with butter. Bake at 350 degrees for 20 to 30 minutes. Top with marshmallows for last 10 minutes of baking. Serves 8.

Mrs. Dean N. McFarland (Donna VanEwyk)

Brandied Sweet Potatoes

6 large sweet potatoes
2 teaspoons cornstarch
½ teaspoon cinnamon
2 teaspoons salt
½ cup sugar
1 cup water
1 tablespoon lemon juice
⅓ cup brandy

Cook unpared sweet potatoes in boiling, salted water 25 minutes or until tender. Drain and cool. In a saucepan mix cornstarch, cinnamon, salt and sugar. Stir in water. Cook over low heat until sauce is clear. Stir in lemon juice and brandy. Peel potatoes; slice crosswise ¼- to ½-inch thick. Put slices into a buttered 9-inch square baking dish; pour sauce overall. Bake at 375 degrees for 30 minutes or until glazed; basting occasionally. Serves 6.

Mrs. Douglas Guilfoile (Paula L. Tiezzi)

Yellow Squash Casserole

3 cups thinly sliced yellow squash (about 4 medium)
1 small onion, sliced
1 (10¾-ounce) can cream of chicken or cream of mushroom soup
1 cup sour cream
1 (6-ounce) box cornbread dressing mix
½ cup butter or margarine, melted

In a saucepan cook squash with onion in as little water as possible until squash is just tender; drain. Add soup, sour cream and spices from dressing mix. In a large bowl mix dressing with butter. Spread half of dressing in a 2-quart casserole dish; cover with squash mixture. Top with remaining dressing. Bake at 350 degrees for 30 minutes or until squash bubbles through dressing. Serves 10 to 12.

Mrs. S. E. "Pete" Covey (Carol Daugherty)

Company Potatoes

1/4 cup butter
1 medium onion, finely chopped
3 tablespoons chopped green pepper
1 tablespoon chopped pimento
2 1/2 tablespoons all-purpose flour
2 cups milk
1/2 teaspoon salt
1/8 teaspoon pepper
3 cups cubed, cooked potatoes
1/3 cup pasteurized process cheese spread

In a medium saucepan cook onion and green pepper in butter for 5 minutes. Add pimento and flour; stir. Add milk; stir and cook until thickened. Season to taste with salt and pepper; add potatoes. Pour into a 1½-quart buttered casserole. Top with cheese. Bake at 350 degrees for 30 minutes. Serves 4 to 6.

Mrs. Albert MacCaffery (Shirley)
Chicago, Illinois

Kitchen Hint: Cook potatoes in salt water for 10 minutes before baking. Shortens cooking time and saves energy.

Delish Cheese Potatoes

Microwave

4 slices bacon or 1/3 cup bacon bits
4 medium potatoes, peeled and thinly sliced
1/4 cup chopped onions
1/4 cup water
1/2 cup mayonnaise or salad dressing
1/3 cup sour cream
1 cup shredded Cheddar cheese
1/4 cup sliced stuffed green olives
1/2 teaspoon salt
1/8 teaspoon pepper

Microwave bacon on High until crisp; set aside. Place potatoes, onion and water in 1½-quart casserole. Cover and microwave on High 12 to 14 minutes or until tender, stirring every 6 minutes; drain. In a medium bowl combine remaining ingredients except bacon. Add to potatoes; mix lightly to combine. Crumble bacon; sprinkle over top. Microwave on High, uncovered, 3 to 4 minutes or until heated through. Serves 4. For 8 servings, double quantities; use 2-quart casserole. Cook potatoes 24 to 26 minutes; heat through 4 to 5 minutes.

Irish Gray
Tampa, Florida

Make Ahead Party Potatoes

9 medium baking potatoes, peeled and quartered
½ cup butter or margarine
1½ teaspoons salt
¼ teaspoon pepper
⅔ cup warm milk
1½ cups shredded Cheddar cheese
1 cup whipping cream, whipped

In a saucepan cook potatoes in boiling water until tender; drain. In a large bowl mash potatoes; beat until fluffy adding butter, seasonings and milk. Pour into buttered 12x8x2-inch glass baking dish. Fold cheese into whipped cream; spread over potatoes. Bake at 350 degrees for 25 minutes until golden brown. May be made ahead, but reserve topping until ready to bake and serve. Serves 8 to 10.

Variation: Add 1 clove crushed garlic, 1 cup sour cream and 1 (8-ounce) package softened cream cheese to whipped potatoes. Omit topping; sprinkle with paprika. Bake as directed.

June Burns
Dunedin, Florida

Fabulous Layered Potatoes

3 tablespoons butter or margarine
6 medium Idaho potatoes, peeled and thinly sliced
1 large onion, thinly sliced
½ tablespoon seasoned salt
2 tablespoons grated Parmesan cheese
½ teaspoon garlic powder

Melt butter in a large skillet with tight lid. Alternate layers of potatoes, onions, seasoned salt, cheese and garlic powder until pan is full. Cover; cook slowly on low to medium heat for ½ hour. Turn if top and bottom browning are desired. Continue cooking another ½ hour. Serves 4 to 6.

Variation: Melt butter in 2-quart casserole and layer as directed. Bake, covered, at 350 degrees for 45 minutes.

Mrs. Lawrence Feltman (Bertha)
Chicago, Illinois

Pittsburgh Potato Casserole

8 potatoes, cooked, peeled and diced
1 (16-ounce) package American cheese, sliced in strips
1 cup mayonnaise
½ cup chopped onion
¼ teaspoon salt, or to taste
⅛ teaspoon pepper, or to taste
½ pound bacon, partially fried and chopped
½ cup sliced stuffed olives

In a large mixing bowl combine first 6 ingredients. Pour into a 12x8x2-inch glass baking dish. Top with olives and bacon. Bake at 325 degrees for 1 hour. Serves 10.

Note: Can be made ahead and refrigerated until baking time.

Mrs. Addison Bender (Josephine Andrews)

Campus Potatoes

Microwave

6 large potatoes, peeled and sliced
1 large onion, sliced into rings
½ cup butter or margarine
¾ teaspoon seasoned salt

In a 2-quart casserole layer potatoes and onions; dot with butter and sprinkle with seasoned salt. Cover; microwave on High for 10 minutes. Stir and cook 10 minutes more. Let stand 5 minutes. Serves 4 to 6.

Ruth Treymann
Bay City, Michigan

Rich Creamed Potatoes

Men love these!

6 medium to large potatoes, cooked
½ cup butter
1 cup whipping cream
½ teaspoon salt, or to taste
⅛ teaspoon pepper, or to taste

Peel potatoes and dice into ½-inch pieces; set aside. In a large saucepan melt butter. Add cream; heat. Add cool potatoes, salt and pepper. Heat mixture and serve. Serves 6 to 8.

Note: Can be made ahead and reheated.

Great with any meat! They never fail and are good for company!

Mrs. J. Wallace Lee (Ida)

Baked Cheesy Potatoes

- 1 (10¾-ounce) can cream of chicken soup
- 1 cup sour cream
- 1 cup shredded sharp Cheddar cheese
- ¼ cup butter or margarine
- 2 tablespoons green onion tops
- 1 (24-ounce) package frozen hash brown squares
- 1 cup crushed potato chips (optional topping)

In a saucepan combine soup, sour cream, cheese, butter and onion; heat until butter melts. Place frozen hash brown squares in a single layer in a 12x8x2-inch baking dish. Pour warm soup mixture over squares. Bake at 350 degrees for 40 to 45 minutes until brown and bubbly. Serves 4 to 6.

Mrs. Fred Boston (Janet)
Mrs. Paul J. Donahue (Sigrid), Dunedin, Florida
Betty Miller, Savannah, Georgia

Potato Patties

- 2 cups mashed potatoes
- 1 egg yolk, slightly beaten
- 2 tablespoons minced onions
- ¼ teaspoon salt
- ⅛ teaspoon pepper
- ½ cup all-purpose flour
- 3 tablespoons shortening

In a medium bowl combine mashed potatoes, egg yolk, onion, salt and pepper. Mix well. Shape into 6 patties; coat with flour. Melt shortening in a skillet until hot. Brown patties slowly so they will have a delicious brown glazed crust. Serves 6.

Variation: Shape mixture into balls; roll in egg white, then in fine bread crumbs or corn flake cereal crumbs. Fry in a skillet or bake in oven at 450 degrees for 15 minutes.

Mrs. William S. Sharpe (Wanda)

Parsley Butter

- ½ cup softened butter
- 1 tablespoon chopped fresh parsley
- 1 teaspoon fresh lemon juice
- Salt to taste
- Pepper to taste

Place all ingredients in a medium bowl; beat at medium speed, scraping bowl often, until light and fluffy. Makes ½ cup.

Suncoast Seasons Committee

Flavor-enhancing spread for potatoes, chicken, cauliflower and other fresh vegetables.

Desserts and Pies

Almond Float

Float:

1 (11-ounce) can mandarin oranges
1 (1/4-ounce) envelope unflavored gelatin
3 tablespoons water
1 (5 1/3-ounce) can evaporated milk
1 1/2 cups water
6 tablespoons sugar
1 tablespoon almond extract

Drain and reserve juice from can of oranges. In small bowl dissolve gelatin in 3 tablespoons water. Heat milk, remaining water and sugar to just below boiling point; add dissolved gelatin and stir until mixed. Cool. Add almond extract; mix. Pour into 9- or 10-inch square pan; refrigerate until set or overnight. Cut into diamond shapes; place in dessert bowls and float in syrup with oranges on top.

Syrup:

1/4 cup sugar
1 to 1 1/2 cups warm water
1 teaspoon almond extract
Reserved juice of the mandarin oranges

Dissolve sugar in warm water; cool. Add almond extract and mandarin orange juice. Serves 4 to 6.

Mrs. Jay Johnston
Princeton, New Jersey

Crustoli

Italian

3 eggs, beaten
2 tablespoons sugar
1 ounce light rum
1 1/2 cups unbleached flour
3 tablespoons water
1/4 teaspoon salt
1 1/2 teaspoons baking powder
2 cups oil, for frying
Powdered sugar

Combine all ingredients except oil and powdered sugar in large bowl; knead until smooth. Roll out 1/4-inch thick on floured board. Cut into triangles; put slit in center and pull top of triangle through slit. Cook in oil a few at a time until golden brown. Drain on paper towels. Sprinkle with powdered sugar. *Do not make in humid weather!* Makes 3 to 4 dozen.

Mrs. Douglas Guilfoile (Paula L. Tiezzi)

Crustoli, Bow Ties, Snowballs and Chruski are basically the same light, melt-in-your mouth pastry. Traditionally made when snow is on the ground!

Traditional English Trifle

5 slices poundcake, cut ½-inch thick or 10 ladyfingers
⅓ to ½ cup raspberry preserves
½ cup sweet sherry, or more according to taste
1 (3-ounce) package black cherry flavored gelatin
½ cup boiling water
Ice cubes or chilled water
1 (16-ounce) can pear halves, drained
Cold custard
1 (16-ounce) can sliced peaches, drained
1½ cups whipping cream, whipped
¼ cup coarsely chopped walnuts

Spread preserves on cake and arrange in the bottom of a deep 3-quart decorative glass serving bowl. Pour sherry over cake. Dissolve gelatin in boiling water; add ice cubes or chilled water to make 1½ cups gelatin. Pour over cake mixture; chill until set (about 1 hour). Dice pear halves and spread over gelatin layer. Pour over half cold custard; smooth top with a spatula. Arrange peach slices pinwheel-fashion on top of custard, slicing thinner if necessary. Pour remaining custard over peaches, smoothing top with spatula. Chill overnight. Before serving spread whipped cream over all and sprinkle with chopped nuts. Serves 8 to 10.

Custard:

6 egg yolks, well beaten
⅔ cup sugar
½ cup all-purpose flour
⅛ teaspoon salt
3 cups milk, scalded
1 tablespoon butter
1½ teaspoons vanilla extract

In a large bowl beat egg yolks, sugar, flour and salt together until thoroughly blended. Very slowly combine milk with egg mixture, beating constantly. Return to heavy saucepan and cook, stirring constantly, over low heat until thick and smooth. Remove from heat; stir in butter and vanilla. Cool to room temperature before using on trifle.

Variation: Can also be made into 10 individual trifles by dividing ingredients between 10 glass serving bowls.

Janet Joyce

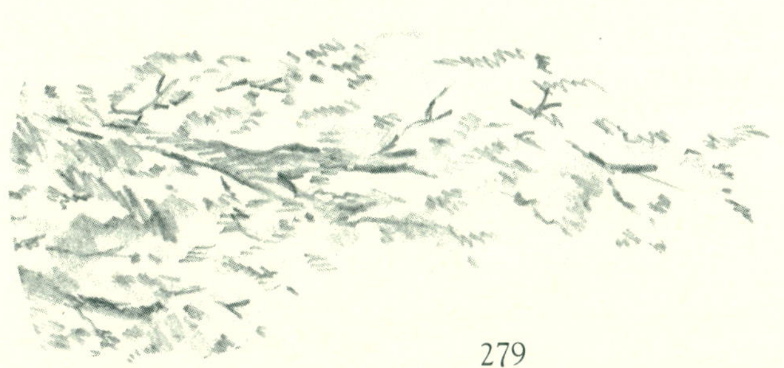

Almond Pumpkin Charlotte

30 single ladyfingers
2 (1/4-ounce) envelopes unflavored gelatin
2/3 cup milk
1/3 cup dark rum
4 eggs, separated
2/3 cup brown sugar
2 cups mashed pumpkin (fresh or canned)
1 teaspoon grated orange peel
1 teaspoon cinnamon
1/2 teaspoon nutmeg
1/2 teaspoon ginger
1/4 teaspoon ground cloves
1 cup whipping cream, whipped with 3 tablespoons sugar
1/2 cup toasted almonds, chopped
Whipped cream, for garnish

Trim the tips of the ladyfingers to fit the height of an 8-inch springform pan. Stand ladyfingers in pan with curved side out; set aside. In a large saucepan combine gelatin, milk, rum, egg yolks and 1/3 cup of sugar. Stir over a low heat for 5 to 10 minutes to make a soft custard. Remove from heat; stir in pumpkin, orange peel and spices; set aside to cool. In a large bowl beat egg whites until soft peaks form. Gradually beat in remaining sugar. Gently fold egg white mixture and whipped cream alternately into pumpkin mixture. Fold in almonds. Turn into prepared ladyfinger-lined pan. Cover with plastic wrap and chill at least 6 hours. When ready to serve, remove springform pan. Pipe rosettes of whipped cream around edges of dessert. Serves 8 to 10.

Janet Joyce

Miniature Cream Cheese Tarts

3 (8-ounce) packages cream cheese
1 cup sugar
1 1/4 teaspoons vanilla extract
3 eggs

Mix cream cheese, sugar and vanilla together until creamy. Beat in eggs, one at a time. Pour mixture into paper cupcake holders in 1 3/4-inch size muffin tins until 3/4 full. Bake at 350 to 375 degrees for approximately 20 minutes (or until crack appears on top). Remove from oven; let stand for 5 minutes.

Topping:

1 pint sour cream
1/4 cup sugar
1/4 teaspoon vanilla extract
1 (21-ounce) can cherry or blueberry pie filling

Mix together sour cream, sugar and vanilla; spoon on top of miniature cupcakes; return to oven for 5 minutes. Top with pie filling when cool. Makes 4 dozen. *Excellent! Great for parties!*

Mrs. Anthony S. Brancato (Georgine E. Palmer)

Black Forest Trifle

A Different Trifle!

Base:

4 (½-inch) slices pound cake
2 tablespoons cherry preserves
½ cup strong black coffee
1 tablespoon Kirsch (cherry liqueur)
1 (16-ounce) can pitted black cherries, drained, reserving liquid
1 (¼-ounce) package unflavored gelatin

Spread preserves on cake slices and arrange in bottom of a deep 2-quart decorative glass serving bowl. Combine coffee and liqueur; pour over cake. Dissolve gelatin in 1 cup of reserved cherry liquid; pour over coffee-soaked cake. Chill until set, about 1 hour. Arrange cherries in a layer on top of cake mixture.

Custard:

2 cups milk, scalded
1 tablespoon cocoa
5 egg yolks
⅔ cup sugar
⅓ cup all-purpose flour
⅛ teaspoon salt
1 tablespoon butter
1½ teaspoons vanilla extract

In a heavy medium saucepan stir cocoa into scalded milk. In a large bowl combine egg yolks, sugar, flour and salt, beating together until smooth. Stirring constantly, very gradually pour milk into egg mixture. Return to saucepan and cook over low heat, stirring until mixture is thick and smooth. Remove from heat; beat in butter and vanilla extract. Cool to room temperature; pour over cherries in bowl. Chill overnight.

Topping:

2 ounces dark chocolate, grated
1 cup whipping cream, whipped

Sprinkle ½ of grated chocolate over custard layer. Spread whipped cream overall. Sprinkle remaining chocolate. Must be prepared ahead. Serves 6 to 8.

Hint: To stop a skin from forming on custard, dust top lightly with sugar.

Mrs. Enid Lythgoe

Betsy's Surprise Dessert

Crust:

2 cups unsalted pretzels, crushed
¾ cup butter, melted
3 tablespoons sugar

Mix pretzels, butter and sugar and pat into bottom of 12x8x2-inch glass baking dish. Bake at 350 degrees for 7 minutes; cool.

Filling:

1 (8-ounce) package cream cheese
1 cup sugar
1 (8-ounce) container non-dairy whipped topping

In a medium bowl beat together cream cheese, sugar and whipped topping. Spread over cooled crust.

Topping:

1 (6-ounce) box strawberry gelatin
1 (8-ounce) can crushed pineapple and juice
1 (16-ounce) package frozen unsweetened strawberries
1 tablespoon lemon juice

Dissolve gelatin in 2 cups hot water; add fruit and lemon juice; chill. When slightly thick, spread on top of filling. Refrigerate several hours. Serves 15.

Note: Should be prepared a day ahead.

Betsy Vetters
Dunedin, Florida

Halva

Greek Style

2 cups water
1 cup sugar
½ cup sweet butter
1 cup farina
¼ teaspoon vanilla extract
1 tablespoon chopped walnuts
¼ teaspoon cinnamon

Heat water; add sugar and stir to dissolve. Do not boil. Melt butter; add farina and brown slightly. Add sugar, water and vanilla; mix well until mixture leaves sides of pan. Pour into 1½-quart ring mold. Let cool slightly; turn into dish while still warm. Sprinkle with walnuts and cinnamon. Cool and slice.

Mrs. Chris Demas (Jeannie)

Huguenot Tart

4 eggs, room temperature
3 cups sugar
½ cup all-purpose flour
5 teaspoons baking powder
½ teaspoon salt
2 cups chopped nuts
2 cups finely chopped, tart apples

Beat whole eggs until very frothy. Add remaining ingredients in above order. Pour into 2 well buttered (bottom and sides) 12x8x2-inch glass baking pans. Bake 45 minutes at 350 degrees until crusty and brown. Serve warm or cold with whipped cream or ice cream. Recipe may be cut in half. Serves 16.

Mrs. Preston Packard (D'Lou)

Black Magic Dessert

Crust:

1½ cups all-purpose flour
¾ cup butter or margarine
½ cup chopped walnuts

In a large mixing bowl cut flour together with butter or margarine until well blended. Add walnuts. Press into a 13x9x2-inch baking dish; bake at 350 degrees for 15 to 20 minutes. Cool completely.

Filling:

2 cups powdered sugar
1 (16-ounce) container non-dairy whipped topping
2 (8-ounce) packages cream cheese, softened
2 (4⅛-ounce) packages instant chocolate pudding
1 tablespoon vanilla extract
3 cups milk

Beat together powdered sugar, 2 cups whipped topping and cream cheese. Spread over cooled crust. Beat instant pudding, vanilla and milk for 2 minutes. (Mixture will be semi-thick.) Pour over cheese layer. Let pudding set. Top with remaining whipped topping. Refrigerate at least 1 hour. Makes 18 servings.

Ruth Treymann
Bay City, Michigan

Variations: Substitute either butter pecan, butterscotch, lemon or pistachio for chocolate pudding. Sprinkle with ¼ cup chopped nuts.

Mrs. Joni Richards, Royal Palm Beach, Florida
Mrs. Vito Grasso (Aurora), Dunedin, Florida

A Different Strudel

½ pound sweet butter
½ pint vanilla ice cream, softened
2 cups all-purpose flour

Mix ingredients and knead until pie crust is soft. Cut dough into 4 balls and refrigerate a few hours.

Filling:

1 teaspoon lemon juice
1 pound jar apricot preserves
1 cup finely chopped walnuts
1 cup shredded coconut
¼ cup cinnamon
½ cup sugar
1 cup chopped raisins
Cinnamon-sugar

Beat lemon juice with apricot preserves; set aside. Mix and blend remaining dry ingredients. Roll out each pastry ball into oblong, very thin pieces. If dough is sticky, dust with flour before rolling. Cut in half crosswise; spread preserves overall; sprinkle in turn with dry ingredients and roll. Pinch edges and place on cookie sheet seam side down. Continue until all dough is used. Cut strudel rolls in diagonal slits 3-inches apart almost through to bottom. Brush tops with egg whites and sprinkle with cinnamon-sugar overall before baking. Bake at 350 degrees for ½ hour or until golden brown. Cool on waxed paper before cutting through. Wrap in foil and place in plastic bags before freezing. Serves 12.

Mrs. Gregory H. Keuroghlian (Nora Ghazikian)

Cherry Cobbler

Microwave

1 (20-ounce) can cherry pie filling
½ teaspoon cinnamon
1 teaspoon almond extract
1 (8-ounce) can crushed pineapple, drained
1 (9-ounce) package yellow or white cake mix
½ cup flaked coconut
½ cup sliced almonds
½ cup margarine, melted

Combine pie filling, cinnamon, and extract in a 1½-quart baking dish. Spread pineapple over cherry mixture. Sprinkle cake mix on top, then coconut and almonds. Pour melted margarine overall. Microwave on High for 13 to 15 minutes or until bubbly. Serve with vanilla ice cream or whipped cream. Serves 6 to 8.

Variation: Toast coconut and almonds, if desired.

Mrs. John W. Vassel, Jr. (Eleanor)

Mom's Apple Dumplings

1½ cups all-purpose flour
½ teaspoon salt
½ cup shortening
4½ tablespoons cold water
6 baking apples, pared and cored
6 tablespoons sugar
¾ teaspoon cinnamon
3 teaspoons butter

Sift salt with flour. Work shortening into flour being careful not to soften more than necessary. Use a fork or 2 knives to cut it in. When the shortening has been worked in until it is of uniform size, add the cold water, slowly, until the mixture becomes a stiff dough which will hold together in 1 ball. (*Short Cut*—Pie crust sticks or mixes may be substituted for the above, if desired.) Roll out dough; cut into 6-inch squares. Place apple on each square. Add 1 tablespoon of sugar, ⅛ teaspoon cinnamon and ½ teaspoon butter to each apple. Fold dough around apple. Prick with fork and place in baking dish. Pour syrup (see recipe below) around dumplings. Bake at 450 degrees 35 to 40 minutes. Serves 6.

Syrup:

1 cup water
½ cup sugar
¼ cup butter

Heat water, sugar and butter until sugar and butter are melted.

Mrs. Jerry Harris (Nancy)

Frozen Fruit Medley

1 (12-ounce) can frozen orange juice
1½ cups sugar
1½ cups water
1 (29-ounce) can peeled apricots with juice
3 bananas
1 (20-ounce) can crushed pineapple, drained

Mix together orange juice, sugar and water. (The blender works wonders!) Mash bananas and apricots together and add pineapple. Stir the two mixtures together. Pour into individual serving containers like small plastic or 6-ounce paper cups and freeze. Serve right from freezer or thaw slightly. Serves 14.

Note: Good anytime, especially in summer! This is good served for a brunch.

Mrs. William Harris (Clara)
Dunedin, Florida

Fresh Fruit Tart

1 (17-ounce) package refrigerator sugar cookies
2 cups real cream whipped topping, thawed
1 cup sour cream
Assorted fresh fruit, sliced

Cut cookie dough into 1/8-inch slices. Arrange dough slices, slightly overlapping, on a foil-lined 14-inch pizza pan or 15x10x1-inch jelly roll pan; press edges to seal. Bake at 375 degrees for 10 to 12 minutes until golden brown. Cool; remove from foil onto serving plate. Fold whipped topping into sour cream; spread over crust and arrange fruit on whipped topping mixture; chill. Spread cooled glaze over fruit. Cut into wedges to serve. Suggested fruits; strawberries, blueberries, apples, banana or peaches. Serves 16.

Glaze:

1/2 cup sugar
1/8 teaspoon salt
1 tablespoon cornstarch
1/2 cup orange juice
2 tablespoons lemon juice
1/4 cup water
1/2 teaspoon grated orange peel

Stir together; cook about 1 minute after mixture boils. Cool.

Mrs. Stanley Kincaid (Pat)
Ozona, Florida

Chocolate Cherry Bars

1 (3 1/8-ounce) package chocolate pudding
1 (18 1/2-ounce) package chocolate cake mix
1 cup drained maraschino cherries, chopped
1 cup chopped nuts
1 cup semi-sweet chocolate chips

Cook pudding according to package directions. To hot pudding add dry cake mix and stir 1 or 2 minutes with beater or mixer. Add cherries and spread in greased and floured 13x9x2-inch pan. Sprinkle on chopped nuts and chocolate chips. Bake at 350 degrees for 30 to 35 minutes; cool. Serves 15 to 20. *Best when made a day ahead.*

Julie Amidon
New Port Richey, Florida

Cherry Cinnamon Cobbler

½ cup sugar
4 tablespoons red cinnamon candies
2 tablespoons cornstarch
½ cup water
1 (16-ounce) can sour cherries

Combine sugar, cinnamon candies, cornstarch, water and cherry juice in saucepan. Cook over medium heat, stirring occasionally until thickened. Stir in cherries; pour into 8x8-inch baking pan.

Topping:

1½ cups all-purpose flour
2 teaspoons baking powder
½ teaspoon salt
6 tablespoons brown sugar, divided
⅓ cup finely chopped pecans
½ cup shortening
1 egg, slightly beaten
2 tablespoons milk
1 tablespoon margarine, melted
¼ teaspoon cinnamon

Mix flour with baking powder and salt in a bowl. Add 3 tablespoons brown sugar and pecans. Cut in shortening until mixture is fine. Combine egg and milk. Add to flour mixture; mix until moistened, adding a few drops of milk if needed. Roll out onto floured surface to a 14x12-inch rectangle. Brush with butter. Combine 3 tablespoons brown sugar and cinnamon; sprinkle over dough. Roll up, starting with 12-inch side. Cut into ¾-inch slices. Arrange on cherry filling. Bake at 400 degrees for 25 to 30 minutes. Pour glaze over warm cobbler. Serves 6 to 8.

Lemon Glaze:

Combine ½ cup sifted powdered sugar and 1 tablespoon lemon juice.

Helen S. Glass

Fresh Peach Crunch

3 cups fresh sliced peaches
1 tablespoon lemon juice
1 cup self-rising flour
1 cup sugar
1 egg
6 tablespoons butter, melted

Place peaches in a 9-inch square baking dish and sprinkle with lemon juice. Mix flour, sugar and egg until lumpy. Spread mixture over peaches. Pour melted butter on top. Bake at 375 degrees for 30 to 35 minutes. Serves 8

Mrs. Thomas Parsons, Jr. (Gerrie)
Tampa, Florida

Celestial Angel Dessert

2 (¼-ounce) envelopes unflavored gelatin
4 tablespoons cold water
1 cup boiling water
½ cup sugar
Juice of 2 lemons
1 (16-ounce) can crushed pineapple, undrained
3 pints non-dairy whipped topping
2 (10x4-inch) oblong Angel Food cakes

Soften gelatin in cold water. Add boiling water; stir until dissolved. Add sugar, lemon juice, pineapple and juice. Chill until almost set; then fold in whipped topping. Stir until thoroughly mixed. Slice each cake into 4 long narrow slices lengthwise. Lay 4 slices in bottom of 13x9x2-inch pan. Cover with half of the filling. Lay 4 more slices on top; spread remaining filling over cake. Chill overnight or at least 3 hours before serving. Serves 12 to 16.

Janet Joyce

Kitchen Hint: To get maximum amount of juice from lemon, warm in water. Press down firmly and roll on hard surface before juicing.

Cheesecake Dreams

⅓ cup light brown sugar, firmly packed
1 cup all-purpose flour
½ cup chopped walnuts
⅓ cup margarine, melted

Preheat oven to 350 degrees. Grease 8-inch square pan. Mix together sugar, flour and walnuts; stir in margarine. Reserve ⅓ cup of crumb mixture. Pat remainder into pan. Bake 12 to 15 minutes.

Filling:

1 (8-ounce) package cream cheese, softened
¼ cup sugar
1 egg
2 tablespoons milk
1 tablespoon lemon juice
1 teaspoon vanilla extract

Beat cream cheese and sugar together using medium speed on mixer. Add remaining ingredients; pour over crust; sprinkle on reserved ⅓ cup crumbs. Bake 25 minutes longer. Cool on wire rack. Cut into 2-inch squares; then cut squares diagonally in half. Makes 32.

Janet Joyce

Kitchen Hint: To soften brown sugar put in a container and cover with a damp cloth and tight lid. In a day or so you will have soft sugar.

Frozen Chocolate Nut Zuccotto

1 (10-ounce) frozen poundcake, defrosted
½ to 1 cup Amaretto or another liqueur
2 cups heavy cream, whipped
½ cup chopped pecans or slivered almonds
½ cup (or more) chocolate chips

Cut poundcake into slices, about ½-inch thick. Cut each slice of cake diagonally into two triangles. Line a 1½-quart round bottomed bowl with the cake triangles. Place slices in the same direction — so that the crust on the cake will make a swirled design. The small long corner of the triangle will be in the center at bottom each time. Reserve 5 or 6 slices for later. Sprinkle the cake with ½ cup of the Amaretto or a bit more. Whip cream until very stiff. Fold nuts into half of the cream; add 1 tablespoon or so of Amaretto. Spread this cream evenly in the cake lined bowl, covering the cake and making a hollow in the center. Put in freezer. Melt chocolate chips. Cool and fold into remaining cream; add 1 tablespoon of Amaretto. Spoon chocolate cream into hollow. Cover with remaining cake slices. Sprinkle these with 2 tablespoons of Amaretto. Put in freezer for several hours or overnight. Place on plate to serve. Comes out easily with knife around edge. May be decorated with whipped cream and nuts. Serves 6 to 8.

Mrs. William Harris (Clara)
Dunedin, Florida

Banana Split Dessert

Great for a summer day!

2 cups graham cracker crumbs
1 cup butter, separated
2 cups sifted powdered sugar
2 eggs
5 bananas
1 (15½-ounce) can crushed pineapple, well drained
1 (8-ounce) container frozen non-dairy whipped topping, thawed
½ (4-ounce) bar semi-sweet chocolate, shredded
⅓ cup chopped nuts
15 maraschino cherries

In a medium bowl toss together graham cracker crumbs and ½ cup melted butter. Press crumb mixture into bottom of a 13x9x2-inch baking pan. In a small bowl beat remaining ½ cup butter until softened. Add powdered sugar; beat until fluffy. Beat in eggs. Spread egg mixture over crumb mixture. Slice bananas lengthwise into halves and arrange over egg mixture. Spoon pineapple over bananas. Spread with whipped topping. Sprinkle with chocolate and nuts. Cover; refrigerate at least 4 hours. Cut into squares to serve. Top each with a cherry. Cover and chill to store. *Elegant!* Serves 15.

Mrs. Jack Wilson (Mary Jane Brown)

Galatoboureko

Filling:

1 cup butter, melted
6 tablespoons all-purpose flour
1 quart milk, warmed
8 egg yolks
1 cup sugar
1 teaspoon vanilla extract

Crust:

½ pound fillo
½ cup butter, melted

Melt butter in saucepan; add flour and stir until smooth. Add warmed milk slowly, stirring constantly. Cook over low heat until it thickens. Remove from heat. In a separate bowl beat egg yolks; add sugar and vanilla extract. Pour slowly into milk mixture. Let stand until cool. Line a 12x8x2-inch glass baking pan with half the fillo sheets, bringing it over the edges and buttering every second sheet. Pour cooled custard over fillo. Then tuck in edges of fillo and use remaining sheets, buttering every second sheet until used. Bake at 325 degrees for 45 minutes. While galatoboureko is baking, make syrup and let cool; pour over hot galatoboureko. Serves 20.

Syrup:

½ cup water
1 cup sugar
2 tablespoons honey
1 tablespoon fresh lemon juice

Boil water and sugar for 5 minutes; then add honey and lemon juice.

Mrs. Charles Nikitas (Theresa)
Williamstown, Massachusetts

Bread Pudding

1 (6-ounce) box zwieback crackers
2 eggs, well beaten
½ cup sugar
1 quart milk
½ cup raisins
2 tablespoons cinnamon

Heat milk in pan; set aside. Grease a 13x9x2-inch glass dish. Lay zwieback in two rows on bottom of dish. In a bowl blend eggs with sugar; add milk and stir. Pour mixture over zwieback. Sprinkle with raisins and cinnamon. Bake at 350 degrees for 30 minutes. Cover and refrigerate, if preferred serve warm. Serves 12-15.

Variation: Add sliced apples to top of zwieback before adding remaining ingredients.

Mrs. George Ghazikian (Gladys)
Springfield, Pennsylvania

Persian Baklava

2 cups finely chopped, blanched almonds
¼ cup sugar
½ tablespoon cardamon
1 pound butter, melted
1 pound fillo, thawed in refrigerator
1 cup finely chopped, unsalted pistachio nuts

Preheat oven to 350 degrees. Mix almonds, sugar and cardamon together; set aside. Brush bottom and sides of a 13x11x1-inch jellyroll pan or equivalent with melted butter. Place 2 fillo sheets in the pan, brush top with melted butter. Continue layering sheets until half the package is used. Spread almond mixture evenly over fillo; sprinkle top with pistachios. Continue layering sheets and buttering until finished. Cut baklava into diamond-shaped pieces. Carefully spoon remaining butter (½ cup or more) over cut pieces to saturate. Bake at 350 degrees for 15 minutes. Check pastry for dryness. If needed add more melted butter and continue baking 25 to 30 minutes. Pour syrup over hot baklava. Makes 45 pieces.

Syrup:

1½ cups water
2 cups sugar
1 to 2 teaspoons lemon juice

Boil water and sugar for 5 minutes or until clear. Add juice; let cool. *Easy to prepare and so irresistably good!*

Mrs. Hagap Keuroghlian (Ofelia)
Northridge, California

Ice Cream Pumpkin Squares

Great for a luncheon!

1 (16-ounce) can pumpkin
1 cup sugar
1 teaspoon salt
1 teaspoon ginger
½ teaspoon nutmeg
1 teaspoon cinnamon
1 cup chopped pecans, toasted
½ gallon vanilla ice cream, slightly softened
36 ginger snaps

Combine pumpkin, sugar, salt, ginger, nutmeg and cinnamon; add chopped pecans. In a chilled bowl fold pumpkin mixture into ice cream. Line bottom of a 13x9x2-inch pan with half of gingersnaps. Top with ½ of the ice cream mixture. Cover with another layer of gingersnaps; add remaining ice cream. Freeze until firm, about 5 hours or overnight. Cut into squares. Garnish with whipped topping and pecan halves. Makes 18 servings.

Mrs. Stanley C. Dawson (Marilyn)
Oak Lawn, Illinois

Galopita

Greek Farina Custard

1 quart milk
1 cup sugar
½ cup butter
1 teaspoon vanilla extract
1 cup farina
6 large eggs, separated
Cinnamon
Maraschino cherries, cut in half

In a large saucepan combine milk, sugar, butter and vanilla. Heat to boiling, add farina stirring constantly for 5 minutes. Beat egg whites until stiff; add egg yolks. Fold into hot farina mixture. Pour into greased 13x9x2-inch pan (or equivalent). Sprinkle with cinnamon and bake 30 to 35 minutes at 350 degrees. While baking custard, make syrup, if desired. Serves 12 to 16.

Syrup I:

1½ cups water
1½ cups sugar

In a small saucepan boil water and sugar until clear. When custard is cooked, pour syrup over top. When cool, cut into diamond shapes. Place half of cherry on top of each.

Syrup II:

1 cup water
1½ cups sugar
1 teaspoon vanilla extract
2 ounces peach or orange liqueur
3 whole cloves
1 (3-inch) cinnamon stick
2 teaspoons orange peel

In a medium saucepan add all ingredients except vanilla extract and liqueur; simmer over low heat for 15 minutes; add vanilla extract and liqueur. Remove from heat; cool.

Hint: Important—Pour warm syrup on cool custard; or cool syrup on warm custard.

Mrs. Harvey Heimann (Jean)

Chocolate Mousse

5 squares semi-sweet chocolate
¾ cup sugar
½ cup water
4 egg yolks
2 tablespoons Cognac or strong coffee
1 cup whipping cream, whipped

Melt chocolate in top of double boiler. In small saucepan combine sugar and water and cook until clear and syrup like. Scrape melted chocolate into blender or food processor fitted with the steel blade and turn on, adding the sugar syrup with machine running. Add egg yolks, one at a time, with machine running; add Cognac or coffee and let cool to room temperature. Fold chocolate mixture into whipped cream. Pour into mold or cups and chill 4 hours. Serves 6.

Note: So good and so quick!

Mrs. Polly Leach
Kerville, Texas

Frozen Fruit Pops

1 ripe banana
⅓ cup honey
1 (6-ounce) can orange juice concentrate, thawed
1 (16-ounce) package frozen strawberries, thawed
2 cups apple juice

Whip all ingredients in blender. Freeze in pop molds or small paper cups. Makes 10 to 12. *A child's delight! And healthful too!*

Mrs. John W. Vassel, Jr. (Eleanor)

Café au Lait Dessert

A quick easy mousse

2 tablespoons gelatin
1½ cups cold water
1 cup boiling water
½ cup sugar
2 cups hot, strong coffee
1 cup whipping cream
2 tablespoons sugar

In a large bowl dissolve gelatin in cold water. Add boiling water, sugar and coffee; stir until sugar is dissolved. Chill until mixture begins to set. Beat at high speed of electric mixer until light and foamy, about 5 minutes. Beat cream and 2 tablespoons sugar until cream is stiff. Fold into gelatin mixture. Pour into 8-cup mold or individual serving glasses. Serves 6 to 8.

Violet T. Bernard

Elsbeth's Chocolate Roll

6 eggs, separated
1/2 cup fine sugar
2 tablespoons unsweetened cocoa
1/2 pint whipping cream
2 teaspoons sugar
1/2 teaspoon vanilla extract

In a medium mixing bowl beat egg whites until stiff; set aside. In a large mixing bowl beat egg yolks and sugar together for 10 minutes; add cocoa and mix. Slowly fold beaten egg whites into yolk mixture. Pour batter into a heavily buttered, lightly floured 15x10x2-inch jelly roll pan, making sure corners are greased well. Bake in preheated oven at 500 degrees for 5 minutes. Take a piece of brown paper the size of the pan; lay on counter and sprinkle with sugar. Turn the chocolate roll onto the brown paper; roll from narrow end while still hot. Cover with damp cloth; cool. Whip cream until peaks form; add sugar and vanilla. Before serving unroll and spread with sweetened whipped cream. Roll again, place on platter and sprinkle with powdered sugar. Serves 10. This recipe is a favorite of all Elsbeth's friends.

Mrs. Joseph Falotico (Elsbeth)

Kitchen Hint: For cream that will not whip, add an egg white and chill. Try again.

Homemade Ice Cream

6 eggs
2 tablespoons vanilla extract
1 cup sugar
1/4 teaspoon salt
1 (14-ounce) can sweetened condensed milk
1 pint whipping cream, whipped
Cold milk, as needed
Freezer salt

In a medium bowl beat eggs; add vanilla, sugar, salt and condensed milk; beat well. Fold whipped cream into mixture. Pour into a 5-quart ice cream freezer; fill to "full" line with cold milk. Pack ice cream freezer with ice and freezer salt. Turn until firm. Makes 5 quarts.

Sandee Pfister
Belleair, Florida

Baklava

1 pound walnuts, finely chopped
1 cup sugar
1 tablespoon cinnamon
1 pound fillo pastry, thawed according to package directions
1 pound sweet butter, melted

Combine nuts, sugar and cinnamon. Into the bottom of a 17x12x2-inch baking pan, layer 8 sheets of fillo pastry, brushing each sheet generously with melted butter. Sprinkle top sheet with some of nut mixture; add two more buttered fillo sheets; sprinkle with nut mixture. Continue adding buttered fillo sheets, sprinkling every second sheet, until all nuts are used. Place remaining fillo on top, buttering each sheet. *Hint:* While assembling baklava have everything prepared before removing fillo from package. Cover unused portion of fillo with a damp cloth while working. With a sharp knife cut baklava into small diamond-shaped pieces. Sprinkle top with a few drops of cold water; bake at 350 degrees for 30 minutes; reduce temperature to 300 degrees; bake 1 hour longer. Cool and pour syrup over baklava.

Syrup:

3/4 cup sugar
3/4 cup honey
2 cups water
1/2 lemon with rind
1 (3-inch) cinnamon stick

Combine ingredients for syrup. Boil 20 minutes. Remove lemon and cinnamon stick; cool. Pour over baklava after it has been baked and cooled. Makes 48.

Mrs. Anthony S. Brancato (Georgine E. Palmer)

Elegant Hot Chocolate Sauce

1/2 cup butter
2 squares unsweetened baking chocolate
1 cup sugar
1/2 pint whipping cream

Melt butter and chocolate in saucepan. Add sugar; boil until dissolved. Stir in whipping cream; boil 8 to 10 minutes, stirring constantly. Serve warm over ice cream or cake; sprinkle with chopped nuts, if desired. Will keep in refrigerator 2 weeks. Just spoon out and melt as needed. Makes 1½ cups.

Mrs. Polly Leach
Kerville, Texas

Swedish Rice Pudding

½ cup rice
4 eggs
⅔ cup sugar
2 cups milk
¼ teaspoon salt
½ teaspoon cinnamon
¼ teaspoon nutmeg

Cook rice and drain. In a medium bowl beat eggs; add sugar, milk, salt, cinnamon, nutmeg and rice. Pour into a well-buttered 1½-quart casserole. Place casserole in pan of hot water. Bake at 350 degrees for 1 hour or until light brown on top. Serves 4 to 5.

When made at Christmas, add 1 whole almond. Whoever gets the almond has good luck for the coming year!

Mrs. Addison Bender (Josephine Andrews)

Raspberry Sauce

1 tablespoon all-purpose flour
1 cup water
1 cup white corn syrup
1 teaspoon vanilla extract
½ teaspoon cinnamon
1 quart fresh raspberries

Mix flour with a small amount of water in a saucepan. Add remaining water, corn syrup, vanilla and cinnamon. Bring to a boil; add raspberries and return to a boil. Pour onto ice cream. Makes about 4 cups.

Variation: Fresh or canned peaches may be used in place of raspberries. If using canned peaches, substitute peach syrup for corn syrup.

Betty Hartley
Tawas City, Michigan

Mocha Sauce

2 egg whites
¼ cup sugar
2 teaspoons instant coffee
½ teaspoon water
¾ cup light corn syrup
⅛ teaspoon salt, or to taste
1 teaspoon vanilla extract

In a medium bowl beat egg whites until soft peaks form; add sugar and coffee. Add water to dissolve sugar and coffee. Beat in vanilla extract and salt, then syrup, beating until smooth and creamy. Serve over ice cream.

Mrs. Charles Nikitas (Theresa)
Williamstown, Massachusetts

Honeyscotch Sundae Sauce

½ cup sugar
¾ cup honey
½ teaspoon salt
¼ cup butter
⅔ cup evaporated milk

Combine ingredients using ⅓ cup evaporated milk. Cook to a soft-ball stage (235 to 240 degrees), then stir in additional ⅓ cup evaporated milk; cook until sauce is thick and smooth, about 3 minutes longer. Makes 1½ cups.

Mrs. Jerry Harris (Nancy)

Old-Fashioned Cornstarch Pudding and Pies

An excellent filling for eclairs!

2 cups milk or half and half
1 cup sugar
2 tablespoons cornstarch
⅛ teaspoon salt or to taste
2 eggs
1 teaspoon vanilla extract
Cherries (optional)

In a quart saucepan warm milk over medium heat. In a small bowl mix together sugar, cornstarch and salt; add eggs and mix well. Add mixture to warm milk; cook until thickened, stirring constantly. Add vanilla; pour into custard dishes. Top with a cherry. Serves 4 to 6.

Note: If mixture lumps, use an egg beater until lumps are gone. If you don't like too sweet, use ½ to ¾ cup sugar.

For Pies:

As a pie filling, add at least 1 more tablespoon cornstarch.

Coconut Cream Pie: Add ¾ to 1 cup coconut.

Chocolate Cream Pie: Add 4 to 5 tablespoons cocoa to dry mixture.

Banana Cream Pie: Line bottom of crust with sliced bananas.

Meringue:

3 egg whites
⅓ cup sugar
¼ teaspoon cream of tartar

Beat egg whites until stiff but not dry. Beat in sugar and cream of tartar gradually and continue until well blended. Spread evenly on pie and bake at 350 degrees for 10 minutes.

Mrs. Louis Doty (Faylene)
Palm Harbor, Florida

Amaretto Satin Pie

1 (9-inch) graham cracker pie crust
4 egg yolks
1/4 box (4-ounces) powdered sugar
1 cup sweet butter, softened
1/3 cup coffee liqueur
1 banana, thinly sliced
1 ounce Amaretto liqueur

In a bowl place egg yolks, sugar, butter and coffee liqueur. (These should be at room temperature.) Place sliced banana on bottom of graham cracker crust. Sprinkle the Amaretto over the bananas; let soak into crust. Use electric beater on high speed to whip egg yolks, sugar, butter and coffee liqueur. Beat for *10 minutes.* (This is important for texture and smooth consistency.) Place mixture in crust spreading evenly over bananas. Refrigerate for several hours. About 15 minutes before serving, take pie out of refrigerator. Top with whipped cream. Serves 8 to 10.

Note: This is a very rich dessert so a small portion is ample.

Sharon Arnold Spencer
Clearwater Beach, Florida

Cream Cheese Cherry Pie

1 (9-inch) baked pie shell or graham cracker pie crust
1 (8-ounce) package cream cheese, softened
1 (14-ounce) can sweetened condensed milk
1/3 cup lemon juice
1 teaspoon vanilla extract
1 (21-ounce) can cherry pie filling

In a medium bowl whip cream cheese until fluffy; gradually add milk; beat well. Add lemon juice and vanilla extract; beat well. Pour into crust; chill 3 to 4 hours. Top with cherry pie filling; chill. Serves 8.

Mrs. Stanley H. Dawson (Ruth)

Macaroon Pie

12 single soda crackers, finely crushed
12 dates, finely chopped
1 cup sugar
1 cup nuts, chopped
3 egg whites

In a large bowl combine crackers, dates, sugar and nuts. In a medium bowl beat egg whites until almost stiff; fold into other ingredients and pour into a greased 9-inch pie pan. Bake at 350 degrees for 30 minutes. Serves 8.

Mrs. Jack Garber (Lois)

Easy Cherry Pie

A Different Cherry Pie!

Crust:

1 cup all-purpose flour
1/2 cup butter, softened
1/3 cup sugar
1/8 teaspoon salt

In a medium bowl mix flour, butter, sugar and salt with your hands; press into a 9-inch pie pan. Place in oven at 350 degrees for 15 minutes.

Filling:

1 (21-ounce) can cherry pie filling
1/4 teaspoon almond extract

Combine pie filling and almond extract. Cool pie shell slightly; pour filling into shell.

Topping:

1 (8-ounce) package cream cheese, softened
1 egg
1/2 cup sugar

In separate bowl beat together cream cheese, egg and sugar. Pour over pie filling. Bake at 350 degrees 30 to 35 minutes until top is firm. Serves 8

Mrs. James McKinley (Lillian)
Chicago, Illinois

Banana Cream Pie

1 (9-inch) pie shell, baked
3 egg yolks, slightly beaten
1/3 cup all-purpose flour or 1/4 cup cornstarch
2/3 cup sugar
1/4 teaspoon salt
2 cups milk, scalded
2 tablespoons butter
1/2 teaspoon vanilla extract
2 medium bananas, sliced

In top of double boiler mix flour or cornstarch, sugar and salt. Gradually add milk; cook over moderate heat, stirring constantly until mixture thickens and boils. Cook 2 minutes; remove from heat. Add small amount to egg yolks. Stir this mixture into remaining hot mixture; cook 1 minute stirring constantly. Add butter and vanilla; cool slightly. Pour over sliced bananas in pie shell. Refrigerate until set, about 1 hour. Serves 8.

Mrs. Dean N. McFarland (Donna VanEwyk)

Buttermilk Pie

1 (9-inch) pie shell, unbaked
3 eggs
½ cup butter, softened
1½ cups sugar
1 cup buttermilk
3 tablespoons all-purpose flour
1 teaspoon vanilla extract

In large mixing bowl beat eggs, slightly. Cream butter and sugar; add to eggs. Add other ingredients; mix well. Pour into pie shell. Bake at 425 degrees for 10 minutes; reduce to 325 degrees; bake 30 minutes or until knife inserted comes out clean.

Mrs. Ronald Gordon (Linda)

Chocolate Peanut Butter Pie

½ cup powdered sugar
¾ cup peanut butter
1 (9-inch) graham cracker pie crust
1 (4⅛-ounce) package chocolate instant pudding
2 cups milk
1 (8-ounce) container non-dairy whipped topping

In medium bowl mix powdered sugar and peanut butter together; blend well. Pour mixture into pie crust. In small bowl mix pudding and milk; pour over peanut butter mixture; top with whipped cream. If desired, sprinkle with graham cracker crumbs. Cool. Serves 6 to 8.

Mrs. Greg Santa (Cathy)

Chocolate Cream Pie

1 (9-inch) pie shell, baked or graham cracker crust
2 egg yolks
1 egg
1¼ cups sugar
⅓ cup cocoa
¼ cup all-purpose flour
1½ cups milk
⅛ teaspoon salt
1 teaspoon vanilla extract
¼ cup butter, softened

In top of double boiler mix egg yolks, egg, sugar, cocoa, flour, milk and salt with wire whisk. Cook over low heat until thick, stirring constantly. Add vanilla extract and butter, continue stirring until butter is completely dissolved. Cool slightly; pour into pie shell; refrigerate. Garnish with whipped cream, if desired, before serving. *Easy!* Makes 1 (9-inch) pie.

Mrs. William Parmer (Jean Glasscock)

Dessert Cheese Pie

Crust:

16 to 18 graham crackers, crushed (2½ cups)
¼ cup butter, melted
2 tablespoons sugar

Filling:

¾ pound cream cheese, room temperature
2 eggs
½ cup sugar
½ teaspoon vanilla extract
Cinnamon

Topping:

1 (16-ounce) carton sour cream
3 tablespoons sugar
½ teaspoon vanilla extract

In a medium bowl mix graham crackers, butter and sugar. Press into 10-inch pie pan. Beat cream cheese, eggs, sugar and vanilla together; pour into pie crust; sprinkle with cinnamon. Bake 20 minutes at 375 degrees; cool thoroughly. Mix sour cream, sugar and vanilla extract. When pie is cool, pour sour cream mixture over top. Bake 5 minutes at 400 degrees; cool again and chill at least 24 hours before serving. Serves 9 to 12.

Mrs. Jack Garber (Lois)

Kitchen Hint: Empty leftover cereal or cookie crumbs into blender. Grind and store in airtight container. Use instead of graham crackers for tasty pie crust or dessert topping.

Baked Egg Custard Pie

1 (9-inch) pie shell, unbaked and chilled
4 eggs
½ cup sugar
¼ teaspoon salt
1 teaspoon almond extract
2½ cups scalded milk
½ teaspoon nutmeg

In a medium bowl beat eggs slightly (do not over beat); add sugar, salt and almond extract. Gradually add scalded (not quite boiling) milk. Pour into shell; sprinkle with nutmeg and bake at 400 degrees for 25 to 30 minutes. Cool pie 10 to 15 minutes at room temperature; then chill before serving. Serves 6 to 8.

Hint: When transferring custard from counter to oven before cooking, leave spoon resting in the mixture; this helps stop the custard mixture from spilling over. Remove spoon before baking.

Janet Joyce

Ricotta Pie

Crust:

1/2 cup butter
2 packages graham crackers, crushed or 2 1/2 cups graham cracker crumbs
1 teaspoon cinnamon

Prepare crust by melting butter; add crushed crackers and cinnamon; press into a 15½x9½x2¼-inch baking dish or two 9-inch pie pans.

Filling:

2 pounds ricotta cheese
4 eggs
2 tablespoons all-purpose flour
1 cup evaporated milk
1 (8-ounce) can crushed pineapple, drained
3/4 (10-ounce) jar cherries, drained and cut in half
1 teaspoon vanilla extract
1 cup sugar

In a large bowl mix ricotta cheese, eggs, flour, milk, pineapple, cherries, vanilla and sugar. Pour into shell and sprinkle remainder of crumbs on top. Bake at 350 degrees for 1 hour. Serves 16 to 24.

Mrs. Giordano Tiezzi (Ida)
Meriden, Connecticut

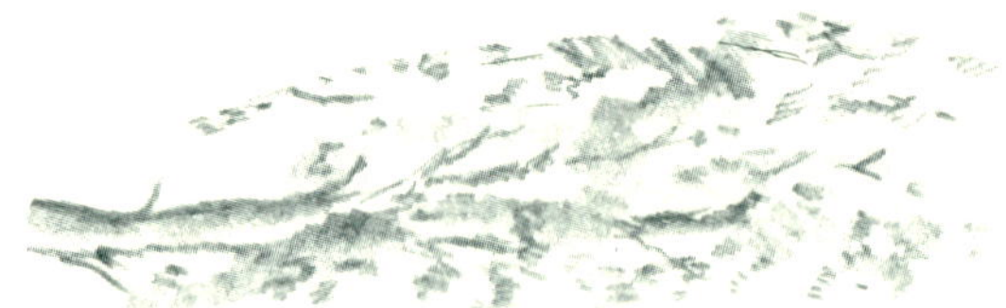

Key Lime Pie

1 (8-inch) pie shell, baked or graham cracker crust
1 (14-ounce) can sweetened condensed milk
1/2 cup lime juice
1 teaspoon grated lime peel
1/4 teaspoon salt
2 eggs, separated
1/4 teaspoon cream of tartar
4 tablespoons sugar

Pour sweetened condensed milk into mixing bowl; add lime juice, peel, salt and egg yolks. Beat until well blended. Turn filling into pie shell. To make meringue, add cream of tartar to egg whites and beat until stiff. Add sugar gradually, beating until smooth and glossy. Spread over lime filling. Bake at 425 degrees 4 to 4½ minutes or until brown. Cool. Serves 6.

Mrs. Paul R. Chabot (Arinda D. Bass)

Key Lime Pie Americana

1 (9-inch) pie shell, baked
1 (1/4-ounce) envelope unflavored gelatin
1/2 cup sugar
1/4 teaspoon salt
4 eggs, separated
1/2 cup fresh lime juice
1/4 cup water
1 teaspoon grated lime peel
2 to 3 drops green food coloring
1/2 cup sugar
1 cup whipping cream, whipped

In a medium saucepan mix gelatin, sugar and salt. Beat egg yolks, lime juice and water; add to gelatin mixture. Cook over medium heat and stir constantly until boiling; (you may use a double boiler) remove from heat. Stir in lime peel and food coloring; chill; stir occasionally until mixture mounds slightly when dropped from a spoon. Beat egg whites; gradually add ½ cup sugar. Beat until stiff and fold into gelatin mixture. Fold half of whipped cream into gelatin mixture and pour into pie shell; chill. Spread with additional whipped cream. Chill. Serves 6 to 8.

Mrs. James Knauff (Alice)
Belleair, Florida

This key lime pie is a treasured recipe in Mrs. Knauff's collection, as her husband, Jim, was affiliated with the Americana in Bal Harbour, Florida.

Marshmallow Fruit Pie

1 cup (16) graham crackers, finely crushed
1/3 cup butter or margarine, melted
24 marshmallows, cut in quarters
1/4 cup milk
1/8 teaspoon salt
1 (20-ounce) can fruit cocktail, drained (2 1/2 cups)
1/2 cup whipping cream, whipped

Preheat oven to 350 degrees. In a large bowl combine graham cracker crumbs and butter; blend well. Pack into bottom and around the sides of a greased 9-inch pie pan. Bake 8 to 10 minutes; cool. Heat marshmallows, milk and salt in the top of a double boiler over hot water until marshmallows are just melted. Chill until mixture begins to thicken. Then fold in 2 cups of the fruit cocktail and all the whipped cream. Pour into crust and chill several hours until firm. Garnish with remaining fruit cocktail and additional whipped cream, if desired. Serves 6.

Mrs. Bill Ritchey (Carol Eddington)

Kitchen Hint: For cream that will not whip, add an egg white and chill. Try again.

Choco-Mint Alaska Pie

A Grande Finale!

1 (9-inch) pie shell, baked
1 (5 1/3-ounce) can evaporated milk
2 (1-ounce) squares unsweetened chocolate
1 cup sugar
2 tablespoons butter or margarine
1 teaspoon vanilla extract
1 quart peppermint ice cream

Combine evaporated milk and chocolate. Cook and stir over low heat until chocolate is melted. Stir in sugar and butter or margarine. Cook over medium heat 5 to 8 minutes more or until thickened, stirring occasionally; stir in vanilla; cool. In a mixing bowl soften ice cream using a wooden spoon to stir and press against side of bowl. Soften just until pliable. Spoon ½ of the ice cream into baked pie shell. Return remaining ice cream to freezer. Cover pie with ½ of the cooled chocolate sauce and freeze. Let remaining chocolate sauce stand at room temperature. Repeat layers with remaining ice cream and sauce, softening ice cream to spread, if necessary. Cover and freeze until firm.

Meringue:

3 egg whites
1/2 teaspoon vanilla extract
1/4 teaspoon cream of tartar
1/3 cup sugar
1/4 cup crushed peppermint candy

Prepare meringue by beating egg whites, vanilla and cream of tartar until soft peaks form. Gradually add ⅓ cup sugar beating to stiff peaks. Fold 3 tablespoons of the crushed candy into meringue. Remove pie from freezer. Spread meringue over chocolate layer, carefully sealing to edge of pastry. Swirl the meringue in a circular motion to make decorative peaks. Place on a baking sheet. Bake at 475 degrees for 3 to 5 minutes or until meringue is golden. Sprinkle with remaining tablespoon crushed candy. Serve immediately. Serves 6 to 8.

Mrs. William R. Barnes (Vickie)

Chocolate Mousse Pie

Absolutely Luscious!

Crust:

3 cups chocolate wafer crumbs
1/2 cup unsweetened butter, melted

Combine crumbs and butter. Press on the bottom and completely up sides of a 10-inch springform pan. Refrigerate for 30 minutes or chill in freezer. A wide flat-bottomed glass is good to compress crumbs.

Filling:

1 pound semi-sweet dark chocolate
2 eggs
4 egg yolks
2 cups whipping cream
6 tablespoons powdered sugar
4 egg whites, room temperature

Soften chocolate in top of double boiler (or in bowl over simmering water). Let cool until lukewarm. Add 2 eggs and mix well; then add 4 egg yolks and mix until thoroughly blended. Whip cream with powdered sugar until soft peaks form. Beat egg whites until stiff but not dry. Stir a little of the cream and egg white into chocolate mixture to lighten; then fold in remaining cream and egg whites until thoroughly mixed. Pour into crust and chill at least 6 hours, or preferably overnight.

Chocolate Leaves:

4 ounces (approximately) semi-sweet chocolate
1 teaspoon vegetable shortening
Camelia or other waxy leaves

Melt chocolate and shortening in top of a double boiler. Using a spoon generously coat underside of 10 or 12 leaves. Place on waxed paper and chill or freeze until firm.

Topping:

2 cups whipping cream
2 tablespoons powdered sugar

Whip remaining 2 cups of cream with sugar until quite stiff. Loosen crust on all sides of pie, using sharp knife. Remove springform. Spread whipped cream over top of mousse. Peel leaves away from chocolate starting at stem end of leaf and decorate top of mousse. Cut pie into wedges with a thin, sharp knife. *A delicious and impressive dessert!* Serves 12 to 15.

Note: This dessert can be prepared ahead and frozen. Thaw overnight in the refrigerator.

Janet Joyce

Kitchen Hint: Refrigerated eggs separate more easily than those at room temperature.

Fresh Strawberry Pie

1 (9-inch) pie shell, baked
1 (3-ounce) package strawberry flavored gelatin dessert
2/3 cup sugar
1 3/4 cups hot water
3 1/2 tablespoons cornstarch
4 tablespoons cold water
1 tablespoon butter
1 1/2 teaspoons red food coloring (optional)
1 quart fresh strawberries, sliced
1/4 cup sugar

Mix gelatin and sugar in a saucepan. Add hot water. Stir to dissolve. Blend cornstarch and cold water together and add to gelatin mixture. Cook over low heat until clear and thick stirring constantly. Remove from heat and add butter. Add red food coloring, if desired, for color. Cool in a pan of ice water. When cool, add fresh strawberries, slightly sweetened with sugar. Pour into pie shell. Chill. Serve with whipped cream. Serves 6

Mrs. Paul Glasscock (Lurlene)
Brandon, Florida

Pecan Pie

A not-so-sweet version

1 (9-inch) pie shell, unbaked
1/4 cup butter or margarine
1/2 cup sugar
1 cup dark corn syrup
1/4 teaspoon salt
3 eggs
1 cup pecan halves

In a mixing bowl cream butter to soften; add sugar gradually and beat until fluffy. Add syrup and salt; beat well. Add eggs one at a time, beating thoroughly after each; stir in pecans. Pour into unbaked pastry shell. Bake at 350 degrees for 50 minutes or until knife inserted comes out clean. Cool. Serves 8.

Mrs. S. E. "Pete" Covey (Carol Daugherty)

Bluegrass Pie

1 (9-inch) pie shell, unbaked
1/2 cup margarine, melted
1 cup sugar
1 cup light corn syrup
2 tablespoons bourbon
3 eggs
1/2 cup chocolate chips
1 cup chopped pecans

In a bowl combine margarine, sugar and syrup; add eggs and bourbon. Fold in nuts and chocolate chips. Pour into pie shell; bake at 350 degrees for 45 minutes. Makes 1 pie.

Mrs. Bruce Simmons (Debbie)
Palm Harbor, Florida

Peach Cream Pie

Pastry:

1 cup sifted all-purpose flour
1 egg yolk
1 tablespoon sugar
½ cup butter, softened
Rind of 1 lemon, grated
⅛ teaspoon salt

In a large bowl mix pastry by hand into a paste; pat evenly into a 9-inch pie pan. Chill until firm.

Filling:

4 (3-ounce) packages cream cheese
½ cup sugar
2 eggs
¼ teaspoon cinnamon
5 fresh peaches
3 tablespoons peach preserves

In a medium bowl mash cream cheese until soft. Beat in sugar, eggs and cinnamon. Pour filling into chilled pastry; bake at 425 degrees for 12 to 15 minutes or until firm. Peel; slice and arrange peaches when pie has cooled. Heat preserves and pour over peach slices. Serves 6.

Mrs. Dean N. McFarland (Donna VanEwyk)

Sour Cream Lemon Pie

1 (9-inch) graham cracker crust
1 cup sugar
¼ cup cornstarch
1¼ cups milk
3 egg yolks, slightly beaten
1 teaspoon grated lemon rind
⅓ cup fresh lemon juice
¼ cup margarine
1 cup sour cream
Whipped cream

In a 2-quart saucepan stir together sugar and cornstarch. Stir in milk until smooth; stir in egg yolks, lemon rind and lemon juice until smooth; add margarine, stirring constantly; boil over medium heat for 1 minute. Pour into large bowl; cover; refrigerate 40 to 50 minutes. Fold sour cream into lemon mixture until well blended. Pour into pie crust; refrigerate 2 hours until firm. Garnish with whipped cream. Serves 8.

Mrs. J. Wallace Lee (Ida)

Kitchen Hint: To get maximum amount of juice from lemon, warm in water. Press down firmly and roll on hard surface before juicing.

Fresh Strawberry Cream Pie

Pastry:

½ cup slivered almonds, toasted
1½ cups sifted all-purpose flour
½ teaspoon salt
½ cup shortening
4 to 5 tablespoons cold water

Set almonds aside. Make pastry by mixing flour, salt, shortening and water; roll ⅛-inch thick; fit loosely into 9-inch pie pan. Trim 1 inch beyond edge; fold under and crimp high. Prick bottom and sides well with fork. Bake at 450 degrees 10 to 12 minutes. Cover bottom of cooled, baked shell with almonds.

Creamy Vanilla Filling:

½ cup sugar
3 tablespoons cornstarch
3 tablespoons all-purpose flour
½ teaspoon salt
2 cups milk
1 egg, slightly beaten
½ cup whipping cream, whipped
1 teaspoon vanilla extract
2½ cups whole fresh strawberries

Combine sugar, cornstarch, flour and salt. Gradually stir in milk. Bring to boiling, stirring constantly. Lower heat; cook and stir until thick. Stir a little hot mixture into egg; return to remaining hot mixture. Bring just to a boil, stirring constantly; cool; then chill. Beat well; fold in whipped cream and vanilla. Fill shell with chilled filling. Slice strawberries in half, reserving a few whole berries for center; arrange sliced berries on top of filling.

Glaze:

½ cup strawberries, crushed
½ cup water
¼ cup sugar
2 teaspoons cornstarch
Few drops red food coloring
Whole berries, reserved, for garnish
Whipped cream, for garnish

In medium saucepan place strawberries; add the water; cook 2 minutes; sieve. Mix the sugar and cornstarch; gradually stir in berry juice. Cook and stir until thick and clear. Tint with red food coloring. Cool slightly; spoon over strawberries. Refrigerate until serving time. Garnish with whole strawberries and whipped cream. Serves 6 to 8.

Mrs. William S. Sharpe (Wanda)

English Walnut Pie

3 egg whites
1 cup sugar
1 teaspoon baking powder
1 teaspoon vanilla extract
1 cup chopped walnuts
20 round buttery crackers, crushed

In a large bowl beat egg whites until they peak; add sugar gradually. Fold in baking powder and vanilla. Fold in nuts and crackers. Bake in greased 9-inch pie pan at 350 degrees for 30 minutes. Serve with whipped topping; garnish with cherries or chipped chocolate. Serves 6.

Gerry Bracken
Clearwater, Florida

Variation: **French Pecan Pie**—substitute 1 cup crushed pecans for walnuts; bake for 20 to 25 minutes. Serve with whipped cream; garnish with grated chocolate.

Mrs. Dean N. McFarland (Donna VanEwyk)

Frozen Pumpkin Pie

1 (10-inch) pie shell, baked or graham cracker crust
1 pint vanilla ice cream, softened
1 (16-ounce) can pumpkin
1½ cups sugar
½ teaspoon salt
1 teaspoon cinnamon
½ teaspoon ginger
¼ teaspoon ground cloves
1 teaspoon vanilla extract
1½ cups whipping cream
1 cup slivered almonds
¼ cup sugar

Spread ice cream in cooled pie shell. Place in freezer. Mix pumpkin with 1½ cups sugar, salt, spices and vanilla extract. Whip 1 cup of whipping cream until stiff; fold into pumpkin mixture. Pour mixture over ice cream layer; cover with aluminum foil; freeze about 4 hours. In a skillet caramelize the almonds with sugar, stirring constantly. Remove from heat when almonds are caramel colored and spread on greased cookie sheet. Break apart when cool. Whip remaining ½ cup cream; spread over pie. Garnish with almonds. Serves 8 to 10.

Hint: Can be made up to a week ahead.

Mrs. Ronald Gordon (Linda)

Applesauce Pumpkin Pie

1 cup pumpkin
½ cup applesauce
½ cup brown sugar
½ teaspoon salt
½ teaspoon ground cloves
1½ teaspoons cinnamon
1½ teaspoons nutmeg
¼ teaspoon ginger
4 eggs, beaten
1¼ cups evaporated milk
1 (9-inch) pastry shell, unbaked

In a bowl combine pumpkin, applesauce, sugar, salt and spices; add eggs to mixture. Slowly add milk, mixing well. Pour into shell; bake at 425 degrees for 45 minutes. Cool and garnish with whipped cream or whipped topping; sprinkle with nutmeg. Makes one 9-inch pie.

Mrs. Paul R. Chabot (Arinda D. Bass)

Pumpkin Chiffon Pie

1 (9-inch) pie shell, baked
1 (¼-ounce) envelope unflavored gelatin
¼ cup cold water
3 eggs, separated
1 cup sugar
1¼ cups canned pumpkin
½ cup milk
½ teaspoon salt
½ teaspoon cinnamon
½ teaspoon ginger

In a small bowl dissolve gelatin in water. In medium saucepan cook slightly beaten egg yolks with ½ cup of sugar, pumpkin, milk, salt and spices. Cook until thick. Add gelatin mixture; stir and cool. In a separate bowl beat egg whites and ½ cup sugar until stiff. Fold into gelatin mixture when it begins to thicken. Pour into pie shell. Store in refrigerator. Serve with whipped cream. Serves 6 to 8.

Mrs. James Long (Eva Fandrich)

Million Dollar Pie

2 (9-inch) graham cracker crusts
1 (14-ounce) can sweetened condensed milk
1 (12-ounce) carton non-dairy whipped topping
¾ cup chopped pecans
¾ cup flaked coconut
1 (20-ounce) can crushed pineapple, drained
2 tablespoons lemon juice

In medium bowl mix milk, whipped topping, pecans, coconut and pineapple. When well mixed, add lemon juice; pour into pie crusts and garnish with cherries or favorite fruit. Refrigerate at least 2 hours before serving. Makes 2 pies.

Gerry Bracken, Clearwater, Florida
Mrs. S. E. "Pete" Covey (Carol Daugherty)
Alice Forrester, Madre, California

Angel Cream Pie

Pie Shell:

1/4 teaspoon salt
1/4 teaspoon cream of tartar
4 egg whites, room temperature
1 cup sugar

In a large mixing bowl combine salt, cream of tartar and egg whites; beat until stiff peaks form. Add sugar beating in a spoonful at a time. Spread in a well-buttered 9-inch pie pan having meringue higher on edge forming a rim. Preheat oven to 400 degrees. Put in pie pan, immediately turn off heat and leave for 5 hours or overnight. *Do not open oven.* Remove pie.

First Layer:

1/2 cup whipping cream, whipped
1/2 teaspoon vanilla extract

Mix cream with vanilla extract; spread over pie shell. Refrigerate several hours.

Filling:

4 egg yolks
4 tablespoons sugar
4 tablespoons lemon juice
1/2 cup whipping cream, whipped

In top of double boiler beat egg yolks until thick and lemon colored. Gradually beat in sugar and lemon juice. Cook and stir over hot water until thick and smooth (about 5 minutes). Cool. Spread filling over layer and top with whipped cream. Chill. Serves 8.

Variation: Try strawberry or raspberry filling. Over first whipped cream layer spread halved fresh strawberries or whole raspberries. Sprinkle lightly with sugar; cover with remaining whipped cream.

Mrs. Dean N. McFarland (Donna VanEwyk)

Variation: Chocolate Filling

1 (4-ounce) package German sweet chocolate
3 tablespoons water
1 teaspoon vanilla extract
1/2 pint whipping cream, whipped

In a small saucepan melt chocolate in water over low heat, stirring constantly. Cool; add vanilla extract. Fold in whipped cream. Pour into pie shell. Decorate top with shaved chocolate. Refrigerate. Serves 8.

Mrs. Charles Christensen (Jeanne)
Oldsmar, Florida

Southern Pecan Pie

1 (9-inch) unbaked pie shell
1 cup white corn syrup
1 cup dark brown sugar
1/3 cup butter, melted
1 to 1 1/2 cups shelled pecans
3 eggs
1/4 teaspoon vanilla extract
1/8 teaspoon salt

In a medium bowl combine all ingredients; mix well. Pour into the pie shell and bake at 350 degrees for 45 to 50 minutes. Cool and serve with whipped cream or vanilla ice cream. Serves 6 to 8.

Mrs. Robert Russ (Carol Hodapp)
Mrs. John W. Vassel, Jr. (Eleanor)

French Pastry Pie Shell

2 cups all-purpose flour
10 tablespoons butter or margarine
1/2 teaspoon salt
1 egg
1 to 2 tablespoons cold water

In a food processor place chopping blade. Add flour, butter and salt. Cover; process until butter is size of course cornmeal, about 5 seconds. Add egg and 1 tablespoon water; process until dough forms a ball, adding more water if necessary. Chill dough at least 30 minutes before rolling out. Makes a double crust pie or two 9-inch pies. If pie shell is to be baked before filling, prick and bake at 450 degrees for 12 to 15 minutes or until light golden brown. Makes two 9-inch pies.

Plain Pastry Pie Shell

1 1/2 cups sifted all-purpose flour
1/2 teaspoon salt
1/2 cup shortening
4 to 5 tablespoons cold water

In a large bowl mix flour and salt, cut in shortening with a pastry-blender until pieces are the size of small peas. Sprinkle water, a tablespoon at a time, over mixture. Gently mix with fork; until all is moistened. Form a ball; let stand several minutes. Divide dough in half. Form two balls. Roll on a lightly floured board making 1-inch larger than pie pan. Bake in a hot oven, 450 degrees, for 12 to 15 minutes for unfilled pie shell. Makes 8 to 9-inch double shell.

Hint: When rolling out pie crust, always roll from the center out to edge. Use light strokes. If edges split, pinch together. When baking pie shell without filling, prick the bottom with a fork.

Suncoast Seasons Committee

Kitchen Hint: To soften dried pastry, place in airtight container for 24 hours with slice of fresh bread. Use club soda instead of water for pie crust.

Cakes

Apricot Brandy Cake

1 cup butter
3 cups sugar
6 eggs
½ teaspoon rum extract
¼ teaspoon almond extract
1 teaspoon orange extract
½ teaspoon lemon extract
1 teaspoon vanilla extract
1 teaspoon butter flavoring
3 cups all-purpose flour
¼ teaspoon baking soda
1 teaspoon salt
½ cup apricot brandy
1 cup sour cream

In a large bowl cream butter and sugar; add eggs, one at a time. Add extracts and flavoring. In a separate bowl sift together the flour, soda and salt. Using electric mixer add dry ingredients to egg mixture, alternating with brandy and sour cream. Bake in a 10-inch tube or Bundt pan at 300 degrees for 1 hour and 10 minutes or until done. Remove from pan and wrap in foil while hot. Serves 12 to 16.

Hint: A double recipe makes 3 loaves (9x5x3-inch)

Note: This cake keeps a long time; gets better the longer it ages.

Mrs. Marian Connell
Nashville, Tennessee

Fresh Apple Walnut Cake

1 cup butter or margarine
2 cups sugar
3 eggs
3 cups sifted all-purpose flour
1½ teaspoons baking soda
½ teaspoon salt
¼ teaspoon mace
1 teaspoon cinnamon
1 teaspoon vanilla extract
3 cups pared, chopped tart apples
2 cups chopped walnuts

Cream butter and sugar together until fluffy. Add eggs, one at a time, beating well after each addition. Sift together flour, baking soda, salt, mace and cinnamon; add gradually. Stir in vanilla, apples and walnuts. Batter will be stiff. Spoon into greased and floured 10-inch tube pan. Bake at 325 degrees for 1½ hours. Let cool in pan for 10 minutes before removing to wire rack. Serves 12 to 16.

Mrs. Robert Haverkos (Ginny)

Grand Marnier Cake

1 (18½-ounce) yellow cake mix
1 tablespoon lemon juice
1 cup orange juice
½ cup Grand Marnier liqueur
1 cup sugar
1 (7-ounce) jar apricot jam

Prepare cake mix according to package directions. Bake in a Bundt cake pan. When cake is done remove from pan to cool. While the cake bakes, combine the next 4 ingredients in a small saucepan. Bring to a low boil; continue to boil until mixture reaches a syrupy consistency; cool. While the cake is still warm, poke many holes in the cake with a straw. Pour the syrup over the cake filling the holes. Brush apricot jam over the cake. Serves 10 to 12.

Jacqueline Crowne
Sarasota, Florida

Angel Sherbet Cake

Cake:

1 package angel food cake mix
2 to 3 pints lemon sherbet, softened
¼ to ⅓ cup crème de menthe

Two weeks before serving bake cake in a 10-inch tube pan; cool. Remove a ¾-inch slice from the top of the cake; reserve top. Hollow out center of cake, leaving ¾-inch of cake on the sides and bottom. Spoon ⅓ of the sherbet into the hollow; make rivers in sherbet with a fork. Pour ½ of creme de menthe into rivers in the sherbet; creme de menthe should not touch cake. Spoon ⅓ of sherbet over; make rivers again and pour remaining creme de menthe over second layer of sherbet. Spoon remaining sherbet on top. Place reserved cake top over last layer of sherbet. Freezer wrap cake and place in freezer. Remove from freezer 2 days before serving and frost.

Frosting:

1 cup evaporated milk
⅛ teaspoon salt
2 (6-ounce) packages semi-sweet chocolate pieces
2 teaspoons vanilla extract

In a small saucepan bring milk and salt to a boil; remove from heat. Stir in chocolate pieces and vanilla extract and continue stirring until completely smooth. Let stand 5 minutes until slightly thickened. Frost cake and refreeze. Serves 12 to 16.

Mrs. Dean N. McFarland (Donna VanEwyk)

Autumn Loaf Cake

1½ cups all-purpose flour
1 teaspoon baking soda
½ teaspoon salt
1 teaspoon cinnamon
½ teaspoon nutmeg
¼ teaspoon ginger
¼ teaspoon ground cloves
½ cup butter or margarine
1 cup sugar
1 teaspoon vanilla extract
2 eggs
¾ cup solid packed pumpkin
¾ cup chocolate chips
¼ cup walnuts, chopped

Sift together first 7 ingredients; set aside. In large mixing bowl cream butter, gradually add sugar; beat until light and fluffy; add vanilla. Blend in eggs; beat well. On low speed add dry ingredients alternately with pumpkin, beginning and ending with dry ingredients. Stir in chips and ½ of the walnuts. Spread in greased 9x5x3-inch loaf pan and sprinkle remaining nuts on top. Bake in preheated oven at 350 degrees for 60 to 70 minutes. Cool; remove from pan and drizzle with glaze. Serves 12 to 15.

Glaze:

½ cup sifted powdered sugar
⅛ teaspoon cinnamon
⅛ teaspoon nutmeg
2 tablespoons milk

Mix ingredients together blending well.

Mrs. Phillip Chabot (Eva)
Royal Palm Beach, Florida

Apple Cake

1 cup sugar
¼ cup oil
2 eggs
1 teaspoon vanilla extract
1 cup all-purpose flour
½ teaspoon salt
½ teaspoon baking powder
½ teaspoon baking soda
½ teaspoon cinnamon
3 cups peeled, sliced McIntosh apples
½ cup chopped nuts
½ cup raisins

Cream together sugar and oil; add eggs and mix well. Add vanilla extract, flour, salt, baking powder, baking soda and cinnamon. Add apples, nuts, and raisins; mix. Put into greased and floured 9-inch square pan. Bake at 375 degrees for 45 minutes or until done. Cool; dust with powdered sugar.

Note: Dough will be heavy.

Mrs. George Palmer (Margaret)
Garfield, New Jersey

Grandma's Applesauce Cake

1/3 cup butter
1 cup sugar
1 1/2 cups sweetened applesauce
2 cups all-purpose flour
2 teaspoons cocoa
1 teaspoon baking soda
1/8 teaspoon salt
1 teaspoon cinnamon
1/2 teaspoon nutmeg
1/2 teaspoon ground cloves
1 cup seedless raisins

Cream together butter and sugar; stir in applesauce. Sift all dry ingredients together and add to first mixture; add raisins that have been dusted with flour. Turn into well greased 9x5x3-inch loaf pan; bake at 350 degrees for 45 minutes or until done. Serves 12. "This recipe was my Great-Great Grandmother, Annie Fox's recipe."

Evelyn Carver
Dunedin, Florida

Kitchen Hint: Shake raisins or chopped dried fruit with some of the flour before adding to cake batter. It will keep them from sinking to bottom of cake.

Lazy-Daisy Cake

2 eggs
1 cup sugar
1 teaspoon vanilla extract
1 cup cake flour
1 teaspoon baking powder
1/4 teaspoon salt
2 tablespoons butter or margarine
1/2 cup milk, heated to lukewarm

Beat eggs until light and frothy; continue beating while adding the sugar, a little at a time; then add vanilla. Sift together flour, baking powder and salt. Add a little at a time to above mixture. Melt butter in saucepan; add milk heating to *lukewarm*. Add this to flour mixture stirring well. (Mixture will be thin and have bubbles on surface.) Pour into a generously greased 9-inch round baking pan. Bake for 20 minutes at 350 degrees. When done, frost. Serves 8.

Frosting:

4 1/2 tablespoons butter, melted
8 teaspoons dark brown sugar
3 tablespoons half-and-half
1 1/2 cups moist coconut

Combine all ingredients and spread on cooled cake. Put under broiler at 500 degrees, about 4 to 5 inches, until golden (a few seconds).

Mrs. Lewis N. McFarland (Blanche)
Villa Park, Illinois

Applesauce Cake

1½ cups applesauce
2 teaspoons baking soda
⅔ cup margarine
1 cup sugar
1 cup raisins
1 cup chopped walnuts
2 cups all-purpose flour
1 teaspoon cinnamon
½ teaspoon nutmeg
½ teaspoon ground cloves
¼ teaspoon mace
¼ teaspoon ginger

Heat applesauce; add baking soda; mix and set aside. Melt margarine; add sugar to dissolve; add applesauce mixture and remaining ingredients. Mix to blend. Pour into a greased 8x8x2-inch pan; bake at 350 degrees for 30 to 35 minutes. Cut into squares and serve with whipped cream. Serves 9.

Variation: For a delicious fruit cake add 1 cup candied fruits and peels and decrease raisins to ½ cup.

Mrs. Gregory H. Keuroghlian (Nora Ghazikian)

Texas Cookie Cake

2 cups sugar
2 cups all-purpose flour
⅛ teaspoon salt, or to taste
3 tablespoons cocoa
½ cup margarine
1 cup water
2 eggs
½ cup buttermilk
1 teaspoon baking soda
1 teaspoon salt

Combine sugar, flour and salt in a large bowl. Heat cocoa, margarine and water in a small saucepan until it boils; add to flour mixture. In a medium bowl beat together eggs, buttermilk, baking soda and salt; add to chocolate mixture. Place in a greased and floured 15x10x1-inch jelly roll pan; bake at 350 degrees for 20 to 25 minutes. Serves 10 to 12.

Icing:

½ cup margarine
3 tablespoons cocoa
6 tablespoons milk
1 (16-ounce) box powdered sugar
1 teaspoon vanilla extract
1 cup nuts, chopped

In a medium saucepan heat margarine, cocoa and milk until margarine melts. Add powdered sugar and vanilla and beat until smooth. Ice cake as soon as it comes from the oven. Cool on rack before serving.

Note: Refrigerate uneaten portion.

Mrs. John G. Dodson (Frankie Armitage)

Chocolate Eclair Cake

22 graham crackers
2 (3 3/8-ounce) packages vanilla instant pudding
3 cups milk
1 (8-ounce) carton non-dairy whipped topping

Butter a 13x9x2-inch pan; line with whole graham crackers. In large mixing bowl combine pudding with milk; mix well. Add whipped topping; blend thoroughly. Pour ½ mixture over crackers. Top with another layer of crackers. Add remaining pudding mixture; cover with crackers.

Topping:

2 (1-ounce) squares unsweetened baking chocolate
1 tablespoon light corn syrup
2 tablespoons butter
1 teaspoon vanilla extract
1½ cups powdered sugar
4 tablespoons milk

In small saucepan dissolve chocolate, corn syrup, butter, vanilla, powdered sugar and milk; mix well. Spread over last layer of graham crackers. Refrigerate several hours or overnight. Serves 10 to 12.

Mrs. James H. Fresh (Bette)
Dunedin, Florida

Mississippi Mud Cake

Cake:

1½ cups all-purpose flour
⅓ cup cocoa
1 cup grated coconut
1 cup chopped pecans
1 cup margarine, melted
4 eggs
1 teaspoon vanilla
2 cups sugar
1 (7-ounce) jar marshmallow cream

Mix first 8 ingredients. Pour into a greased 13x9x2-inch pan. Bake at 350 degrees for 30 minutes. Remove from oven; spread marshmallow cream over hot cake. Allow to cool before frosting.

Frosting:

½ cup margarine
3 to 5 teaspoons milk
⅓ cup cocoa
1 (16-ounce) box powdered sugar
1 teaspoon vanilla

Combine ingredients in a bowl; mix until smooth, using 3 teaspoons milk. Add more, if necessary. Spread over cake. Serves 16 to 20.

Mrs. Anthony Castrogiovanni (BeBe)

All-American Texas Sheet Cake

1 cup margarine
1 cup water
4 tablespoons cocoa
2 cups sugar
2 cups all-purpose flour
½ teaspoon salt
2 eggs
½ cup sour cream
1 teaspoon baking soda

In a large heavy saucepan bring first 3 ingredients to a boil. Remove from heat. Add sugar, flour and salt; beat well. Add eggs, sour cream and baking soda; beat well. Pour into greased jelly roll pan and bake 20 minutes at 375 degrees. Spread frosting on warm cake. Serves 15.

Frosting:

½ cup margarine
4 tablespoons cocoa
4 to 6 tablespoons milk
1 pound powdered sugar

Bring margarine, cocoa and milk to a boil in heavy saucepan. Remove from heat. Beat in powdered sugar a little at a time until spreading consistency.

Variation: Substitute ½ cup buttermilk or ½ cup milk and 1½ teaspoons vinegar for sour cream, plus 1 teaspoon vanilla; add with eggs.

Mrs. S. E. "Pete" Covey (Carol Daugherty)
Mrs. Jack Garber (Lois)

Orange Cake

Cake:

1 cup sugar
½ cup shortening
2 eggs, beaten
1 cup raisins
Peel of 1 large orange
1 cup sour milk or buttermilk
1 teaspoon baking soda
2 cups all-purpose flour

Grease and lightly flour a Bundt or 10-inch tube pan. In a large bowl cream sugar, shortening and eggs. Grind raisins and orange peel; add to batter. Stir in milk, baking soda and flour; mix well. Bake at 350 degrees for 45 minutes to 1 hour.

Icing:

1 cup sugar
½ cup orange juice

Combine sugar and orange juice. Spoon over warm cake.

Mrs. Edward W. Roos (Mildred Seagren)

Grandma's Chocolate Cake

2 cups sugar
3/4 cup shortening
2 eggs
1 cup sour milk
6 heaping tablespoons cocoa
1 cup boiling water
2 cups all-purpose flour
2 teaspoons baking soda
1 teaspoon vanilla extract
1/4 teaspoon salt

In a large bowl cream sugar and shortening; beat in eggs and sour milk. Mix cocoa in boiling water. Gradually add cocoa mix and flour to bowl, alternating each. Add baking soda, vanilla extract and salt. Do not overbeat. Bake in 2 greased and floured 9-inch round pans at 350 degrees for 30 minutes. When cool, frost. Serves 8 to 10.

7-Minute Frosting:

2 egg whites, unbeaten
1 1/2 cups sugar
2 teaspoons light corn syrup
1/3 cup cold water
1/8 teaspoon salt
1 teaspoon vanilla extract

Place all ingredients except vanilla extract in top of a double boiler. Beat 1/2 minute with electric mixer to blend. Place over boiling water. Cook, beating constantly with electric mixer, until frosting forms peaks, about 7 minutes. Do not overcook. Add vanilla extract. Remove from heat; beat an additional 2 minutes or until of spreading consistency. Frost cake.

Hint: Best made on a sunny day!

Variation: In a small bowl beat 1 (3-ounce) package cream cheese until soft. Beat in small amount of frosting; fold cream cheese mixture into frosting. Blend thoroughly. Do not beat.

Mrs. Jack Garber (Lois)

Westerner Pound Cake

1 1/2 cups margarine or butter, room temperature
1 (16-ounce) box powdered sugar
6 eggs, room temperature
2 cups all-purpose flour, sifted
1 teaspoon lemon juice
1 tablespoon vanilla extract

Cream margarine; add powdered sugar; beat until fluffy. Add eggs, one at a time, beating well after each addition. Sift flour 3 times and add gradually to batter. Add flavorings and mix well. Bake in a 10-inch greased and floured tube pan at 325 degrees for 1 1/2 hours. Cool 4 minutes, then invert pan. Serves 10 to 12.

Note: Serve plain; frosted with whipped cream; fruit or ice cream.

Jane Stipe

Chocolate Chip Date Cake

1 cup dates, chopped
1½ cups boiling water
1 teaspoon baking soda
½ cup shortening
1 cup sugar
2 eggs, well beaten
1¼ cups, plus 3 tablespoons, all-purpose flour
¼ teaspoon salt
¾ teaspoon baking soda

In a small bowl pour water over dates and 1 teaspoon baking soda; allow to cool. Cream shortening with sugar; add eggs and cooled date mixture. Sift together remaining ingredients and combine with date mixture; mix well. Pour into a greased 13x9x2-inch pan. Serves 12 to 15.

Topping:

1 (6-ounce) package chocolate chips
½ cup pecans, chopped
½ cup sugar

Mix together ingredients and sprinkle over top of cake batter; bake at 350 degrees for 40 minutes.

Variation: Add 1 teaspoon cocoa to flour before sifting.

Mrs. Eugene Kraegel (Dawn), Marietta, Georgia
Mrs. Donald Street (Mavis)

Kitchen Hint: Break eggs into measuring cup before measuring shortening. Empty cup, then measure shortening. It will not stick.

Toffee Candy Bar Cake

2 cups brown sugar
2 cups all-purpose flour
½ cup butter or margarine
1 teaspoon baking soda
½ teaspoon salt
1 egg
1 cup milk
1 teaspoon vanilla extract
½ cup chopped pecans
1 (6¾-ounce) package of 6 toffee candy bars, chopped coarsely

In large bowl mix sugar and flour thoroughly. Cut in butter as for pie crust. Reserve 1 cup of this mixture. Add salt and baking soda to remaining mixture. Add egg, milk and vanilla and beat until blended. Pour into greased 13x9x2-inch pan. Sprinkle reserved crumbs, nuts, and candy bars on top. Bake at 350 degrees for 35 minutes. Serve with whipped cream. Makes 35 bars.

Mrs. Joe Hensley (Joann)

Sour Cream Pound Cake I

1 cup butter
3 cups sugar
6 eggs
3 cups all-purpose flour
1 cup sour cream
1/4 teaspoon baking soda
1 teaspoon almond or lemon extract
1 teaspoon vanilla extract

Cream butter and sugar until very creamy. Add eggs, one at a time; beating well after each. Sift flour three times. Add baking soda to sour cream and stir. Add alternately with flour a little at a time. Beat well; add flavorings. Pour into a well greased and floured 10-inch tube pan. Bake at 350 degrees for 1 hour, or until cake tests done. When cool, ice with burnt pecan icing. Serves 18 to 20.

Mrs. Annie B. McClellan, Wetumpka, Alabama
Mrs. J. J. Suddath Jr. (Eleanor Picken)

Icing:

1/2 cup margarine
1 teaspoon butter flavoring
2 to 4 tablespoons milk
1 (16-ounce) box powdered sugar
1/2 to 1 cup pecans, toasted and chopped

In a large bowl cream margarine. Add flavoring, milk and sugar; beat until smooth and of spreading consistency. Stir in pecans. Makes 1 cup.

Mrs. J. J. Suddath Jr. (Eleanor Picken)

Sour Cream Pound Cake II

2 3/4 cups sugar
1 cup butter or margarine
6 eggs
3 cups all-purpose flour
1/2 teaspoon salt
1/4 teaspoon baking soda
1 cup sour cream
2 teaspoons orange brandy
1/2 teaspoon vanilla extract

Cream together sugar and butter until light and fluffy. Add eggs, one at a time, beating well after each addition. Sift together flour, salt and baking soda; add to cream mixture alternating with sour cream, beating after each addition. Add brandy and vanilla; beat well. Pour into greased and floured 10-inch tube pan. Bake at 350 degrees for 1 hour or until cake tests done. Cool 15 minutes; remove from pan. When cake is cool, frost or sprinkle with powdered sugar. Serves 24.

Helen S. Glass

Florida Pound Cake

1 cup butter
2 cups sugar
2 cups all-purpose flour
5 eggs
1 tablespoon vanilla extract

Cream butter and sugar; add eggs, one at a time, beating well after each addition. Add flour and vanilla extract. Pour batter into greased and floured 10-inch Bundt or tube pan. Bake at 325 degrees for about 1 hour or until done. Serves 10 to 12.

Variation: 1 tablespoon lemon extract or almond extract may be substituted for vanilla extract.

Mrs. Denver Bass (Eunice), Dunedin, Florida
Joan Dickerson

Brandy Butter Sauce:

1/4 cup sugar
2 tablespoons cornstarch
1/2 cup butter
1 1/4 cups water
1 tablespoon brandy

In small saucepan combine sugar and cornstarch; add butter, water and brandy. Cook over medium heat, stirring constantly, until thick and bubbly (6 to 8 minutes); boil 1 minute. Serve warm over pound cake or ice cream. Makes 1 3/4 cup.

Suncoast Seasons Committee

Sour Cream Poppy Seed Cake

1 (12-ounce) can poppy seed filling
1 cup shortening
1 1/2 cups sugar
4 eggs, separated
1 teaspoon vanilla extract
1 cup sour cream
2 1/2 cups all-purpose flour, sifted
1 teaspoon baking soda
1 teaspoon salt

In a large bowl cream shortening and sugar until fluffy. Add poppy seed filling and egg yolks, one at a time. Blend in vanilla extract and sour cream. Sift together dry ingredients and add slowly to the poppy seed mixture. Fold in stiffly beaten egg whites. Pour into an 8-cup greased tube pan; bake at 350 degrees for 1 1/4 hours or until done. Serves 16.

Miss Rita Fandrich
Lakeland, Florida

Coconut Pound Cake

1½ cups vegetable oil
2½ cups sugar
5 eggs
3 cups all-purpose flour
½ teaspoon salt
1 teaspoon baking powder
1 cup milk
2 teaspoons coconut flavoring
1 (3½-ounce) can flaked coconut

In a large bowl beat oil and sugar together on high speed of mixer for 10 minutes. Reduce speed and add eggs, one at a time. Sift dry ingredients; add alternately with milk to oil mixture. Fold in coconut and flavoring. Pour into 10-inch tube cake pan. Place in cold oven; turn heat to 300 degrees; bake for 1½ hours. While hot, prick cake with fork; pour buttermilk glaze over cake. Cool in pan. Serves 16 to 20.

Buttermilk Glaze:

1 teaspoon baking soda
½ cup buttermilk
1 cup sugar
½ cup margarine

In a small saucepan dissolve baking soda in buttermilk; add sugar and margarine. Cook slowly over low heat for 7 or 8 minutes.

Mrs. William S. Sharpe (Wanda)

Aunt Stelle's Fruit Cake

4 cups pecans
12 ounces candied cherries
16 ounces candied pineapple
1¾ cups all-purpose flour
1 cup butter or margarine
1 cup sugar
5 large eggs
½ teaspoon baking powder
2 ounces lemon extract
2 ounces vanilla extract

Chop nuts and fruit into medium-sized pieces. Sprinkle with ¼ cup flour; set aside. Cream butter and sugar until fluffy. Add well beaten eggs and blend. Sift remaining flour and baking powder together and fold into egg-butter mixture. Add vanilla and lemon. Mix well. Stir in fruit and nuts. Grease a 10-inch tube pan or two 9x5x3-inch loaf pans. Line with brown paper and grease again. Pour batter into pan or pans. Place in a cold oven and bake at 250 degrees for 3 hours for tube pan or 2 hours for loaf pans. Cool in pans on rack.

Note: This recipe is really great for those who don't like fruit cake. Makes one 10-inch tube pan or two 9x5x3-inch loaf pans.

Mrs. Ross H. Suddath (Estelle)
Tampa, Florida

Old-Fashioned White Fruit Cake

- 2 cups sweet butter
- 2 cups sugar
- 12 eggs
- 4½ cups all-purpose flour
- 1 (16-ounce) container mixed glazed fruits
- 1 pound walnuts, coarsely chopped
- 1 (16-ounce) box dates, cut into halves
- 1 (16-ounce) box golden raisins
- 4 or 8 ounces of extra glazed cherries may be added if desired
- French imported brandy

Cream butter and sugar well; add eggs, three at a time, then gradually add 4 cups of flour. Put fruits, nuts, dates and raisins in a large bowl and mix in ½ cup flour; add to batter and mix well. Bake at 275 degrees in 1 (10-inch) tube pan for 2½ hours and 1 (9x5x3-inch) loaf pan for 1½ hours.

Hint: Use extra large bowl for batter.

Note: Before storing, pour 2 ounces of brandy over ring and 1 ounce over loaf. Wrap in double layer aluminum foil. Make about one month ahead of time to age fruit cake. Pour brandy over cake about every ten days.

Mrs. Anthony S. Brancato (Georgine E. Palmer)

This is an old family recipe of a friend and was "handed down" in the old way—1 pound each of butter, sugar, eggs, flour, fruit, walnuts, dates and raisins. It is reputed to be from the 1800's.

Cherry Pound Cake

- ½ pound butter or margarine
- 2 cups sugar
- 4 eggs
- ¾ cup milk
- 3 cups all-purpose flour
- 1½ teaspoons baking powder
- 1 (8- or 10-ounce) jar maraschino cherries, chopped
- ¼ cup cherry juice

In a large bowl cream butter and sugar. Add eggs, one at a time, beating well after each addition. Add milk, flour and baking powder. Beat with electric mixer until smooth. Fold in cherries and cherry juice. Pour into large greased and floured 10-inch tube pan. Bake at 350 degrees for 1 hour. Serves 10.

Optional: It is good with a glaze made from 1 cup powdered sugar mixed with 3 to 4 teaspoons milk or cherry juice.

Evelyn Link
Palm Harbor, Florida

Orange Pound Cake

1 cup butter, softened
2 cups sugar
6 eggs
3 cups self-rising flour, sifted
2 tablespoons orange extract

In a large bowl cream butter and sugar. Add eggs, one at a time, beating well after each addition. Add flour gradually; add orange extract; mix batter well. Pour into a greased and floured 10-inch tube pan. Bake at 325 degrees for 1 hour and 15 minutes. Serves 16 to 24.

Variation: Try lemon extract!

Mrs. Ronald Gordon (Linda)

Strawberry Ribbon Cake

2½ cups all-purpose flour
2 cups sugar
3 teaspoons baking powder
1 teaspoon salt
1½ cups milk
⅔ cup shortening
3 eggs
2 teaspoons vanilla extract
⅛ teaspoon red food coloring

Grease and flour two 8x8x2-inch pans. Measure all ingredients, except red food coloring, into a large mixer bowl. Blend ½ minute on low speed, scraping bowl constantly. Beat 3 minutes on high speed, scraping bowl occasionally. Pour ½ of batter into one pan. Stir food coloring into remaining batter; pour into second pan. Bake at 350 degrees for 35 to 40 minutes. Cool layers in pans on wire racks for 10 minutes; turn out onto racks and cool completely. Split each cooled layer in half; put together alternating pink and yellow with part of the frosting. Use remainder of frosting on top and sides of cake. Serves 10 to 12.

Frosting:

4 ounces cream cheese
4 tablespoons butter or margarine
⅓ cup mashed fresh strawberries
1 pound powdered sugar

In medium bowl blend cream cheese with butter until fluffy. Beat in strawberries; stir in 2 cups sifted powdered sugar until smooth. Measure out scant 1½ cups of mixture for filling. Beat remaining powdered sugar into rest of mixture for frosting.

Note: Frozen strawberries may be used, but consistency of the frosting will need to be adjusted.

Helen S. Glass

Almond-Brittle Torte

1½ cups sifted all-purpose flour
¾ cup sugar
8 large eggs, separated
¼ cup cold water
1 tablespoon lemon juice
1 teaspoon vanilla extract
1 teaspoon cream of tartar
1 teaspoon salt
¾ cup sugar

Sift flour and sugar into bowl; make well in center; add egg yolks, water, lemon juice and vanilla. Beat until smooth. Beat egg whites with cream of tartar and salt just until very soft peaks form. Add remaining sugar gradually, 2 tablespoons at a time. Continue to beat until stiff meringue forms. Fold first mixture gently into the meringue. Pour batter into an ungreased 10-inch tube pan. Carefully cut through the batter, going around tube 5 or 6 times with a knife to break air bubbles. Bake at 350 degrees about 50 to 55 minutes or until top springs back when lightly touched. Invert pan 1 hour or until cool. Remove cake. Split crosswise into 4 equal layers. Assemble torte with whipped cream and almond-brittle topping as directed. Makes 1 torte.

Candy Topping:

¾ cup sugar
½ teaspoon instant coffee
2 tablespoons light corn syrup
2 tablespoons water
1½ teaspoons baking soda, sifted
3 cups whipping cream
1 tablespoon sugar
2 teaspoons vanilla extract
½ cup blanched almond halves, toasted

While cake bakes, fix candy-brittle part of topping. In a saucepan mix first 4 ingredients. Cook to hard-crack stage (285 to 290 degrees). Remove from heat and add baking soda at once. Stir vigorously, but only until mixture blends and pulls away from sides of pan. Quickly pour foamy mixture into buttered 8x8x2-inch pan. Do not spread or stir. Cool. Tap bottom of pan to remove candy; crush into crumbs. When cake is thoroughly cool, whip cream with sugar and vanilla. Spread half between layers and remainder over top and sides. Cover with candy crumbs; trim with almond halves by poking in porcupine style all over cake.

Mrs. William S. Sharpe (Wanda)

Kitchen Tip: To cool cake baked in a tube pan, place pan over neck of a soda bottle.

Queen Anne Cake

2/3 cup shortening
1 3/4 cups sugar
2 eggs
2 egg yolks (reserve whites)
1/4 cup milk
2 1/2 cups all-purpose flour
2 1/2 teaspoons baking powder
1 teaspoon salt
1 (12-ounce) can apricot nectar, separated
1/2 teaspoon lemon extract

In large mixing bowl cream shortening; add sugar; blend well. Add 2 eggs and 2 egg yolks; beat for 1 minute. Add milk; mix until blended. In separate bowl mix flour, baking powder and salt. Alternately add flour mixture and 1 cup apricot nectar to large bowl; add lemon extract; blend well after each addition. Pour into 3 greased and floured 9-inch cake pans. Bake at 350 degrees for 25 to 30 minutes.

Filling:

1/4 cup cornstarch
1 (12-ounce) can apricot nectar plus reserved
2 teaspoons lemon juice

In small saucepan mix cornstarch with 1/4 cup apricot nectar; mix well. Add additional 1 3/4 cups apricot nectar. Cook over medium heat until thick; add lemon juice; cool.

Fluffy Frosting:

2 egg whites, reserved
3/4 cup sugar
2 tablespoons water
1/4 teaspoon salt
1/4 teaspoon cream of tartar
1/4 teaspoon vanilla extract

In top of double boiler over boiling water, beat the first five ingredients with an electric mixer until peaks form. Remove from heat; add vanilla extract; beat until spreading consistency.

To assemble cake:

Spread filling between bottom and middle layers (filling should be 1/4-inch from side edges). Add top layer and refrigerate while making frosting. Frost sides and top and refrigerate several hours or overnight. Makes a 9-inch 3-layer cake.

Note: This recipe uses two 12-ounce cans apricot nectar.

Mrs. George Palmer (Margaret)
Garfield, New Jersey

M-J's Original Cheesecake

2 graham crackers, crushed
1 (16-ounce) carton ricotta cheese or small curd cream style cottage cheese
2 (8-ounce) packages cream cheese, softened
2¼ cups sugar
4 eggs, slightly beaten
⅓ cup cornstarch
2 tablespoons lemon juice
1 tablespoon vanilla extract
½ teaspoon almond extract
½ cup butter, melted
Less than ¼ cup milk
1 (16-ounce) carton sour cream

Grease a 9x3¼-inch springform pan; dust with graham cracker crumbs. Sieve cottage cheese or ricotta into a large mixing bowl; add cream cheese. Beat at high speed of electric mixer until well blended and creamy. Beating at high speed blend in sugar, then eggs. Reduce to low speed; add cornstarch, lemon juice and extracts. Beat until blended. Add melted butter, milk and sour cream; blend on low speed. Pour into prepared pan; bake in preheated oven at 325 degrees for 1 hour and 10 minutes, or until firm around edges. Turn off oven; let cake stand in oven 2 hours. Remove and cool completely on wire rack. Chill; remove sides of pan. If desired, top with fruit glaze. Serves 20.

Fruit Glaze:

1 (10-ounce) package frozen strawberries, drained (reserve juice)
¼ cup sugar
2 tablespoons cornstarch

In a saucepan combine reserved strawberry juice, sugar and cornstarch. Place over low heat; bring to a boil; cool. Add strawberries. Coat each berry and place on top of cake.

Note: The secret to a creamy cheesecake is a lot of beating; so you can never beat it too much!

Mrs. Paul Jasinski (Mary Jo)
Miami, Florida

Mandarin Orange Cake

2 cups sugar
2 cups all-purpose flour
2 teaspoons baking soda
½ teaspoon salt
2 eggs
2 (11½-ounce) cans mandarin oranges, drained

Sift together dry ingredients. In a separate bowl beat eggs. Add oranges and dry ingredients to eggs; beat for 4 minutes with an electric mixer; pour batter into a greased and floured 13x9x2-inch baking pan. Bake at 350 degrees for 30 to 35 minutes. Serves 16.

Topping:

3/4 cup brown sugar
3 tablespoons milk
2 tablespoons butter, softened
1/2 pint whipping cream

While cake is baking, combine sugar, milk and butter. Heat to a boil. Pour over cake as soon as it comes from the oven. When cake is cool, serve with whipped cream.

Mrs. Brian Cook (Lee)
Dunedin, Florida

Variation: Use three 8-inch round cake pans well greased and floured.

Filling:

1 (20-ounce) container non-dairy whipped topping
1 (20-ounce) can crushed pineapple, drained
1 (4 3/4-ounce) box instant vanilla pudding

Prepare filling by combining whipped topping, pineapple and pudding.

Mrs. Addison Bender (Josephine Andrews)

Hawaiian Yum Cake

2 cups sugar
2 eggs
2 cups all-purpose flour
2 teaspoons baking soda
1 teaspoon vanilla extract
2 cups crushed pineapple, undrained
1/2 cup chopped pecans

In a large bowl cream the sugar and eggs. Mix in the flour, baking soda, vanilla extract, pineapple and pecans. Bake in a greased 13x9x2-inch pan at 350 degrees for 40 minutes. Spread with Hawaiian Yum Cake icing. Serves 12 to 24.

Note: Keep cake refrigerated.

Hawaiian Yum Cake Icing:

1/2 cup butter, softened
1 (8-ounce) package cream cheese, softened
1 teaspoon vanilla extract
2 cups powdered sugar
1/2 cup chopped pecans

In a medium bowl cream butter and cream cheese. Mix in vanilla and powdered sugar. With a spoon stir in the pecans; spread on top of cake.

June Burns
Dunedin, Florida

Luscious Coconut Cake

1 (18½-ounce) package yellow butter recipe cake mix
1¾ cups sugar
2 (8-ounce) cartons sour cream
3 (6-ounce) packages frozen coconut, thawed
1 (9-ounce) carton frozen whipped topping, thawed

Prepare cake mix according to package directions, making two 9-inch layers. When completely cool, split both layers. Combine sugar, sour cream and 2 packages coconut, blending well. Chill. Reserve 1 cup of sour cream mixture for frosting; spread sour cream mixture with whipped topping. Blend until smooth. Spread on top and sides of cake. Sprinkle third package of frozen coconut overall. Seal cake in an airtight container; refrigerate for 3 days before serving. Serves 12 to 18.

Note: : Can also be frozen.

Mrs. Mark Fuller (Louise), Eros, Louisiana
Jane Stipe

Kitchen Hint: To beautify a cake, tint the coconut. Fill half a screwtop jar with coconut, add a few drops of diluted food coloring, cover and shake until evenly tinted.

New York Bakery Sponge Cake

6 large eggs
2 cups sugar
1 teaspoon vanilla extract
2 cups all-purpose flour
2½ teaspoons baking powder
⅛ teaspoon salt or to taste
1 cup milk, scalded
1 (3½-ounce) package instant vanilla pudding
½ pint whipping cream, whipped
1 teaspoon vanilla extract
3 tablespoons sugar
2 cups strawberries, sliced

Beat eggs, sugar and vanilla for 15 minutes on medium speed. Sift together flour, baking powder and salt. Place cover on pan of milk and cool. Add milk and flour alternately to egg mixture. Pour into an ungreased 13x9x2-inch oblong pan or a 10-cup angel food cake pan. Bake at 350 degrees for 50 minutes. Invert pan immediately after removing from the oven; cool. Prepare pudding according to package directions. Split cake and fill with pudding. Whip cream with vanilla and sugar; spread on top of second layer and top with sliced fruit. Serves 18 to 24.

Variation: Angel Cake—slice plain cake and serve with whipped cream and strawberries or use other fruit in season.

Mrs. Vito Grasso (Aurora)
Dunedin, Florida

Blueberry Cheesecake Macadamia

Superb Dessert—Guests will call it, divine!

Crust:

1 (3½-ounce) jar Macadamia nut pieces, crushed in blender
1 cup all-purpose flour
¼ cup brown sugar, firmly packed
½ cup sweet butter, softened

Combine all ingredients. Mix well; press onto bottom of a 10-inch springform pan. Bake in preheated oven at 400 degrees for 10 to 15 minutes. Reduce oven to 350 degrees.

First Layer:

3 (8-ounce) packages cream cheese, softened
1 teaspoon vanilla extract
1 cup sugar
4 eggs, room temperature

Crumble cheese in large bowl. Add remaining ingredients; beat at high speed with electric mixer until blended and smooth, approximately 5 minutes. (Food Processor may be used.) Pour over crust. Bake at 350 degrees for 40 minutes until set (not completely firm). Remove from oven; cool for 10 minutes.

Second Layer:

1 cup sour cream
2 tablespoons sugar
½ teaspoon vanilla extract

Combine sour cream, sugar and vanilla. Spread over top of cheesecake. Bake at 350 degrees for 5 minutes. Cool; spread blueberry topping over. Refrigerate before serving.

Topping:

2 cups fresh or frozen blueberries
1 tablespoon cornstarch
2 to 3 tablespoons cold water

Mix cornstarch with cold water to form a smooth paste. Stir in blueberries; cook until thickened. Let cool; spread on cake. Cool 1 hour; then refrigerate. Serves 12.

Mrs. J. Wallace Lee (Ida)

Scandinavian Almond Cake

3/4 cup butter
1 cup sugar
3 egg yolks
1 teaspoon almond extract
2 1/4 cups sifted cake flour
2 teaspoons baking powder
1/4 teaspoon salt
3/4 cup milk
3 egg whites
Powdered sugar

Cream butter and sugar and beat until light and fluffy. Add egg yolks, one at a time, beating well after each addition. Mix in almond extract; set aside. Sift flour, baking powder, and salt together. Add to creamed mixture alternately with milk, beginning and ending with dry ingredients. Beat egg whites until soft peaks form; fold into batter. Turn into greased and floured 10-inch Bundt pan. Bake at 325 degrees for 45 to 50 minutes. Dust with powdered sugar. Serves 12.

Mrs. Lawrence J. Tierney, Jr. (Sue)

Open Face Fruit Cake

Peach, Plum or Apple

1/2 cup butter or margarine, softened
1/2 cup sugar
2 eggs
1 cup all-purpose flour
1 teaspoon baking powder
1/4 teaspoon salt (omit if using margarine)
Fresh fruit in season
1 tablespoon sugar
1/2 teaspoon cinnamon

Cream butter and sugar; beat in eggs. Sift together flour, baking powder and salt; add and mix thoroughly. Dough will be very soft. Spoon into 13x9x2-inch ungreased baking pan. Cut fruit into slices and place close together on top of dough. Sprinkle with sugar and cinnamon. Bake at 375 degrees for 30 minutes or 350 degrees for 40 minutes.

Crumb Topping (Optional):

1/2 cup butter or margarine, melted
1/4 to 1/2 cup sugar (to taste)
1 cup plus 2 tablespoons all-purpose flour

Mix all ingredients; sprinkle over cake before baking. Before serving, if desired, dust with powdered sugar. Serves 12.

Mrs. Anthony S. Brancato (Georgine E. Palmer)

Berog

Russian Tea Cake

4 cups all-purpose flour
1½ teaspoons baking powder
1 cup sweet butter, softened
¾ cup sugar
3 egg yolks
1½ teaspoons vanilla extract
1 cup whipping cream
1 (16-ounce) jar tart jam, (red raspberry, plum, apricot) beaten

Sift flour and baking powder together; set aside. In a large bowl beat butter and sugar at high speed until light and fluffy. Add one egg yolk every 5 minutes during beating; add vanilla and flour mixture alternately with cream to make a very soft dough. Grease a 13x9x2-inch pan and an 8x8-inch pan. Reserve 1 cup dough; divide and press remaining dough evenly in pans. Form edging of cakes by rolling small amounts of dough, pencil thick, and place around edge of cakes. Reserve any remaining dough for garnishing. Spread jam on dough evenly. Decorate jam with remaining dough in desired shapes. Bake at 300 degrees for 30 minutes or until lightly brown. Cut into squares. Store in plastic container or freeze. Makes 40 pieces.

Note: You will have two finished cakes.

Mrs. Henry Anmahian (Jannet)
Vienna, Virginia

Sand Kuchen

1 cup butter, softened
2 cups sugar
6 eggs
2 cups all-purpose flour, separated
½ heaping teaspoon baking powder
⅛ teaspoon salt
Rind of 1 lemon, grated
Juice of ½ of lemon
3 tablespoons rum

In a large bowl cream butter and sugar well. Add eggs, one at a time, mixing 5 minutes between each egg. Set aside 3 tablespoons of the 2 cups of flour. Add remaining flour, salt, lemon peel, lemon juice and rum and mix well. Combine baking powder and 3 tablespoons of flour; add to mixture. Pour into 10-inch Bundt pan. Bake at 350 degrees for 1 hour. Serves 10 to 12.

Elsie Fandrich
Clearwater, Florida

Kitchen Hint: To get maximum amount of juice from lemon, warm in water. Press down firmly and roll on hard surface before juicing.

Dobosch Torte

1 (16-ounce) pound cake
1 (6-ounce) package semi-sweet chocolate chips
1/4 cup hot coffee
2 tablespoons powdered sugar
4 egg yolks
1/2 cup butter
2 tablespoons dark rum

Slice pound cake into six or seven thin horizontal slices. Set aside. Pour chocolate chips into an electric blender; blend at high speed for 6 minutes. Scrape chocolate down sides of blender; add hot coffee. Blend an additional 6 minutes. Add powdered sugar, egg yolks, butter and rum. Blend for 30 seconds. Spread between layers and spread on top and sides of cake. Refrigerate. To serve slice in very thin slices. Freezes beautifully. *Small portions make excellent gifts.* Serves 15 to 20.

Mrs. George Engblom (Eileen)

Nut Torte

1 tablespoon butter
3/4 cup breadcrumbs plus crumbs to sprinkle on pan
3 cups ground walnuts or pecans
3/4 cup sugar
8 eggs, separated
1 cup water, boiled and cooled to lukewarm
4 tablespoons sugar
2 teaspoons vanilla extract

Butter a 10-inch tube pan and sprinkle with 1/4 cup of breadcrumbs. In a large bowl beat egg yolks and sugar until thick and lemon-colored. Mix with remaining breadcrumbs and nuts. Beat egg whites until stiff and carefully fold into egg and nut mixture. Pour into tube pan and bake at 250 degrees for 50 minutes, or until a toothpick comes out clean. Remove from oven and cool in pan. When cake is cool, cut into 3 layers. Mix lukewarm water, 4 tablespoons sugar and vanilla, pour over each layer. Spread icing between layers and on top and sides of torte.

Icing:

1 1/2 cups sweet butter
3/4 cup sugar
2 egg yolks, beaten
1/2 cup strong coffee (or a little more depending on individual taste)

Slowly combine sugar and butter; beat together until light and fluffy. Add cooled coffee a few drops at a time; continue to beat. Add egg yolks and beat thoroughly. Serves 16

Hint: Make ahead. Serve at room temperature.

Mrs. John Leja (Audrey)
Dunedin, Florida

Oatmeal Cake

1 cup quick-cooking oatmeal
1½ cups boiling water
½ cup margarine
1 cup sugar
1 cup brown sugar
2 eggs, beaten
1⅓ cups all-purpose flour
1 teaspoon baking powder
½ teaspoon baking soda
½ teaspoon salt
¾ teaspoon cinnamon

Add boiling water to oatmeal; set aside to cool. In a large bowl beat together margarine and sugars. Add eggs and beat thoroughly. Slowly add dry ingredients. Stir in oatmeal. Pour mixture into greased and floured 13x9x2-inch pan. Bake at 350 degrees for 30 to 35 minutes. Serve warm or cold.

Topping:

1 tablespoon margarine
½ cup brown sugar
¼ cup evaporated milk
1 teaspoon vanilla extract
1 cup flaked coconut

Mix ingredients and pour over hot cake. Place cake under broiler for 3 minutes. Serves 15.

Mrs. Stanley H. Dawson (Ruth)

Graham Cracker Cake

Cake:

1 (16-ounce) box graham crackers, crushed
2 teaspoons baking powder
1 cup butter or margarine
2 cups sugar
5 eggs
1 cup milk
1 teaspoon vanilla extract
1 (3½-ounce) can coconut flakes

Lightly grease and flour three 9-inch cake pans. Add baking powder to graham crackers. Combine with remaining ingredients; add eggs, one at a time. Pour into cake pans. Bake at 350 degrees for 20 to 25 minutes.

Frosting:

½ cup margarine
1 (16-ounce) box powdered sugar
1 egg
1 teaspoon vanilla extract
1 (15¼-ounce) can crushed pineapple, drained

Mix together margarine, sugar, egg and vanilla. Top each layer of cake with ⅓ can pineapple. Frost over pineapple. Makes 3 cakes.

Mrs. Ronald Gordon (Linda)

Carrot Cake I

2 cups self-rising flour
2 cups sugar
1 teaspoon cinnamon
3 cups (6 medium) grated carrots
1½ cups oil
4 eggs
1 teaspoon vanilla extract
1 (15½-ounce) can crushed pineapple, drained

Preheat oven to 325 degrees. Grease and lightly flour 10-inch tube pan. In large bowl blend flour, sugar, cinnamon, carrots, oil, eggs and vanilla; fold in pineapple. Pour batter into prepared pan. Bake at 325 degrees for 90 minutes or until toothpick inserted comes out clean; cool 10 minutes. Remove from pan; cool completely. Serves 12 to 16.

Frosting:

1 (8-ounce) package cream cheese
1 (16-ounce) box powdered sugar
1 tablespoon fresh lemon juice

In medium bowl blend frosting ingredients. Spread over cake.

Mrs. Horst P. Bothmann (Ingrid)

Cloud-Topped Peach Cake

Breadcrumbs, for dusting
1 cup sifted cake flour
1 teaspoon baking powder
¼ teaspoon salt
2 eggs
1 cup sugar
½ teaspoon vanilla extract
½ cup milk
1 tablespoon butter
Fruit Fresh

Preheat oven to 350 degrees. Butter a 9-inch cake pan well. Dust lightly with fine breadcrumbs. Sift together flour, baking powder and salt. In small mixer bowl beat eggs at high speed for 3 minutes. Gradually add sugar and vanilla. Beat until very thick. Heat milk and butter to a boil. On low speed, beat hot milk into eggs. Beat until smooth. Add dry ingredients and beat until flour is blended. Pour into prepared pan. Bake 30 minutes at 350 degrees. Cool in pan 2 minutes. Turn onto cake rack and invert onto serving plate. Pour syrup over hot cake. Cool completely.

Syrup:

⅔ cup sugar
⅓ cup boiling water
¼ teaspoon almond or rum extract

Mix sugar and water. Boil 1 minute without stirring. Cool to room temperature. Add almond extract.

Topping:

1/4 cup peach preserves
6 peaches, peeled and sliced, sprinkle with Fruit Fresh
1/4 cup sugar
1/4 cup water

Spread peach preserves over top of cake. Bring sugar and water to boil. Add a layer of peach slices. Cover and cook until barely tender. Drain on paper towels. Repeat with remaining slices. Arrange peaches in a ring around edge of cake. Fill center with remaining peach slices which have been chopped.

Whipped Cream:

1 cup whipping cream
1/4 cup powdered sugar
1 teaspoon vanilla extract
1/4 cup slivered almonds, toasted

Whip cream, sugar and vanilla until stiff. Spoon over center of cake. Sprinkle with toasted almonds. Serves 8 to 10.

Variation: 1 to 2 tablespoons light rum may be added to syrup.

Mrs. Mark Fuller (Louise)
Eros, Louisiana

Kitchen Hint: For cream that will not whip, add an egg white and chill. Try again.

Gooey Butter Cake

Crust:

1 (18 1/2-ounce) package yellow cake mix
1/2 cup butter, softened
2 eggs

Mix together cake mix, butter and eggs. Pour into ungreased 13x9x2-inch pan.

Topping:

1 (8-ounce) package cream cheese, softened
2 eggs
1 (16-ounce) package powdered sugar

Reserve 1/2 cup powdered sugar. Beat remaining ingredients until smooth. Pour on top of crust. Bake at 325 degrees for 45 minutes. Sprinkle with reserved powdered sugar. Makes 24 two inch squares.

Note: Serve warm or cold

Mrs. Harvey Heimann (Jean)
Janet Joyce

Carrot Cake II

2 cups sugar
4 eggs
1½ cups salad oil
3 teaspoons cinnamon
2 teaspoons baking soda
1 teaspoon salt
2 tablespoons vanilla extract
2 cups all-purpose flour
3 cups grated raw carrots

Combine all ingredients except grated carrots; mix well. Stir carrots into batter. Pour into three 8-inch layer pans or a 13x9x2-inch pan. Bake at 325 degrees for 30 minutes. Serves 12 to 16.

Frosting:

½ cup butter or margarine, softened
1 (8-ounce) package cream cheese, softened
1 (16-ounce) box powdered sugar
1 cup chopped nuts

Cream butter or margarine and cream cheese. Add sugar and beat until smooth. Stir in nuts. Frost cake.

Mrs. Ronald Gordon (Linda)

Swedish Nut Cake

2 cups sugar
2 eggs
1 (20-ounce) can crushed pineapple, undrained
2 teaspoons baking soda
1 teaspoon salt
1 teaspoon vanilla extract
2 cups all-purpose flour
½ cup chopped walnuts

Mix and pour into a greased 13x9x2-inch pan. Bake at 350 degrees for 35 minutes. Serves 10 to 12.

Topping:

½ cup butter, softened
1 (8-ounce) package cream cheese, softened
1¾ cups powdered sugar
1 teaspoon vanilla extract
½ cup chopped walnuts or pecans

Combine and spread on hot cake. Cover with foil; refrigerate from 24 to 48 hours.

Mrs. Robert Baker (Alice)
Hebron, Indiana

Friendship Cake with Brandied Fruit Starter

Fruit Starter:

1 (20-ounce) can pineapple chunks, drained
1 (17-ounce) can sliced peaches, drained
1 (10-ounce) jar whole maraschino cherries, drained
1¼ cups sugar
1¼ cups brandy

Combine all ingredients in a clean non-metal bowl; stir gently. Cover and let stand at room temperature 3 weeks, stirring fruit twice a week. Makes enough for cake.

Cake:

1½ cups brandied fruit
1 (18½-ounce) box yellow or white cake mix
⅔ cup oil
1 cup pecans or walnuts, whole
4 eggs
1 (3⅛-ounce) box instant vanilla pudding

Mix all ingredients together, adding fruit last. Pour into a greased and floured 10-inch Bundt pan. Bake at 350 degrees for 50 to 60 minutes. Glaze or sprinkle with powdered sugar. Serves 24.

Mrs. Douglas Guilfoile (Paula L. Tiezzi)

Friendship Fruit Starter can be made with rum in an apothecary jar and given to friends at Christmastime to spread holiday cheer.

Pecan Cake

2 cups butter, softened
2 cups sugar
6 eggs, well-beaten
1 (2-ounce) bottle lemon extract
4 cups all-purpose flour
1½ teaspoons baking powder
2 cups raisins
4 cups whole pecans

Cream butter and sugar in large mixing bowl; add eggs and extract, beating well. Sift together flour and baking powder and mix with raisins and nuts. Add to creamed mixture; gently blend all together. Pour into a well-buttered and floured 10-inch tube pan. Bake at 275 degrees for 2 hours. Serves 12.

Mrs. Harvey Heimann (Jean)

Kentucky Prune Cake

2 cups self-rising flour
1½ cups sugar
1 teaspoon baking soda
1 teaspoon cinnamon
1 teaspoon nutmeg
1 teaspoon allspice
1 teaspoon salt
1 cup vegetable oil
3 eggs
1 cup buttermilk
1 cup chopped pecans
1 cup cooked, pitted prunes
1 teaspoon vanilla extract

In a large bowl blend flour and sugar. Sift the remaining dry ingredients into the flour mixture. Add the remaining 6 ingredients, beating well after each addition. Pour batter into a lightly greased and floured 13x9x2-inch baking pan. Bake at 350 degrees for 1 hour. Prepare Sauce.

Sauce:

1 cup sugar
2 tablespoons light corn syrup
½ cup buttermilk
½ cup butter
⅓ teaspoon baking soda
½ teaspoon vanilla extract

Mix ingredients together in a saucepan and bring to a boil. Pour hot sauce over cooled Kentucky Prune Cake. Serves 12.

Mrs. Alpha Amburgey
Holiday, Florida

Caramel Frosting

4 tablespoons margarine
1½ cups brown sugar, firmly packed
6 tablespoons milk
1¾ to 2 cups sifted powdered sugar

In a saucepan combine margarine and brown sugar; cook over low heat for 2 minutes; stirring constantly. Add milk; stir and cook until mixture boils. Remove from heat and cool; add powdered sugar until desired spreading consistency is reached. Frosts 9-inch layer cake or 13x9x2-inch cake.

Note: Great used on spice cake or chocolate fudge cake.

Mrs. Jack Garber (Lois)

Kitchen Hint: To soften brown sugar put it in a container and cover with a damp cloth and tight lid. In a day or so you will have soft sugar.

Nut Cake

$2^3/4$ cups all-purpose flour, sifted
2 teaspoons baking powder
1 teaspoon salt
1 cup butter, softened
$1^3/4$ cups sugar
4 eggs
2/3 cup milk
2 teaspoons vanilla extract
2 cups nuts, finely chopped

Grease and flour 10-inch Bundt pan. Mix flour, baking powder and salt. Beat butter, sugar and eggs until fluffy. Stir in dry ingredients; add the milk, a little at a time. Add vanilla and 1 cup of nuts. Pour batter into pan. Bake in preheated oven at 350 degrees for 1 hour, or until top springs back when lightly pressed. Cool in pan for 15 to 20 minutes. Loosen cake and let completely cool on rack. Frost top or serve topped with whipped cream.

Note: You can use your favorite nut for this cake. Serves 16.

Frosting:

1/2 cup butter
1/4 cup milk
1 (16-ounce) box powdered sugar

In saucepan melt butter; remove from heat; add milk and sugar. Blend until smooth. Spread on cake; sprinkle remaining 1 cup nuts on frosting.

Mrs. Horst P. Bothmann (Ingrid)

Date-Nut Cake

1 cup dates, chopped
1 teaspoon baking soda
2 tablespoons butter
1 cup boiling water
1 cup sugar
1/2 teaspoon salt
1 egg
$1^1/2$ cups all-purpose flour
1/2 cup chopped nuts
1 teaspoon vanilla extract

Place dates in a large mixing bowl. Add baking soda and butter. Pour boiling water over mixture. Set aside and allow to cool. When mixture has cooled, stir in sugar, salt, egg, flour, nuts and vanilla. Pour into greased 13x9x2-inch pan. Bake at 350 degrees for 20 to 25 minutes. Frost with vanilla-butter frosting. Serves 12.

Frosting:

1/2 cup margarine or butter, softened
1 (16-ounce) box powdered sugar
2 teaspoons vanilla extract
1/4 cup milk

Mix together until spreading consistency.

Mrs. Dean N. McFarland (Donna VanEwyk)

Pumpkin Pie Cake

Crust:

1 (18½-ounce) yellow cake mix, separated
½ cup margarine, melted
2 eggs, beaten

Reserve 1 cup of dry cake mix for topping. Combine remaining dry cake mix, melted margarine and eggs. Press into prepared 9x13x2-inch pan.

Filling:

1 (1-pound 13-ounce) can pumpkin
3 eggs
⅔ cup milk
½ cup firmly packed brown sugar
1½ teaspoons cinnamon
¼ cup white sugar

Blend pumpkin, eggs, milk, brown sugar, cinnamon and white sugar; pour over crust.

Topping:

1 cup cake mix (reserved from crust ingredients)
½ cup sugar
½ cup nuts
¼ cup margarine, softened

Mix reserved 1 cup dry cake mix with sugar, nuts and margarine. Crumble the topping and sprinkle on top of filling. Bake at 350 degrees for 50 to 55 minutes. Serves 15.

Note: Do not use mix with pudding added. Can be served with non-dairy whipped topping or ice cream.

Mrs. S. E. "Pete" Covey (Carol Daugherty)

Chocolate Icing

1 cup sugar
3 tablespoons cornstarch
7 tablespoons cocoa
⅛ teaspoon salt
1 cup boiling water
3 tablespoons butter
1 teaspoon vanilla extract

Mix sugar and cornstarch together in a 2-quart saucepan. Add cocoa and salt. Add boiling water; stir to mix; cook over low heat until mixture thickens. Remove from heat; stir in butter and vanilla extract. Spread on hot cake. Frosts one 13x9x2-inch.

Note: This icing remains soft.

Jane Stipe

Cookies and Candies

Apple-Orange Brownies

6 tablespoons butter or margarine
1 cup firmly packed brown sugar
1 egg, beaten
½ cup applesauce
1 teaspoon shredded orange peel
1 teaspoon vanilla extract
1¼ cups all-purpose flour
1 teaspoon baking powder
½ teaspoon salt
½ teaspoon baking soda
½ cup chopped pecans

In a saucepan combine butter and sugar; heat until butter is melted. Stir in egg, applesauce, orange peel and vanilla extract. In a large bowl combine flour, baking powder, salt and baking soda. Stir in applesauce mixture and nuts. Spread in a greased 12x8x2-inch baking pan. Bake at 350 degrees for 25 minutes. Makes 36.

Orange Glaze:

1½ cups powdered sugar
2 tablespoons orange juice
½ teaspoon vanilla extract

In a small bowl combine all ingredients; stir until smooth. Pour over warm brownies.

Mrs. Hugh F. Smith, III (Mary Jo)
Dunedin, Florida

Pumpkin Bars

2 cups pumpkin
4 eggs, beaten
1 cup salad oil
2 cups all-purpose flour
2 cups sugar
⅛ teaspoon salt
1 teaspoon baking soda
1 teaspoon baking powder
2 teaspoons cinnamon

In a large bowl mix pumpkin, eggs and oil. In a separate bowl mix remaining ingredients and add to pumpkin mixture. Bake at 350 degrees in an ungreased jellyroll pan or on a large cookie sheet for 20 to 25 minutes.

Frosting:

3 ounces cream cheese, softened
6 tablespoons butter
½ cup powdered sugar
1 teaspoon vanilla extract
1 teaspoon milk

In a small bowl mix together all ingredients. Spread on warm bars. Makes 30.

Mrs. Brian Cook (Lee)
Dunedin, Florida

Brownies

1/2 cup shortening
1 1/2 (1-ounce) squares baking chocolate
1 cup sugar
2 eggs, slightly beaten
1/2 cup all-purpose flour
1/4 teaspoon baking powder
1/2 teaspoon salt
1 teaspoon vanilla extract
1/2 cup chopped nuts

Combine shortening and chocolate in top of a double boiler; cook until melted. Stir sugar and eggs into batter; remove from heat. Sift flour and baking powder with salt and beat into mixture. Add vanilla and chopped nuts. Pour into a greased 8x8-inch pan; bake 25 to 30 minutes at 325 degrees or until brownies pull away from sides of pan. Frost while warm.

Frosting:

1/2 (1-ounce) square baking chocolate
2 2/3 tablespoons margarine
1 1/2 cups powdered sugar
1 teaspoon vanilla extract
1 to 2 tablespoons milk

Melt chocolate and margarine. Add sugar, vanilla and enough milk to make good spreading consistency. Makes one 8-inch square pan. Serves 9.

Note: Brownies are best one day old. These brownies freeze beautifully.

Mrs. Robert Russ (Carol Hodapp)

Martha's Cookies

A Cookie Jar Favorite

2 cups brown sugar
10 tablespoons butter
2 eggs
1 teaspoon vanilla extract
1 cup nuts, chopped
2 cups all-purpose flour
2 teaspoons baking powder
1/8 teaspoon salt

In a medium bowl cream butter and sugar. Add eggs and vanilla; mix well. Combine flour, nuts, baking powder and salt; stir into creamed mixture. Pour into a waxed paper-lined 13x9x2-inch baking pan. Bake at 350 degrees for 30 minutes. Do not overcook. Cookies should rise, then fall when they are done. Remove from pan onto a piece of waxed paper sprinkled with powdered sugar. Cut into 1-inch squares while still hot. Sprinkle with powdered sugar. Cookies will be chewy. Makes 40 cookies.

Mrs. A. W. Picken, Sr. (Sarah)
Columbus, Georgia

Kitchen Hint: To soften brown sugar put in a container and cover with a damp cloth and tight lid. In a day or so you will have soft sugar.

Swedish Nut Wafers

4 tablespoons sweet butter
3/4 cup sugar
1 egg, well beaten
2 tablespoons milk
1 teaspoon vanilla extract
1 1/3 cups all-purpose flour
1 teaspoon baking powder
1/2 teaspoon salt
1/3 cup chopped walnuts

Preheat oven to 325 degrees. Lightly butter a cookie sheet or jelly roll pan. With an electric mixer cream butter; gradually beat in sugar until light and fluffy. Add egg, milk and vanilla extract; beat well. Mix together flour, baking powder and salt; beat into the first mixture. Spread dough on cookie sheet as thin as possible; just enough to cover the bottom. Sprinkle with nuts; press them gently into the dough. With a sharp knife, mark into cookie-sized rectangles. Bake about 12 minutes or until lightly browned. Cut through rectangles while still warm. Makes 4 dozen.

Mrs. John Vignola (Franca)
Dunedin, Florida

Toffee-Nut Bars

Crust:

1/4 cup shortening
1/4 cup butter, softened
1/2 cup brown sugar, packed
1 cup sifted all-purpose flour

In a bowl thoroughly mix together shortening, butter and sugar; stir in flour. Press and flatten with spoon to cover bottom of 13x9x2-inch baking pan. Bake 10 minutes at 350 degrees; then spread with almond-coconut topping. Return to oven and bake at 350 degrees for 25 minutes, or until topping is golden brown. Cool slightly; cut into bars. Makes 30.

Topping:

2 eggs
1 cup brown sugar, packed
1 teaspoon vanilla extract
2 tablespoons all-purpose flour
1 teaspoon baking powder
1/2 teaspoon salt
1 cup shredded coconut
1 cup almonds or other nuts, chopped

In a medium bowl beat eggs; stir in sugar and vanilla. Combine flour, baking powder and salt; stir into egg mixture. Add coconut and almonds; combine thoroughly. Pour over crust.

Mrs. Donald Behm (Marion)

Marble Mocha Walnut Squares

Crust:

1 cup graham cracker crumbs
1/4 cup unsweetened cocoa
1/4 cup sugar
1/4 cup margarine, melted

Filling:

2 tablespoons instant coffee
1 teaspoon hot water
1 (14-ounce) can sweetened condensed milk
2/3 cup chocolate syrup
1 cup chopped walnuts
1 pint whipping cream, whipped
1/4 cup chocolate syrup

In a small bowl combine graham cracker crumbs, cocoa and sugar. Stir in melted margarine; pat into bottom of 9x9-inch square pan; refrigerate. In a medium bowl combine coffee and water; stir in condensed milk. Add 2/3 cup chocolate syrup; mix well. Fold in nuts and whipped cream. Pour mixture into crust. Drizzle 1/4 cup chocolate syrup over top; gently stir to marble. Freeze 6 hours or until firm. Serves 9.

Mrs. William Harris (Clara)
Dunedin, Florida

German Style Brownies

Microwave

2 tablespoons margarine
1/3 cup brown sugar, firmly packed
1/2 cup coconut
1/3 cup chopped walnuts

Topping:

1/2 cup sugar
1/2 cup chocolate syrup
1/2 cup all-purpose flour
1/2 teaspoon vanilla extract
1/4 teaspoon salt

In a round, microwave, 10-inch pan melt margarine 1 minute on High. Add brown sugar, coconut and walnuts; mix well and pack solid in pan. Microwave 1 minute on High; set aside. In a small bowl mix all topping ingredients; pour over brownie mix. Microwave for 6 minutes on High, turning pan once after 3 minutes. Let stand 5 minutes; then turn out on a plate. Makes 15 to 20.

Mrs. Robert B. Thomson (Eunice)
Holiday, Florida

Chip-Topped Date Bars

½ cup sifted all-purpose flour
½ teaspoon salt
¼ teaspoon baking soda
¾ cup butter
1 cup sugar
2 eggs
1 (7-ounce) package dates, chopped
1 cup chocolate chips
½ cup coarsely chopped pecans
1 tablespoon firmly packed brown sugar

In a small bowl sift flour with salt and baking soda. In a separate bowl cream butter and sugar until light and fluffy. Add eggs one at a time, beating well after each addition. Add flour mixture gradually; fold in dates. Spread in a greased 13x9x2-inch pan. Sprinkle with chocolate chips; press them into mixture. Sprinkle nuts and brown sugar on top. Bake at 350 degrees for 25 to 30 minutes, until golden brown. Cut into bars. Makes 24 bars.

Mrs. Robert Haverkos (Ginny)

Crisp Orange Cookies

1 cup butter
1 teaspoon vanilla extract
1 egg, unbeaten
1 teaspoon baking soda
½ teaspoon salt
1½ cups powdered sugar
1 tablespoon grated orange rind
2 cups all-purpose flour
1 teaspoon cream of tartar
Powdered sugar

Mix all ingredients in a medium bowl. Drop from a teaspoon 1-inch apart onto cookie sheet. Bake at 375 degrees for 8 minutes or until lightly browned. Remove from oven; cool; sprinkle with extra powdered sugar. Makes 4 to 5 dozen.

Mrs. Joe Hensley (Joann)

Kitchen Hint: Cookies too soft? Heat them in an oven at 300 degrees for 5 minutes. To hard? Place in an air-tight container overnight with slice of fresh bread or apple slices.

Chinese Christmas Cookies

1 (12-ounce) package semi-sweet chocolate chips
1 (12-ounce) package butterscotch chips
1 (5½-ounce) can chow mein noodles
1 cup cashew nut halves

In a double boiler melt chocolate and butterscotch chips over hot, not boiling, water. Remove from heat; add noodles and cashews. Drop by teaspoonfuls onto waxed paper; let dry. Makes 3 dozen.

Mrs. Harvey Heimann (Jean)

Pineapple Bars

1 1/2 cups sugar
4 eggs, well-beaten
1/2 cup margarine, melted
1 1/2 cups all-purpose flour
1 cup chopped nuts (optional)
1/2 teaspoon baking soda
1/2 teaspoon salt
1 (16-ounce) can crushed pineapple, drained

In a large bowl beat sugar into eggs. Add remaining ingredients; beat thoroughly. Pour batter into a greased 13x9x2-inch pan; bake at 350 degrees for 30 to 35 minutes. Cool before cutting. Makes 2 dozen.

Note: Flavor improves with refrigeration.

Mrs. Jack Garber (Lois)

Wedding Wafers

1/2 cup sweet butter
1/2 cup margarine
5 tablespoons sugar
1 tablespoon water
2 teaspoons vanilla extract
2 cups all-purpose flour, sifted
1/2 teaspoon salt (optional)
1/4 cup finely chopped pecans
Powdered sugar

Cream butter, margarine, and sugar. Beat until well blended; add water and vanilla extract. Sift flour and salt together; gradually add to creamed butter. Add nuts; mix well. Put dough in refrigerator until a little stiff. Form into 1-inch balls and flatten with prongs of fork on a greased cookie sheet. Bake at 325 degrees for 15 minutes. When cool sprinkle with powdered sugar. Makes 5 to 6 dozen.

Mrs. Edward Jaenicke (Helen)
Villa Park, Illinois

Coconut Dreams

1/2 cup butter or margarine
1 cup all-purpose flour
4 tablespoons powdered sugar
1 1/2 cups brown sugar
1/4 teaspoon salt
2 tablespoons all-purpose flour
3/4 cup coconut
2 eggs, beaten
1/4 teaspoon baking powder
1 cup chopped nuts
1 teaspoon vanilla extract

In a small bowl mix butter, flour and powdered sugar; pat into a 13x9x2-inch pan. Bake at 350 degrees for 12 minutes. Combine remaining ingredients; spread over shortbread. Return to oven; bake 20 minutes. Cut into bars. Makes 32 bars.

Mrs. Richard Davis (Lana)
Dunedin, Florida

Butterscotch Chocolate Bars

½ cup butter
1½ cups graham cracker crumbs
1 (6-ounce) package butterscotch chips
1 (6-ounce) package chocolate chips
1 cup chopped nuts
1 cup flaked coconut
1 cup sweetened condensed milk

Melt butter in a 13x9x2-inch baking pan, tilting pan to spread butter over bottom and sides. Add graham cracker crumbs to cover bottom of pan and pat down. Sprinkle a layer of butterscotch chips, chocolate chips, nuts and coconut over graham crackers. Pour sweetened condensed milk over top. Bake at 350 degrees for 30 minutes or until coconut is golden brown. Cut into squares. Makes 42 to 48 squares.

Mrs. Ernest Habig (Margie)
Dunedin, Florida

Italian Nut Delights

½ cup sweet butter, softened
⅓ cup sugar
1 egg, separated
¼ teaspoon vanilla extract
¼ teaspoon almond extract
1 cup sifted all-purpose flour
½ teaspoon salt
¾ cup chopped walnuts or pecans, colored
½ cup apricot jam

In a medium bowl cream butter. Beat in sugar, egg yolk and extracts. Sift flour with salt; add to creamed mixture. Form 36 small balls, using about ½ tablespoon of dough for each ball. Dip into slightly beaten egg white; roll lightly in nuts. Place on buttered cookie sheets. With fingertip, make depression in center of each cookie. Bake at 300 degrees for 25 minutes. While warm, fill centers with jam. Makes 3 dozen.

Colored Nuts:

Add green food coloring to 2 teaspoons warm water. Add nuts; blend thoroughly. Place nuts on cookie sheet and bake at 350 degrees for 8 minutes. Cookies freeze well.

Mrs. Dean N. McFarland (Donna VanEwyk)

Chocolate Madeleins

2 eggs, separated
1/2 cup sugar
1/2 cup cocoa
1/2 cup sifted all-purpose flour
1 teaspoon baking powder
1/8 teaspoon salt
1/2 cup butter, melted
1 teaspoon vanilla extract
4 (1-ounce) semi-sweet chocolate squares

In a medium bowl beat egg yolks, sugar and cocoa. Fold in flour, baking powder and salt; add butter and vanilla. Beat egg whites to soft peaks; fold into yolk mixture. Brush madelein molds with melted butter; fill each shell 2/3 full. Bake at 425 degrees for 10 to 15 minutes, until risen and firm. Can be frosted with melted semi-sweet chocolate squares, if desired. Makes 24.

Mrs. Horst P. Bothmann (Ingrid)

Scottish Shortbread

1 pound butter, room temperature
1 cup sugar
6 cups all-purpose flour, sifted twice

In a medium bowl cream butter and sugar until light and fluffy. Gradually mix in flour, using a wooden spoon and stirring until dough forms a ball. Using hands press dough evenly onto a 15x11x2-inch cookie sheet. Cover with waxed paper and smooth out using light pressure from a rolling pin; discard waxed paper. Mark shortbread into 3x1-inch rectangles. Prick entire surface with a fork; bake at 300 degrees for 40 minutes or until top is lightly browned. When cooled, store in an air-tight container. Makes 33 cookies.

Zena Duncan
Dunedin, Florida

Gingersnaps

1 1/2 cups shortening
2 cups sugar
2 eggs
1/2 cup light or dark molasses
4 cups sifted all-purpose flour
1/2 teaspoon salt
4 teaspoons baking soda
2 teaspoons cinnamon
4 teaspoons ginger

In a large mixing bowl cream shortening and sugar until light and fluffy. Beat in eggs; add molasses and dry ingredients. Roll into 1-inch balls; dip in sugar. Place 2 inches apart on a greased cookie sheet. Bake at 375 degrees for 13 to 15 minutes. Makes 7 dozen.

Mrs. Horst P. Bothmann (Ingrid)

Crunchy Chocolate Chip Cookies

3 1/3 cups sifted all-purpose flour
1 teaspoon baking powder
1/2 teaspoon salt
1 1/2 cups butter or margarine, softened
1 cup sugar
3/4 cup firmly packed dark brown sugar
1/4 cup hot water
1 egg
1 teaspoon vanilla extract
1 (6-ounce) package semi-sweet chocolate chips
1 1/2 to 2 cups corn flakes

Grease 2 cookie sheets. Sift flour, baking powder and salt onto waxed paper. Beat butter and sugars in a large bowl with electric mixer until light and fluffy. Beat in water, egg and vanilla. Gradually stir in flour mixture. Gently stir in chocolate chips and corn flakes. Drop mixture by heaping teaspoonfuls, 1-inch apart, onto prepared cookie sheets. Bake at 375 degrees 8 to 10 minutes or until cookies are set and golden brown. Cool on cookie sheets several minutes. Transfer to wire rack; cool completely. Store in tightly-covered container. Makes 7 dozen.

Mrs. Bill Ritchey (Carol Eddington)

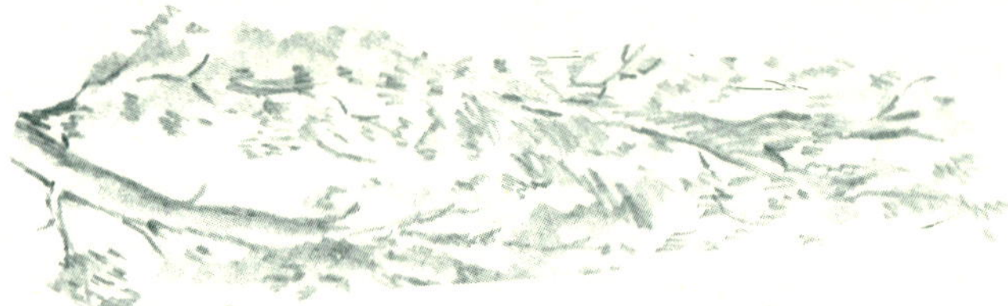

Anise Cookies

1 cup butter
1 1/2 cups sugar
6 eggs
1 (1-ounce) bottle anise extract
4 cups all-purpose flour
5 teaspoons baking powder
1/2 teaspoon baking soda
1 teaspoon salt

In large bowl cream butter with sugar. Add remaining ingredients; stir until well combined. Drop by teaspoonfuls onto ungreased cookie sheet. Bake at 350 to 375 degrees for 15 minutes. Makes 7 dozen.

Sugar Glaze:

1/4 to 1/3 cup milk, heated
1 1/2 to 2 cups powdered sugar
Colored sprinkles

Stir hot milk into powdered sugar to desired consistency in medium bowl. Glaze cookies. Sprinkle with colored sprinkles.

Suncoast Seasons Committee

Scandinavian Cookies

1 cup butter
½ cup brown sugar
2 egg yolks, lightly beaten
2 cups sifted all-purpose flour
2 egg whites
1 cup finely chopped pecans
½ cup strawberry jam

In medium bowl cream butter and brown sugar; mix in egg yolks and sifted flour. Chill for 2 hours. Roll into walnut-size balls. Dip balls into egg whites, then into chopped nuts. Place on greased cookie sheet and make a depression in center, using thumb or thimble. Bake 5 minutes at 300 degrees. Remove from oven and press center down again; put about ½ teaspoon of strawberry jam into center of each cookie. Return to oven and continue baking for 15 minutes longer. Cool. Makes 2 to 3 dozen.

Mrs. Robert Hall (Barbara)

Sandies

1 cup margarine
¼ cup powdered sugar
2 teaspoons vanilla extract
2 teaspoons water
2 cups all-purpose flour
1 (6-ounce) package semi-sweet chocolate chips
2 tablespoons water
1 cup chopped nuts

Cream margarine with sugar in medium bowl; blend in vanilla and 2 teaspoons water. Add flour and mix well; chill 1 hour. Shape dough into small fingers; place on cookie sheet. Bake at 325 degrees for 20 minutes or until lightly browned. In top of double boiler melt together chocolate chips and 2 tablespoons water. Dip tips of cookies in chocolate and then in nuts. Makes 6 dozen.

Suncoast Seasons Committee

Norwegian Spritz Cookies

1 cup butter
⅔ cup sugar
3 egg yolks, beaten
2½ cups cake flour
2 teaspoons rum or brandy
½ cup finely chopped blanched almonds

In a medium bowl cream butter and sugar. Stir in egg yolks; add flour and rum or brandy; chill dough a few hours. Fill cookie press and form into desired shapes. Decorate with chopped almonds. Place cookies on an ungreased cookie sheet. Bake at 350 degrees for 8 to 12 minutes. Makes 3 dozen.

Mrs. Carl Ness (Myrtle)
Dunedin, Florida

Teatime Tassies

Pastry:

2 (3-ounce) packages cream cheese
1 cup sweet butter
2 cups all-purpose flour

In a medium bowl combine all ingredients; mix with hands. Roll into a ball; chill covered, for 1 hour. Form into 1-inch balls; press to fit into ungreased miniature muffin tins.

Filling:

1½ cups light brown sugar
2 tablespoons butter, melted
2 teaspoons vanilla extract
⅛ teaspoon salt
2 eggs, beaten
1⅓ cups chopped pecans

In a medium bowl combine sugar, butter and vanilla; mix well. Add salt and eggs; mix well. Fold in nuts; pour into uncooked shells. Bake at 350 degrees for 20 to 25 minutes. Makes 4 dozen.

Mrs. Dean N. McFarland (Donna VanEwyk)
Mrs. Robert Haverkos (Ginny)

Chocolate Honey Bits

1 cup all-purpose flour
1½ teaspoons baking powder
¼ teaspoon salt
½ teaspoon cinnamon
½ teaspoon allspice
½ cup shortening
1 egg, well beaten
⅓ cup honey
2 tablespoons water
1 cup chocolate chips
½ cup raisins

In a medium bowl sift flour, baking powder, salt, cinnamon and allspice. In a large bowl cream shortening; add egg; mix well. Add honey and water to creamed mixture. Stir in dry ingredients; mix well. Gently stir in chocolate chips and raisins. Drop by teaspoonfuls onto a lightly greased and floured cookie sheet. Bake at 350 degrees for 8 to 10 minutes or until lightly browned. Makes 3½ dozen.

Variation: ¼ cup of corn syrup may be substituted for honey, but omit water and increase flour to 1½ cups and baking powder to 2 teaspoons.

Mrs. Charles Shupe (Jewel)
Park Forest, Illinois

Springerle Cookies

4 cups all-purpose flour
2 teaspoons baking powder
2 cups sugar
4 eggs, beaten
2 teaspoons boiling water
2 tablespoons anise seeds

Sift flour with baking powder; set aside. Add sugar gradually to beaten eggs. Pour boiling water over anise seeds; add to egg mixture. Sift in dry ingredients. Chill several hours or overnight. On lightly floured surface, roll out dough ¼-inch thick. Using floured cookie cutters, cut out cookies. Let dry 4 to 6 hours at room temperature. Bake at 375 degrees for 12 to 15 minutes on lightly greased cookie sheet. Makes 50 to 80.

Note: Cookies should be white when coming out of oven and will probably be hard. They are best if kept for 2 weeks before eating.

Mrs. Dean N. McFarland (Donna VanEwyk)

Cathedral Cookies

1 (12-ounce) package chocolate chips
2 tablespoons butter
2 eggs, beaten
1 (10-ounce) package colored miniature marshmallows
1¾ cups chopped nuts
Powdered sugar

Melt chocolate chips and butter in top of double boiler. Add beaten eggs until cooked. Do not overcook. Cool. Add marshmallows and nuts. Shape dough into rolls about 6-inches long and 1½-inches thick. Roll in powdered sugar. Wrap rolls individually in aluminum foil and store in refrigerator or freezer. Slice the rolls crosswise when ready to serve. Makes 4 dozen.

Note: Very colorful. Give the appearance of stained glass.

Mrs. Hartwell Hatton
Montgomery, Alabama

Honey-Nutters

1 cup chunky peanut butter
⅔ cup honey
½ cup instant non-fat dry milk
16 graham crackers, crushed
½ to 1 cup toasted wheat germ or coconut

In a medium bowl combine peanut butter, honey and dry milk. Add graham crackers to mixture. Make little balls by rolling a teaspoonful between the palms of your hands. Roll in wheat germ or coconut to coat. Makes 4½ dozen. *Taste improves if made a day ahead.*

Mrs. Jerry Harris (Nancy)

Shortbread Cookies

2 cups butter, softened
1 cup powdered sugar
3³/₄ cups all-purpose flour
2 tablespoons cornstarch

In a large mixing bowl cream butter; slowly add sugar. Add flour and cornstarch; mix until fluffy. Drop by teaspoonfuls onto waxed paper covered cookie sheet. Bake at 350 degrees for 15 minutes. Cool and frost.

Frosting:

¹/₃ cup vegetable shortening
3 cups powdered sugar
1¹/₂ teaspoons vanilla extract
Milk to desired consistency

Mix together shortening, sugar and vanilla. Add small amounts of milk until mixture reaches a smooth spreading consistency. Makes 5 dozen.

Mrs. Horst P. Bothmann (Ingrid)

Linzer Tarts

Great at Christmas Time!

³/₄ pound butter
6 tablespoons sugar
4 egg yolks
4 cups all-purpose flour
1 teaspoon baking powder
1 teaspoon vanilla extract
2 egg whites
¹/₂ cup walnuts, finely chopped
1 (12-ounce) jar raspberry preserves

In a large bowl cream butter, sugar and egg yolks. Sift flour and baking powder together; blend into butter mixture along with vanilla. Divide dough into 4 pieces. Roll ¼ of dough at a time into ¼-inch thicknesses on a floured board. Cut into rounds using a 2-inch biscuit cutter. Use a thimble to cut holes in center of ½ of the cookies. Combine holes into remaining dough; roll and cut as before. Bake on an ungreased cookie sheet at 350 degrees for 8 to 9 minutes or until lightly brown. Brush top half of cookies (ones with holes) with egg white; then dip into nuts. Spread raspberry preserves on bottom half of cookies. Put top in place, making a sandwich. Makes 2 to 3 dozen.

Note: The same dough makes wonderful cut-out cookies for children. Decorate as desired.

Mrs. Anthony S. Brancato (Georgine E. Palmer)

Rugelach

Pastry:

1 (8-ounce) package cream cheese, room temperature
1 cup sweet butter, room temperature
2 cups all-purpose flour
1/4 teaspoon salt
1/2 teaspoon baking powder

In a medium bowl cream together cream cheese and butter. In a separate bowl combine flour, salt and baking powder. Add to creamed mixture; mix well. Divide dough into four portions; wrap individually in plastic wrap. Chill overnight.

Filling:

1/2 cup sugar
1/2 cup chopped raisins
1/2 cup finely chopped walnuts
1 teaspoon cinnamon

In a small bowl mix ingredients; set aside. Remove one portion of dough at a time from refrigerator. On a lightly-floured board roll ball into a 10-inch round. Using a sharp knife or pizza cutter, cut into 12 wedges. Sprinkle 1/4 of the filling over the 12 wedges. Starting at the wide end, roll each wedge into a crescent. Place on ungreased cookie sheet. Bake at 350 degrees for 10 minutes, or until pastry is set. Continue with remaining dough. If desired, sprinkle with powdered sugar. Makes 48 pastries.

Mrs. George Palmer (Margaret)
Garfield, New Jersey

Cherry Cookies

1/2 cup butter
1/4 cup sugar
1 egg, separated
1 tablespoon grated orange rind
1 tablespoon lemon juice
1 cup sifted all-purpose flour
1/8 teaspoon salt
1 cup finely chopped nuts
6 candied cherries

In a mixing bowl thoroughly cream butter and sugar. Add egg yolk, orange rind and lemon juice; mix. Add flour and salt; mix to smooth paste; chill until firm. Roll dough in palms of hands to form small marble-sized balls. Dip each ball in slightly beaten egg white; roll in chopped nuts. Arrange on a greased cookie sheet; press 1/4 candied cherry on each ball. Bake at 350 degrees for 20 minutes. Makes 2 dozen.

Mrs. Leon Lewis (Dorothy)
Walnut Creek, California

Lebkuchen

The Almond-decorated Cookies from Nürnberg, the Famous German City of Toys

½ cup honey
½ cup molasses
¾ cup brown sugar, packed
1 egg
1 tablespoon lemon juice
1 teaspoon grated lemon rind
2¾ cups all-purpose flour
½ teaspoon baking soda
1 teaspoon cinnamon
1 teaspoon ground cloves
1 teaspoon allspice
1 teaspoon nutmeg
⅓ cup cut-up citron
⅓ cup chopped nuts

For Decorating:

⅔ cup citron, for topping
10-ounce package blanched almond halves

Combine honey and molasses in saucepan; bring to boil. Stir in sugar, egg, lemon juice and rind. Stir together flour, baking soda, cinnamon, cloves, allspice and nutmeg; blend into honey-molasses mixture. Add citron and nuts. Chill dough overnight. Roll out chilled dough ¼-inch thick on lightly floured board. Cut 2-inch rounds; place on greased baking sheet. Press on blanched almond halves around the edge like petals of a daisy. Place a piece of citron in the center. Bake 10 to 12 minutes or until just set in a preheated oven at 400 degrees. Immediately brush with icing. Remove from baking sheet. Cool and store in airtight container with orange or apple slices for a few days to mellow.

Icing:

1 cup sugar
½ cup water
¼ cup powdered sugar

Blend sugar and water in a small saucepan. Boil to 230 degrees on a candy thermometer. Remove from heat; stir in powdered sugar. If icing becomes sugary while brushing cookies, reheat slightly, adding a little water until clear again. Any leftover icing may be used on fruitcake or other fruit bars. Makes 6 dozen.

Note: Cookie cutters may also be used, if desired.

Mrs. James Long (Eva Fandrich)

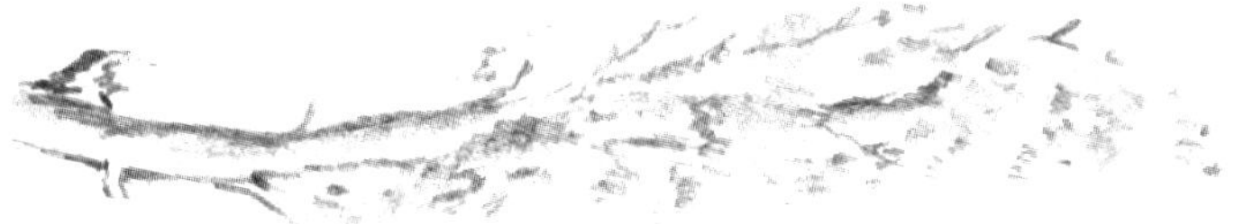

Pride of Iowa Cookies

Oatmeal

1 cup brown sugar
1 cup sugar
1 cup shortening
2 eggs
2 cups all-purpose flour
½ teaspoon salt
1 teaspoon baking soda
1 teaspoon baking powder
1 teaspoon vanilla extract
1 cup coconut
3 cups quick-cooking oats
½ cup chopped nuts

In a large mixing bowl cream sugars and shortening until fluffy. Add eggs; beat until mixed. Sift together flour, salt, baking soda and baking powder, mixing well. Combine with creamed mixture. Add vanilla; stir in coconut, oats and nuts. Drop by large teaspoonfuls onto greased cookie sheet. Flatten with bottom of glass dipped in sugar. Bake at 375 degrees for 8 minutes, or until lightly browned. Makes 7 dozen.

Mrs. Richard Benkusky (Judy)

Crunchy Peanut Chocolate Bars

1½ cups crunchy peanut butter
1½ cups graham cracker crumbs
1 (16-ounce) box powdered sugar
1 cup melted butter
2 (8-ounce) plain milk chocolate bars

In a medium bowl mix all ingredients except chocolate bars; press mixture firmly into a 13x9x2-inch pan. Melt chocolate bars; pour over mixture in pan. Cool completely; cut into bars. Makes 5 dozen.

Mrs. Jimmie Bryan (Donna)

Date Nut Balls

1 cup chopped dates
1 cup sugar
1 cup chopped pecans
½ cup butter
1 tablespoon light corn syrup
1 egg, well beaten
¼ teaspoon almond extract
½ teaspoon vanilla extract
2 cups oven-toasted rice cereal
1 to 1½ cups powdered sugar

In a deep large saucepan combine first 6 ingredients. Cook for 8 minutes over medium heat, stirring constantly. Do not overcook. Remove from heat; stir in extracts and then cereal; set aside until cool enough to handle. Mixture will be sticky. Dust hands with powdered sugar; form into ½-inch balls. Drop into a bowl of powdered sugar; roll until well coated. Makes 4 dozen.

Mrs. Wilford R. Poe (Mollye Redmon)

Simit

A Crispy Finger Cookie

4 cups all-purpose flour
2 teaspoons baking powder
¾ teaspoon salt
2 tablespoons sugar
½ cup butter
¾ cup shortening
½ cup water
½ cup milk
1 egg, beaten
½ teaspoon water
½ cup sesame seeds

In a large bowl sift flour with baking powder, salt and sugar. In a small saucepan melt butter, shortening, water and milk. Make a hole in the dry ingredients and gradually add liquids, mixing together as you pour. Knead slightly to make a semi-soft dough. Make walnut-sized balls; then roll and stretch dough to form mini-shaped cigars. Place on an ungreased cookie sheet. Brush tops with a mixture of beaten egg and water; sprinkle generously with sesame seeds. Bake at 350 degrees for 30 minutes or until lightly browned. Makes 3 to 4 dozen.

Mrs. Gregory H. Keuroghlian (Nora Ghazikian)

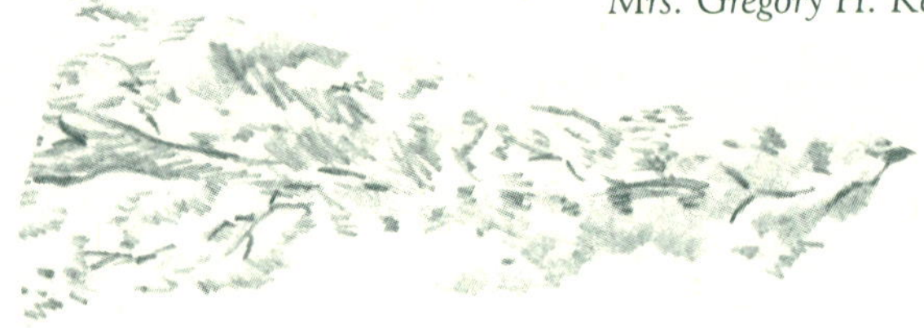

Strufoli

4 eggs, beaten
½ cup salad oil
2 teaspoons salt
2½ cups all-purpose flour, separated
1 teaspoon baking powder
½ cup salad oil
1¾ cups honey
½ cup coarsely chopped walnuts or almonds
Nuts, candied green and red cherries or nonpareils

In a large bowl combine eggs, oil and salt; blend well. Gradually stir in 2 cups flour and baking powder; mix well by hand. Knead in remaining flour. Turn dough onto lightly-floured surface; cut into 20 equal portions. Using palms of hands, roll each piece into a pencil-shaped stick. Cut into ¼-inch pieces with floured knife. Heat ½ cup oil in skillet to 370 degrees on a thermometer. Cook a few strufoli at a time, turning with a slotted spoon, until lightly golden. Drain on paper towels. Stir strufoli in honey; place on rack to allow honey to drip. Decorate with nuts and cherries or nonpareils. Makes 200.

Mrs. Vito Grasso (Aurora)
Dunedin, Florida

Gladys' Chocolate Cookies

¼ cup butter or margarine
2 (1-ounce) squares baking chocolate
1 cup sugar
2 eggs
1 cup all-purpose flour
1½ teaspoons baking powder
1 teaspoon vanilla extract
½ cup powdered sugar

In top of double boiler melt butter and chocolate. Stir in sugar; remove from heat. Add eggs, one at a time; beat well. Sift flour with baking powder; add to chocolate mixture. Add vanilla extract; cover and refrigerate overnight. Roll dough into walnut-sized balls; dip in powdered sugar. Place 2 inches apart on a cookie sheet. Bake at 350 degrees for 12 to 15 minutes. Makes 3 dozen.

Mrs. Gladys Bledsoe Duncan
Dunedin, Florida

High Energy Candy Balls

4 tablespoons honey
4 tablespoons wheat germ
4 tablespoons crunchy peanut butter
4 tablespoons shredded coconut
3 to 4 tablespoons wheat germ

Mix first 4 ingredients together; refrigerate for 1 hour. Form into 1-inch balls. Roll in wheat germ; refrigerate. Makes 1 dozen balls.

Mrs. Jerry Harris (Nancy)

Fruit Drop Cookies

½ cup shortening
1 cup brown sugar
1 egg
1¾ cups sifted all-purpose flour
½ teaspoon salt
½ teaspoon baking soda
¼ cup sour milk
¾ cup coarsely chopped pecans
1 (8-ounce) package candied cherries
1 cup dates, chopped
48 pecan halves

In a large bowl mix all ingredients except pecan halves. Drop by teaspoonfuls onto greased cookie sheets. Place ½ pecan on each cookie. Bake at 375 to 400 degrees for 8 to 10 minutes. Makes 4 dozen.

Note: To sour the milk, have the milk at 70 degrees. Place 1 tablespoon of lemon juice or distilled white vinegar in the bottom of a measuring cup. Fill to ¼ cup with sweet milk; stir; let stand for 10 minutes.

Mrs. Ernest Habig (Margie)
Dunedin, Florida

French Butter Cream Cookies

½ cup butter
½ cup shortening
1½ cups sifted powdered sugar
1 teaspoon vanilla extract
1 teaspoon salt
1 egg
2½ cups all-purpose flour
1 teaspoon baking soda
1 teaspoon cream of tartar

In a large mixing bowl cream butter with shortening. Add powdered sugar gradually, continuing to cream. Add vanilla, salt and egg; beat thoroughly. Add flour, baking soda and cream of tartar; mix well. Divide dough in half; chill thoroughly, at least 1 hour. On lightly floured surface roll out dough, one half at a time, ¼-inch thick. Refrigerate remaining half until ready to roll out. Cut out cookies, using floured cookie cutters. Place 2 inches apart on ungreased cookie sheet. Bake at 350 degrees for 12 to 15 minutes. Cool; decorate as desired. Makes 3 dozen.

Mrs. Dean N. McFarland (Donna (VanEwyk)

Cinnamon Pecans

2 egg whites
½ cup sugar
¾ teaspoon cinnamon
1 pound pecan halves

In a medium bowl whip egg whites until foamy; set aside. In a small bowl combine sugar and cinnamon. Toss pecan halves in egg whites, then in sugar and cinnamon mixture. Toast in oven at 225 degrees, gently turning occasionally, for 20 to 30 minutes; cool. Freeze or store in tightly-sealed container. Makes 1 pound.

Mrs. James Berfield (Sue Mautz)

Peanut Brittle

2 cups sugar
1 cup light corn syrup
1 cup water
2 cups peanuts
¼ teaspoon salt
1 teaspoon butter
¼ teaspoon baking soda
¼ teaspoon vanilla extract

In heavy saucepan combine sugar, corn syrup and water. Cook slowly, stirring until sugar dissolves. Cook to soft ball stage, 238 degrees on a candy thermometer. Add peanuts and salt. Cook to hard crack stage, 290 degrees, stirring constantly. Remove from heat; add butter, baking soda and vanilla; stir slightly. Pour evenly into a well-greased 15x9x2-inch jellyroll pan. Cool partially by lifting around edges with knife. When cool, break into pieces. Makes 2 pounds 5 ounces.

Mrs. Dean N. McFarland (Donna VanEwyk)

Currant-Coconut Crescents

1 cup butter
$2^{1}/_{2}$ cups all-purpose flour
1 (8-ounce) carton sour cream
2 cups sugar
$^{1}/_{4}$ teaspoon cinnamon
2 cups currant jelly
1 cup raisins
1 cup nuts, chopped
2 cups flaked coconut
3 drops lemon juice

In a large bowl and using a pastry blender, cut butter into flour until lumps are the size of peas. Mix in sour cream; refrigerate overnight. In a small bowl mix sugar and cinnamon. Divide pastry into 6 parts. Sprinkle cinnamon-sugar mixture on pastry cloth or counter; roll one part of pastry into a circle. Spread with jelly. In a medium bowl mix raisins, nuts, coconut and lemon juice. Sprinkle $^{1}/_{6}$ of raisin mixture over jellied pastry. Cut like a pizza; roll into crescents. Repeat with remaining pastry. Bake at 400 degrees for 8 to 10 minutes, until lightly browned and bubbly-thick, but not burned. Remove immediately from pan to wire rack. Makes 72.

Mrs. William S. Sharpe (Wanda)

Pecan Candy Rolls

1 (7-ounce) jar marshmallow cream
1 (16-ounce) package powdered sugar
1 teaspoon vanilla extract
1 (14-ounce) package assorted vanilla and chocolate caramels
3 tablespoons water
1 to $1^{1}/_{2}$ cups chopped pecans

In a mixing bowl combine marshmallow cream, powdered sugar and vanilla, mixing well with hands. Shape mixture into 5 (4x1-inch) rolls. Mixture will be very dry. Chill 2 to 3 hours. Combine caramels and water in top of a double boiler; cook until melted. Dip rolls in melted caramel; roll each in pecans. Chill 1 hour. Cut into slices to serve. Makes 5 rolls.

Mrs. Robert Haverkos (Ginny)

Glazed Nuts

1 egg white
1 cup sugar
$^{1}/_{2}$ cup butter, melted
$^{1}/_{8}$ teaspoon salt
1 pound whole pecans, shelled

In a medium bowl beat egg white. Gradually add sugar, then butter and salt. Mix in pecans. Spread in a single layer on cookie sheet. Bake at 300 degrees for 30 minutes; stirring occasionally. Makes 1 pound.

Mrs. William S. Sharpe (Wanda)

Caramel Corn

2 cups firmly packed light brown sugar
½ cup light corn syrup
½ pound butter or margarine
¼ teaspoon cream of tartar
1 teaspoon salt
1 teaspoon baking soda
6 quarts freshly popped corn

In a 2½-quart saucepan combine brown sugar, corn syrup, butter, cream of tartar and salt. Heat to boiling, stirring over medium-high heat. Stirring constantly, boil rapidly to hard-ball stage (260 degrees on candy thermometer), about 5 minutes. Remove from heat. Stir in baking soda quickly, but thoroughly, and pour at once over popcorn in a large roasting or baking pan. Stir gently until all kernels are coated. Bake in preheated oven at 200 degrees for 1 hour, stirring 2 or 3 times during baking. Turn out at once onto waxed paper; spread apart and allow to cool completely. Break apart and store in a tightly-covered container. Makes 6 quarts.

Mrs. Brian Cook (Lee)
Dunedin, Florida

Strawberry Delights

1 (14-ounce) can sweetened condensed milk
2 cups flaked coconut
2 teaspoons almond extract
2 (3-ounce) packages strawberry gelatin dessert
¼ cup powdered sugar, sifted
½ teaspoon milk
4 drops green food coloring

In a medium bowl mix condensed milk, coconut, almond extract and 1 package gelatin. Stir until thoroughly blended; allow to stand in refrigerator for 1 hour, or until set. Using 1 tablespoonful of mixture at a time, form into strawberry-shaped balls. Roll in remaining gelatin. Combine powdered sugar, milk and food coloring to make a stiff paste. Give each berry a green "stem". Refrigerate for 1 hour before serving. Makes 60 strawberries.

Mrs. Frank Peck (May)
Hamilton, Ontario, Canada

Peanut Butter Bon Bons

1½ (16-ounce) boxes powdered sugar (6 cups)
1 cup butter or margarine
2 cups peanut butter
1 (12-ounce) package semi-sweet chocolate chips
3 ounces paraffin wax

In an extra large bowl combine sugar, butter and peanut butter; mix well. Form into 1-inch balls; refrigerate for several hours or overnight. In double boiler melt chocolate chips and paraffin wax. Dip chilled peanut balls into chocolate mixture. Makes 5 dozen.

Variation: Try crunchy peanut butter; and double-dip bon bons with chocolate mixture.

Mrs. Ronald Gordon (Linda)

Easter Bird Nests

1 (16-ounce) bag melting chocolate
2 to 3 cups flaked coconut or crispy rice cereal
1 cup small jelly beans

In top of double boiler melt chocolate. When fully melted, stir in coconut until mixture holds its shape. Drop by tablespoonfuls onto waxed paper, forming circles. Make an indentation in the center of each circle; add 3 to 4 jelly beans. Allow to cool and harden; wrap individually in cellophane to fill Easter baskets. Makes 40 to 44 nests.

Note: Melting chocolate may be purchased in many colors.

Carol Dawson Clarke
Columbus, Mississippi

Peanut Bark

1 (12-ounce) package semi-sweet chocolate chips
5 tablespoons evaporated milk, warmed
1 cup salted or unsalted peanuts

In a double boiler melt chocolate over hot, not boiling, water; stir until smooth. Remove from heat; immediately stir in milk and peanuts until blended. Pour onto waxed paper; flatten with a spatula. Chill a few minutes or until firm. Cut into irregular pieces. Makes 1 pound.

Mrs. George Engblom (Eileen)

Frozen Chocolate Frangoes

1 cup butter, softened
3 cups powdered sugar
4-ounces unsweetened chocolate, melted
¾ cup chopped walnuts or pecans
4 eggs
1 teaspoon vanilla extract
1 teaspoon peppermint extract
¼ cup chopped walnuts or pecans

In a mixing bowl cream butter and sugar. Add chocolate, ¾ cup nuts, eggs and extracts. Spoon into 24 double cupcake liners. Top with remaining nuts. Freeze. Makes 2 dozen.

Phyllis Taylor
New Concord, Ohio

Mamie Eisenhower Fudge

4½ cups sugar
1 (13-ounce) can evaporated milk
6 tablespoons butter
⅛ teaspoon salt
1 (12-ounce) package chocolate chips
3 (1⅓-ounce) bars German baking chocolate
1 pint marshmallow creme
2 cups chopped pecans or walnuts

In a saucepan boil sugar, milk, butter and salt for 6 minutes. In a large bowl mix remaining ingredients, except nuts. Gradually pour hot syrup over mixture. Beat with electric mixer until chocolate is melted; add nuts. Pour into 2 buttered 8-inch square pans. Refrigerate for several hours to harden. Makes 5 pounds.

Mrs. Edwin Everett (Barbara)

New Orleans Creamy Pecan Pralines

1 cup sugar
1 cup light brown sugar
1 (5⅓-ounce) can evaporated milk
2 cups pecan halves

In a saucepan over medium heat combine sugar, evaporated milk and a few pecans. Stir only around sides while mixture boils to soft-ball stage. Remove from heat; stir in remaining pecans. Spoon onto buttered foil or waxed paper to desired size. Makes 4 dozen.

Note: For dark pralines use all light or dark brown sugar.

Mrs. Anthony Castrogiovanni (BeBe)

From the Famous

Macaroni and Cheese

½ pound macaroni
1 teaspoon butter
1 egg, beaten
1 teaspoon dry mustard
1 teaspoon salt
1 tablespoon hot water
1 cup milk
3 cups shredded sharp cheese

Boil macaroni in water until tender; drain thoroughly. Stir in butter and egg. Mix mustard and salt with hot water; add to milk. Add cheese, leaving enough to sprinkle on top. Pour into buttered 1-quart casserole; add milk; sprinkle with reserved cheese. Bake at 350 degrees for about 45 minutes or until custard is set and top is crusty. "President Reagan's favorite!" Serves 6 to 8.

Mrs. Ronald Reagan (Nancy)
The First Lady
White House
Washington, D.C.

Pumpkin Pecan Pie

4 eggs, slightly beaten
2 cups canned or cooked, mashed pumpkin
1 cup sugar
½ cup dark corn syrup
1 teaspoon vanilla extract
½ teaspoon cinnamon
¼ teaspoon salt
1 9-inch pie shell, unbaked
1 cup chopped pecans

Combine all ingredients except pecans. Pour into pie shell; top with pecans. Bake at 350 degrees for 40 minutes or until set. Serves 8.

"With Best Wishes."

Nancy Reagan

Mrs. Ronald Reagan (Nancy)
The First Lady
White House
Washington, D.C.

Lemon Bars

"For Lemon Lovers of America!"

1 cup margarine
2 cups powdered sugar
2 cups all-purpose flour
4 teaspoons lemon juice
Rind of 2 lemons, grated
4 eggs, well beaten
2 cups sugar
1 teaspoon baking powder
4 tablespoons all-purpose flour
1 cup shredded coconut (optional)

Mix margarine, powdered sugar and flour. Spread (batter is stiff) in a 15x10x1-inch jelly roll pan. Bake 15 minutes at 350 degrees, "until pale tan or paler." Cool. Mix remaining ingredients. Pour over crust. Bake for 25 minutes at 350 degrees.

"This is a favorite of ours—I borrowed the recipe from my dear friend, Antoinette Hatfield, wife of Senator Mark O. Hatfield."

Mrs. George Bush (Barbara)
Vice President's House
Washington, D. C.

Vice President's Spinach Salad

2 pounds fresh spinach, chopped
10 hard-cooked eggs, sliced
1 pound bacon, fried and crumbled
1 medium head lettuce, shredded
1 cup sliced shallots
1 (10-ounce) package frozen peas, thawed and uncooked
2½ cups mayonnaise
2½ cups sour cream
¼ teaspoon salt
⅛ teaspoon pepper
1 teaspoon Worcestershire sauce
1 tablespoon lemon juice, or to taste
½ cup shredded Swiss cheese

Place first six ingredients in layers in large glass salad bowl. Blend mayonnaise, sour cream, salt, pepper, Worcestershire sauce and lemon juice. Pour over first six ingredients; sprinkle Swiss cheese on top. Cover and chill 12 hours. Do *not* toss. Serves 16. "This is a favorite of Vice President George Bush."

Barbara Bush

Mrs. George Bush (Barbara)
The Vice President's House
Washington, D. C.

Flank Steak à la Carter

1½ pounds flank steak
¼ cup soy sauce
¼ cup red or white wine

In shallow dish marinate steak in mixture of soy sauce and wine for 1 hour or longer, turning occasionally. For medium rare, broil steak for 5 minutes on each side, basting once with marinade. Let rest for a couple of minutes before slicing in thin slices across the grain. Serves 3 to 4.

Hint: Always salt steak after it is cooked to avoid toughening.

"With best wishes!"

Rosalynn Carter

Mrs. Jimmy Carter (Rosalynn)
Plains, Georgia

Chocolate Ice Box Dessert

1 (9-inch) angel food cake, sliced in half
6 eggs, separated
1 (12-ounce) package chocolate chips
4 tablespoons sugar
6 tablespoons water
2 teaspoons vanilla extract
1 teaspoon salt
2 cups whipping cream, whipped

Line a 9-inch square cake pan with waxed paper; place a layer of cake in pan. Melt chocolate chips in double boiler; add sugar and water; mix well. Be sure sugar melts. Remove from heat and stir the chocolate mixture gradually into beaten egg yolks; beat until smooth. Cool chocolate mixture; add vanilla and salt and mix. Beat egg whites until stiff; fold whites into cooled chocolate mixture; fold in whipped cream. Place a layer of chocolate mixture on the sliced cake; cover with second cake half. Cover entire cake with chocolate mixture. Refrigerate overnight. Serves 9 to 12.

Note: May be refrigerated overnight, frozen and used later; being sure to chill overnight before freezing. Cake slices better, if frozen.

"The recipe is one that the Ford family has always enjoyed."

Mrs. Gerald Ford (Betty)

Lady Bird's Spiced Tea

6 teaspoons tea (or 8 tea bags)
2 cups boiling water
1 (6-ounce) can frozen lemon juice
1 (6-ounce) can frozen orange juice
1½ cups sugar
2 quarts water
1 (3-inch) cinnamon stick

In a teapot pour boiling water over tea and let cool. Strain and pour into a 4-quart saucepan; add juices, sugar, water and cinnamon. Simmer for 20 minutes. If too strong, add water. Add extra sugar to taste. Serve hot. Serves 16 to 20 cups.

"I like to serve this to guests on a cold winter's day here at the LBJ Ranch, just as I did at the White House."

Lady Bird Johnson
Stonewall, Texas

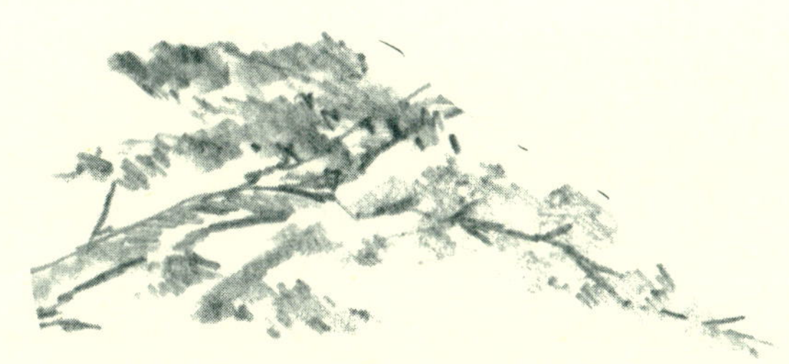

Dilled Okra Pickles

Enough okra to fill 4 to 5 pint jars
2 bunches dill or ½ teaspoon dill seed in bottom of each jar
4 to 5 hot red peppers
4 to 5 hot green peppers
4 to 5 garlic cloves
1 quart undistilled white vinegar
1 cup water
½ cup plain salt

Sterilize 4 to 5 pint jars. Without bruising, carefully pack okra tightly into jars. Top each jar with 2 to 3 sprigs dill, 1 of each hot pepper and 1 clove garlic. In a small pan boil vinegar, water and salt. Pour over jars of okra to top; seal jars. Refrigerate for 2 weeks. Serve icy cold. Makes 4 to 5 pints.

Note: If okra is bruised, the pickles will not be crisp.

Lady Bird Johnson

Lady Bird Johnson
Stonewall, Texas

Orange Dessert Squares

A Favorite of Governor Bob Graham

2/3 cup sugar
1/2 cup butter or margarine, softened
2 eggs, separated
2 cups self-rising flour
3/4 cup milk
4 teaspoons grated orange rind

In medium bowl beat sugar, butter, and egg yolks at medium speed until light and fluffy; add flour alternate with milk at low speed, beginning and ending with flour. Beat egg whites until stiff but not dry; fold egg whites and orange rind into batter; pour into greased 13x9x2-inch baking pan. Bake at 375 degrees for 20 to 25 minutes or until golden brown. Cool and serve with orange sauce. Serves 15 to 18.

Orange Sauce:

2/3 cup sugar
1 tablespoon cornstarch
1/4 teaspoon salt
1 cup boiling water
1 teaspoon butter or margarine
4 teaspoons grated orange rind
1/2 cup fresh orange juice

In a small saucepan mix together sugar, cornstarch and salt; pour boiling water over mixture, stirring constantly. Cook over moderate heat until mixture boils and thickens. Add butter, orange rind and juice.

Governor Bob Graham
Governor's Mansion
Tallahassee, Florida

Florida Seafood Casserole

1/2 pound crabmeat
1/2 pound Florida lobster
1 pound shrimp
1 cup mayonnaise
1/2 cup chopped green pepper
1/4 cup minced onion
1 1/2 cups finely chopped celery
1/2 teaspoon salt
1 tablespoon Worcestershire sauce
2 cups potato chips, crushed
1/8 teaspoon paprika

Mix all ingredients together, except potato chips. Fill a 13x9x2-inch baking dish with mixture and completely cover with potato chips; Sprinkle with paprika. Bake at 400 degrees for 20 to 25 minutes or until done. Serves 12 as luncheon dish.

Note: The addition of 1 tablespoon or more of lemon juice will enhance the flavor.

GREAT SEAL OF THE STATE OF FLORIDA
IN GOD WE TRUST

Governor Bob Graham
Governor's Mansion
Tallahassee, Florida

Paula's Favorite Pound Cake

2¾ cups sugar
1 cup butter
6 eggs
3 cups sifted all-purpose flour
½ teaspoon salt
¼ teaspoon baking powder
1 cup sour cream
½ teaspoon lemon extract
½ teaspoon orange extract
½ teaspoon vanilla extract
¼ cup powdered sugar

Cream sugar and butter until fluffy. Add eggs, one at a time, beating well between each addition. Sift together flour, salt and baking powder. Add to creamed mixture alternately with sour cream. Add extracts and beat well after each addition. Bake in greased and floured 10-inch Bundt pan for 1 hour 10 minutes or until done at 350 degrees. Cool for 15 minutes before removing from pan. When cooled, dust lightly with powdered sugar. *"This is delicious! Thank you for requesting my favorite recipe. I welcome the opportunity to be of service."* Serves 12 to 16.

Senator Paula Hawkins
Senator from Florida
Washington, D.C.

Cheese Grits

1 cup grits
4 cups boiling water
¼ pound butter or margarine
2 tablespoons seasoning salt
Garlic, to taste
12 ounces Cheddar cheese, shredded
2 eggs, slightly beaten

Cook grits in boiling water until thick. Add butter, seasonings and cheese, stirring until melted. Stir eggs into grits mixture. Pour into greased 1½-quart casserole; bake 1 hour at 325 degrees. Serves 6.

Note: Placing a sheet of aluminum foil under the pan seems to prevent it from sticking.

"Thank you for your letter requesting one of Mrs. Brown's favorite recipes. Kentucky has many delicious traditional foods, and a favorite of hers is Cheese Grits. This dish is served for both formal and informal occasions. Best wishes and thank you again for writing."

Phyllis George Brown
Governor's Mansion
Frankfort, Kentucky

Mayor Bonner's Favorite Cranberry Bread

2 cups sifted all-purpose flour
1½ teaspoons baking powder
½ teaspoon baking soda
½ teaspoon salt
1 cup sugar
2 tablespoons shortening, melted
Grated rind and juice of 1 orange plus fresh or diluted frozen juice to make ¾ cup
1 egg, beaten
1 cup raw cranberries, cut into halves

In a bowl stir together first 5 ingredients; mix thoroughly next 3 ingredients; fold in cranberries. Pour into greased 9x5x3-inch loaf pan. Bake at 350 degrees for 50 to 60 minutes or until toothpick inserted in center comes out clean. Serve day after baking and refrigerating. Makes 1 loaf.

"Best wishes in this endeavor."

Mary Bonner

Mary Bonner, Mayor
Dunedin, Florida

Kathy Kelly's Chicken

¼ cup chipped beef
4 slices bacon
4 chicken breasts, boned and skinned
1 (10¾-ounce) can cream of mushroom soup
1 cup sour cream

Spread beef on bottom of 9x9x2-inch pan. Wrap 1 slice of bacon around each piece of chicken; put on top of beef. Mix soup and sour cream; spread on top of chicken. Bake, uncovered, at 275 degrees for approximately 3 hours. Do *not* let it brown; cover with foil for last ½ hour. Serves 4.

"Thanks so much for writing. Good luck!"

Kathy Kelly

Kathy Kelly
Mayor of Clearwater

Sausage Bread

2 pounds sweet or hot Italian sausage
1 large clove garlic, minced
1/2 teaspoon basil
1/2 teaspoon oregano
1/4 teaspoon salt
1/8 teaspoon pepper
1/2 pound fresh mushrooms, sliced
1 (4-ounce) can tomato sauce
1 (1-pound) loaf bread dough (yours or purchased from store)
1 (8-ounce) package mozzarella cheese, shredded

Remove sausage from casing; simmer in large skillet, draining frequently, for about 30 minutes. Add garlic, seasonings, mushrooms and tomato sauce; cover and cook an additional 15 minutes. Roll out bread dough fairly thin; spread with sausage mixture, and sprinkle on cheese. Roll jelly roll fashion. Bake on a lightly greased cookie sheet at 350 degrees for 30 minutes. Remove from oven; cool 30 minutes. Slice into ½-inch pieces. Makes 12 pieces.

Note: Prepare sausage bread a day ahead; freeze without slicing. Prior to serving, slice while still frozen; place on cookie sheet and place under broiler 5 to 10 minutes or until crisp.

Mayor Sandy J. and Diane Francisco
Oldsmar, Florida

Hot Seafood Spread

2 (8-ounce) packages cream cheese
4 tablespoons butter
1/4 cup mayonnaise
1 (6 1/2-ounce) can crabmeat
1 (6 1/2-ounce) can minced clams, drained
1/8 teaspoon Worcestershire sauce
Dash hot pepper sauce

Combine all ingredients in a 1-quart saucepan; mix well. Cover; simmer 2 hours on very low heat. Place in a fondue pot over low flame; spread on party rye, pumpernickel bread, crackers or melba toast. Makes 4 cups.

"Thank you for thinking of us."

Diane Francisco

Mayor Sandy J. and Diane Francisco
Oldsmar, Florida

Refritos Frijoles

Refried Beans

- 1 (12-ounce) package pinto beans
- 1 teaspoon salt
- 1/4 teaspoon hot pepper sauce
- 1/4 cup milk
- 1/2 cup shredded sharp Cheddar cheese
- 2 tablespoons oil
- 1/2 cup milk
- 1/2 cup shredded sharp Cheddar cheese
- 1/4 teaspoon hot pepper sauce, or to taste

In a large pan soak beans in water flavored with salt and hot pepper sauce for several hours or overnight. Bring beans to a boil and simmer until soft (2 to 3 hours). During cooking add milk and cheese. Drain beans reserving liquid. Heat oil in a large skillet over medium heat; add beans; cook a few minutes. Add reserved liquid, gradually, and mash and mash and mash. Add small amounts of milk (amout may vary depending on liquid left when cooking beans), hot pepper sauce and cheese while continuing to mash. Adjust flavoring to taste. Serve with tortillas and fresh fruit. Serves 6.

"Congratulations to you and the members who work diligently for the young people of the area. No other endeavor could be more needed or worthy. Best wishes to you and your club."

Gabe & Maggie

Gabe and Maggie Cazares
Pinellas County Commissioner

Mexican Enchiladas

- 1 (10-ounce) package corn tortillas
- 2 to 3 tablespoons vegetable oil
- 1 (10-ounce) can mild enchilada sauce, heated
- 12 ounces shredded sharp Cheddar cheese
- 1 medium onion, chopped
- 2 cups shredded lettuce
- 2 cups diced tomatoes
- 2 oranges, sliced

In skillet over medium heat soften tortillas in 2 tablespoons oil. Add more oil, if needed. Dip tortillas in enchilada sauce; remove to oven-proof platter or baking dish. Sprinkle each with cheese and onion; roll tortilla. Pour enchilada sauce overall. Cover with foil and heat for 20 minutes at 300 degrees. Serve with lettuce and tomatoes. Add hot enchilada sauce, if desired. Garnish with oranges. Serves 4 to 6.

PINELLAS COUNTY FLORIDA
BOARD OF COUNTY COMMISSIONERS

Gabe and Maggie Cazares
Pinellas County Commissioner

Nana's Green Beans

2 pounds fresh green beans, cleaned
4 tablespoons olive oil
1 clove garlic
1 teaspoon basil
2 tablespoons chopped onion
2 tablespoons minced parsley
½ teaspoon sugar
½ teaspoon pepper

In 4-quart sauce pan cook whole beans in salted water until tender; drain well. In skillet heat olive oil; add remaining ingredients and cook until onion is soft. Remove garlic; pour mixture over beans and toss lightly. Reheat slowly; serve warm. Serves 6.

"This string bean dish is an old family recipe." Mary Jane Martinez

Mayor Bob and Mary Jane Martinez
Tampa, Florida

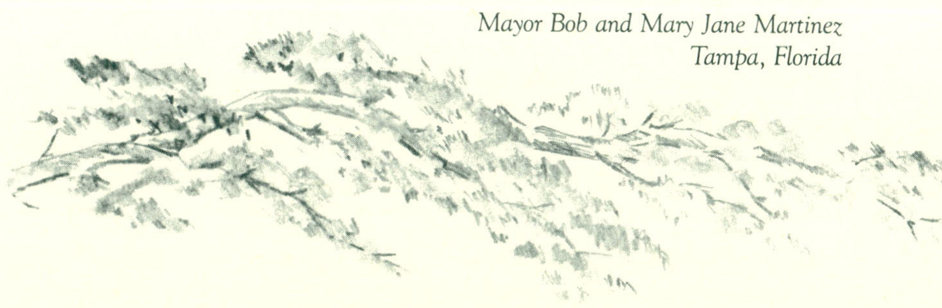

Shrimp Mold Spread

1 (10¾-ounce) can tomato soup
3 (3-ounce) packages cream cheese
1 cup finely minced shrimp
1 cup mayonnaise
⅓ cup finely chopped celery
⅓ cup finely chopped onion
⅓ cup finely chopped green pepper
1 (¼-ounce) envelope unflavored gelatin
3 to 4 tablespoons warm water
⅛ teaspoon hot pepper sauce

Heat tomato soup; cut up cheese; add to soup. Stir until melted and smooth. Add remaining ingredients. Pour into 1½-quart mold which has been lightly greased with mayonnaise or vegetable oil. Refrigerate and allow 3 to 4 hours to set. Serve with an assortment of crackers. Makes 4½ cups.

Note: Best results if made day before. "Very attractive appetizer if fish mold is used."

CITY OF TAMPA FLORIDA ORGANIZED JULY 15 1887

Mayor Bob and Mary Jane Martinez
Tampa, Florida

Rumanian Meat and Peppers

3 tablespoons shortening
1½ pounds beef, cut into cubes
1½ pounds veal, cut into cubes
4 onions, chopped
2 teaspoons salt
½ teaspoon pepper
½ cup boiling water
6 green peppers, cut into thin slices
4 tomatoes, cut into thin slices
2 cloves garlic, crushed
Snipped parsley sprigs

Melt shortening in Dutch oven, brown meat and onions; add seasonings and water; cover; cook 1½ hours. Toss vegetables with meat. Bake covered 15 minutes, then uncovered 15 minutes at 375 degrees. Serves 10 to 12. Delicious served over rice or noodles!

"Here is the recipe which you requested for your cookbook. Thank you for including me."

Mayor Corinne Freeman
St. Petersburg, Florida

The Princess' Fudge

¼ cup butter
2 cups sugar
4 tablespoons water
1 (14-ounce) can sweetened condensed milk

In a large saucepan (preferably non-stick) put sugar, butter and water; stir gently until sugar is dissolved. Add the condensed milk; bring to boil. Simmer on very low heat until mixture thickens and browns, about 30 minutes. Stir occasionally during simmering. Remove from heat; beat well. Pour onto greased cookie sheet; wait until mixture sets; cut into squares.

"The Princess of Wales has asked me to write and thank you so much for your very nice letter. Her Highness was most touched by your kind thought in writing and asks me to send her very sincere thanks." Yours sincerely, Lavinia Baring, Lady-in-Waiting."

Princess of Wales
Buckingham Palace
London, England

The Weatherman's Pound Cake

1 cup butter, at room temperature
½ cup shortening
5 eggs, at room temperature
3¼ cups light brown sugar
3½ cups all-purpose flour
½ teaspoon baking powder
1 cup milk

In a large bowl cream together butter and shortening; add eggs, one at a time, creaming after each addition. Add sugar. Sift flour and baking powder together. Add alternately with milk to mixture. Bake in greased and floured 10-inch tube pan for 1¼ to 1½ hours at 325 degrees. Serves 12 to 20.

Frosting:

1 cup chopped pecans
½ cup butter, softened
1 (16-ounce) box powdered sugar
3 to 4 tablespoons milk

Toast pecans in butter in a broiler pan until well browned. Cool slightly; add sugar and enough milk to thin to spreading consistency. Spread on top of cake. Some should drip down sides and center, but spread only on top.

"Good luck with the book."

Willard H. Scott
TODAY'S Weatherman

Ann's Meat Loaf

2 pounds ground round steak
2 eggs
1½ cups breadcrumbs
¾ cup ketchup
1 teaspoon monosodium glutamate
½ cup warm water
1 (1.37-ounce) package dry onion soup mix
2 strips bacon (optional)
1 (8-ounce) can tomato sauce

Mix first seven ingredients thoroughly, put into 9x5x3-inch loaf pan. Cover with 2 strips of bacon, if you like that flavor. Pour tomato sauce over meat mixture. Bake 1½ hours at 350 degrees. Serves 8.

Ann Landers

Baked Salmon à la Martin

4 pieces salmon
2 tablespoons butter
1/4 cup chopped fresh mushrooms
1/4 cup chopped bacon
1/4 cup chopped shallots or green onions
1/8 cup chopped fresh parsley
1/4 teaspoon salt
1/8 teaspoon pepper

Prepare four 12x12-inch sheets of oil paper, or plain paper brushed with 1/8 cup olive oil. In medium skillet sauté mushrooms, bacon and shallots in butter. Spread this mixture in center of each sheet of paper; add parsley. Salt and pepper both sides of salmon; roll salmon tightly in paper, making certain the ends of the paper are tightly closed. Place in a 9x9x2-inch generously greased casserole; bake at 350 degrees for 25 minutes. Serves 4.

Note: Halibut, turbot, cod or sole (any fish, for that matter) can be used in place of salmon. Adjust baking times accordingly.

Mary Martin

Mary Martin

Pig Pickin' Cake

Cake:

1 (18½-ounce) box butter cake mix
1 (11-ounce) can mandarin oranges and juice
½ cup oil
4 eggs

In large bowl mix all ingredients together. Place in 13x9x2-inch cakepan. Bake at 325 degrees for 30 to 35 minutes; cool. Serves 24.

Frosting:

1 (3-ounce) package vanilla instant pudding mix
1 (8-ounce) carton non-dairy whipped topping
1 (20-ounce) can crushed pineapple and juice

In large bowl mix all ingredients together; spread on cooled cake; refrigerate.

Note: If you use a regular cake mix, add about ½ cup melted margarine to other ingredients in the cake mix.

Barbara Mandrell

Blonde Brownies

Pat and Shirley's Favorite!

1/3 cup butter or shortening, melted
1 cup light brown sugar
1 egg, slightly beaten
1 teaspoon vanilla extract
1 cup all-purpose flour
1/2 teaspoon baking powder
1/8 teaspoon baking soda
1/2 cup chopped nuts
1 (6-ounce) package chocolate chips

Cream butter and sugar; add egg and vanilla extract. Sift together dry ingredients. Add to sugar and egg mixture gradually; add nuts. Spread into an 8x8-inch greased pan and sprinkle chocolate chips over top. Bake at 350 degrees for 25 to 30 minutes. Cool; cut into squares. Makes 16.

Pat and Shirley Boone

Chess Pie

1 (8-inch) pie shell, unbaked
1/2 cup butter or margarine
1 1/2 cups sugar
3 eggs, beaten
1 tablespoon cider vinegar
1 tablespoon vanilla extract
1/4 teaspoon salt

Preheat oven to 300 degrees. Combine butter and sugar in a saucepan; cook over medium heat, stirring constantly until very smooth. Remove from heat; add eggs and mix thoroughly. Stir in vinegar, vanilla extract and salt. Beat to blend ingredients. Pour into pastry shell. Bake for 45 or 50 minutes or until done. Serves 6.

Minnie Pearl

Minnie Pearl

Dolly's Five Layer Dinner

2 cups sliced raw potatoes
2 cups ground beef, browned and drained
1 cup sliced onion
1 cup minced green peppers
2 cups cooked tomatoes
1/2 teaspoon salt
1/4 teaspoon pepper
Green pepper, for garnish

In a greased 2-quart casserole layer all ingredients, starting with meat and ending with tomatoes; season each layer with salt and pepper. Garnish with green pepper slices. Bake for 2 hours at 350 degrees. Serves 8 to 10.

Dolly Parton

Dolly Parton

Fresh Peach Soufflé

1½ cups fresh peaches, peeled and pitted, or frozen, adding no sugar
¾ cup macaroon crumbs
3 tablespoons Amaretto liqueur
½ cup butter
½ cup sugar
4 egg yolks
5 egg whites, stiffly beaten

Crush peaches; combine with crumbs soaked in Amaretto. In medium bowl cream together butter and sugar. Add egg yolks, one at a time, beating well after each addition. Combine egg and macaroon mixtures; fold in egg whites. Pour mixture into a buttered and sugared soufflé dish; bake at 350 degrees for about 35 minutes, or until it is well puffed. Serves 6 to 8.

Carol Burnett

Turkey Fillets with Pistachio Nuts

1 cup butter
6 turkey fillets, cut from breast, approximately 4 to 6 ounces each
½ teaspoon salt, or to taste
⅛ teaspoon pepper, or to taste
4 shallots, finely chopped
4 large mushrooms, sliced
2 tablespoons all-purpose flour
⅓ cup dry white wine
⅔ cup chicken broth
2 egg yolks
½ cup whipping cream
⅓ cup shelled, chopped pistachio nuts
¼ teaspoon dried tarragon
1 tablespoon lemon juice

Melt ¼ cup butter in large skillet. Season turkey with salt and pepper; sauté until golden; remove from pan; set aside. Adding more butter as needed, sauté shallots for 5 minutes, add mushrooms; sauté 5 minutes more. Sprinkle in flour; stir and cook for 3 minutes; stir in wine and broth; cook until slightly thickened. Return the fillets to the pan; cover and cook for 15 minutes on low heat. Beat the cream and the egg yolks together. Add some of the hot sauce to cream mixture; then stir into the hot sauce. Stir until thickened. Add pistachios, tarragon and lemon juice. Correct seasonings, if necessary. Place fillets on hot serving platter; cover with hot sauce. Serves 6.

Carol Burnett

Carol Burnett

Crab Allando

Tomato Sauce:

2 cups fresh crushed tomatoes
1 tablespoon butter
12 ounces crabmeat (use body of crab)
1 tablespoon basil (dry) or 2 tablespoons fresh chopped basil
1 tablespoon chopped garlic clove
1 teaspoon salt or to taste
½ teaspoon pepper
⅛ teaspoon monosodium glutamate

In a medium skillet sauté tomatoes in butter; add remaining ingredients; simmer 15 to 20 minutes. Set aside.

Fettucine Sauce:

½ cup butter, softened
1 egg yolk
¼ cup whipping cream
½ cup freshly grated Parmesan cheese
⅛ teaspoon pepper

In small bowl beat butter until fluffy. Continue beating while adding egg yolk and then cream. Beat in cheese; season with pepper. Set aside.

Fettucine:

1 pound fettucine
½ teaspoon salt
12 crab legs cooked (optional)

Prepare fettucine in boiling, salted water until tender; drain. In large pan combine fettucine and fettucine sauce; cook briefly until sauce becomes a very creamy consistency. Add tomato sauce; heat through while tossing thoroughly. Serve immediately with 2 crab legs per person. Serves 6.

Note: Serve with hot French bread and white wine.

Vicki Lawrence

Vicki Lawrence

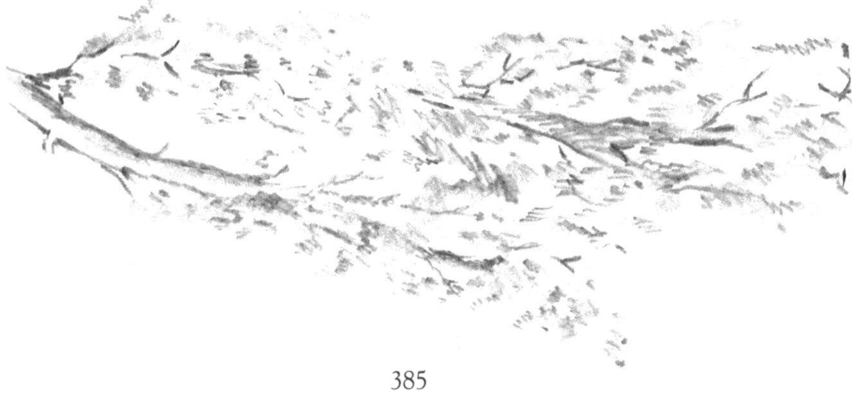

Molded Gazpacho Salad

3 (1/4-ounce) envelopes unflavored gelatin
2 cups water
1 (14 1/2-ounce) can stewed tomatoes and liquid
2 (8-ounce) cans tomato sauce
1/2 cup wine vinegar
1 tablespoon Worcestershire sauce
10 to 12 drops hot red pepper sauce
1 1/2 teaspoons salt
1/2 teaspoon ground cumin
1 clove garlic, crushed
1/2 cup finely chopped onions
2/3 cup finely chopped celery
3/4 cup seeded and finely chopped cucumber
1 cup finely chopped green pepper
Lettuce leaves and lemon wedges for garnish, if desired

In a small saucepan soften gelatin in water; heat, stirring constantly, until gelatin is dissolved. Remove from heat; set aside. Drain tomatoes, reserving liquid; chop tomatoes. In a medium bowl combine gelatin mixture, chopped tomatoes and reserved liquid, tomato sauce, wine vinegar, Worcestershire sauce, hot pepper sauce, salt and cumin; stir to combine thoroughly. Add garlic, onion, celery, cucumber and green pepper; refrigerate until mixture molds on a spoon when stirred. Turn into an oiled 6-cup mold; refrigerate until firm, about 4 hours. Invert mold onto a serving platter lined with lettuce leaves and garnish with lemon wedges. Serves 10 to 12.

Mitzi Gaynor

"Wunnerful Wunnerful" Creamed Chicken

1 tablespoon butter
1 medium fryer chicken, skinned and cut up
1/2 teaspoon salt
1/4 teaspoon pepper
1 small onion, sliced
2 tablespoons water
1 cup whipping cream (or more if extra gravy is desired)

In skillet melt butter; add chicken. Keep stirring to sear, but not brown. Add onion; let simmer about 1 minute. Add water; cover and simmer slowly for 30 minutes. If more water is needed during cooking, add just enough to keep meat stewing. After 30 minutes remove cover; add cream. Simmer for 5 minutes and season. Delicious served with rice. Serves 4.

Note: Be sure not more than a tablespoon of water is left in pan before adding cream. Stir meat in cream a couple of times during last 5 minutes.

Lawrence Welk

Zucchini

1 medium onion, chopped or sliced
1 clove garlic, minced
2 tablespoons butter
1 tablespoon olive oil
2 medium fresh tomatoes, chopped
4 medium zucchini, sliced
½ teaspoon salt
⅛ teaspoon pepper

In large skillet sauté onion and garlic in butter and olive oil. Add tomatoes, zucchini, salt and pepper; cover and simmer for 20 minutes. Serve with steak or chops and salad. Serves 3 or 4.

Note: You can use this as a meat dish by adding 1 pound cooked ground beef and topping with ½ to 1 cup shredded Cheddar or mozzarella cheese. Place under broiler until cheese is melted and slightly browned.

Michael Learned

Michael Learned

Hungarian Chicken

3 or more onions, thinly sliced
2 tablespoons butter
6 to 8 chicken pieces, boned
1 teaspoon salt
¼ to ½ teaspoon cayenne pepper
4 tablespoons all-purpose flour
1 (16-ounce) container sour cream

Sauté onions in butter. Line bottom of 13x9x2-inch casserole with onions. Place chicken over onions, with heavier pieces on bottom; sprinkle with salt and cayenne pepper. Cover tightly with foil; bake at 350 degrees for about ½ hour or until chicken is tender. Remove from oven; drain off any excess fat. Sprinkle with flour; spread sour cream overall. Bake another ½ hour. Serves 4 to 6.

Note: Tastes even better the next day. "I usually serve this with rice, peas with ham bits and salad. You can substitute veal."

Michael Learned

Chili Tex

1 (15-ounce) can chili and beans
1 cup shredded Cheddar cheese
1 medium onion, chopped
1 (20-ounce) can white or yellow hominy

In a 2-quart casserole arrange in alternate layers chili, cheese, onions and hominy. Top with cheese; bake at 350 degrees until onions are tender and cheese is thoroughly melted. Serves 6.

Dale Evans Rogers
Victorville, California

Chilaquiles

Sour Cream and Tortillas

12 tortillas, cut into eighths
2 tablespoons oil
1 medium onion, chopped
1 (28-ounce) can tomatoes, chopped
2 tablespoons Salsa Jalapeño, or chili powder or to taste
1 teaspoon oregano, rubbed between palms of hands
½ teaspoon salt
½ cup grated Romano cheese
½ pound Monterey Jack or American cheese, cubed
1 (8-ounce) carton sour cream
4 ounces American cheese, coarsely grated

In a skillet fry tortillas lightly in oil; drain on absorbent paper. For the sauce sauté onion in hot oil; add tomatoes, Salsa Jalapeño, oregano and salt. Cook 10 to 15 minutes; set aside. Butter a 2-quart casserole. Alternate layers of tortillas, sauce, Romano cheese, Monterey cheese and sour cream. Repeat until all ingredients have been used, ending with a layer of sour cream. Bake covered at 325 degrees for 1 hour. Sprinkle with grated American cheese; bake uncovered for 10 minutes. On the side you can serve finely chopped raw onions, finely chopped cilantro, fried chorizo (Mexican sausage), taken out of its casing and well drained in paper towel. Serves 6 to 8.

Eddie Albert

Chicken Wings Pacifica

3 pounds chicken wings
½ cup butter or margarine
1 cup soy sauce
1 cup brown sugar
¾ cup water
½ teaspoon dry mustard

Arrange wings in shallow baking pan. Heat butter, soy sauce, sugar, water and mustard until butter and sugar melt. Cool; pour over wings and marinate at least 2 hours, turning once or twice. Bake in same pan at 375 degrees for 1¼ to 1½ hours, turning occasionally. Drain on paper towels. Serves 6.

Betty White

Betty White

Rooney's Blueberry Delight

1 (7-ounce) box vanilla wafers, crushed
2 tablespoons butter
1½ cups powdered sugar
3 eggs, separated
1 (21-ounce) can blueberry pie filling
1 (16-ounce) container non-dairy whipped topping

Spread half the wafer crumbs in a 13x9x2-inch buttered glass pan, reserving the other half for the top. Cream butter with sugar; beat until creamy. Add egg yolks to the mixture, one at a time, beating well after each yolk. In a separate bowl beat 3 egg whites into stiff peaks. Add egg whites to the cream mixture, a little at a time. Spread mixture over crumbs. Spread berries over cream mixture. Spread whipped topping over top. Spread remaining crumbs over top. Refrigerate for 24 hours. Serves 24.

Mickey Rooney

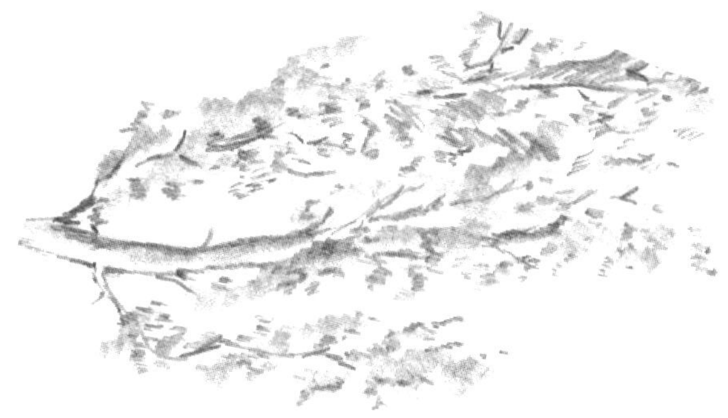

Fresh Peach Sherbet

5 medium peaches, peeled and sliced
¼ teaspoon almond extract
¾ cup sugar
1 teaspoon lemon juice
1 cup sour cream

Place 4 peaches in blender container; add almond extract, sugar, lemon juice and sour cream. Blend at high speed until smooth. Pour into shallow pan or ice cube tray. Freeze until almost firm. Turn into large mixing bowl and break up; beat until smooth but not melted; freeze again. At this point sherbet can be packed into a 1-quart mold or returned to ice cube trays and frozen. To serve unmold on platter; let stand 15 minutes before serving. Spoon into dessert glasses; top with slices of reserved peach. Makes 3½ cups.

Ruth Buzzi
Beverly Hills, California

Chicken Salad à la Rogers

2 cups cooked chicken (white meat)
3 dill pickles
½ cup chopped walnuts
¼ cup slivered or chopped almonds
¾ cup mayonnaise
4 scallions, chopped (optional)
½ teaspoon salt
⅛ teaspoon pepper
Lettuce

Remove the chicken from the bone, rather than cut it. Peel pickles with a potato peeler; chop. Mix first four ingredients lightly with mayonnaise of choice. Add scallions, if desired. Season with salt and pepper, or to taste. Serve on a bed of crisp lettuce. Serves 6.

"I'm pleased to share one of my very favorite recipes with you. This is a delicious recipe for luncheons and light suppers. Marianne and I enjoy it often, and our guests love it as well. Happy Eating!"

Kenny Rogers

Chicken with Wine and Vegetables

Tom Selleck's Favorite

1 tablespoon butter
1 medium onion, sliced
¼ teaspoon salt
⅛ teaspoon pepper
4 chicken breasts, boned and halved
½ cup all-purpose flour
2 tablespoons butter
8 whole mushrooms
1 (16-ounce) can artichoke hearts
1 cup orange juice
1 cup Marsala wine or dry white wine
1 cup ginger ale
2 tablespoons lemon juice

In a skillet brown onion in butter; salt and pepper chicken. Roll in flour to cover. Brown quickly in remaining butter. Place onions in bottom of Dutch oven; layer chicken and mushrooms. Mix liquid ingredients; pour over. Cook covered for 1 hour at 325 degrees. Add artichoke hearts; cook for ½ hour more. Serve with brown rice. Serves 4.

Tom Selleck

From Suncoast
Restaurants

Benihana Magic Mustard Sauce

3 tablespoons dry mustard
2 tablespoons hot water
½ cup soy sauce
2 tablespoons sesame seeds, toasted
1 clove garlic

In a small bowl blend mustard and water into a paste. Pour paste into blender; add remaining ingredients and process about 1 minute or until smooth. Makes 6 servings, 2 tablespoons each.

Hint: To toast sesame seeds, spread seeds in pie pan and toast in oven at 350 degrees for 10 to 15 minutes.

Note: Use as a dipping sauce for Hibachi chicken or steak or as a dressing for beans or alfalfa sprouts.

Benihana of Tokyo
Tampa, Florida

Benihana Salad Dressing

¼ cup chopped onion
½ cup peanut oil
2 tablespoons rice wine vinegar
2 tablespoons water
1 tablespoon chopped fresh ginger root
1 tablespoon chopped celery
1 tablespoon soy sauce
1½ teaspoons tomato paste
1½ teaspoons sugar
1 teaspoon lemon juice
⅛ teaspoon salt, or to taste
⅛ teaspoon pepper, or to taste

Combine all ingredients in blender or processor using the steel blade; process until smooth. Makes 6 generous servings. Store in covered container in refrigerator. Serves 6.

Benihana of Tokyo
Tampa, Florida

Brazilian Snow

1 pint best quality vanilla ice cream, softened slightly
4 to 6 rounded tablespoons freshest coffee, roasted but unground
Whipped cream for garnish
Cherries for garnish

Grind coffee in a small nut grinder as finely as possible. Sprinkle about ⅓ of coffee over ice cream. Scoop up ice cream, one scoopful at a time. Try to mix without overhandling ice cream. As you finish one layer of ice cream, sprinkle more coffee over the top; continue until most of coffee and all ice cream are in serving dishes. Garnish with whipped cream; sprinkle with coffee and cherry. Serve at once! Serves 4.

"Remember that coffee loses its flavor soon after it is ground. It shouldn't be used again after 5 or 10 minutes if you want the maximum fresh coffee taste!"

Bern's Steak House
Tampa, Florida

Fillet of Rainbow Trout in Leek Sauce

¼ cup chopped shallots
1 cup julienne-cut strips of leeks, light part only
¾ cup butter
⅛ teaspoon salt
⅛ teaspoon pepper
2 cups white wine
1 cup water
8 (3-ounce) fillets of boneless and skinless trout
2 tomatoes peeled, seeded and cut into thin strips
1 cup whipping cream
1 tablespoon Beurre Marniere

Sauté shallots and leeks in butter for 3 minutes. Add salt, pepper, white wine and water. Bring to a simmer for 5 minutes. Place trout fillets into liquid and poach gently for 4 to 5 minutes. Remove the fish from pan to warm serving platter. Add tomatoes and cream to fish stock; simmer over low heat and stir. Stir Beurre Marniere into sauce until cream sauce consistency is achieved. Top each serving of 2 fish fillets with sauce and serve. Serves 4.

Bon Appétit
Dunedin, Florida

For Beurre Marniere: Mix thoroughly 3 parts of butter to 2 parts of flour and use to thicken sauce by stirring constantly.

Roast Beef Salad

1 pound eye of round beef, medium well roasted, diced into 1/3-inch pieces
2 ripe tomatoes, skinned and diced into 1/3-inch pieces
2 dill pickles, diced into 1/3-inch pieces
1 medium onion, diced into 1/3-inch pieces
1/2 cup olive oil
1 cup ketchup
2 tablespoons horseradish
1 tablespoon Dijon mustard
2 tablespoons wine vinegar
1/2 teaspoon salt
Freshly ground pepper to taste
1 cup thinly sliced cucumbers
1/2 cup alfalfa sprouts

In a medium bowl toss beef, tomatoes, pickles, onions, olive oil, ketchup, horseradish, mustard, vinegar, salt and pepper. Refrigerate well before serving. Serve on slices of cucumber; top with alfalfa sprouts. Serves 4.

Bon Appétit
Dunedin, Florida

Chicken Breast Grand Hotel

8 (5-ounce) boneless chicken breasts
1/2 teaspoon salt
1/4 teaspoon pepper
1/2 teaspoon rosemary leaves
2 tablespoons all-purpose flour
2 tablespoons butter
2 tablespoons brown sugar
1 (4-ounce) can whole-berry cranberry sauce
Juice of 1/2 lemon
1 cup red wine
1 tablespoon cornstarch dissolved in 1 tablespoon water
Pinch of cinnamon
8 kiwi slices for garnish
8 servings rice or pasta

Season chicken with salt, pepper and rosemary; roll in flour. In large skillet sauté in butter until tender and yellow; place chicken in 13x9x2-inch casserole and keep warm in oven. In same skillet dissolve brown sugar; add cranberry sauce, lemon juice and wine. Bring to a light boil; add dissolved cornstarch and cinnamon. Cover chicken with sauce; place one kiwi slice on each chicken breast. Serve with pasta or rice. Serves 8.

Bon Appétit
Dunedin, Florida

Artichokes Vinaigrette

2 (8-ounce) cans hearts of artichokes
2/3 cup olive oil
1/2 cup finely chopped green pepper
1/2 cup julienne-cut carrots
1/3 cup lemon juice
1/3 cup vinegar
2 garlic cloves finely pureed
1/2 teaspoon salt
1/4 teaspoon pepper
1/4 cup grated Parmesan cheese

Combine all ingredients except cheese; marinate at room temperature for 4 hours. Sprinkle cheese on individual portions before serving. Serves 6 to 8.

Bon Appétit
Dunedin, Florida

Creole Remoulade Sauce

4 tablespoons Creole mustard
4 tablespoons mayonnaise
1 tablespoon olive oil
1 tablespoon paprika
2 tablespoons lemon juice
1 cup finely chopped celery
1/8 teaspoon salt, or to taste
1/8 teaspoon pepper, or to taste
1/8 teaspoon Worcestershire sauce, or to taste

Combine all ingredients and refrigerate until very cold. Makes 1 cup.

Note: For cold meat or poultry—but especially good with shellfish!

Bon Appétit
Dunedin, Florida

Stuffed Mushrooms

20 large mushrooms
2 tablespoons butter
1/2 cup finely chopped green onions
1/2 cup creamy clam chowder
1/2 cup sour cream
1 pound fresh lump crabmeat
1/8 teaspoon salt, or to taste
1/8 teaspoon pepper, or to taste
1 teaspoon English mustard
Juice of 2 lemons
Pieces of fresh squid, optional

Wash mushrooms and remove stems. Chop stems into fine pieces; sauté in butter. Add onion, chowder and sour cream. Bring to light boil. Add crabmeat, salt, pepper, mustard and lemon juice. Remove from heat and fill mushrooms with the mixture. Bake at 350 degrees for 15 minutes. Remove mushrooms from oven and top with pieces of squid. Broil 30 seconds before serving. Makes 20.

Bon Appétit
Dunedin, Florida

Fettucine Fruites des Mer

- 1/3 cup olive oil
- 12 jumbo shrimp (approximately 3/4 pound)
- 1 pound scallops
- 1/3 cup white wine
- 3 cloves garlic, minced
- 1/4 cup freshly squeezed lemon juice
- 1/3 cup fish stock or clam juice
- 1/8 teaspoon pepper, or to taste
- 1/8 teaspoon rosemary, or to taste
- 1/8 teaspoon basil, or to taste
- 1 pound fettucine, cooked *al dente*
- 6 ounces Romano cheese, freshly grated

In a medium skillet heat olive oil until aroma can be sensed. Add shrimp and scallops and sauté until firm; remove from pan. Pour white wine into hot skillet; add garlic, lemon juice and stock. Season with pepper, rosemary and basil, stirring until sauce is just boiling. Remove from heat; add shrimp and scallops stirring in gently. Serve immediately over fettucine cooked according to package directions. Sprinkle with Romano cheese. Serves 4 to 6.

Brothers, Too
Tampa, Florida

Al dente means slightly firm, not overcooked. A state which still offers some resistance when bitten.

Blue Lagoon Lobster Salad

- 2 cups cooked lobster
- 2 ripe pineapples
- 2/3 cup diced celery
- 1/2 cup coarsely chopped macadamia nuts
- 1/4 cup shredded coconut
- 1/3 cup mayonnaise
- 1/4 cup diced kiwi fruit
- Additional kiwi for garnish

Drain and cut lobster into bite-sized pieces. Cut pineapple in half lengthwise. Remove fruit from each half and save shells. Cut pineapple into chunks. Combine lobster, pineapple chunks, celery, macadamia nuts, coconut, mayonnaise and kiwi fruit. Fill the pineapple halves with mixture and garnish with sliced kiwi. Serves 4.

Note: White grapes may be substituted for kiwi.

Brothers, Too
Tampa, Florida

Cold Avocado Crab Soup

2 avocados, peeled
1 (6½-ounce) can crabmeat, drained
¼ cup minced celery
½ cup sour cream
⅛ teaspoon salt, or to taste
⅛ teaspoon pepper, or to taste
⅛ teaspoon hot pepper sauce, or to taste
1 cup whipping cream
⅓ cup sliced, toasted almonds

Dice 1 avocado into ¼-inch cubes. Puree the other avocado in a blender or food processor. Combine crabmeat, celery, sour cream, salt, pepper, hot pepper sauce, whipped cream and the avocados. Mix thoroughly; chill for several hours. If the consistency is too thick, before serving thin with whipping cream. Garnish with toasted almonds. Serves 4 to 5.

Brothers, Too
Tampa, Florida

Chicken and Yellow Rice

Valencia Style

2½ pounds chicken, quartered
½ cup Spanish olive oil
1 medium onion, thinly sliced
2 cloves garlic, minced
1 green pepper, thinly sliced
¼ cup whole cherry tomatoes
4 cups chicken broth
1 tablespoon salt
⅛ teaspoon Spanish saffron
⅛ teaspoon yellow food coloring
1 bay leaf
½ pound Spanish Valencia rice or Spanish yellow rice

In clay casserole brown chicken in olive oil; remove chicken. In casserole braise onion, garlic, green pepper and tomatoes. Place chicken in casserole; add chicken broth; bring to a boil. Add salt, saffron, food coloring, bay leaf and rice; bring to a boil. Cover casserole and bake at 350 degrees for 20 minutes. Serves 2.

Garnish:

½ cup small peas, cooked
6 slices Spanish pimento
¼ to ½ cup fresh parsley leaves
2 to 3 eggs, hard-cooked
4 asparagus tips

Top casserole with garnishes and serve.

Columbia Restaurant
Tampa, Florida

Spanish Bean Soup

8 ounces garbanzo beans
1 ham bone
1 beef bone
8 cups water
1 tablespoon salt
4 ounces salt pork
1 medium onion, finely chopped
1 chorizo (Spanish sausage)
2 potatoes, cut into quarters
1/8 teaspoon saffron, or to taste
1/4 teaspoon paprika

Wash garbanzos; soak overnight with a tablespoon of salt in sufficient water to cover. When ready to cook, drain the salted water from the beans. Place in a 4-quart soup kettle; add 2-quarts of water, ham and beef bones. Cook for 45 minutes over slow heat, skimming foam that forms at the top. Cut salt pork in thin strips and fry slowly in a skillet. Add chopped onion and sauté lightly. Add to the beans along with potatoes, paprika and saffron. Add salt to taste. When potatoes are done, remove from heat; add chorizo that has been cut into thin round slices. Serves 4.

Note: May be served over boiled rice and topped with finely chopped onions.

The Columbia Restaurant
Tampa, Florida

Red Snapper "Alicante"

2 to 3 large Spanish onions, sliced into rings
2 pounds Red Snapper fillets
4 green peppers, sliced into rings
1/2 cup Spanish olive oil
1 teaspoon salt
1/8 teaspoon pepper
3/4 cup brown beef stock gravy
1 cup white Spanish wine
1 to 2 cloves garlic, minced

Place onion rings in bottom of 13x9x2-inch casserole; place fish on top of onions. Place pepper rings on top of fish. In a bowl mix together remaining ingredients; pour over casserole. Bake at 350 degrees for approximately 25 minutes. Serves 4.

***Garnish:* (optional)**

1/4 cup sliced toasted almonds
8 large shrimp, cooked and cleaned
8 pieces eggplant, breaded and fried
Fresh parsley sprigs

The Columbia Restaurant
Tampa, Florida

Filet Steak Columbia

1 filet steak, cut 1-inch thick
1/8 teaspoon salt, or to taste
1/8 teaspoon pepper, or to taste
2 strips bacon
1/2 green pepper, chopped
1/2 medium onion, chopped
1 tablespoon oil
1/4 cup tomato sauce
1/4 cup brown gravy
1/4 cup red wine

Salt and pepper filet steak and wrap in two strips of bacon. Sauté onion, green pepper and tomato sauce in 1 tablespoon of oil for 10 minutes. Add brown gravy and wine; heat until hot. Broil steak to desired doneness and place in casserole. Pour hot sauce over it; bake at 450 degrees for 2 minutes. Serves 1.

The Columbia Restaurant
Tampa, Florida

Pompano Papillot

8 small fillets of pompano (approximately 1 pound)
1/2 cup butter
1 onion, finely chopped
1/2 cup all-purpose flour
2 cups milk
2 egg yolks
1/8 teaspoon nutmeg
1 teaspoon salt
1/8 teaspoon hot pepper sauce, or to taste
3 tablespoons dry white wine
1/2 pound small boiled shrimp
1/2 pound crabmeat
4 (10x10-inch) squares parchment paper

Melt butter in 2-quart saucepan. When foam subsides, sauté chopped onion over medium heat for 5 minutes. Add flour; stir well with wooden spoon until mixture bubbles. Add milk, nutmeg, salt and hot pepper sauce to roux, stirring continually to make smooth sauce. Carefully whisk some hot sauce into egg yolks. Return to rest of sauce. Mix shrimps, crabmeat and wine into sauce. Cook over medium heat for approximately 2 minutes. Cover; set aside. On center of buttered square of parchment paper, spread 2 heaping tablespoons of seafood dressing; place 1 fish fillet on dressing; add another 2 heaping tablespoons of dressing, one more fillet and more dressing. Fold over paper crimping edges very tightly. Brush melted butter over paper; bake 30 minutes at 350 degrees. Serves 4.

The Columbia Restaurant
Tampa, Florida

Parchment paper can be found in gourmet specialty shops or housewares department of any department store.

Spanish Custard

3 cups sugar
½ cup boiling water
6 eggs
1 teaspoon vanilla extract
2 teaspoons anisette extract
⅛ teaspoon salt
2 cups boiling milk

Boil 1 cup of sugar and water until brown; pour the mixture into six individual custard molds or bowls. In medium bowl beat eggs; add remaining sugar, vanilla, anisette and salt. Beat again; add boiling milk little by little. Strain mixture through cloth or china collander. Pour mixture into molds; place molds in water-filled baking pan and bake at 350 degrees for 30 minutes. Do not let water boil or custard will be filled with holes. Cool molds in refrigerator. To serve press edges of custard with spoon to break away from molds; turn molds upside down on individual dessert plates. Serves 6.

The Columbia Restaurant
Tampa, Florida

Cream of Onion Soup

2 Spanish onions, grated
1 small carrot, grated
1 quart chicken stock
¼ cup butter or margarine
4 tablespoons all-purpose flour
1 pint light cream, hot but not boiling
1 teaspoon pepper, or to taste
1 bunch parsley, chopped
Grated Parmesan cheese

Cook onions and carrots in chicken stock until tender (about 10 minutes). In a large heavy pot melt margarine; mix in flour and cook over medium heat for 2 minutes, stirring constantly; remove from heat and stir in vegetable mixture, using 1 cupful first to blend into roux then adding remainder. Return to heat and stir until mixture boils and thickens. Allow to cool slightly and process in blender, 2 cups at a time. At this point soup can be placed in a large soup toureen, or returned to pot. Stir in hot cream; add pepper and salt. Serve in soup cups sprinkled first with parsley and then Parmesan cheese. Serves 8 to 10.

Heilman's Beachcomber
Clearwater Beach, Florida

Shrimp Rockefeller

4 pounds fresh or frozen shrimp (20 per pound size)
1/8 teaspoon salt
1/8 teaspoon white pepper
1/8 teaspoon cayenne pepper
1 lemon, cut in half
1 pound frozen spinach, thawed and cut into 1-inch squares
6 green onions, trimmed and chopped
1 bunch parsley, finely chopped
1 bunch celery, chopped
1 clove garlic, chopped
1 tablespoon salt
1 teaspoon white pepper
3 tablespoons Worcestershire sauce
1/2 pound butter

Be sure shrimp are thoroughly thawed. Place in pot and cover with water. Add salt, pepper and both pieces of lemon; heat only to boil. Immediately pour through a collander. Run cold water over shrimp and peel and devein while warm; set aside. Melt butter in heavy-bottomed pot and add drained spinach. Simmer for about 10 minutes and add all remaining ingredients including spices and simmer for about 1 hour, uncovered, stirring occasionally. Be sure that celery is cooked through enough so that it is not crisp. Set aside. Prepare Mornay sauce.

Mornay Sauce:

1/2 pound butter
3/4 cup all-purpose flour
1 quart milk, heated to boiling point
1 teaspoon salt
1/2 teaspoon white pepper
1/8 teaspoon cayenne pepper, or to taste
1 pound Swiss Gruyère cheese, grated
3 ounces Parmesan cheese, grated
1 tablespoon butter, melted
Paprika

Melt butter and blend in flour over heat. Meanwhile make sure milk is very hot without boiling. Remove pot with butter and flour mixture (roux) from heat; pour the hot milk into pot. Stir vigorously at this point with wire whisk until roux is completely dissolved. Place pot back on high heat and continue stirring. As sauce is thickening add salt, pepper, cayenne pepper and grated cheese. Allow sauce to come to a boil momentarily. Taste and adjust seasoning if necessary. Remove from heat immediately and pour into another container. Makes 6 cups.

Cover bottom of a 2- to 3-quart casserole with spinach mixture. Lay all the shrimp over spinach. Ladle the sauce over shrimp and then sprinkle with grated Parmesan cheese; dot with butter and sprinkle with paprika. Bake in preheated oven at 425 degrees for 20 minutes. Serves 8.

Heilman's Beachcomber
Clearwater Beach, Florida

Lemon Pie

1½ cups sugar
3 cups water
3 to 4 ounces cornstarch
1 teaspoon salt
4 egg yolks
½ cup fresh lemon juice
1 tablespoon lemon rind (use only the yellow of the rind)

Combine sugar, water, cornstarch and salt in double boiler and cook until clear. In a separate bowl combine egg yolks, lemon juice and rind. Pour into cooked clear mixture in top of double boiler and let cook an additional 5 to 10 minutes. Pour into baked pie shell while still hot. Top with a favorite meringue and brown. Makes one 9-inch pie.

Heilman's Beachcomber
Clearwater Beach, Florida

Fevillete de Homard et Crevette en Couronne

Puff Pastry with Lobster and Shrimp Crowned

Lobster Bisque:

½ cup chopped onion
½ cup chopped celery
½ cup chopped parsley
¼ cup chopped carrot
¾ cup butter
2 cups white wine
2 ounces brandy, reduced
2 quarts fish stock
1 (4-pound) lobster
2 tomatoes, chopped
4 peppercorns
1 bay leaf
¼ cup rice
1 cup whipping cream
3 tablespoons sherry

In a saucepan make mirepoix by sautéing onion, celery, parsley and carrot in ½ cup butter until soft. Deglaze the pan with wine and brandy. Add mixture to a kettle with fish stock, lobster, tomatoes, peppercorns, bay leaf and rice. Cook 30 minutes; remove lobster, bay leaf and peppercorns. Remove meat from lobster; dice body meat and mince tail and claw meat. Reserve ½ of lobster meat. Pass remaining ½ of lobster meat and bisque mixture through a fine sieve; set aside. Add ¼ cup cold butter; mix thoroughly with mortar and pestle, if necessary. Makes 2 quarts.

Note: If using just lobster bisque as soup du jour, simmer bisque, covered, for 5 minutes just to heat through. For each 8-ounce serving; use 2 tablespoons cream and 1 teaspoon sherry.

Puff Pastry:

1 frozen patty shell or 1 (4-inch) round puff pastry, rolled 1/2-inch thick
1 egg yolk

Brush with egg yolk; bake patty shell or puff pastry round at 375 degrees 10 to 15 minutes or until golden brown. Serves 1.

Seafood mixture:

2 tablespoons butter
1/2 teaspoon chopped shallots
2 tablespoons sliced mushrooms
1/8 teaspoon chopped garlic
4 to 5 shrimp, peeled and butterflied
1/2 cup lobster meat
8 ounces bisque with cream and sherry already added
1/8 cup lemon juice
1/4 teaspoon chopped parsley
1/8 teaspoon salt
1/8 teaspoon pepper

Sauté shallots, mushrooms and garlic in butter. Add remaining ingredients; fold in 4 ounces of bisque. Simmer for 3 minutes at low heat.

To Assemble:

Cut off top of cooked pastry and hollow out. Remove shrimp from seafood mixture; spoon remainder into pastry shell. Arrange shrimp in pastry so tails point to the center like a "crown". Top with a sprig of parsley. Pour remaining 4 ounces of bisque around the pastry to make an "island" effect. Place top of pastry on the side leaning against top of the stuffed pastry shell. Serves 1.

Note: For puffy pastry and seafood mixture increase by the number of people being served.

Pasquet Restaurateur
St. Petersburg, Florida

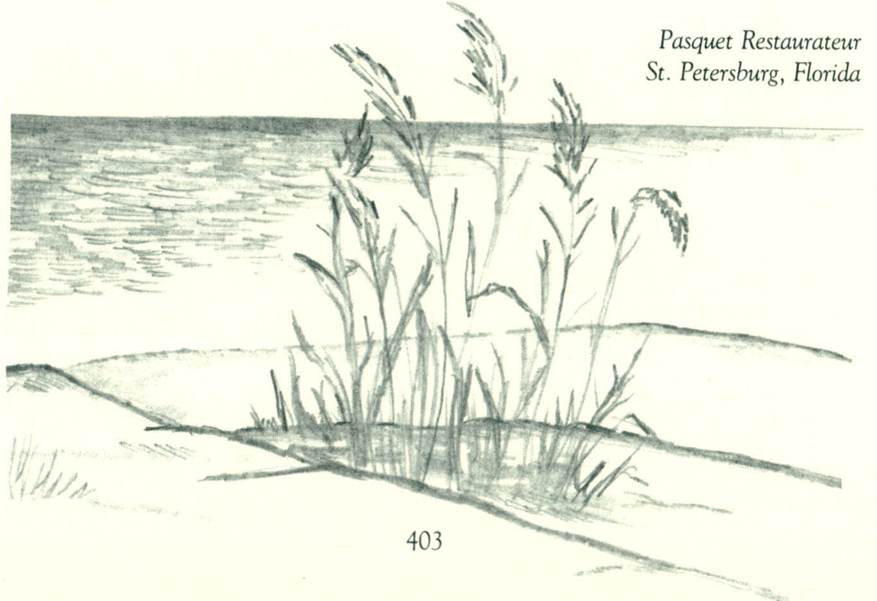

Consommé à la Madrilene

2 pounds beef, cubed
1/4 cup butter or margarine
1 knuckle bone
2 quarts water
3 stalks celery with leaves
3 carrots, peeled and cut into chunks
2 leeks, sliced lengthwise
2 medium onions, stuck with 3 cloves
4 sprigs parsley
1 bay leaf
1 tablespoon salt
6 peppercorns
1 clove garlic
1/4 teaspoon thyme
1 cup tomato puree
1/2 teaspoon basil
Lemon slices, for garnish

Brown beef cubes in butter in large heavy kettle; add bone and water. Cover and bring to boil for 5 minutes. Skim top of liquid. Reduce heat; simmer for 1 hour, skimming top occasionally. Add remaining vegetables and seasonings except tomato puree and basil. Cover; simmer 2 hours longer. Discard bone and vegetables; reserve meat for another use. Strain through several thicknesses of cheese cloth. Return strained liquid to kettle. Add tomato puree and basil. Simmer 30 minutes more. Serve hot with thin slices of lemon on top in small soup tureens. Makes 6 servings.

Ritz Restaurant
Clearwater, Florida

Baked Wild Rice

With Onions, Carrots and Mushrooms

1 cup wild rice
1 tablespoon salt
4 tablespoons butter
1/2 cup minced carrot
3/4 cup minced onion
1/2 pound mushrooms, rinsed and chopped
2 tablespoons minced shallots
1 teaspoon salt
1/2 teaspoon freshly ground pepper
2 teaspoons fresh thyme
1 bay leaf
1 1/2 cups beef stock

Place the rice in a bowl with sufficient water to cover. Allow to soak for 1 hour. Drain and discard water. In a medium pot boil 1½ quarts of water; add 1 tablespoon salt and rice. Cook for 5 minutes after water returns to boil. Drain; set aside. Melt butter in a 9- or 10-inch skillet. Add all vegetables at once and simmer for 10 minutes over low heat until soft. Stir in rice and continue to cook for 2 minutes more. Add salt, pepper, thyme, bay leaf and beef stock. Transfer the mixture to a 2-quart casserole. Cover and bake at 375 degrees for 35 to 40 minutes or until liquid is absorbed. Serves 6 to 8.

Ritz Restaurant
Clearwater, Florida

Shredded Carrots

With Orange Juice

8 tablespoons butter
1 pound peeled carrots, shredded
Grated rind and juice of 1 large navel orange
½ teaspoon salt
⅛ teaspoon freshly ground pepper
4 large spinach leaves, washed, or 4 hollowed-out orange halves

In a medium skillet melt butter. When hot, add the shredded carrots and orange rind; sauté together over high heat for 2 minutes, turning frequently with a slotted spoon. Add the orange juice and reduce the liquid over high heat for 1 or 2 minutes longer; season with salt and pepper. Serve on a fresh spinach leaf or in hollowed-out orange halves. Serves 4.

Note: If made ahead of time, remove carrots to a bowl with a slotted spoon. Reduce the liquids in the skillet to 1 tablespoon and reserve to reheat. Sauté the carrots in 1 tablespoon butter over high heat for 1 minute or until hot; add reserved liquid; stir and serve.

Ritz Restaurant
Clearwater, Florida

Fresh Snow Peas

With Shallots and Basil

1 pound fresh snow peas
4 tablespoons butter
¼ cup glacé de viande
2 tablespoons minced shallots
2 tablespoons chopped fresh basil
⅛ teaspoon salt, or to taste
⅛ teaspoon fresh ground pepper, or to taste

Clean snow peas by removing the string-like fibers on both edges. In a vegetable steamer steam the snow peas for 1 or 2 minutes, or until they are barely tender. Make sure the water level comes below the steamer. Drain and set aside. Melt the butter in a 10- to 12-inch skillet. When foam begins to subside, add the glacé de viande and shallots; simmer over medium heat for 1 to 2 minutes or until shallots are soft. Add snow peas to skillet; raise the heat and stir constantly with a wooden spoon for about 1 minute. Make sure the shallots and butter evenly coat the snow peas. Season with salt and pepper to taste. These may be reheated just before serving by quickly sautéing over a high heat for 30 seconds until peas are hot. Spoon out the peas and sprinkle each portion with fresh basil. Serves 8.

Ritz Restaurant
Clearwater, Florida

Glacé de Viande is a meat glaze obtained by boiling down stock from meats or poultry reducing it to a syrup that becomes hard jelly when it is cold. (See Salmagundi Section for recipe.)

Pumpkin Rum Mousse

1 (1/4-ounce) envelope unflavored gelatin
1/4 cup rum
5 eggs, separated
3/4 cup sugar, divided
1 tablespoon grated lemon rind
1/4 teaspoon salt
1 cup cooked, mashed pumpkin or canned pumpkin
3/4 teaspoon cinnamon
1/2 teaspoon ginger
1/4 teaspoon allspice
1 cup whipping cream
Candied ginger (optional)

In top of double boiler sprinkle gelatin over rum; stir to soften. In a small bowl combine slightly beaten egg yolks, 1/2 cup sugar, lemon rind and salt; mix well. Add to softened gelatin. Cook, stirring constantly, over simmering water until gelatin is dissolved and mixture thickens slightly. Remove from heat. Chill until mixture thickens. In a large bowl combine pumpkin, cinnamon, ginger and allspice. Stir in thickened gelatin mixture. Beat egg whites until soft peaks form. Gradually add remaining 1/4 cup sugar, beating until stiff peaks form. Fold gently but thoroughly into gelatin mixture. Whip cream until well thickened. Fold in whipped cream until well blended. Spoon into lightly oiled 2-quart mold or individual molds. Cover and chill at least 3 hours. Unmold on to plate and garnish with whipped cream or candied ginger. Serves 6.

Ritz Restaurant
Tampa, Florida

Riverhouse Cornbread

Onion Hoe Cake

1 cup self-rising flour
2 cups self-rising white corn meal
1 1/2 cups chopped green onions, lightly packed
2 tablespoons sugar
2 1/4 cups cold milk
Oil for frying

Mix dry ingredients thoroughly; stir in milk to make a medium batter. Using a heavy skillet drop 1 tablespoon of batter at a time into *hot oil* 1/4 inch deep. Turn only once as a pancake; drain on paper towels. Finished breads should be about 1/2 inch thick, golden brown, with a curled edge. A perfect compliment to seafood or vegetables. Makes 3 to 4 dozen.

"According to Southern legend, these corn cakes were first made by slaves in the field, cooked on the heads of their weeding hoes. Thus the name 'Hoe Cake'."

Riverhouse Restaurant
Tarpon Springs, Florida

Salmagundi

Salmagundi

A culinary term derived from the French word *SALMIGONDIS,* "hotchpotch." It is used to describe a stew made from leftover meats, seasoned with wine vinegar, pickles, etc., or a salad plate of diced meats, pickled vegetables and other salad ingredients, arranged, not tossed, and served with a dressing. Any mixture, medley or miscellany.

Rose Potpourri

¾ cup dried rose petals
10 drops rose oil
2 tablespoons orris root
¼ cup dried zinnia petals

Combine ingredients in large apothecary jar with tightly fitting lid. Store for 4 or 5 weeks, stirring every 2 or 3 days, to allow to mature. To use; measure 1 tablespoon potpourri into a 2x4-inch sachet bag; tie with a colorful ribbon. Delicate flowery fragrance, perfect for lingerie drawers. Makes 1 cup or 16 sachets.

Wintergreen Potpourri

¾ cup dried marigold petals
¼ cup dried geranium petals
2 tablespoons dried mint leaves
¼ cup dried lemon peel
5 drops wintergreen oil

Pungent spicy aroma, suitable for kitchens.

Wood Sachet

½ tablespoon sassafrass roots
¼ cup dried orange peel
¼ cup dried lemon peel
¼ cup allspice
¼ cup anise

Pleasing woodsy scent for your closets.

Note: Sassafras and orris root can be purchased from Drug or Health Food stores.

Flowers for use in potpourri should be gathered early in the morning; pick the freshest blossoms, separate the petals and spread them out on paper towels in the bottom of a large shallow cardboard box. Place in a dry shady spot for 3 or 4 days or until they are thoroughly dry.

Suncoast Seasons Committee

Winter Holiday Boil

10 to 12 large bay leaves
3 (3-inch) cinnamon sticks, broken in half
3 whole star anise
1 tablespoon whole cloves
1 tablespoon whole allspice
¼ cup chopped dried orange peel

Mix all ingredients together and wrap in a 6-inch circle of cheesecloth or seasonal print fabric; tie with yarn or string. To use, heat 1 quart of water in a heavy saucepan or crockpot add bag of spices; allow to simmer all day to make a delightful spicy aroma. Add more water as necessary. May be re-used; store in a glass jar in refrigerator.

Makes a lovely Christmas gift!

Mrs. Ronald Bliss (Judy)

Microwave Dried Herbs

Herbs which dry well in a microwave oven include chives, dill, marjoram, mint, oregano, parsley, rosemary, sage, savory, sweet basil and thyme.

Place 3 paper towels on a 9-inch glass pie plate. Make a wreath shape using approximately ½ cup of the herb. Cover with another paper towel. Microwave on high power 3 to 3½ minutes, rotating plate after 1½ minutes. Remove paper towels; allow herbs to cool; crumble leaves, discard stems. Place in airtight containers. Store in refrigerator or freezer. Because herbs have a low moisture content do not microwave more than ten batches consecutively, then allow the oven to rest. Alternate two pie plates to avoid heat build-up.

Note: Herbs should be gathered early in the day to ensure highest aromatic content. Leaves are easier to handle if left on the stems. Be sure your herbs are perfectly dry or they will "cook" rather than dehydrate.

Suncoast Seasons Committee

Strawberry Jam

3 cups fresh strawberries
3 cups sugar

Place strawberries and sugar in large saucepan; bring to boil and continue to boil for 7 to 10 minutes. Skim off white top as it cooks. Cook until jam becomes thick and form clumps when dropped from spoon. Cool in a 13x9x2-inch glass baking dish. Stir mixture several times during the day as it cools. It will thicken. Refrigerate or seal in sterilized glass jars.

Mrs. William Harris (Clara)
Dunedin, Florida

Queen of Scots Marmalade

6 large thick-skinned oranges
2 lemons, sliced as thinly as possible
6 cups water
6 cups sugar

Peel oranges close to flesh; slice peel into thin strips about ¾-inch long. Dice orange flesh, discarding seeds. Place orange peel, flesh, lemon and water into a large thick-bottomed saucepan. *Do not use cast iron as this will discolor fruit.* Simmer over low heat until peel is soft and white part is almost clear (about 1 hour); remove from heat. Allow mixture to rest in a cool place for about 12 hours to blend flavors. Measure fruit mixture, (should be about 6 cups) return to saucepan. Stir in 1 cup of sugar for each cup of fruit mixture, be sure to blend well. Over a low heat bring very, very slowly to boil, stirring with a wooden spoon. When mixture boils, raise heat to medium; stir constantly until all sugar is dissolved; taste to be sure marmalade is not gritty. Continue to boil rapidly to jellying point; this should take about 25 minutes; test set on a plate. Pour marmalade into hot sterilized jars; seal with paraffin then cap. Store in a cool dark place; refrigerate after opening. Makes 6 to 8 pints.

Janet Joyce

When Mary Queen of Scots was a girl, she was ill and was sent to France to recover. Her future father-in-law told his cook to make something to tempt her appetite. The cook picked some oranges from the castle grove and combined the citrus with sugar in a sort of jam. She liked it and it was named Mariemalade.

Kitchen Hint: To test the set of jellies and preserves drop ¼ teaspoon of mixture on to a plate and place in refrigerator for 1 minute. Touch the drop lightly with one finger; if the surface crinkles the jelly is done.

Surinam Cherry Preserves

4 cups sugar
$1\frac{1}{2}$ cups water
4 cups seeded Surinam cherries
$\frac{1}{2}$ cup lemon juice

In a large heavy saucepan combine sugar and water. Bring to boil; add cherries and lemon juice. Continue to boil, stirring occasionally, until mixture thickens (20 to 25 minutes). Pour into hot sterilized jars and seal.

Suncoast Seasons Committee

Surinam cherries grow on an evergreen shrub, generally planted as a hedge in Central and Southern Florida. During spring and summer the bush produces red berries about 1-inch in diameter, shaped like miniature Chinese lanterns. Fruit has a piquant flavor and makes delicious preserves.

Orange Marmalade with Amaretto and Almonds

$\frac{1}{2}$ cup orange marmalade
1 tablespoon blanched slivered almonds
1 tablespoon Amaretto liqueur

Mix ingredients together; serve with croissants or scones. Can be stored in covered jar in refrigerator.

Suncoast Seasons Committee

Raspberry Preserves with Kirsch and Hazelnuts

$\frac{1}{2}$ cup raspberry preserves
1 tablespoon chopped hazelnuts
1 tablespoon Kirsch liqueur

Mix ingredients together; serve with croissants or scones. Can be stored in covered jar in refrigerator.

Suncoast Seasons Committee

Maple Flavored Syrup

No Preservatives

4 cups sugar
$\frac{1}{2}$ cup brown sugar
2 cups water
1 teaspoon vanilla extract
$\frac{3}{4}$ teaspoon maple flavoring

In a saucepan combine all ingredients. Cook slowly for 10 minutes. Makes 1 quart.

Mrs. Ronald D. Kimball (Hope)

Calamondin Marmalade

Fruit Stock:

4 cups calamondins, firm and free of blemishes
Water

Wash fruit; cut into halves and remove seeds. Slice thinly or put through a food chopper. Measure fruit; place in large saucepan. For each cup of fruit add 3 cups water. Bring to a full boil; boil 15 minutes stirring occasionally. Marmalade may be cooked immediately. Otherwise, let fruit stock stand overnight or refrigerate up to 1 week.

Marmalade:

3 cups fruit stock
3 cups sugar

Bring fruit stock to a boil in a large saucepan. Add sugar; stir to dissolve. Cook rapidly to 220 degrees on a candy or jelly thermometer, stirring constantly. Remove from heat; cool to 190 degrees. Pour into clean jars and close with self-sealing lids. Makes 3 cups.

Mrs. Denver Bass (Eunice)
Dunedin, Florida

A calamondin is a very small fruit that looks like a tangerine and is very sour. Use only when fully ripe.

Lemon Curd

½ cup butter or margarine
1½ cups sugar
Finely grated rind of 1 lemon
Juice of 2 large lemons (½ cup)
6 eggs, lightly beaten

Melt butter in top of double boiler over simmering water; using a wooden spoon stir in sugar until no longer gritty. Remove from heat; add lemon peel, juice and eggs, blending well. Cook over boiling water until mixture thickens (15 to 20 minutes). Pour into sterilized jars and seal while still hot. Store in refrigerator. Makes 3 cups. Use as a filling for tiny tarts or as a spread on muffins, biscuits or pound cake.

Jacky Joyce
Palm Harbor, Florida

Kitchen Hint: When pouring hot preserves into glass jars, place empty jars in a warm oven to heat; otherwise, they may crack.

Half-Sour Cucumbers

5 to 6 cups cold water
3/4 cup white vinegar
1/4 cup salt
2 teaspoons sugar
1 1/2 teaspoons pickling spice
2 to 3 sprigs fresh dill
2 cloves garlic
12 small pickling cucumbers, washed

In a 1-gallon jar combine all ingredients. Allow to stand at room temperature 24 to 48 hours. Store in refrigerator. Makes 1 gallon. *These are wonderful!*

Mrs. Gregory H. Keuroghlian (Nora Ghazikian)

Frozen Dill Pickles

4 cups unpeeled cucumbers, sliced
2 teaspoons salt
2 tablespoons water
2 cups sliced onion

Brine:

3/4 cup sugar
1/2 cup cider vinegar
1 teaspoon dry dill weed

In a large non-metal bowl layer cucumber and onion slices. Combine salt and water; sprinkle over cucumbers and onions. Let stand at room temperature 2 hours or longer; mix occasionally. Drain, but do not rinse. Return to bowl. Combine sugar, vinegar and dill weed; pour over cucumbers and onions. Let stand until liquid covers cucumbers. Divide into 2 small freezer containers; freeze. Defrost just before serving. Makes 2 quarts.

Mrs. Richard Benkusky (Judy)

Sweet Pickles

1 quart (14-ounce) jar whole dill pickles
2 cups sugar
1/2 cup water
1/2 cup vinegar
2 teaspoons celery salt
1 teaspoon alum

Drain and slice pickles. Add 1 cup sugar; mix well. Refrigerate overnight. Pour water and vinegar into a medium saucepan; add 1 cup sugar, celery salt and alum. Drain refrigerated pickles; pour hot mixture over. Place pickles in a jar; cover; store in refrigerator. Makes 1 quart 14 ounces.

Mrs. Robert A. Anderson (Sharon)
Nashville, Tennessee

Spiced Mango Chutney

5 large ripe mangoes, peeled and diced
1 large onion, chopped
2 hot red peppers, chopped
2 green peppers, chopped
1 clove garlic, minced
1 tablespoon salt
1 pound golden seedless raisins
1 cup grapefruit juice
1 cup wine vinegar
1 pound brown sugar
1 tablespoon mustard seed
1 teaspoon allspice
1 teaspoon cinnamon
1 teaspoon ground ginger
½ cup coarsely chopped pecans

In a large bowl combine mangoes, onion, peppers, garlic, salt, raisins and grapefruit juice. Let stand overnight. Drain well. Place in a large saucepan; add vinegar, sugar, mustard seed, allspice, cinnamon and ginger. Bring to boil; continue to boil gently for 30 minutes. Stir in pecans. Pour into hot sterilized pint jars and seal. Makes about 6 pints. Delicious accompaniment to meat.

Mrs. Thomas J. Robertson (Muriel)
Palm Harbor, Florida

Curried Four Fruit Sauce

⅓ cup butter
¾ cup brown sugar
4 teaspoons curry powder
5 maraschino cherries, whole or sliced
1 (16- to 17-ounce) can pear halves
1 (16- to 17-ounce) can peaches or apricots halves or slices
1 (20-ounce) can pineapple chunks

In a small skillet melt butter; add sugar and curry. Drain and dry fruit and place in a 1½-quart ungreased casserole; add butter mixture. Bake uncovered at 325 degrees, just until it bubbles. Serve warm with meat, such as, ham or beef roast. Serves 6 to 8.

Note: Flavor even better if dish stands covered in refrigerator and is reheated.

Mrs. Horst P. Bothmann (Ingrid)
Mrs. Joseph Holder (Martha)

Piquant Pecans

6 tablespoons butter
1/8 teaspoon minced garlic
2 drops hot pepper sauce
1 pound pecan halves
1/2 teaspoon chili powder
1/2 teaspoon salt
1 teaspoon seasoned salt

In a large skillet melt butter; add garlic. Let stand a few minutes. Add hot pepper sauce; mix. Toss pecans in mixture, coating well. Remove and spread evenly on cookie sheet. Bake at 325 degrees for 15 minutes, turning every 5 minutes. In a bowl mix together remaining seasonings; sprinkle over pecans. Return to oven for 4 minutes. Toss pecans once more; return to oven for 3 minutes. Toss again; cool. Pack in an air-tight container. Store in a cool, dry place. Will keep easily for 6 weeks. Makes 4 cups.

Marion Palmer
Cincinnati, Ohio

Granola

1 pound instant oats
2 cups wheat germ
1 cup brown sugar
1 cup shredded coconut
1 cup nuts
1/2 cup sesame seeds
1/2 cup sunflower seeds
1 cup oil (corn, peanut, sunflower or soy)
1 teaspoon salt
Dried fruit (raisins, dates or apricots)

In a large bowl combine all ingredients except fruit. Mix well making sure brown sugar is free of lumps. Spoon mixture into a roasting pan. Bake at 325 degrees for 1 hour or until golden brown, stirring every 10 minutes. Cool before adding dried fruit. Refrigerate or freeze. Makes 8 cups.

Mrs. Richard Benkusky (Judy)

Escalloped Pineapple

4 cups fresh breadcrumbs, leave on some crusts, if desired
1 (20-ounce) can chunk or crushed pineapple, undrained
3/4 cup butter
1 cup sugar
3 eggs, beaten

Mix breadcrumbs and pineapple together in a 1½-quart casserole; set aside. Melt butter and pour over sugar and beaten eggs; mix. Pour egg mixture over breadcrumbs and pineapple. Bake at 325 to 350 degrees for 45 minutes to 1 hour until lightly browned. Serve hot or cold with ham or pork. Serves 6 to 8.

Ina Zook
Dunedin, Florida

Cranberry Relish

1 (16-ounce) package fresh cranberries
4 unpared apples, quartered and cored
2 unpeeled oranges, quartered and seeded
1 (8-ounce) can crushed pineapple with juice
1 cup broken walnuts or pecans
1 cup sugar, or to taste

With a meat grinder grind first 3 ingredients; mix together in a large bowl until blended. Add pineapple, nuts and sugar; stir and chill. Makes approximately 2 quarts.

Note: Keeps well in refrigerator or can be frozen.

Mrs. James Long (Eva Fandrich)

Vermouth and Lime Sauce

1/8 cup finely chopped onion
1 teaspoon butter
2/3 cup fish stock
1/4 cup Vermouth
2/3 cup whipping cream
½ fresh lime
Salt and pepper to taste

In a large skillet, heat butter; saute onion for one minute. Add fish stock, Vermouth and reduce by half. Add cream and reduce until a syrupy consistency is achieved. Add lime and seasoning to taste. Serves 2 to 4. Serve immediately over baked fish.

Head Chef Tommy Gordon
Stakis Dunblane Hydro Hotel
Stirling, Scotland (Sister City of Dunedin, FL)

Index

C

SUNCOAST SEASONS
Post Office Box 1453
Dunedin, Florida 34697-1453

Please send me ________ copies of *Suncoast Seasons* at $13.95 per book plus $1.75 postage and handling per book. (Florida residents include $.84 sales tax per book.)

Name ______________________________

Address ______________________________

City ______________ State ____________ Zip Code ____________

Make checks payable to SUNCOAST SEASONS.

SUNCOAST SEASONS
Post Office Box 1453
Dunedin, Florida 34697-1453

Please send me ________ copies of *Suncoast Seasons* at $13.95 per book plus $1.75 postage and handling per book. (Florida residents include $.84 sales tax per book.)

Name ______________________________

Address ______________________________

City ______________ State ____________ Zip Code ____________

Make checks payable to SUNCOAST SEASONS.

SUNCOAST SEASONS
Post Office Box 1453
Dunedin, Florida 34697-1453

Please send me ________ copies of *Suncoast Seasons* at $13.95 per book plus $1.75 postage and handling per book. (Florida residents include $.84 sales tax per book.)

Name ______________________________

Address ______________________________

City ______________ State ____________ Zip Code ____________

Make checks payable to SUNCOAST SEASONS.